The Political Life of Memory

The Political Life of Memory examines the representation of Birsa Munda's political life, memory politics and the making of anti-colonialism in contemporary Jharkhand. It offers contrasting features of political imaginations deployed in developing memorial landscapes. The framing of Birsa in the heroic narrative through a grand scale of memorialization, often in the form of the built environment, curates a selective version. This isolates the scope of elaborating his political ideas outside the confines of atypical historical records and their relevance in the contemporary context. This book argues that everyday politics through affective sites such as memorials and statues produce political visions, emotions and opportunities. It shows how such symbolic sites are often strategically placed and politically motivated to inscribe ideologies. This process outlines how the state and Adivasis use memory as a political tool to lay claims to the past of the Birsa movement.

Rahul Ranjan is postdoctoral research fellow at Oslo Metropolitan University (OsloMet), Oslo, Norway. Currently he is working on a collaborative project titled 'Riverine Rights: Exploring the Currents and Consequences of Legal Innovations on the Rights of Rivers', funded by the Norwegian Research Council. His interests broadly encompass the fields of political ecology, environmental studies, anti-colonial politics and South Asia studies. He has edited the volume *At the Crossroads of Rights: Forest Struggles and Human Rights in Postcolonial India* (2022).

The Political Life of Memory

Birsa Munda in Contemporary India

Rahul Ranjan

CAMBRIDGE
UNIVERSITY PRESS

University Printing House, Cambridge CB2 8BS, United Kingdom

One Liberty Plaza, 20th Floor, New York, NY 10006, USA

477 Williamstown Road, Port Melbourne, vic 3207, Australia

314 to 321, 3rd Floor, Plot No.3, Splendor Forum, Jasola District Centre, New Delhi 110025, India

103 Penang Road, #05–06/07, Visioncrest Commercial, Singapore 238467

Cambridge University Press is part of the University of Cambridge.

It furthers the University's mission by disseminating knowledge in the pursuit of education, learning and research at the highest international levels of excellence.

www.cambridge.org
Information on this title: www.cambridge.org/9781009337908

© Rahul Ranjan 2022

This publication is in copyright. Subject to statutory exception and to the provisions of relevant collective licensing agreements, no reproduction of any part may take place without the written permission of Cambridge University Press.

First published 2022
Reprint 2023

Printed in India by Avantika Printers Pvt. Ltd.

A catalogue record for this publication is available from the British Library

ISBN 978-1-009-33790-8 Hardback

Cambridge University Press has no responsibility for the persistence or accuracy of URLs for external or third-party internet websites referred to in this publication, and does not guarantee that any content on such websites is, or will remain, accurate or appropriate.

For Maa and the *memory* of Birsa Munda

Contents

List of Figures	ix
Preface	xiii
Acknowledgements	xxv
List of Abbreviations	xxix

Part I Context and Theory

1. Introduction — 3

Part II 'Historical Memory'

2. Claiming the Munda *Raj* from the Margins: Land, Missionaries and the Making of the Birsa *Ulgulan* in Chota Nagpur (1845–1900) — 49

Part III Ethnography of Memory, Objects and Resistance

3. Memories Set in Stone: Political Aesthetics and the Statue of Birsa Munda in Post-colonial Jharkhand — 93

4. 'Burying the Dead, Creating the Past': The Making of Memorials, Stone Slabs and Birsa Munda in Jharkhand — 153

5.	Echoes from the Graveyard: *Pathalgadi*, Birsaites and the Landscape of Memory	207
6.	Conclusion	258

Appendix	264
Glossary	266
Bibliography	269
Index	290

Figures

1.1	Birsa Munda's statue at Birsa Memorial in Ranchi, Jharkhand	4
1.2	Birsa Munda captured by the police at the end of the 1890s	10
1.3	Gossner School in Chaibasa, West Singhbhum district, where Birsa Munda received his first lesson	11
2.1	Gossner Evangelical Lutheran Church, Ranchi	57
2.2	A map depicting the representation of religions of the world, where grey stands for heathens, used by missionaries in the 19th century	58
3.1	Ulgulan Foundation pamphlet	109
3.2	*Pahan*s wearing white *karia* and women draped in traditional *khanria* performing the rituals of Sarhul around a *sal* tree	120
3.3	A *pahan* performing an elaborate ritual with stems of *sal*	121
3.4	Birsa Munda's statue showing him in shackles at Birsa Chowk, Ranchi	123
3.5	Landscape of Ulihatu, Khunti district—an unending patch of forest and hills	129
3.6	Billboard displaying the prime minister of India, Narendra Modi (*left*), and the then chief minister of Jharkhand, Raghubar Das (*right*), from the right-wing Bharatiya Janata Party (BJP) government, promoting the Ayushman Bharat scheme that seeks to offer 'free health service to 57 lac [5.7 million] families for up to 5 lac [half a million] cost'	130

3.7a	The main gate of Birsa Munda's house extended by a courtyard used by women to dry grains	132
3.7b	A statue of Birsa Munda inside a room of Birsa's house depicting the timeline of his life	133
3.8	People gathered at Birsa Munda's house to observe his death anniversary, 9 June 2018	134
3.9	The main statue of Birsa Munda in Ulihatu, Khunti district	136
4.1	Birsa Munda's *samadhi sthal* located at Kokar distillery, Ranchi	160
4.2	A stone slab acknowledging Sudesh Mahto's contribution to the construction of Birsa Munda's *samadhi sthal*	161
4.3	A stone slab at Birsa Munda's *samadhi sthal*, with information on the members who built it	161
4.4	Bindrai and her friend displaying their *tendu patta* bowls	163
4.5	A newspaper reporting the procession of Birsaites with Mahto and the police, a day after Birsa Munda's birth anniversary and Jharkhand Foundation Day (15 November)	165
4.6	The statue of Birsa Munda inside his *samadhi sthal*, Ranchi	166
4.7	A mural of Birsa Munda's *ulgulan*—sculpted by Amitav Mukherjee on the wall of Birsa's *samadhi sthal*—depicting a scene of hideout under the cave of Sail Rakab, Khunti district	167
4.8	A billboard—erected on the eve of Independence Day at Harmu Chowk in Ranchi, 2018—illustrating the aesthetic vision of nationalism in which Birsa Munda is equated to Indian soldiers to demonstrate his contribution to the nation	172
4.9	A stone slab in the middle of a field representing the *sasandiri* practice in Sail Rakab village, Khunti district	178
4.10	The constellation of hills surrounding the lush green landscape of Sail Rakab, Khunti district	179
4.11	A stone slab on Dombari Hill bearing the names of people who were killed on 9 January 1900	181
4.12	Birsaites gathered at Dombari Hill to commemorate the memory of their ancestors, 9 January 2017	184
4.13	Birsaites on their way to the Dombari hilltop in Sail Rakab, Khunti district	184
4.14	The memorial pillar on Dombari Hill with a symbol of the sun in the middle	186

4.15	The statue of Birsa Munda at the entrance of the Dombari Buru gateway	187
4.16	The compound that hosts the stage and the statue beside the gateway to Dombari Hill—alternatively used by children who attend the school (the building in the background with maroon shutters)	191
5.1	Stone slabs depicting *sasandiri* in Khunti district	210
5.2	Members of the Adivasi community in Khunti district performing ceremonial rituals to erect a burial stone	211
5.3	A *pathalgadi* stone slab displaying Article 244 of the Constitution of India and declaring the area as 'non-judicial'	217
5.4	Map of Jharkhand's forest cover	220
5.5	A land document outlining the status of 'deemed forest'	222
5.6	A land-bank report	223
5.7	Protest against the Supreme Court judgment on the Forest Rights Act (FRA), July 2019	225
5.8	Protest against the Forest Rights Act (FRA) judgment	226
5.9	A *pathalgadi* slab in Sail Rakab, Khunti district	228
5.10	A *pathalgadi* slab in Khunti district	232
5.11	A newspaper clipping capturing the congregation of Adivasis on the eve of a *pathalgadi* installation	235
5.12	A Birsaite recounting her story of everyday life of remembering Birsa	238
5.13	Birsaites congregated at Birsa Munda's house to observe the anniversary of his death, 9 June 2019	239
5.14	A Birsaite household in Khunti district	240
5.15	A document explaining Birsa Munda's history and the traits of Birsaism	242
5.16	A Birsaite house in Khunti district	243

Preface

Braiding together narratives of life experiences, processes of remembering and flattened ideas of time steeped in memory is often an act of defiance against coded histories. It defies submission to linear representation of events that often use emotive, personalized accounts as appendices to descriptions, casting them away from the body of content. Memory, in turn, is a language that speaks for those who are not written into histories. Writing on memory renders the words as if they were shores to waves, oscillating between the slippages of the past and a vast texture of imagination. Writing on memory, in effect, is about drawing on words from feeling, seamlessly. Much of the South Asian landscape, and India in particular, is replete with registers of resistance movements that have shown how collective memory has shaped political ideas about belonging. In recounting these events there is a tendency, especially within historical writings, to draw on figures and icons who were the *primus motor* of the Indian nation-state project. This process of writing renders those individuals and communities who struggled at the margins against the Raj, and today in post-colonial India, as residual or at best a footnote in the description.

In this sense, writing on historical figures is also a double-edged sword. On the one hand, it accentuates heroic tales of those individuals who reveal their contribution to popular fronts within nationalist movements. On the other, it presents history as forms of events frozen in time. Combining the two leads to a methodical explanation of the past that not only occludes the voices of those who speak from the margin, but also appropriates hegemonic structures of speech as the only legible form in the historical register. In this sense, memory is a form of resistance against history. Memories involve processes of 'inscription and reinscription, coding and recoding', making memory textured and distributive in nature.[1] *The Political Life of Memory* allows me to tell a story of transition—one where shifts in power continue to shape new forms of struggles and memory politics.

This book explores subaltern memory politics in Jharkhand, a region of eastern India. I mobilize the idea of the subaltern to demonstrate the use of dominant forms of memory that erase marginal voices. I consider the 'subaltern' as a word, a conceptual tool, for ethnographic research that 'enables us to look at the lifeworld of subalterns from within it'.[2] As a lived experience, subalternity is a key tool that presents an alternative imagination. Similarly, in the book, the subaltern memory is cast as a subversive tool to highlight the possibilities and limits of memory politics. For the ethnographic use of the category, I draw from Philip Zehmisch's recent work.[3] The word *subaltern* is a complex term defined by incommensurability—that is, subaltern subjects are made visible only through either the 'texts of counter-insurgency or elite documentation that gives us the news of the consciousness of the subaltern'.[4] This proposition is challenged in this book by extending Neil Lazarus's conceptualization, which considers 'incommensurability' as a form of fetishization—ignoring the relation between theory and practice.[5]

The book therefore uses the term in two ways. First, it refers to subalterns as a social group of people and community that are systematically disempowered by the elites. Drawing on Antonio Gramsci, who used it as a military term to describe uneven development and unorganized social groups consisting in the fringes of history, this book situates the tension and struggle for power in the state of Jharkhand. Second, it refers to the the concept of the subaltern through re-reading philosophical rendering of Gayatri Chakravorty Spivak's work, where the subaltern is a site of subversion that is entangled in the multiple discursive chords of colonial power. Subalterns, in this sense, are deemed people who cannot speak because their voices are systematically excluded or violently erased from the dominant mode of representation.

In no sense and at no point does this book give into the rhetoric that subalterns cannot speak. Contrary to this, the book demonstrates how speech is always present but continually not heard or forcefully erased—often because it contains reflection of nefarious power structures in India defined by caste and the consistent racialization of the Adivasi as the 'Other'. In this way, the question of 'Can the subaltern speak?' is inverted to show how they speak and how we fail to hear because we lack structures of hearing; it is not the absence of their speech.

In rendering this, the book offers an account of political ethnography of memory amongst Adivasis and the state by focusing on an iconic figure, Birsa Munda, who staged a protest against British officials, missionaries and *zamindar*s (landowners) at the end of the 19th century in colonial Chota Nagpur. I refer to Evelyn Brodkin's latest work, which has oriented disciplines such as political science towards ethnography as a mode of doing research on politics. Brodkin's idea of ethnography as 'tools of inquiry that are particularly well-suited to research that seeks to contextualize political behaviours and beliefs and examine the processes through which they are shaped and expressed in real-life settings' allows the book to trace the conflict of memory.[6] For a long time Indian political science, which is interested in studying elite behaviours and political parties, amongst others, has refused to engage with subaltern icons and ways in which these icons structure subalternity, political spaces and representation. The book humbly pursues this by employing the methods of ethnography, which is explained in the following section.

The book traces the colossal impression of the Birsa rebellion—popularly known as the Birsa *ulgulan*, a colloquial word meaning 'great tumult'—on the sociopolitical and cultural milieu of this region. Ranging from folk songs to statues, Birsa's presence in the public sphere and, increasingly, in the built environment is indelible. This presence, however, is marked by a unique political mobility—allowing regional as well as national parties to use him to signpost the way to their own political campaigns and agendas. Every election in the Jharkhand state and now increasingly at the national level brings a renewed interest in Birsa and his legacy.

This book is therefore not a study of the history of Birsa Munda. Neither is it about the Adivasi or state politics. In no sense does it represent the voice of the Adivasis or claim any ownership of it. Rather, it is a specific inquiry into the politics of Birsa's memory and, by extension, an attempt to carve out a space to approach politics outside of electoral studies. It uses an inversion tool through which the background (memory) becomes the foreground (politics). In laying out palpable tensions within the state—defined by its history of protest, Maoists and land-rights movements—the book renders memory as a key methodological tool.[7] Memory functions as a narrative tool that traces the invocation of historical fissures and their accentuation with different political injections.

In this book, memorials, statues, stone slabs and forms of subaltern 'speech' represent embodied forms of memory. In this process, various social compositions shape the remembering and forgetting—making history felt, lived and seen all at once.[8] In this way of telling history as we live and experience it, the book looks at memory 'not only for what is remembered (facts, data) but also for how it is remembered, that is, for the quality and meaning the past assume'—placing the narratives and the meaning that memory holds in the present day.[9]

Broadly speaking, memory is an image of the past. It is a 'representation' of historical facts and not *history* itself. History is about linear progression based on a successive set of events. Memory combines the facts and impressions of the past with experiences. It personalizes the historical recounting of the events. Memory contains an acute sense of political implication as it ruptures the hegemonic accounts produced by history. History at best is an account of the past; memory is textured narratives of the past.

As a caveat, this book is not a work of memory of violence and trauma—the use of memory-studies literature serves *only* as a point of reference to highlight the significance of the debate between history and memory. Significantly, the book defines memory as an idea, which requires distributing our attention to 'all forms of human remembering (from neuronal processes to media representations) that take place within sociocultural contexts, within frameworks made by the *animal symbolicum* (symbol-making capacity)'—allowing the establishment of a relationship between community and that community's past.[10] Memory in this book therefore presents a proposition of the past and how it is produced and mobilized through different sites in the present. In this process, the book shows how these sites are reposed with certain forms of remembering and forgetting through the active participation of political actors.[11] At the same, I also show how memory becomes a militant trope in challenging the hegemonic structures of remembering as well (see Chapter 5).

Memory emerges in two forms in this book. First, it approaches acts of speech and the role of symbolism through narratives that focus on Adivasis and everyday politics. Second, it represents memory as embodied sites such as statues and memorials that are controlled by the state and political elites to mobilize people within the political spectrum. These strands are supplemented with oral history, adding texture to the writing on Birsa. Memory and oral history decentre the opposition between 'written and oral sources' because they are not mutually exclusive'.[12] In fact, both data and speech in this book have 'common characteristics as well as autonomous and specific functions which only either one can fill'.[13] It foregrounds the importance of speech, emotion, anger and grief. Memory makes history and facts by admitting to feelings.[14]

A Note on Subaltern Memory

In exploring the landscape of the memory of Adivasis and their representation in Jharkhand, the book proposes to devise a methodological tool that combines the effective use of memory studies with subaltern-studies literature to offer what I call *subaltern memory*.[15] In this book, subaltern memory is a conceptual tool that investigates the use of various aesthetic and affective sites such as statues and memorials made for political use. It explores the contours of representation through a close examination of the built environment and subaltern speech. Such sites become both artefacts for public display and 'repertoire of different agents of mediation'.[16]

Effectively used as a place for symbolic performance, bereavement and commemoration, affective sites are also spaces for political performance. Subaltern memory, then, contests the institutionally governed and popular public images of the past. It contains the disruptive potential to resist the 'official histories' that 'create and maintain the unity and continuity of a political body by imposing an interpretation on a shared past and, at the same time, by silencing alternative interpretations of historical experiences'.[17] Subaltern memory becomes 'counter-histories', an insurgent category to approach 'silences and to undermine the unity and continuity of memory that official histories produce'.[18] It mobilizes the 'remembering of the past within the framework of collective memory' in order to forge an identity.[19] Subaltern memory is a medium to understand the changes in cultural milieu and shapes the 'concretion of identity'.[20]

Adivasis use symbolic sites of subaltern memory—*pathalgadi*, for instance—to articulate their political consciousness. These symbolic sites of subaltern memory and landscapes become 'figures of memory'.[21] In this book, subaltern memory therefore investigates the complex process of representing the past in the context of Jharkhand and does not necessarily focus only on forms of episodic violence.[22] Through an ethnographic inquiry it recognizes the 'pragmatic, entangled and contemporary forms of indigenous cultural politics' and articulates sites of indigeneity that remain outside the fold of the official register.[23]

In doing so, the book examines three specific material objects: statues, mausoleum sites (*samadhi sthal*s) and stone slabs. It reviews four statues, one mausoleum site, one memorial pillar and two stone slabs. These objects contain a specific ideological standpoint and distinct aesthetical appeal to give descriptions of Birsa's memory. The historical significance of their location and associated political performance have led to their selection. Amongst them, two statues and the mausoleum site are in Ranchi. One other statue is in Ulihatu—this statue holds an essential position to describe two interrelated arguments in the book: the political aesthetic and expansion of capital through heritagization of the past (see Chapters 3 and 4). All stone slabs are in the villages of Sail Rakab and Ulihatu. The contemporary resistance movement—the Pathalgadi that situates the historic struggle of *jal, jungle aur jameen* (water, forest and land) into the mainstream political discourse—prompts the choice of these slabs (see Chapter 5).

There are various instances, or rather long descriptions, in the chapters that may appear to readers as tangential or a departure from the aims and scope of the book, that is, memory politics of the Birsa movement. However, I use these descriptions as a way to explain tangential and discursive ideas in order to capture various forms of intimate entanglements of my collaborators, interviewees and friends' social habitus. These descriptions offer an insight into enclaved and personalized accounts of memory that often emerge from experience, encounter and recall. They encapsulate powerful traces of everyday memory in non-eventful and variegated acts. In doing so, I use the first-person narrative to emplace not only my access to the 'field' but also the privileges that enable it (see Chapter 5).

In order to make writing accessible to a wide readership, this book provides translations for some of the core concepts used by the community and individuals to describe the cosmic structure that governs their lifeworld. It intentionally uses Mundari words in various places to accentuate the importance of language that forms the value system and cosmic formations of the community. Terms such as 'Adivasi' start with capital letters and are not italicized. It is not italicized to normalize the use of the word and to recognize its political potential.

Emplacing the Self and the Method

Although I partly grew up in a flood-hit region of Bihar that brought a yearly halt to schooling and long spells of darkness, my caste location eventually allowed me for schooling elsewhere. In this passage, I frequented Ranchi through childhood summers at my grandparents' home and went to finish two years of high school here, but an intimate encounter with the state was never fully available to me. However, a metaphor to explain my interest in the state politics emerges from a typical anthropological *encounter* caused by the disruptions of the state government and imposition of president's rule during my school days. This disruption was punctuated with protests and caused me to seek an entry into the political dynamics of the state, which had been unstable for a while. Essentially trained as a political scientist, I undertook a period of fieldwork in the peri-urban area of Ranchi to explore the tension around land rights in the state for my MPhil degree. Young and driven, I soon realized the scale of the problem was colossal. In this process of undertaking research, I came across Birsa Munda repeatedly during the fieldwork.

The cultural romanticism surrounding Adivasis—which portrays them as nature-loving, isolated and unruly both in the popular imaginary cast by various racialized stereotypes and in political campaigning—is in remarkable dissonance with their lived realities. Contrary to this assailable portrayal of their lives, Adivasis stake their claims both by using both the language of the law as well as by drawing on their own reserve of knowledge—one that is regularly sabotaged. In staking their claims, they flatten the most primal thrust of the Indian modernity project which is sustained on projections of their backwardness. My motivation behind this book therefore stems from meetings and living with frontline activists and informal labour forces whose lives are defined by uncertainties, far removed from academia—a place from where I write. The book is rooted in solidarities with Adivasis and activists who continually stage their resistance against the force of the neoliberal state that recklessly justifies violence against them. Some of these activists—often named in the book, other times silent—helped me gain critical insight into the 'field'.

Preface

As I write, some of the aforementioned activists are serving jail sentences, while others such as Stan Swamy lost his life fighting for Adivasis as repression in India intensifies. The manufactured realities about the lives of Adivasis as relics of the past, almost as counterpoints to the modern project of Hindu nation-making, in turn sustain this imagery. The state of India draws legitimacy from this portrayal. In fact, Indian modernity is imagined through the prism of this construction and the mobilization of different forms of abjection allowing the Indian state to intervene on behalf of Adivasi development. Their otherization is a condition of the development of the Indian state. The state of Jharkhand brings this narrative to the fore by continually refusing to make the Adivasis the writers of their own history and custodians of the present, denying them aspirations and rights and, at best, facilitating erasure of their memory. These aspirations far exceed the constitutional and federal imagination often enforced by the state and academics who, in their writings, insist on using data as feelings.

While working there in 2015, I was shown a clear tension in the region: the unresolved problems of land (often defined by remarkable material inequalities) and their intimate connection to memory. Interviews undertaken for a project on land acquisition were replete with constant references to Birsa as a symbol of the popular fronts of resistance movements. Gradually, a network of people, their trust and the dearth of literature on memory politics convinced me to undertake this project, which over the subsequent years became a product of my doctoral thesis. Apart from continual visits to protests since 2015, I undertook an organized fieldwork for this book in two phases. The first phase of fieldwork (which drew upon the network of people I had met during my MPhil's pilot study) took place in Ranchi and Khunti district from September to December 2017. I returned to archival research in London for three months to explore the contours of the past that led up to the Birsa rebellion. The archival reserve of the Christian Mission Society (CMS) documents commissioned at the University of Birmingham, which enriched the historical memory in this book (see Chapter 2), has so far been little used. The second round of fieldwork was undertaken from April to December 2018 in Ranchi, Ulihatu and Sail Rakab.

With a notorious reputation due to the presence of Maoists and their ongoing conflict with the army, the fieldwork in this region remained challenging to conduct. Any hesitation to use a recorder while in the field, and the lack thereof, is mine. As momentary suspicion and anxieties caused by militancy and the active presence of the state formed clouds above, the support and willingness of the people inspired me to continue.

The ranges of visuals of landscapes and interviews that are used in the book were collected in these villages. These visuals, amongst others, bear witness to the insidious power of memory and political campaigning. I have chosen to focus on two places for their specific relevance to the protagonist of my book. Not only was Birsa Munda born in Khunti, but his memory and teachings also continue to shape the political movements in this region. Both Ranchi and Khunti have a specific role within the political landscape of the state. The former plays an administrative role as a capital city that has primary institutions, civil societies, newspaper offices and the state archive. Most of the elite interviews were conducted in Ranchi. The latter is a crucial point of historical and contemporary struggles—for there is something profoundly interesting about the political temper in this region. It forms a vital source of interviews, landscape visuals and sites of memory.

The selection of material objects (statues and memorials) as sources occurs for two specific reasons. First, the historical records of the Birsa movement are limited and atypical. Objects that reflect his memory have not been studied in the same way as the official records in the existing literature on contemporary memory politics. In fact, this book makes an intervention on the discourse of indigeneity by using objects as a lens through which to capture the politics of Jharkhand. Therefore, material objects play a significant role in shaping public and collective memory through various commemorative practices.

As an account of political ethnography, I have declared certain personal stakes as a researcher in this project. As a non-Adivasi and upper-caste Hindu scholar endowed with the privilege of undertaking this project, I write the book from a place of solidarity—one that grows stronger over time. This solidarity is not patronage. No one has asked for it. I extend it as a submission to learn and listen to Adivasis; to be able to speak with, not for, them; and to be able to write alongside, not on, them. Most importantly, the people who speak loudly and clearly in this book are participants, not respondents—to resist the passive and docile ascription used by academics for people and communities who allow them an entry. In fact, I was a participant in this profound experience, almost a galaxy of knowledge that Adivasis and their lifeworld contains—one that is now violently repressed, erased or stolen.

Above all, I write from a place of solidarity as a way to teach myself to attend to voices, to listen and to learn. I repeat: In no sense does this book represent Adivasis. This book is a form of writing in solidarity. Writing from a place of solidarity has widened the scope of representation to imagine moving towards 'collective theorization'.[24] People who are interviewed in this book, especially Adivasis, therefore contain in themselves a world of knowledge to which my writing stands miniscule to explain their experiences.

In doing this, the book uses the ethnographic method to approach the environment of memory that encapsulates the relationship between human and object as the background of material inequalities that shape Hindu caste society and its aggression against Adivasis. By the *environment of memory*, I mean to suggest a wide range of objects and non-human worlds (such as forest and water) that explain the broader context of meaning-making within the Adivasi lifeworld. Ethnography occupies a political tool of description in this book.[25]

Personally, writing ethnography is a humbling exercise. It not only removes us from our deepest fear but also exposes the most intimate prejudice. It brings us closer to believing in each other's stories in the vast schema of *thinking of and about* life struggles. Trust in this process was a defining aspect of the research. It is, in some sense, a gateway to my ethnographic inquiry that explains both the limits and scope of research. As a thin terrain, trust may also mislead, disappear or get suspended. Jharkhand, the context of this research, is fraught with intense militancy, political instability and protests; trust is a far-fetched language to communicate. It then 'not only supposes, but actively demands reliability, and can be extremely unforgiving when it is not forthcoming'.[26] One way towards building this trust could be simply sitting for days, spending months with people—sometimes with deafening silence, waiting, and sometimes by sharing *hadia* (rice beer) and chai.[27] These waiting silences are routes towards trust—a sort of non-verbal passage, where a 'smile, a twinkle in the eyes, a shrug, a straightening of the back' forms a world of communication.[28] But at no point is trust tangible. At best, capturing it is a transient experience. In other words, ordinary acts of care and arduous forms of waiting form the texture of description.

Notes

1 Michael Rothberg, 'Between Memory and Memory: From Lieux de Mémoire to Noeuds de Mémoire', *Yale French Studies*, nos. 118–19, Noeuds de Mémoire: Multidirectional Memory in Postwar French and Francophone Culture (2010): 3–12, p. 8.

2 See Philip Zehmisch, *Mini-India: The Politics of Migration and Subalternity in the Andamans Islands* (New Delhi: Oxford University Press, 2017).

3 See Antonio Gramsci, *Selections from Prison Notebooks: Antonio Gramsci*, trans. Quintin Hoare and Geoffrey Nowell Smith (London: Lawrence and Wishart, 1971); Gayatri Chakravorty Spivak, 'Can the Subaltern Speak?', in *Marxism and the Interpretation of Culture*, ed. Cary Nelson and Lawrence Grossberg, pp. 271–313 (Chicago: University of Illinois Press, 1988); Zehmisch, *Mini-India*. The word *jharkhand* comes from *jhar* (grove) and *khand* (country). Chota Nagpur, Santhal Pargana, South Bihar and three bordering states, Chhattisgarh, West Bengal and Odisha, were initially proposed in the Jharkhand movement to carve out the state. However, the actual formation was done *only* with the South Bihar districts.

4 Gayatri Chakravorty Spivak, *The Spivak Reader: Selected Works of Gayatri Chakravorty Spivak*, ed. Donna Landry and Gerald MacLean (New York: Routledge, 1996), p. 204.

5   Neil Lazarus, 'Introducing Postcolonial Studies', in *The Cambridge Companion to Postcolonial Literary Studies*, ed. Neil Lazarus, pp. 1–16 (Cambridge: Cambridge University Press, 2004), p. 10.

6   Evelyn Z. Brodkin, 'The Ethnographic Turn in Political Science: Reflections on the State of the Art', *American Political Science Association* 50, no. 1 (January 2017): 131–34, p. 131.

7   Inspired by Mao Zedong, who laid out the path of revolution in rural China, the radical left, also known as the Communist Party of India (Maoist) (CPI[M]), was formed in India. The CPI(M), which includes the People's War, the Party Unity and the Maoist Communist Centre, aimed to target the bourgeoisie by forging an alliance with the larger social base of the proletariat, including peasants.

8   Jeoffrey Cubit, *History and Memory* (Manchester: Manchester University Press, 2007).

9   Astrid Erll, Nünning Ansgar and Sara B. Young, *Cultural Memory Studies: An International and Interdisciplinary Handbook* (Berlin: Walter de Gruyter, 2008), p. 7

10 See Astrid Erll, 'Travelling Memory', *Parallax* 17, no. 4 (2011): 4–18, p. 6

11 James Young, in his study, has shown how the production of 'sites of memory' requires the active agency of individual and group. James Young, *The Texture of Memory: Holocaust Memorials and Meaning* (New Haven: Yale University Press, 1993).

12 Alessandro Portelli, 'The Peculiarities of Oral History', *History Workshop Journal* 12, no. 1 (1981): 96–107.

13 Ibid.

14 Svetlana Alexievich, *Second-Hand Time* (New Delhi: Juggernaut Books, 2016), p. 28.

15 'Subaltern memory' is a common term to represent a vast schema of struggles led by subaltern groups. For instance, Timothy Brennan, in his essay, discusses subaltern memory as a key tool for the rise of subaltern studies. However, this book uses 'subaltern memory' to describe the narratives of Adivasis and the politics of memory set out in Jharkhand. See Timothy Brennan, 'Subaltern Stakes', *New Left Review* 89 (2014): 67–87.

16 Linda Steiner and Barbie Zelizer (eds.), 'Competing Memories: Reading the Past against the Grain: The Shape of Memory Studies', *Critical Studies in Mass Communication* 12, no. 2 (1995): 213–39, p. 232.

17 Jose Medina, *The Epistemology of Resistance: Gender and Racial Oppression, Epistemic Injustice, and Resistant Imaginations* (Oxford: Oxford University Press, 2013), p. 289.

18 Ibid.

19 Astrid Erll, *Memory in Culture*, trans. Sara B. Young (London: Palgrave Macmillan, 2011), p. 17.

20 Jan Assmann, 'Collective Memory and Cultural Identity', *New German Critique* 65 (Spring–Summer 1995): 125–33.

21 Ibid.

22 See Gyanendra Pandey, *Remembering Partition: Violence, Nationalism and History in India* (New Delhi: Cambridge University Press, 2001); Urvashi Butalia, *The Other Side of Silence* (Chapel Hill, NC: Duke University Press, 2000).

23 James Clifford, 'Indigenous Articulations'. *Contemporary Pacific* 13, no. 2 (2001): 469–90, p. 472.

24 For collective theorization and ethics in research, see Adam Gary Lewis, 'Ethics, Activism and the Anti-Colonial: Social Movement Research as Resistance', *Social Movement Studies* 11, no. 2 (April 2012): 227–40.

25 Matthew Carey, *Mistrust: An Ethnographic Theory* (Chicago: HAU Books, 2017).

26 Ibid.

27 Pooja Parmar, *Indigeneity and Legal Pluralism in India: Claims, Histories, Meanings* (New Delhi: Cambridge University Press, 2016), p. 17.

28 Talal Asad, in his writing, describes ethnography as a political tool that contains seeds of radical politics. As a method, I mobilize ethnography in the book in the same fashion. See Talal Asad (ed.), *Anthropology and the Colonial Encounter* (New Jersey: Humanities Press, 1975).

Acknowledgements

A network of support in the field helped me conduct the research. It consists of members from civil societies, filmmakers, journalists, Adivasis and friends. Central to the book is the exemplary support of people who collaborated as participants—most of whom are anonymized and stripped of their actual names in view of their privacy and safety. Anonymous names, places and identities form the basis of defiance to remain silent in an atmosphere where routine violence against disenfranchised Adivasis is the norm.[1] Such a network of support, sustained by a sense of solidarity, provided refuge and supplemented the process of writing the narratives of memory.

I am thankful to Gunjal Munda, Rupesh, Meghnathji, Samar Bosu, Gaya Munda, Abhay Sagar Minz and Anurag Faizal for their outstanding support which helped me navigate through the various parts of the region. Anjana Singh, a *saathi* and participant, has expressed sustained interest in my work, helped me in conducting a part of my fieldwork and provided corrections too. Asoka Sen gave clarity to the project as I crisscrossed the region of eastern India. He fed and comforted me as I felt lost, an endearing act of care. I am also thankful to my relatives and friends, especially Nana and Nisha, for making my stay in Ranchi a pleasant one as I frantically rushed back and forth during my time there.

My doctoral supervisor, Corinne Lennox, offered ingenious insights and unwavering support. She carefully read the drafts and gave comments. Her heart full of love for students often far exceeds her formal obligations as a supervisor. Thanks to Corinne for seeing me through the thick and thin of emotions. With his kind supervision, James Chiriyankandath has offered his historical precision to the drafts and supported me personally. Damien Short, Daniel Rycroft and Paul Havemann entered the scene at different points to support this project with their incisive comments. Damien, Chloe Pieters and Elaine Walters, particularly, have been kind to me for years and offered a lot of opportunities. Subir Sinha often lent most generous support with his eye for detail in politics and his welcoming home, with Kashmiri chicken and Bihari camaraderie in times of crisis. Rashmi Varma and her scholarly work have significantly shaped my thinking and this project. Andrew Wyatt (University of Bristol) and Rahul Rao (University of St Andrew) were very kind and helpful in examining this manuscript in its thesis form at the School of Advanced Study, University of London. My MPhil supervisor, Vidhu Verma (Jawaharlal Nehru University, New Delhi), really pushed me forth to pursue my interest and instilled in me the most astute professional ethics. Three anonymous reviewers at Cambridge University Press offered critical insights to help develop the argument and structure of this book. Thanks are due to Adam King, whose eye for detail and copyediting has helped rid this book of mistakes.

Kenneth Bo Nielsen in Oslo has offered his generous support, opened the door to his home and extended the invitation to talk at the University of Oslo that eventually materialized into my postdoc elsewhere in the same city. Several friends during the long spell of life in London came to offer support—Lily (for being a great support), Jose (for always reassuring his faith in the work with an element of fun), Sonya, Uncle, Aunty (for making London a home, reassuring their love as I felt lost), Daniela Zanini (for offering a shared space to register endless complaints and worries), Ida Mensa (for being the best flatmate and an endearing friend in London), Jena (for all the kindness and warmth), Aparna and Prerna (for being genuinely kind in listening to my rants and sharing care), Kiran (my long-lost sister, for feeding me biryani and sharing love) and, especially, Shruti Amar who made my stay upon arrival in London a warm and beloved one. I will always be thankful to Shruti for opening the doors of her home to me.

Friends in India offered their support by taking calls at odd hours—and for this, I am thankful to Sidhant, who spoke through the night until daybreak in India to settle my anxiety, and to Mayank, who helped me through the best and worst of times. Thanks are due to Cihnnita, Rajat, Nisha, Khusbu, Manjesh and Priya for their endearing love and care, and to Sandy, Ishleen, Shahiskant *bhaiya* and Neha for their friendship. All of these wonderful people are invaluable. Swastee Ranjan has been exceptionally patient in listening to my drafts of this book's chapters. Her critical insight and unwavering support have kept the radical fringes of my intellectual ideas alive. Shailesh has been a great source of strength and inspiration. Nithin has shown some of the most extraordinary support in multiple crises during my stay in London—for his warmth stays today. Separated by the Atlantic, I also thank my two friends in the United States—Linette Park and Will Mosley—whose scholarship on Blackness and race has been instrumental to the critical thinking in my work.

Acknowledgements

Without funding, research is challenging. To this end, I am thankful to the Louise Arbor Studentship, the Yusuf Ali Fund, the Stefanie International Travel Bursary and the Dame Lilian Penson Fund, and to the conference grants and awards from the Institute of Commonwealth Studies, School of Advanced Study, University of London. Several grants to attend workshops including the School of Criticism and Theory at Cornell University, the Modern South Asia Workshop at Yale University, the Writing Activism at Oxford University and the Asia-Net at the University of Oslo offered the opportunity to present several drafts of chapters at different stages. The chapter on statue has already been published by the *Journal of Global South*.

I finish this manuscript as a Postdoctoral Research Fellow at Oslo Metropolitan University, Norway, which is generously supported by the Research Council of Norway. I am thankful foremost to Axel Borchgrevink for allowing me to draw out time to revise the manuscript and to Catalina Vallejo Piedrahita (a sweet friend), John McNeish and Elizabeth Macpherson for their laudable support and encouragement me to finish this book.

Palak Rao (Polu) offered endearing comfort as I swam through a sea of emotions, often marked by joy, grief and love—and sometimes all of them at once. Nishant Sirohi brought his unwavering friendship folded in love. Both came together to hold me tight as the city of Oslo deepened isolation during Covid-19.

My gratitude also goes to Isabelle (a refuge in the university space and a *chai* friend when I was lost), Randi Havnen (for her compassionate love and care), Elise, Benedicte, Thorgeir and Tonje for extending kind and generous support in days when Covid-19 made life incredibly challenging. Tom Griffith, Hilde Arntsen and Hanne Svarstad supported my project in the department at OsloMet as I wrestled with the review process and life in Oslo. A heartfelt thanks is due to Arnendu Majumdar (Amit), Shampa and Ontique for making Kringsjå feel less lonely and their food that brought home close. Thanks are due to two lovely friends, Camelia Dewan and Anwesha Dutta, for their ingenious support through the long spell of Arctic darkness. Ursula and Daniel Münster brought comfort and kindness to Oslo with their love, insights, encouragement and food.

Needless to say, coming abroad has been a long journey. On this journey, my family has offered love and faith in my work. My elder brother, Ashutosh, has shown his support at various stages and maintained my confidence in pursuing this project. Bhabhi has shared her care and laughter. My father has supported this intellectual journey by any means possible. My younger brother, Rishav (Chotu), a gift to our family, kept me motivated with his early morning calls as I lived flitted between Delhi, London and now Oslo, strung apart from home.

This book is for Maa, Ranjana, who stood for me as life cast long spells of failures, shame and struggles as both a child and an adult. I drew strength in her fearless pursuits, a sort of unfailing resilience in the face of life. Far from submitting to the gendered norms that structure our lives, she taught me to challenge them. I never became a feminist from books because I lived with one who inhabited ideals that shaped my worldviews. Without my Maa, I would have never come this far to write this work.

Finally, the book is dedicated to Birsa Munda and his struggles that long live to inspire us. I also owe intellectual calibre and grit to pursue this project to Ram Dayal Munda, whose writings have taught me to pause, absorb and attend to the world of Adivasis fraught with layers of knowledge to which I stand student for my entire life. Adivasi artist Lakhinder Hassa has designed the book cover. He is an artist based in Jharkhand, and he designed the cover through interaction with me about the book. The painting on the front cover depicts the continual struggle of Adivasis to secure their rights. The green patch under the sheets represents Jharkhand, which was once colonized by the British (represented by the red sheet). The stones represent the burial ground as a marker of their memory.

Any misrepresentation or mistake in this book is mine. *Johar!*

Oslo
March 2022

Note

1 Adivasis are, of course, not disfranchised in the *de jure* sense.

Abbreviations

AJSU	All Jharkhand Student Union Party
ASI	Archaeological Survey of India
BJP	Bharatiya Janata Party
BL	British Library
BSP	Bahujan Samajwadi Party
CAG	Comptroller and Auditor General
CAMPA	Compensatory Afforestation Fund Management and Planning Authority
CMS	Christian Mission Society
CNTA	Chota Nagpur Tenancy Act
CPI	Communist Party of India
CPI(M)	Communist Party of India (Maoist)
EIC	East India Company
FRA	Forest Rights Act
GoJ	Government of Jharkhand
IOR	India Office Records
JCC	Jharkhand Coordination Committee
JJM	Jharkhand Janadhikar Mahasabha
JMM	Jharkhand Mukti Morcha
LAA	Right to Fair Compensation and Transparency in Land Acquisition, Rehabilitation and Resettlement Act

MoTA	Ministry of Tribal Affairs
NAI	National Archives of India
NBA	Narmada Bachao Andolan
PESA	Panchayats (Extension to the Schedule Areas)
PVTG	Particularly Vulnerable Tribal Group
RSS	Rashtriya Swayamsevak Sangh
SP	Samajwadi Party
SPG	Society for the Propagation of the Gospel
SPTA	Santhal Pargana Tenancy Act
UNWGIP	United Nations Working Group on Indigenous Populations

Part 1

Context and Theory

The basis of the whole movement is a feeling on the part of the Mundas that they are the true owners of the soil; that they appointed the maharaja and that all non-aboriginals are interlopers and land-grabbers: to this must be added to the fact, on which I have more than once dwelt, that the Munda is altogether incapable of making a good case for himself in our law courts, while he is always beset by people of his race and outsiders, ready to swindle him out of his land, and all his other rights.
—H. C. Streatfield, Esq., Deputy Commissioner of Ranchi [1]

Their cry is the same as that of the old sardari malcontents' viz., that the Raj is theirs and not ours, and that they intend to fight for it and get it.
—A. Forbes, Esq., CSI, Commissioner of the Chota Nagpur Division [2]

At that moment [colonial India], when Birsa fought against the Empire, we, then, had one East India Company (EIC). The EIC against which Birsa rose to seek independence of his Jal, Jungle and Jameen. Today, we are in independent India, and now 18 years into new Jharkhand, there is an attack from all quarters. There was one East India Company and now we have many.
—Dayamani Barla, in an interview [3]

Notes

1. Extract from a letter from H. C. Streatfield, Esq., Deputy Commissioner of Ranchi, dated Camp Bangaon, 4 January 1900, IOR/L/PJ/6/532, J&P 224, India Office Records, British Library, London.
2. Ibid. From A. Forbes, Esq., CSI, Commissioner of the Chota Nagpur Division to the Chief Secretary to the Government of India, Bengal, IOR/L/PJ/6/532, J&P 268, British Library, London.
3. Dayamani Barla, in personal interview with the author, Ranchi, 22 October 2018.

Chapter 1

Introduction

Vignette: Birsa Munda and His Memory

'Ek photo le lijiye; agle baar photo laeyega. Diwaal par lagaenge Birsa baba ko.'[1] During a sultry and dry summer in Ranchi, Jharkhand, Bijo, an Adivasi who works for less than 5,000 rupees (70 dollars) a month in the Ranchi bazaar, finds inspiration from the memorial of Birsa Munda. His skin was undulating from his cracked feet, a witness to Adivasi labour often erased from the register of the 'India Shining' story. The fragrance of *hadia* (rice beer) took hold of us as Bijo insisted on narrating Birsa's legendary past to me. In the rapidly urbanizing landscape of Ranchi, it is common to encounter a set of aluminium pots spread out at the edge of a busy road under a tree with someone (usually a woman) handing out *hadia* on *sal* leaves to the working class. Most who find themselves here, in fellowship with each other after a rough day of work as *rejas* (casual labourers), quaff bowls of *hadia*, sometimes to cherish their culture, other times to quell their melancholy. For most city dwellers, *hadia* remains a displeasing sight that reflects the 'uncultured' traits of Adivasis, while others, more militant, such as the Maoists, see it is an aberration in 'becoming cadres'.[2] Bijo's description of Birsa's memory in this memorial, a place now controlled by the Municipal Corporation of Ranchi, radiated immensely his heritage and gleaming pride. In post-colonial Jharkhand, where 28 per cent of people are Adivasis (officially recognized as a Scheduled Tribe), memory-making has emerged as the new politics (Figure 1.1).[3]

Birsa Munda is perhaps the most venerated figure—at least symbolically, as an anti-colonial icon. Although the political landscape is fraught with his memory, its colossal presence has not gained serious traction in the nationalist, subaltern historiography or popular literature. Born into a poor peasant family in 1875, he was soon personified as the figure of *abua disum* (father of the land) for his

Figure 1.1 Birsa Munda's statue at Birsa Memorial in Ranchi, Jharkhand

Source: Photograph by the author.

political acumen, millenarian characteristics and exceptional capacity to mobilize the root cause of exploitation. He consolidated Adivasis located at the margins of the British Raj and reposed his faith in the cause of securing his land. He was an ordinary Adivasi who came to occupy a historical prominence in the Chota Nagpur region—reinforcing his pride in fellow Adivasis' past and their struggle for its protection.[4] His unfailing political vigour and capacity to resist the colonial state and the massive spectre of power controlled by *zamindar*s (landlords) make him a prominent figure whose movement came to create an empire of memory for Adivasis. His *ulgulan* displays an impressively political encounter of Adivasis with the British establishment and feudal lords in the colonial history of India. His story emerged primarily as that of an icon in the register of the anti-colonial movement, which left a remarkable imprint on the political history of the region and the cultural milieu of the Adivasis.[5]

This book examines the representation of Birsa Munda's political life, the use of his persona and the mobilization of anti-colonial thought in contemporary Jharkhand. In doing so, it offers contrasting features of memorialization that emerge from the process of Birsa's canonization in the contemporary cultural and political milieu. Various political templates are used to develop these memorial landscapes. They seek to display Birsa in the heroic tales and *shahid* (martyr) narratives instituted through the use of the built environment. The narrative portrays a selective version, often the anti-colonial one, isolating the possibility to elaborate his political ideas outside the confines of atypical historical records and their significance within the contemporary context.

So far the scholarship on Birsa Munda remains limited to the archival reconstruction of the event and does not offer reflections on its relationship with the emerging turn to memory politics in the state.[6] This book therefore positions *memory* as a tool of both appropriation and resistance, representation and disruption. It does this by using three case studies of material memory that represent the legacy and spirit of Birsa Munda: *samadhi sthal*s (mausoleum sites), statues and stone slabs.

Today, however, his memory is evident in the form of landscape, at intersections and within cultural milieu. Political parties at the national as well as regional levels, civil societies and communities honour his memory. This makes for a widespread presence, ranging from a portrait hung in the Indian parliament (the only Adivasi leader so honoured) to statues in a tea garden in Assam and at the Ranchi airport, amongst other places.

Recent scholarship by Uday Chandra claims that the Birsa *ulgulan* was 'neither anti-colonial nor proto-nationalist'; my book shows the resurgence of both anti-colonialism and proto-nationalism through the process of memorialization.[7] I argue that an exclusive emphasis on the representation of Birsa as *only* an anti-colonial figure removes the possibility to understand the continual struggles and the emergent form of memory politics. It also animates anti-colonialism as a form of historical phenomena, an anachronistic description of the political idea.

The book therefore moves away from the analysis of established scholarship in two ways. First, it situates the historical reasons for the Birsa movement by using new findings from the archival research (Chapter 2). Second, it illustrates the processes involved in the appropriation of Birsa's memory as a tool of political mobilization for struggles of *jal, jungle aur jameen* (water, forest and land). Crucially, the latter delineates a perspective on the contemporary political landscape, underlining how the issue also highlights the relationship between rights-based advocacy and the emerging climate crisis.[8]

To explore these points, I pose a few questions. How do people relate to representation of the *past*? How do the state, political elites and civil society perceive, produce and control the memory of Birsa Munda for political purposes?[9] In what ways do objects such as statues, memorials and stone slabs become embodied forms of memory? How does memory become a tool of politics for the subalterns to resist and negotiate with the modern state? How do the subaltern groups mobilize the memory and their 'oppositional, placed-based'[10] value against the 'essentialised forms of otherisation'?[11] What is the relationship between memory, subaltern and capital? In what ways does the case study of Birsa Munda explain the struggles or provide the conceptual apparatus to examine the process of subalternization of indigenous peoples?

Anti-colonialism and Birsa Munda

The idea of anti-colonialism dominates as the key theme in the literature and within the popular representation of the Birsa movement. However, it remains underwhelmingly discussed within the body of work on Birsa. While Chandra's reading of the archival records suspects the possibility of defining the movement as purely anti-colonial, this book construes the *representation* and use of anti-colonialism in contemporary Jharkhand as a form of political tool to underscore the potential of ethnic nationalism—by extension, also a means to circumvent the logic of resistance. In other words, it moves away from the understanding of colonialism as formulated in the prevalent accounts on Birsa as merely a form of spatially defined and temporally limited phenomena, which, after the culmination of the colonial period, somehow led to a transition to equality.

In this book, I insist on showing how the effects of colonialism are evident in the ways in which the modern nation state has become a participant 'in a moral and cognitive venture against oppression' and draws on colonial dispositions to imagine or extend the expansion of capital.[12] The modern state and its tools of modernity, fraught with the Hindu-caste imagination, are preconditions to imagining Adivasis and their pasts. They allow the insidious entry of capital to find new currencies by exploiting temporal differences and graded inequalities.

Moreover, anti-colonialism is often perceived within nationalist writing as an ideological standpoint against the limited notion of colonialism. It is limited in the scope of defining a struggle (often temporally)—removing the capacity to imagine a universal basis for struggle. In turn, colonialism becomes a historical phenomenon rather than an epistemic and ideological formation. Such instantiation fails to capture the continued forms of domination which require and represent the 'limited notion of post-colonial justice framed within the institutional construct of the state'.[13]

As a result, the book adheres to a certain definitional framework for these broad ideas. First, colonialism demonstrates an unequal relationship that is justified in using violence and coercion. In effect, the book draws on Aimé Césaire's work, where he writes: 'Between colonizer and colonized there is only room for forced labor, intimidation…. No human contact, but relations of dominations and submission [turning] the indigenous man into an instrument of production…. Colonization = "thingification".'[14] This conceptualization supports the subsequent chapters in fully developing the ideological formation and historical background to Birsa Munda and his rebellion (see Chapter 2). Second, the idea of anti-colonialism is a radical engagement with the past and present to identify various forms of domination. Anti-colonialism therefore is not about accepting a simplified political foreclosure—that is, nationalism—designed to support the restricted interests of dominant groups. Anti-colonial thought is about focusing on the 'actualization of freedom itself'.[15] It demonstrates a position from which we continually disrupt ideological forms of domination and power. Anti-colonial thoughts and ideas stand in opposition to any normative ideals that seek validity through the limited notion of national territory or draw on sectarian identity politics. On the contrary, anti-colonial ideas thrive on forging solidarity through emancipatory politics—where the common interest lies in liberation from oppressive structures, not merely from foreign invasion but also from internal colonizers—a microcosm of which was evident in Birsa's movement.

Birsa sought this claim by the 'space of sharing' with the Sardar movement (see Chapter 2).[16] He drew upon available resources in dialogue with ongoing movements to resist the foreign invasion by *diku*s (outsiders) and the internal occupation by *zamindar*s, missionaries and the Raj. Priyamvada Gopal, in her magisterial work on anti-colonialism, has shown that the 'spaces of sharing' that emerged through 'dialogism of the encounters' helped make sense of universal claims (such as liberation and independence).[17] Any portrayal of anti-colonialism as a closed network of dominant and ruling ideological formations organized around a religion, nation and identity to rule the masses is prone to appropriation and risks slipping into retrogressive ideals. Therefore, anti-colonial thought at best disavows any foreclosures to national boundaries or conservative ideological formations.

Unlike the historical writings of other indigenous peoples that strive to 'articulate their own reality and experience, their own personal truth as an alternative to the homogenization and silence that is required of them within mainstream', the history of Adivasis and of Birsa Munda continues to remain marginal within Indian historiography.[18] In places where it has received attention, the voices of Adivasis are significantly muted, neither heard nor spoken about. Therefore, the book combines the use of the theoretical framework, ethnographic data and philosophical thirst for concepts and ideas that inform the research on subaltern history. This allows the book to situate various facets of memory politics associated with Birsa Munda. In doing so, it studies material objects such as statues, memorial and movements that cast dominant forms of remembering and forgetting about Birsa Munda and his movement.

Memory and Birsa Munda

Memory is a key tool in this book to approach contemporary politics in Jharkhand. As a methodological tool, it highlights the persistence of colonialism: the effects of power and the limits of representation. It represents an inherent contradiction of politics in Jharkhand through examining sites of memory. In this, it moves away from the dominant strands of memory work that focus on eventful and violent episodes (such as the Partition or the Holocaust) and do not clearly mobilize memory, as is seen in the memory studies' corpus on violence.

This book offers a careful study of memory in everyday politics by using materials that are mnemonic, resistant and provocative in nature. The use of these materials is an expression of creative political articulation that seemingly operates on the affective level of political discourse.[19] Here, memory functions as a mode of politics where the past of the subaltern Adivasis is constantly externalized from their present.

I offer an analysis of Birsa's memorialization through extensive research (consisting of surveys of memorial landscape, in-depth interviews and archival research) that demonstrates contesting narratives of subaltern memory against the dominant forms of remembering and forgetting. This means situating the struggle and negotiation of subaltern Adivasis through the everyday politics of memory. Here, the 'everyday forms of resistance' as a category become, as James Scott writes, the 'most vital means by which lower classes manifest their political interests'.[20]

The everyday politics of memory, I argue, is displayed not always in the form of physical use of power but sometimes also through affective sites such as memorials and statues that produce feeling and political opportunity. Strategically placed and politically motivated, such symbolic sites insidiously inscribe ideologies and often emerge as the dominant form of remembering. Upon ascertaining the space of memorialization, it is sustained by concerted political rituals that commemorate the memory of the past. Therefore, the everyday politics of memory represents how the state and Adivasis use memory as a political space to lay claim on the past of the Birsa movement.

The book offers a perspective on how Birsa Munda has emerged as a malleable figure who is appropriated, mobilized and, importantly, represented in various contexts. I show how his characterization through memorial practices offers an interesting insight to understand two strands of memory politics. First, I show the use of memory in politics at the national and regional levels. The latter captures a contradiction in a broad range of interest-based Adivasi constituencies that at the same time are both mineral-rich and poverty-stricken. The book highlights the micro-level working of ideologies that penetrate through forested areas to emerge as register of control. The memorialization of Birsa becomes a medium for the state to seek entry into these spaces. Second, I show how memory also emerges as a tool for capital formation (see Chapter 4). These sites seek to generate opportunities through the process of heritagization. It makes landscape a site of power that not only externalizes the participants in the memory from the creation of his memorial site but also, especially in the state of Jharkhand, applies the language of tourism and restoration of the past.[21]

Scope of the Book and Area of Contribution

As a project deeply rooted in interdisciplinary methods, theories and approaches, this book specifically engages with scholarship from the subaltern studies collective, and memory, post-colonial and anthropological studies, with a key focus on contemporary politics in Jharkhand. I have chosen to focus on Jharkhand because it demonstrates the inherent contradictions of the Indian independence movement and the process of decolonization. As I show throughout the book, Jharkhand foregrounds the perils of post-colonial violence and the model of internal colonialism. In doing so, it allows the readership to imagine broader conflicts and debates on subaltern and indigenous peoples' struggles in other parts of the world. It helps to evaluate and create new forms of political imaginaries in thinking about memory as a template to explain subaltern politics.

In particular, the book contributes towards a collective corpus of writing called 'Adivasi studies' that is intimately interwoven into the critical concerns of indigenous, post-colonial studies. These studies, however, are limited to the East Indian states, often fixated on the historical dimension and lacking insights into the wider net of memory politics and newer forms of extractivism.[22] The book extends this corpus of work by making an intervention through the emergent category of memory. It does so in order to underline the significance of Adivasi studies and mainstream the political potential of this collective, which remains significantly buried or wilfully ignored within disciplinary approaches.

The Canon: Birsa Munda and His Brief Biography

Historically born out of political movements, the idea of the Adivasi was exemplified in Birsa's own lifetime. In the last quarter of the 19th century, Birsa Munda and his rebellion marked an era of resistance and resilience. Born on 15 November 1875 in Ulihatu (present-day Khunti district in Jharkhand), Birsa Munda was one of the four children of his father, Sukhram Munda.[23] Growing up in a hostile atmosphere of the constant disruption that emerged from land disputes, new legislation and the coming of missionaries, Birsa attended a German missionary school at Chibasa in his formative years (see Figures 1.2 and 1.3). During this period, he learned the tenets of Christianity that influenced the formation of his religion—the Birsa *dharam* (religion), a significant religious identity that continues to survive amongst the Birsaites (see Chapter 5).

Figure 1.2 Birsa Munda captured by the police at the end of the 1890s

Source: S. C. Roy, *The Mundas and Their Country* (Calcutta: Kuntaline Press, 1912).

Introduction

Figure 1.3 The Gossner School in Chaibasa, West Singhbhum district, where Birsa Munda received his first lesson

Source: Photograph by the author.

Soon after, he was expelled from the school for protesting against Father Notrott, who had made objectionable remarks about his people.[24] Moving from one place to another in search of a living, Birsa 'apostatized to the Roman Catholics [that is, converted to Roman Catholicism] and remained with them for a short while lapsing into heathenism'.[25] He moved away from the Roman Catholics and began to seek places of refuge to develop his ideas. In due course, he drew himself closer to Anand Panre (a leader of the Sardari *ladai*) and began practising Vaishnavism under his influence.

Under the influence of Anand Panre, Birsa also began participating in the famous Sardari *ladai*, or Sardar agitation, an agrarian movement. It emerged from the dissatisfaction amongst Adivasis regarding the 'restriction imposed upon their traditional rights'.[26] The discussion of a series of laws that were enacted provides a detailed account of the movement in Chapter 2. In the following years, he organized his own religion, the Birsa dharam, whose followers came to be known as Birsaites and continue to live in Porahat and the Khunti district of Jharkhand. His personal life experiences—he was baptized Christian and later became a Vaishnaivite—

influenced his new religion. Adi Dharma, as proposed by Ram Dayal Munda, represents a consolidated version in the wider schema of the Adivasi theological belief system. Various names also depict the same, such as Bongaism. This book prefers to use 'Adi Dharma' to explain the religious worldview of Adivasis unless I quote from other accounts.

Significantly, Birsa's teachings included practices that are readily found in other religions, such as abstaining from the consumption of meat, wearing the 'sacred thread' and adhering to cleanliness.[27] Birsaites also mobilized the folk culture from the Munda society, invoking myths and songs. The use of these symbols, myths and songs came to display an elementary form of 'messianic' or 'millenarian' beliefs in various writings on Birsa.[28] This process both consolidated and perhaps weakened the movement from within. It weakened it through a specific drift towards the mainstream religious traits, including rituals and practices appropriated from Hindus. It gave little or no space for Adivasi cultural norms.

Nonetheless, with his exceedingly charismatic persona, Birsa succeeded in attracting people into the fold of Birsaism. Self-fashioned and revered as the 'messenger of god', Birsa incarnated himself as Birsa *bhagwan* (god).[29] Kumar Suresh Singh's account offers folk songs that commemorate this spiritual element of his religion.[30] Birsa astutely combined his visionary ideas with spiritual elements to develop a mode of political consciousness for his community. For the officials and missionaries in particular, this was not worthy of attention. Soon after, the Dharti Aba (Father of Earth, as Birsa became known) acquired the form of a political ideologue—as recounted in the writings of John-Baptist Hoffman:

> He made himself interesting by playing the *fakir* (saint) for some time. I distinctly remember how the known Sardars were urging the common crowd to go on the pilgrimage to Birsa Bhagwan. At first I took no notice of what I considered for some weeks as *mere acts of semi-savage foolishness*. I did not fully realize the danger of an armed rebellion, because I could not get myself to believe that these people, *usually timid* under what I know to be sometimes shocking oppression, could muster up courage enough to rise in arms.[31]

Vivid use of language that attributes 'semi-savage foolishness' as a defining feature of Birsa and his people suggests the colonizing gaze of the mission that supplemented the repression against the Adivasi by *zamindars*. Birsa was highly cognizant of this sentiment and used it effectively in mobilizing his community against outsiders. His political ideas came to pose threats to not only British officials but also missionaries and *zamindar*s. For Birsa, 'British officers, German missionaries and even the Romans, as they called the Catholics, all these Europeans, wore but one and the same hat' and 'nothing was expected from them'.[32] Much of this clearly illustrates the striking level of political understanding held by Birsa. His growing popularity amongst the Adivasis led to a long-standing period of legal battles in which he was frequently moved in and out of jail. However, he was captured after his uprising in February 1900 and died in prison in Ranchi on 9 June 1900. I give a detailed account of his movement in Chapter 2, but the movement in effect provoked a massive legal response and the creation of the iconic legislation known as the Chota Nagpur Tenancy Act (CNTA) in 1908.

Thereafter, the movement became proverbial. Authors and journalists variously wrote about it. The following section discusses its historiography. It lays out the discussion on the movement's reception by different disciplinary and theoretical frameworks.

Historiography of the Movement

Various writings emerged on the Birsa Munda movement in the years after the rebellion. Amongst the frameworks used to analyse the movement, revitalization and millenarianism seemed to dominate. Having roots in Christianity, the millenarian movement is deemed religious, social and political in its intention to bring transformation. In explaining the movement as millenarian and revitalizing, Michael Adas writes: 'They have varied widely in scale, ranging from localized and spontaneous outbursts to well-organized rebellions that have engulfed the whole societies.'[33] To analyse this framework, he chooses the Birsa rebellion as the manifestation of revitalization and claimed:

> The British represented, after all, a lowland-based empire. Consequently, the 'Pax Britannica' in nineteenth century Chota Nagpur was periodically shattered by riots…. These protest groups culminated in the prophetic rebellion led by Birsa Munda, who promised *supernatural solutions* for problems that human efforts had not been able to resolve…. The Sardars gradually transformed Birsa's amorphous and unrealistic eschatological preaching into an ideology of the rebellion.[34]

Adas's analysis of the movement chimes with various other writings. For instance, the work of S. C. Roy was perhaps one of the first accounts, besides Hoffman's, that offered a history of the region by emphasizing the changes that were brought about. Roy believed that the gradual transformation of the land-tenure system, beginning in the 16th century, posed threats to the social cohesion of the Munda tribe, noting that from 1676 the oldest *pattah*s, or leases, granted to the *jagir*s (servants) by *raja*s (kings) seemingly also suggested their absolute ownership of the property. This could be fairly contested as most of the scribes and draftsmen working together to prepare the documents, who were both literate and had served in the court of the *maharaja*s, were from Behar. These men, Roy believed, 'naturally employed the set forms for such documents they had known in use in their own country'.[35] With the gradual expansion of these *jagirdar*s under the helm of *raja*s, they established a legitimate proprietorship over the matter of supplies. These supplies eventually came to take the form of 'money' or, as Roy maintained, 'the foreign idea of rent' legitimized under the *raja*s' tenure. The *khuntkatti* Mundas[36] rebelled against this new system of rent.

However, some deem Roy's account concerning tribes and 'their regional difference and economic organisation' to be incoherent.[37] Moreover, his pursuit of an Indian anthropology made 'tribes' specimens for Indian modernity. It bore influences of the colonial vision, as Sangeeta Dasgupta writes:

> Late nineteenth and early twentieth-century anthropology had defined itself unambiguously as the study of 'primitive' societies. As a discipline that was created 'by Europeans, for a European audience' to study 'non-European societies dominated by European power', it had produced practitioners in the second half of the nineteenth and early decades of the twentieth century, most of whom belonged to the West.[38]

This is an important observation to illustrate the ways in which Adivasis and the Birsa movement were represented in writings—primarily as a revitalization movement, relics of the past characterized by incapacity and a dearth of reason. Similarly, Surendra Prasad Sinha, in his book *Life and Times of Birsa Bhagwan*, considered the Birsa movement as a revitalization that emerged from the 'refusal of Birsa to acknowledge any authority superior to him. He was himself the prophet of Singbonga, the Dharti Aba of his people.'[39] Considering the 'intelligence of Munda leaders to discover the futility of local British Courts and enactments and Missionary assistance', Sinha believed that 'Birsa Bhagwan led a final showdown and promulgated the slogan of White men, Quit Chotangapur'.[40] Interestingly, his analysis claims that the Sardari agitation and the Birsa movement had two distinct aims. To expand it, he argued: 'Sardari agitation was a political agitation … to recover ancient rights under the direct control of the Administration. Sardar had with Christianity imbibed the idea of peasant proprietorship.'[41] In contrast, Birsa's movement was intended to end Victoria's *raj* (rule) and start his own

Introduction

raj.[42] However, Sinha does not offer any source to support his claims. Further to this, Sachchidanda also concedes: 'The history of tribal of Chotanagpur from the middle of 19th century has been marked by a number of such revitalisation movements.'[43] He considered the Birsa movement as 'the embodiment of the social, economic and religious unrest among the Mundas'.[44] Recognizing Birsa's 'religion as a combination of Munda belief, Hinduism and Christianity', Sinha believed that Mundas saw a 'prophet' and 'saviour' in him, and this combination became the strength of the rebellion later.[45]

The millenarian framework was deeply steeped in central conceptual concerns in order to understand the movement. These writings, while forming crucial reserves to access the past, often underplayed the impact of the agrarian shift in the society that led to civil unrest and the rise of Birsa.

In this context, Singh's pioneering work provided extensive detail and sources to shed new light that remains valuable even today. Motivated by an encounter with the early morning chants of Birsaites in 1960 in Khunti district, Singh began his work on folklore collected from Birsaites.[46] Singh's work shows how the Birsa movement was 'a blend of armed resistance and the revitalization movement'.[47] He pinpoints the breakdown of the 'agrarian structure and rise of the feudal state system' as the defining factors.[48] The agrarian breakdown explains the causal relationship it shared with the emergence of Birsa. The changes in the land system affected the Munda social institutions of *parha* (self-governance amongst Adivasis) and *panchayat* (village council).[49] The decline of these institutions coincided with the introduction of laws and people (outsiders) that jeopardized the Munda societal organization. This led to an assertive reclamation by Mundas, and the Birsa movement emerged as the point of inflection: 'the revitalization movement'.[50] Tracing the gradual development of the Birsa movement from the Sardar agitation, Singh writes:

> Stimulated by the memory of the 'golden' past of the tribe free from the *diku*s, their enemies, as expounded in mission schools, they at one stage urged to be taken under direct British administration; they were not disloyal to the Crown, not even to the Raja of Chotanagpur in the beginning. There were three phases through which Sardar agitation evolved into the Birsa movement: the agrarian phase (1858–81), the revivalistic (1881–90), and the political phase (1890–95). The substratum of the movement, however, remained agrarian.[51]

Birsa, as is claimed here, combined the elements of 'both religious and secular leadership'.[52] Singh's analysis is the most comprehensive account of the movement that combines the use of official records and testimonial references—not only situating Birsa as a folk hero but also recognizing his enormous political strength. Birsa moved from being a 'Sardar agitator to a prophet through a *transfiguration*—in the course of which he was entrusted with the mission to recover the rights for his people which was typical of such divinely inspired leadership'.[53] The spectre of 'millenarianism', however, remains dominant in his work too—what Adas calls 'eschatological preaching into an ideology'.[54] The subaltern history in such analysis is marked with the elements of mysticism and religious enchantments. The use of mysticism is perceived, at least within the literature on Birsa, as lacking the political consciousness amongst the subalterns.

The use of political consciousness seeks entry into the historiography with Ranajit Guha's *Elementary Aspects of Peasant Insurgency in Colonial India*.[55] In the foreword to its latest edition, James Scott identifies Guha's work on 'peasant insurgency in a dialectical with forms of domination'.[56] Scott writes: 'The presumed cultural, economic, and social inferiority of the tribal, the peasant, the outcast[e] in a complex indigenous and colonial order—their subaltern status—is precisely the relationship that forms the basis for all acts of subordination, resistance, refusal and self-assertion.'[57] Discerning the language of 'pre-political', a dominant theme within the Western as well as the nationalist frameworks to analyse the peasant insurgency, Guha shows how the peasantry expresses its political consciousness through the strategic use of mysticism and affect.[58]

Guha believed that no less than 110 known peasant insurgencies, including the Birsa *ulgulan*, constantly 'ruptured' the developing state through 'seismic upheavals until it was to learn to adjust to its unfamiliar site by trial and error and consolidate itself by the increasing sophistication of legislative, administrative and cultural controls'.[59] Insurgency, he thought, was the 'necessary antidote of colonialism'.[60] However, the peasants were denied 'recognition as the subject of history', and such denial was 'codified into the dominant historiography'.[61] Therefore, to draw peasants as the makers of their rebellion within historiography, Guha used the word 'insurgency'. The word 'insurgency' is a critique and a rejection of a framework that recognizes rebellion 'as purely spontaneous—an idea that is elitist as well as erroneous. It is elitist because it makes mobilisation of the peasantry altogether contingent on the intervention of charismatic leaders, advanced political organizations or upper classes.' Guha's diction of political consciousness emerges as a reaction to the usage of the term 'pre-political' by Eric Hobsbawm to describe societies that are not fully industrialized. Guha describes Hobsbawm's use of 'pre-political' for bandits as expressing a phenomenon and strength that 'have been devoid of any explicit ideology'.[62]

Guha's work located the effective use of religious manifestation as the 'political consciousness' of the movement. The display of political consciousness took the form of '*reassemblements*, i.e., masses for war as a formidable strategy against the Raj'.[63] In explaining the strategy to manifest their consciousness, Guha writes:

> Sometimes Mundas would overrule their leader and impose their collective will on him [Birsa].... In March 1898, they firmly and persistently resisted his advice in favour of religious and reformist agitational procedure. In fact, the cumulative upshot of these assemblies was 'the triumph of neo-Sardars' strategy of revolt over the peaceful means of struggle initially advocated by Birsa. A genuine instrument of rebellion as a mass event, they mobilized the Munda peasantry for a war on the Raj. Mobilization of this kind often assumes a religious form.... The communal visits to 'ancestral places' undertaken by Birsa's followers on his advice exceeded the limits of Sardar revivalism and developed into a series of carefully planned risky ceremonial marches to inspire the Mundas for the coming Ulgulan.[64]

Guha insisted that the role of religion functioned as a medium to express and mobilize the virtue of politics—that is, the struggle against power. This is important to consider as often it is noted that religion, at least within the dominant Western framework, is perceived as lacking logic.[65]

Recovering the expression of subaltern agency in such cases is an impossibility. Gyan Prakash signals this danger too. In describing the elite discourse, he writes that peasants are considered 'an embodiment of myths and superstitions existing outside the domain of modernity and reason'.[66] Such perceptions relied on the idea that 'what lies outside the realm of reason—the superstitious peasant—is also knowable'.[67] This posed an irresolvable paradox where 'on the one hand, it projects the subaltern as an irrational other beyond authoritative reason and understanding; on the other hand, it claims that the subaltern is completely knowable and known as an embodiment of irrationality'.[68] In this way, the Birsa *ulgulan* was also a manifestation of incommensurable subaltern political consciousness which inscribed itself on the cultural milieu of Adivasis.

Background to the Book: Concepts and Context in Colonial India

Explaining and maintaining conceptual differences is of key interest in this book. For instance, in this section it outlines the genealogy of terms such as 'tribe' and 'Adivasi' and the differences or similarities they offer. The term 'tribe' was invented by the colonial administration and continues to remain significant in post-colonial India, primarily used as a category to segregate and govern the population and drawing them into the Western fold of Darwinism that assigns evolutionary traits to humans from certain societies. The examination of texts produced during the 19th century is revealing. For instance, *The Tribes and Castes of Bengal* by H. H. Risley, *Castes and Tribes of Southern India* by E. Thurston and *The Tribes and Castes of Central Provinces of India* by R. V. Russell, amongst other publications, illustrate the processes of categorization, often cementing the fluid, amorphous category of people into different 'tribes'.[69]

This was supplemented by the publication of the Indian census of 1881, which laid out the conception of 'tribe' and caste (even as it existed before) as a formal vocabulary in the administrative use. It effectively offered a glossary of the population with an 'unclear line of division between caste and tribe'.[70] Nonetheless, it succeeded in lending a language to the census for producing colonial subjects of governance. In fact, the District Gazetteers began to use the word 'tribe' more frequently to describe the population that had previously been known by their community.[71] The use of the word 'tribe' has had a massive effect on the ways in which the tribal community was separated from the concept of caste.

Unlike the category of tribe, caste is a socially constructed and religiously inscribed category that is defined by the conception of purity and hierarchy in Hindu society. However, caste is inseparable from definitions of tribe. Caste represents a violent form of social system that supports various kinds of discriminatory practices and enforces abjection of bodies that are deemed lower in the social order. These orders gain supremacy from religious texts such as the Manusmriti, which ranks some humans as inferior to others within caste Hindu society.[72] The caste system has had a history of violence, which continues to this day. Violence is perpetrated by ascribing to caste the idea of purity of body and access to society. In the continuum of caste–tribe, Alpa Shah describes the Adivasis as a community occupying relatively independent or autonomous status that has 'much more direct access to land and forest resources'.[73] This spared Adivasis from the direct oppression waged by upper-caste Hindus, but it inscribed other forms of abuse—namely, being represented as 'savage', 'wild', and so on.[74] Meanwhile, Virginius Xaxa writes: 'Its rootedness also lies in the fact that term "tribe" in India has emerged not only in relation to social backwardness or stage of development, but also in opposition to a structure of society characterised by caste.'[75] However, the tribe cannot be separated solely based on division of roles assigned in the *varna* system. Romila Thapar suggests that with such a 'juxtaposition of tribe and caste or of clan and state, the encroachment on the tribe by caste society frequently resulted in its incorporation into the state'.[76] Besides, these are not incidental points of difference set against the backdrop of a complex and heterogeneous course of migration throughout the country, but they in fact eulogize a mythical unity of the past.

In effect, the colonial administration drew upon these existing norms of society—that is, norms that were Brahmanical in nature. It is erroneous to suggest that 'tribalness' was invented by the British administration for official process and as such was absent in pre-colonial India. The characterization of 'tribe', or a tribal attribute, finds resonance in the older Hindu caste order. Vinita Damodaran's analysis disputes this proposition by showing how the idea of Aryan invasion remains central to the definition of the non-Aryans, who are often cast in a negative light as the 'other'.[77] Damodaran explains this as follows:

> Colonial epistemology thus built both on Brahmanical notions of caste and drew on 18th- and 19th-century ideas of race…. For these colonial administrators the 'tribal' model with its essential unity, clear body of customary law and unambiguous legitimacies was better suited to the task of maintaining public tranquillity. Victorian anthropology in this period was dominated by ideas of socio-cultural evolution.[78]

This analysis lays out a fundamental flaw in the methodology used to interrogate concepts such as 'tribe'. Outlining the inheritance of knowledge from pre-colonial India, Damodaran warns us of the danger of ascribing colonial disposition to concepts that are steeped in traditional hierarchies. While 'tribal' as a category of governance emerged from an effort to cope with colonial anxiety, it also obfuscated the porous boundaries of tribe and caste. In the same context, Beteille writes:

> The *permeability of the boundary* in India, in the Islamic world and perhaps also in China obliges us to adopt a flexible rather than a rigid attitude towards the definition of tribe…. The traditional social order tolerated or even encouraged the proliferation of borderline cases, but the modern state cannot afford to do so. It demands clear categories in place of ambiguous ones.[79]

This emphasis on the dilution of permeability functions as the precondition for ordering and governing society within the modern colonial state. A key feature of colonial modernity in India was the creation of the census—this offered a chronicle of a population in order to segregate them on the hard lines of castes and tribes. The consolidation of categories that swayed in spaces of fluid boundaries was coupled with new methods of obtaining and producing knowledge about the community.

These new legal interventions generated huge resistance. Specifically, the Chota Nagpur region witnessed various upsurges against the changing frontiers of the legal system, including the land system. The community, in relation to *rajas*, which loosely defined the ownership of land, later came to be explained by the medium of intermediaries and legislations. The development of 'tribe' necessitated the process of legislation. Chota Nagpur had different land-tenure systems that were jeopardized by the advent of the British legal system, including the *khuntkhattidar*, a predominant tenancy status granted to those who were descendants and clearers of the jungle.

It must be emphasized how the notion of tribe was not static in terms of tenancy rights. Sanjukta Das Gupta has demonstrated the historical evolution of the 'tribe' as an agent within land rights which actively negotiated with the colonial state.[80] In assessing a case from the CNTA and the resettlement of the Kolhan region (1914–18), Gupta asserts that the 'local administration drew attention to the communal character of the Ho village organization and attempted to reinterpret and define custom, as it existed in Kolhan'.[81] In this process of settlement, the Hos (a tribe) 'frequently disputed interpretations and definitions. They actively negotiated with the colonial government on these issues with varying degrees of success.'[82]

The process of securing 'self-interest' within the changing legal framework, Gupta perceived, was a 'silent revolution'.[83] Essentially, it illustrates how 'tribe' as a category is problematic if it is reduced to the invention of colonial rule. She opines:

> Moreover, to argue that colonial rule 'invented' tribe out of an essentially mobile and uncodified pre-colonial system not only negates the significance of the complex socio-economic organisations and indigenous institutions of these communities, but also tends to minimize long-term structural continuities. Such an approach denies minority ethnic groups their agency in reshaping traditions and social practices and their own destinies; it assumes that these groups were merely puppets on a string, manipulated solely by colonial policies.[84]

Explicit in this argument is the role of agency that has played a significant role in the history of 'tribe' in the region. It also shows how the history of this region is enmeshed in the complex role of communities and the making of the colonial state. The urgency of developing the legislative measures, however, emerged as a response to resistance, including the Birsa Munda movement—a key concern of this book. But before elucidating the resistance, the following section briefly outlines the key difference that exists between the tribe and the Adivasi. The latter is used as a defining concept across this book.

Adivasi: A New Political Vocabulary

The Sanskrit word *adivasi* is made up of the word s *adi* (past) and *vasi* (inhabitant), meaning an inhabitant of the past. Various accounts suggest different origins and uses of the term—far removed from the definition *relics of the past*. David Hardiman, whose work offers early accounts of Adivasi politics, defined it primarily as a political identity.[85] The idea thereafter gained a political life and traversed the country. In the context of Chota Nagpur, the word staged primal grievances that were tied to questions of identity and land. It came into frequent usage within the Chota Nagpur Unnati Sabha (Chota Nagpur Improvement Society). Soon after, a visionary Adivasi political leader, Jai Pal Singh Munda, focused on streamlining the urgency to consider Adivasi political and social conditions in the newly emergent nation.[86] As an elected president of the Adivasi Mahasabha (Great Council of the Indigenous Peoples) in January 1932,[87] Jai Pal Singh Munda, in his presidential speech at the All India Adivasi Mahasabha, made a call for unity amongst Adivasis.[88] In this new emerging political order, Adivasis in the region clearly articulated their specific political demand against internal colonization. He noted:

> We aborigines, sir ... as descendants of the earliest known owners of Indian soil and with more hoary traditions of sovereignty in the land ... are entitled to as much or perhaps greater indulgence and an equal, if not a larger, share in the government of our own people.... These alien landlords despise us as 'Mlechhas' and despicable creatures—more brutes than men, and actually stigmatise us as 'Kols' which we understand is a Sanskrit term for 'pigs'. But we too, sir, are human beings with a long past—longer than that of any other The following reference is missing race in India, with a native genius for democratic government.[89]

Two strands of thinking emerged from this speech. First, it instituted a distinctive identity of Adivasis—a place of political order ruled and governed by Adivasis. Second, it emphasized the role of internal colonialism. The latter is useful for the scope of this book as well. The model of internal colonialism explains the continued struggle of Adivasis to achieve Birsa Munda's dream of Munda *raj* as well as new forms of the exploitative system that pervades in the contemporary Jharkhand. As an expression, Munda *raj* literally denotes the rule of Mundas. It is also, I believe, a political tool that Birsa invoked during his movement to awaken political consciousness amongst his people (see Chapter 2).

This establishes that the word 'Adivasi' is a political identity that shapes and defines a mode of self-identification and assertion different from the colonial vocabulary of 'tribe'.[90] It is used as a medium of political assertion by a section of people prominently located in East India, specifically in Jharkhand.[91]

Contemporary Articulations of the Birsa Movement

In the recent past, a few writings have responded to the historiography on Birsa Munda and his movement in the contemporary landscape. Shah's essay, for instance, attends to the work of Guha on the Birsa Munda movement.[92] Her work is rooted in the ethnographic exploration of political conditions and the structuring of Adivasi lives in contemporary Jharkhand.[93] She 'revisits the question of the significance of what people were doing in becoming a part of movements which have been variously labelled devotional, millenarian, prophetic and anti-colonial'.[94] In explaining the question, Shah believes: 'The issue is not simply one of interpretation but also one of theory and praxis, a theory of what they call politics and the place of religion within it.'[95] This provocative claim in the essay is also a departure point for her work—that is, 'the Birsa Munda movement was not an anti-colonial rebellion of tribal freedom fighters per se'.[96]

The anti-colonial framework which dominates the historiography overlooks the complex interaction between the church and the colonial state. Shah argues that it essentially 'segregated the religious from politico-economic underwritten by agrarian politico-economic change' and the movement was 'analytically not contiguous with the secular forces who resurrect it today as their historical antecedent—in this case Maoist insurgents'.[97] That it subsequently led to the expansion of the right wing through religious sects, such as the Shiv *charcha*, works 'as a force of integration against the fragmentation brought into people's lives by the spread of Maoist revolutionaries in conjunction with the postcolonial state'.[98]

Shah interestingly highlights that 'both K. S. Singh and Guha fail to read between the lines of colonial records'.[99] This in turn also allowed Hoffman, a key figure in the history of this region, to 'downplay the threat to the Church and stress instead that Birsa was a threat to the colonial state in order to bring its force to crush the Birsaites'.[100] Ultimately, the movement in the form of insurgent writing ends in 'side-lining religion [prophetic] from politics' and 'Guha was thus able to stress the political role of Birsa and create a "Birsa Munda Rebellion" as the basis for the grammar of his *Elementary Aspects of Peasant Insurgency*'.[101] This is drawn to show two distinct examples of Birsa Munda and Shiva Charcha in contemporary landscape, where Shah argues:

> Birsa Munda and Shiv Charcha … marked people's creative search for order in a time of rapid social transformation, disintegration and alienation caused by institutional authorities, whether it was the Jesuits and the State at the beginning of the 1900s, or the Maoists and the State a hundred years later … it is this search for an abstraction, for the holism of religious-economic-political life in particular that reunited people in action against the disintegration brought into their lives. It is these processes that enabled the spread of millenarian or prophetic sects that have been resurrected by the institutional left but are also all too easy a prey of the extreme institutional right.

Shah warns us of the use of 'sacral polity' enmeshed within the larger fabric of this region.[102] Similarly, Chandra also makes an interesting entry in the discussion through a compelling examination of archives. In his pursuit, Chandra moves away from his claim that 'Guha's account of Birsa's *ulgulan* depended entirely on the prior research of Singh's research' and reconstructs the narrative by relying on his archival findings.[103] Importantly, he claims that 'Shah is concerned primarily with the relationship between the Maoist left and subaltern religiosity today' and 'leaves no scope to appreciate what later subalternists would call entanglements of power and resistance'.[104] Instead he argues: 'It is vital to understand the agrarian and state-centric character of social protest as well as the nature of religious change prior to and during the Birsaite Ulgulan.'[105] He shows that 'Munda activists and rebels, far from seeking to overthrow colonial rule reworked the terms of their subjecthood under British overlordship, and in fact, actively deepened the process of state-making in these margins of modern India'.[106] Chandra shows how the Adivasis trusted in the government when seeking justice in restoring their lost *raj*. He argues:

> [T]he onus was on the British government to restore the *Munda Raj* by evicting those hostiles to the Sardars, whether dikus or Christian missionaries. It was not the case, as Ranajit Guha presumed without the slightest shred of evidence that 'the Birsaite Ulgulan [was] launched with the declared aim of liberating the Mundas from British rule'.[107]

The Iconography of Birsa and the Spectre of Memory

While the existing accounts offer fascinating insights in their attempts to reconstruct Birsa's past and its effects in the contemporary landscape, they remain hesitant in attending to the traces of memory—one which is affective in shaping political imaginaries and memorial practices in the state. It remains steeped in what Sherry Ortner calls 'ethnographic refusal', which is a 'refusal of thickness, a failure of holism or density which itself may take various forms' and, in this case, the refusal of the colossal spectre of memory politics.[108] Perhaps this refusal has less bearing on the approaches of existing accounts, and more on the nature of memory as transient and affective. At most, it requires the suspension of our desire to ascertain the past as a form of evidence. This refusal also remains in the approach to gathering sources that often, at least in the existing literature on Birsa, rely on coded forms of evidence—either speech acts (interviews) or documents (archives). Although these are crucial sources, they are just as limited in developing contours of representation so widely spread out.

In this regard, this book signals towards Daniel Rycroft's work, which is provocative in pushing the limits of our imagination about the past. His work shows how the history of iconography, with close references to the portraiture of Birsa Munda, is 'foregrounded as a means to interpret the *emergent* relationship of Indian anthropology to "the Mundas" and to "the nation"'.[109] It demonstrates how the portraiture shaped the *politics of visibility*—a key theme that also underscores this book (see Chapters 3, 4 and 5) allowed Birsa to emerge in the popular imagination of the nation. Examining a range of work including 'a haunting yet compelling portrait of the Adivasi freedom fighter Birsa Munda' drawn by Upendra Maharathi, a Congress-oriented artist and advocate of national cultural heritage, Rycroft re-reads the photographs as generative of various forms of aesthetic appeal—devotional, prophetic healer, rebellious through subsequent use and circulation.[110] This led to the opening of 'sites of Munda consciousness away from the *ulgulan* itself to incorporate the political heritage and political/aesthetic culture associated with the movement'.[111]

The political use of Birsa's memory—a point often construed as an appendix to the description in the existing writings—suggests the need to mainstream memory as politics. Rycroft's work is therefore helpful in thinking about how the 'integration' of Munda pasts was driven by political needs, especially the Government of India Act (1935) and the Indian National Congress (1940).[112]

Extending this cultural politics of visuals into the fields of memory—where processes of remembering and forgetting animated by various structures of power, including the state, offer an opportunity to map the political life of Birsa Munda—

not only extends our sensibilities to attend to the affective register of politics but also foregrounds emerging claims of Adivasi movements (see Chapter 5).

This book therefore marks a departure from shifting imaginaries of Birsa on the plains of memory. It shows how using the lens of memory highlights different narratives of anti-colonial politics that are produced in everyday politics. It demonstrates how political strands of anti-colonialism are presented as a form of selective history to attain the ambition of political parties, often limiting the broader scope of the Birsa movement that explains the ongoing tension: land conflict, mineral extraction and dispossession, amongst others. The selective invocation of the historical past represents a misleading idea that anti-colonialism is merely a form of struggle against a foreign colonizer—in this case, the British. It completely occludes a wide range of violence suffered by Adivasis. Contrary to using the historical past in a sedimented form, the book foregrounds anti-colonialism as a form of 'radically democratic [thoughts] that asks questions of domestic/ indigenous tyrannies' and challenges frontiers of the imagination produced by ideas of a nostalgic past (see Chapter 4).[113]

Jharkhand's Political Struggle

Years after, the Birsa movement became a major point of reference in conceiving the idea of the Jharkhand movement within the micro-history of the Indian state. Significant to both the Indian struggle for independence and the idea of statehood is a striving towards independence from outsiders—an awakening of decolonization. While one took the form of an aspiration to seek liberation from the shackles of the British Raj on a nation-wide scale, the other aspired to seek independence from a peculiar form of colonization spearheaded by internal rulers. National independence remains elusive as a project of power transfer from one power elite to another in post-colonial India—where 'nationalism as a product of European political history is borrowed in the colony'.[114] In other words, James Chiriyankandath writes: 'Colonialism, by globalizing the European template of an international system constituted of sovereign nation-states, determined that the primary object of anti-colonial nationalism would be the transformation of colonies into independent nation-states within a system that bore the deep impress of the erstwhile colonizer.'[115] Indeed, this idea gained traction for resistance movements against outsiders. Therefore, the scope to define movements such as Birsa's became limited to the confines of anti-colonialism.

However, it also incited an urge to seek separate statehood for Jharkhand from as early as the 1930s, during the operation of the Simon Commission. Such aspirations were marked by the specific illustration of historical place from where Adivasis spoke. Jai Pal Singh Munda, in his speech, made this poignantly clear when he said:

> Sir, I am proud to be a *jungli*, that is the name by which we are known in my part of the country. Living as we do in the jungles, we know what it means to support this Resolution. As a *jungli*, as an Adibasi, I am not expected to understand the legal intricacies of the Resolution. This Resolution is not going to teach Adibasis democracy. You cannot teach democracy to the tribal people; you have to learn democratic ways from them. They are the most democratic people on earth.[116]

Responding to the chairman of the Constituent Assembly in 1946, Jai Pal Singh Munda invoked the identity of 'Adibasi' as the cornerstone claimant in the making of the Indian Constitution. Far flung from rhetoric used by the nationalist parties claiming to triumph the cause of the marginalized, Munda took the charge to establish the claims of Adivasis as the parallel of First Nations, the indigenous peoples of India, and foregrounded what Pooja Parmar calls an attempt towards 'undoing historical wrongs'.[117] He charted his way through this modern document, the Constitution of India, to stake claims for the 'place of Adivasi' in the nation.[118] Conversely, his spectacular mobilization of indigenous claims established how 'for indigenous peoples the *self-identification* goes beyond the attachment to the cultural attributes of a community and extends to the special relationships with the lands where cultural attributes are formed'.[119] This is reflected on a large tribal population in India, who have been subject to a governance model that is the driven logic of 'internal colony'. Hence, the assertion of territorial independence is significant for decolonizing both the nation and internal colonies.[120] In this process, the outsider became a point to define regionalism in the initial years of the movement.

As early as the 1920s, Jharkhand was conceptualized as a separate state through the formation of the Chota Nagpur Improvement Society. The Unnati Sabha consisted of the first generation of those educated in the English medium, mostly Christians who were key members in foregrounding claims of indigeneity. At the heart of the Unnati Sabha was a vision that only tribals should represent the issues of the tribals in Chota Nagpur, and evidently the emphasis was built towards gaining self-reliance of the tribals for their socio-economic improvement. Unfortunately, the Sabha failed to mobilize the masses as it remained within the defined boundaries of participation—mainly consisting of Christian missionaries.[121] In 1938, the Adivasi Mahasabha was formed to widen the social base of the organization to create a pan-tribal identity. It led to an advanced political mobilization directed towards the demand for a separate state formation.

In fact, the idea of Jharkhand was proposed even before the arrival of the Simon Commission in 1927, and it was the Mahasabha's political support that accelerated the pace of the movement.[122] Jai Pal Singh took the post of president in the Mahasabha and organized various meetings for Adivasis; he staged protests against the Indian National Congress party at the helm of the Indian national movement as 'exploitative and anti-Adivasi'.[123] Offensive anti-Bihar slurs in popular media such as 'Bihari bandar nacho' (Bihar's monkey should dance) accompanied these developments.[124]

Interestingly, Jai Pal Singh harnessed the image of Birsa Munda as the symbol of 'Adivasi Risorgimento'.[125] In reviving the Birsa cult, Singh faced opposition from missionaries and officials. L. N. Rana, in his analysis, thinks of it as way through which 'Congress utilized this situation to its advantage and eulogised Birsa as anti-British and anti-Christian'.[126] In 1949, the Adivasi Mahasabha was dissolved to form the Jharkhand Party after the independence of India from the British Empire. The party pursued the cause of forming a new state of Jharkhand. In 1952, the Jharkhand Party contested the first state election in independent India. The party won 32 out of 325 seats and became the main opposition in the Bihar legislative assembly.[127] The party's share of seats eventually declined to 20 seats in the election of 1962, and, finally, a merger with Congress led to its weakening. I do not intend to suggest that the party collapsed. In fact, it remained functional under the leadership of N. E. Horo, an ex-parliamentarian. Horo attempted to revive the party and the Jharkhand movement by helping the oppressed to train themselves in mass movement.[128]

Eventually, several radical parties and groups of intellectuals emerged as potential leaders in the wider spectrum of the Jharkhand movement. Parties such as the Jharkhand Mukti Morcha (JMM), the Birsa Seva Dal and the Communist Party of India (Marxist–Leninist) were amongst these. Each of these parties took up a radical posture to revive the Jharkhand movement—also characterizing Birsa under their guise and according to political need.[129] Invariably, these parties, driven by their vision but united by the desire of seeking independence, encountered the massive spate of violence which unfolded in Bihar.[130]

Regional Parties and the Trope of Cultural Revivalism

A sustained radical response emerged from the JMM in 1972.[131] In a mineral-rich state, the JMM built its political vision by targeting the politics of extraction. Louise Tillin, in her work, attests to the political tone of the party by suggesting that 'the JMM had a radical agrarian programme working among Santhal *adivasi* beyond the traditional areas of Jharkhand Party activity in Chotanagpur, and non-tribal

Kurmi-Mahtos'.[132] This allowed the landed proprietors, despite their differences with the JMM, to join it.[133]

In the following decades, the social and political base of the Jharkhand movement was broadened with the coming of new political contestants such as the Bharatiya Janata Party (BJP) and the All Jharkhand Students Union (AJSU). The AJSU, headed by Surya Singh Besra, was a group of young students who drew inspiration from the Assam Student Party. There is another party called the AJSU Party led by Sudesh Mahto, who is a protagonist in the memorialization of Birsa (see Chapter 3). The AJSU Party must not be confused with the AJSU. The latter led several demonstrations across the states, which were not always supported by other parties, the JMM included. The party believed in violent protest, as Tillin highlighted through an interview with Besra in which he said: 'I totally believed that in the Gandhi-wadi way I cannot achieve Jharkhand. So, I have to follow the Subhas Chandra Bose (revolutionary method) path.'[134]

Coincidentally, intracultural revivalism played a crucial role in mobilizing people for the Jharkhand cause. Various parties used different templates. For instance, the JMM sought to assert a metaphor that catered to a landscape charged with environmental romanticism. Damodaran's account shows how 'the JMM in the 1970s found expression in the festival of the sacred grove, which was to become one of the most important markers of Chotanagpuri identity'.[135] For the JMM, it became a 'site where larger and more powerful hegemonies were constituted, contested and transformed'.[136]

Figures such as R. D. Munda emerged as key leaders in the struggle for the separate state. Combining the legacy of Jai Pal Singh and Birsa Munda, R. D. Munda emerged as the political visionary for imagining the new state. He drew extensively on the legacy of Birsa and later invoked the idea of 'cultural revivalism' as the basis of the Jharkhand movement. He perceived the Birsa movement as the 'period of open revolt' against the imposition of various legal measures.[137] Upon returning from a period of education in Chicago, he mobilized people under a new rubric of culture that combined songs, ethnic identity and language. He went on to become the vice-chancellor of Ranchi University and opened its department of tribal languages, which remains a key centre for Adivasi culture and language. He sought to reclaim the lost identity of Adivasis and encouraged cultural formation as the way to assert demands for a new state.[138] In this process, Birsa Munda was reinstated as the political template for cultural revivalism for parties to argue for the aspiration of Adivasi ethnic statehood.

Parties across the ideological spectrum realized that the formation of Jharkhand statehood could be fulfilled if they came together. Gradually, the Jharkhand

Coordination Committee (JCC), a leading organization led by activists, in 1987 sought a consolidation. Subsequently, the JCC was constituted in 1989 to investigate various claims that sought the formation of a separate state.[139] The JCC represented a coalition of more than 60 cultural and political parties, including the JMM. It accommodated the non-tribal as well. Birsa Munda and his memory became iconic to this coalition in these cultural and political spaces.[140] Parties reproduced Birsa's image as a cultural and political icon through affective sites: statues and portraiture, both of which were mediated by the state and national polity.[141]

The memory of Birsa Munda yet again emerged as the central force in the articulation of everyday politics. Different phases rejuvenated his memory to reflect the different images of the past, making memory an artefact of political consciousness within the region. Samar Bosu Mullick makes a similar point about the role of collective memory of Birsa:

> The reason why the parties formed under the leadership of the indigenous peoples carrying the name of Jharkhand insist on the formation of a state with the cultural area of Jharkhand may be seen in the persistence of a *collective memory* of Jharkhand as their ancestral homeland. Their claim, therefore, continues despite the fact that the reality has been changing fast drastically against their interests. However, opening the doors of the various Jharkhand parties to the non-tribals also may either be seen as a strategy for winning the head of game counting and fundraising under the bourgeoisie democracy or as an expression of an emerging Jharkhandi nationality encompassing both the indigenous peoples and the non-indigenous early settlers of the region.[142]

The invocation of collective memory within the movement ties the notion of ancestral homeland of indigenous people, the Adivasis, and lays out the problems with other narratives—often emerging from the *dikus* and the *sadans* (residents). The collective memory articulates the *past* as not only an event but also a form of continuous struggle, a reminder to mainstream the effects of outsiders on the Adivasi landscape. Furthermore, it has been seen how the consolidation of parties to demand a separate state also coincided with the internationalization of Adivasi identity. This was marked from 1985, when several activists participated in meetings of the United Nations Working Group on Indigenous Populations (UNWGIP), 'seeking recognition for India's *adivasi* communities as indigenous'.[143] These meetings framed the question of Jharkhand within the global discourse of indigenous peoples, where 'rights have also become a major aspect of contestation and restitution in indigenous peoples' interactions with the state and other communities'.[144] In turn, the 'international space has been important for transnational mobilization and efforts to establish global norms on indigenous rights'.[145] Leaders such as R. D. Munda used this platform to establish grievances.

However, as different groups' demand for a separate Adivasi identity emerged, this was followed by the BJP's claim for statehood under the rubric of *vananchal* (forest-dwelling state), primarily because BJP leader Inder Singh Namdhari preferred *vanvasi*s (forest dwellers), a mythical craft drawn out of Hindu epics, rather than the long-standing Adivasi heritage in the region. Predominant in nationalist writings, the figure of Adivasi represents a 'backward Hindu'. This is led by the belief that the Adivasi or tribal community practise animism—drawing them close to Hinduism. The cultivation of this idea has profoundly influenced the Jharkhand movement led by the right-wing parties. It continues to have an effect in Adivasi regions—including through practices of Shiv *charcha* and the burgeoning of schools. Historically, it gained strength from the rise of the Hindu nationalist Sangh Parivar (Family of Organizations).[146]

Following the differing opinions and rounds of talks, the Jharkhand proposal made on 4 September 1989 was accepted.[147] However, the following two decades witnessed various political changes. Statehood was replete with factional politics, allowing various parties such as the BJP to form ties with other non-Adivasi, non-Christian allies to make claims for the state. The formation of the new state was also compromised by unresolved questions of inequalities and political ideologies that shape the lives of Adivasis, who continued to remain marginal in the state.

On 15 November 2000, Jharkhand emerged as a separate state through the Bihar Reorganization Act and joined the Indian Union as its 28th state. The act stipulates 'the State of Jharkhand comprising the following territories of the existing State of Bihar, namely: Bokaro, Chatra, Deogarh, Dhanbad, Dumka, Garhwa, Giridih, Godda, Gumla, Hazaribagh, Kodarma, Lohardaga, Pakur, Palamau, Ranchi, Sahebganj, Singhbhum (East) and Singhbhum (West) districts, and thereupon the said territories shall cease to form part of the existing State of Bihar'.[148] The statehood recognition coincided with Birsa Munda's birthday—a day formerly commemorated as Jharkhand Diwas, or Jharkhand Day.

The territorial settlement of the state—carved out of another state—was strategic and led to a reduced number of people being recognized as both Jharkhandi and Adivasi. Mullick claimed that 'had the original areas of Jharkhand, which encompasses neighbouring states such as West Bengal, Madhya Pradesh and Odisa, been awarded, then Jharkhand would have had a majority population of Indigenous Peoples'.[149] At present, the Scheduled Tribes constitute only 26.3 per cent of the 32,966,238 in the state.[150] Since 2000, the state has been having trouble in forming a stable government. It has had 10 chief ministers and three spells of president's rule, with Raghuvar Das of the BJP being sworn in 2016 as the chief minister.[151]

The unresolved question of ethnicity, statehood and persistent movement against land-grabbing defines the political sphere of Jharkhand. It continues to be a fervent issue that generates agitation, protests and shutdowns. In an article I examined legislations such as the Land Acquisition Act and the subsequent amendments that empower the state to use dated provisions in issues of land transfers. Based in Nagri village, the case of land acquisition rendered many *raiyat*s (tenants) as outseen, mostly women landowners. A noticeable attempt at diluting protective legislation, including the CNTA, that came after—and due to—the Birsa rebellion stirred up fresh protests and the spectre of unresolved tensions in the state (see Chapter 3).[152]

Against such a backdrop of conflict between the state and Adivasis over land, political parties in the state advanced their interests by appropriating different forms of cultural rubric, including the memory of Birsa. The ideological warfare, however, is set out against a background of tension that governs the competing claims of the state, the Maoists and the industrial lobbies. This complex process of staking claims—more clearly about the resources—makes the landscape of Jharkhand both interesting and a matter of great research within a broader field of study. In approaching the state-making and everyday politics of memory, this book foregrounds the study within broader theoretical discussions on subaltern politics and how it may help in understanding the issue more broadly. The following section outlines the same.

Theoretical Foundation of the Book

The book foregrounds the idea of the subaltern in order to analyse the contemporary political dynamics of Jharkhand as an ethnic state that cultivate memory by invoking the image of the past. I mobilize the notion of the subaltern as a form of description to maintain that subaltern is not an identity. It is, as Gayatri Chakravorty Spivak rightly says, 'a position without identity. It is not a class.'[153] Similar to the idea of indigeneity which challenges 'the logics of colonialism that underwrite liberal democracies in order to question Euro-American constructions of self, nation-state', the subaltern studies collective as a corpus of writings has highlighted the significance of small histories and the silences of archives.[154]

The collective began in the late 1970s with Ranajit Guha as the founder of the school.[155] Thereafter, it became a tool to reformulate historical events, ideas and thoughts.

It was invested in examining the hegemonic narrative of the elite that had dominated the historiography of the Indian colonial experience. Using 'elite' as a defining term, it established the failure of the colonial state to achieve a 'hegemonic ruling culture', which led to an externalization of the state from the ruled.[156] Guha predominantly classifies the historiography into two-fold elitist categories, namely colonial elitism and bourgeois nationalist elitism.[157] The intellectual engagement of the collective, however, 'exceeded the disciplines of history' and often 'participated in a contemporary critique of history and nationalism, and of orientalism and Eurocentrism in the construction of social science knowledge'.[158] It primarily aimed to *write history from below*. David Ludden recalls this attempt as a rejection of 'official nationalism' and developing an approach 'transnationally, as did its readership and its critical appreciation'.[159]

While delineating a perspective on 'history from below', it recognized the place of the 'particular' within the 'global'.[160] The subaltern collective project sharpened such claims, as Gyandendra Pandey argues,

> ... not only simply to recover a neglected underside of human experience, and to announce that subaltern groups also counted in the unfolding of history, but to rethink the pattern of historical development as a whole, grasp the contradiction that lay at its heart and outline political possibilities that had been lost to view or remained to be elaborated.[161]

This illuminates the importance of recognizing the unique position of the Indian society in that it had not fully realized or experienced capitalism and was transitioning from a feudal system defined by the caste system. Perhaps another point that came to pose a crucial critique of the school is undermining the function of caste in a society that is folded with the production of capital and creates geographies of difference based on Brahmanical values. However, the subaltern groups in contemporary India stage their issues, often using rights-based claims, and engage with the post-colonial state to negotiate their demands and challenge Brahmanical orders. Partha Chatterjee divides the claims of the subaltern groups into two fissures: civil and political society.[162]

While the former rests their claim through the liberal itinerary and values of the formal institutions of citizenship, often rights-based claims, the latter is defined by governmental policies that undercut governance-based policies. Welfare emerges as one of the key vocabularies of political society and enables a political space of negotiation between the subaltern groups and the state. Groups such as Adivasis become targeted as 'demographic categories of governmentality'.[163]

This book therefore uses the work of the collective as a lens through which to understand the effects of colonialism enmeshed with caste order and routine violence against the marginalized in contemporary India. Subaltern theories in this book are interlaced with post-colonial thoughts and situate a much wider debate that remains crucial to this study. In doing so, it draws on Robert Young's formulation of post-colonialism 'not only as a disciplinary field, nor [as] a theory which has or has not come to an end' but also as an attempt 'to reconstruct Western knowledge formations, reorient ethical norms, turn the power structures of the world upside down, refashion the world from the below.'[164] In some sense, I locate the emerging tension of the subaltern in the post-colonial literature as a figure that inherited 'inter-related histories of violence, domination, inequality, and injustice, … and live without things that most of those in the West take for granted'.[165]

Responding to Young, in particular, but also to Vivek Chibber's innocuous commentary against post-colonialism, Subir Sinha and Rashmi Verma suggest in their thought-provoking article: 'Young is emphatic that there is "no need to rediscover a new theory", what is important is the need to 'locate the hidden rhizomes of colonialism's historical reach, of what remains invisible, unseen, silent or unspoken'.[166] They think that the effort to 'revive' or 'refashion' post-colonial theory through the stances of visibility represents an older commitment.[167] In suggesting so, it is 'no radical rethinking but an enlargement effort' and therefore the attempt should be to go 'beyond the formulae of incorporating' in order to think about addressing new problems.[168] They highlight the creative tension between the two as follows:

> As a framework for analysing imperialism and colonialism, postcolonial theory in its dominant formation has made productive use of notions of contingency, incommensurability, ambivalence and hybridity in order to take down the grand narratives of colonialism and cultural essence (and less frequently capitalism).... Thus, while Marxism provides an overarching analysis of capitalist society, postcolonial theory's analytic approach has been largely premised on deconstructing what it considers to be overarching power of Western capitalism, imperialism and 'modernity'.[169]

Without undermining the usefulness of either, they think that both schools of thought (Marxist and post-colonialist) have 'politically progressive direction, an invitation to continue the conversation rather than to close it'.[170] Furthermore, they challenge the 'assumption of stability in the category of "the universal" which some Marxists invoke in opposition to postcolonial theory's emphasis on difference and particularity'.[171]

Weaving Theory as Method

The book situates the recurring tensions in post-colonial and subaltern theories in the wake of memory politics to understand subalternity as a process necessitated by identities that are often essentialized—making categories such as Adivasi the classical 'resisting subjects' in the imaginary of both Marxists and the post-colonial (read subaltern).[172] I appropriate subalternity in this book as the key tool to explore various positionalities from which people and institutions produce forms of knowledge and use memory as a tool of politics. In doing so, I show how subaltern groups are now very much part of the hyper-visible and global flow of the economy, where their 'backward' disposition prepares the ground for intervention through development projects. In other words, they are 'no more cut off from lines of access to the centre'.[173] I move away from the fixation on the subaltern project and the search for universalism that pose an obstacle in learning from groups such as Adivasis, who are located in a 'set of power relations that are situated in a specific context'.[174] I undertake this project as an exploratory task that uses ethnographic and archival material to situate the emergent category of memory.

In this book, memory therefore disrupts hegemonic ideological standpoints by examining objects (statues and memorials), speech and myriad forms of representation. These sites function as affective registers which conceal material inequalities through the ritual of memorialization. They become affective sites of 'epistemic violence' which not only occlude the speech of the subalterns by denying their ownership of the past or heritage but also systemically diminish them as participants in this process of memorialization.[175] I seek to display how an ethnographic enquiry into these objects (see Chapters 3 and 4), resistance movements that deploy memorial artefacts (see Chapter 5) and their relationship with communities in turn shapes and informs the lifeworld[176] of the subalterns and the state.

In foregrounding this, I show what Alf Nilsen argues is an 'interface between conjunctural opportunities (use of dominant order such as law by subalterns) and structural constraints' (restrictions or limitations of institutions) to locate the various contours of struggle led by Adivasis as memory politics spreads across the state.[177] In fact, when analysing the rapidly changing nature of the state, negotiation by subaltern groups and practices of domination—effectively moving away from the simplistic binaries of 'civil' and 'political' to lay out the complexities

Introduction

of the struggles—this book uses memory as an act of speech. The appropriation of memory is crucial to defining this process. The ambition of this book is to lay out the working of the state and its use of different forms of knowledge and its pursuit of violence to attain the subalternization of memory. The book shows that the subaltern group not only mobilizes methodical tools (law) to clearly stake their claims but also uses memorial forms of speaking that are gestural in nature—often threatening the hegemonic order of speaking. In other words, the subaltern groups appropriate the hegemonic language to challenge or pose limits to speaking as only forms of communication. In this process, they appropriate symbols—artefacts of memory (for instance, graveyards) (see Chapter 5)—to signal how voices that are deemed legitimate within 'epistemic boundaries of hegemony' are capable of being exposed through symbolic markers of memory.[178]

In this book, I offer contesting narratives of politics that are embedded in complex networks of negotiations and emphasize the 'indigenous agency within circumstances after colonialism'.[179] Invariably, this opens the scope for the book to discuss the implication of *thinking* about the wider debate on the relationship between the idea of indigeneity, the subaltern and post-colonialism.[180] The book shifts from the idiosyncratic approach of treating evidence as a form of truth in itself to recognizing temporalities of memory defined by material inequality. It traces these temporalities by basing its analysis on both episodic (the Birsa movement) and fragmentary (*pathalgadi* [erection of stone slabs]) articulations from within the protracted fields of historical inquiry.

While rooted in specific inquiries at the micro-level functioning of memory-making practices and resistance, this book reflects on the larger question of nationalism against the backdrop of the competing claims of ownership, resource and mineral politics. It uses the theoretical formulation to explain the problem—sometimes merely as a form of description, while at others as the analytical framework for discussions on ideas and thoughts.

Structure of the Book

The book contains six chapters divided by three broad thematic parts. The first part, 'Context, Theory, and Methodology', offers an introduction, which serves as the context to the study. Chapter 1 introduces the reader to the background, structure and format of the study—outlining the historiography, contemporary debates and theoretical underpinning.

Chapter 2 features the second theme of the book—'the historical memory'. In this chapter, I use extensive archival material procured from the India Office Records at the British Library, London; the Christian Missionary Society at the

Cadbury Library, Birmingham; and the State Archive of Jharkhand, Ranchi, to show the typical nature of micro-histories that are limited by records and defined by memory.

The last thematic part, 'Ethnography of Memory, Objects and Resistance', consists of three chapters. In Chapter 3, I present an ethnographic exploration of statue-making (of Birsa Munda) practices situated in the wider political and cultural milieu of Ranchi and Khunti district. In this, I trace the process of identity politics—often involving Adivasi and non-Adivasi leaders affiliated to state parties and their engagement with burgeoning practices of memorialization without accommodating for rising tensions around land rights.

Chapter 4 offers an extensive engagement with practices of commemoration associated with Birsa Munda. In doing so, I focus on two sites of memory: the *samadhi sthal* in Ranchi and the memorial pillar at Dombari Buru in Sail Rakab village. These two sites are considered as the most defining memorial landscapes that attract both politicians and Adivasis to observe the death of Birsa and his followers. The chapter also highlights, through field narratives, the displacement of subaltern Adivasi voices in the muffling notions of commemoration endorsed by the political elite.

Chapter 5 offers an interesting case study of a recent movement called Pathalgadi. I use the movement to establish the historical traces of memory—moving back to archival records, showing its implication on the contemporary nature of Adivasi struggle. In doing so, I argue that *pathalgadi* draws inspiration from the historical practice of *sasandiri* (burial practice), showing new ways of thinking about memory-as-politics and harvesting the legacy of Birsa.

Chapter 6 concludes the book by posing the question on the limitation of memory politics. I suggest imagining new political imperatives that stem from forging solidarity alongside the mobilization of identity-based (Adivasi) claims, which accommodates for material inequalities that are shaped by the entrenched structure of class and caste.

Notes

1. 'Take one of my photos. When you come back next time, please bring a printed copy. I will hang it next to my bed and feel inspired.' Bijo, in a personal interview with the author, Ranchi, 12 September 2018. I have translated all interviews quoted in the text.

2. See Alpa Shah, 'Alcoholics Anonymous: The Maoist Movement in Jharkhand, India', *Modern Asian Studies* 45, no. 5 (2011): 1095–1117, https://doi.org/10.1017/S0026749X1000020X (accessed on 15 July 2019).

3   Jharkhand is home to 33 million people, of whom 13 million are poor. In 2012, 40 per cent of the population were living below the poverty line, and significant among those are Adivasis in rural areas, with 55.3 per cent living in poverty. See C. Rangarajan, *Report of the Expert Group to Review the Methodology for Measurement of Poverty* (New Delhi: Planning Commission, Governement of India, 2014). Prominent among other areas are the state's southern and eastern districts that host high concentrations of Adivasis. For a detailed analysis, see K. M. Singh, M. S. Meena, R. K. P. Singh, Abhay Kumar and Anjani Kumar, 'Rural Poverty in Jharkhand, India: An Empirical Study Based on Panel Data', MPRA Paper, Munich Personal RePEc Archive, Munich, 2012, https://mpra.ub.uni-muenchen.de/45258/ (accessed on 30 July 2019). According to global standards of poverty, 82 per cent of Dalits and Adivasis fall below the poverty line. Adivasis are worse off. See K. P. Kannan, 'How Inclusive Is Inclusive Growth in India?', *Indian Journal of Labour Economics* 55, no. 1 (2012): 33–60. The word *adivasi* is used to denote the indigenous peoples of India. However, it is limited to only certain areas. Later in the chapter, I have shown the political use and contestation of the term.

4   Hilary Standing, 'Munda Religion and Social Structure', PhD dissertation, SOAS University of London.

5   See Kumar Suresh Singh, *Birsa Munda and His Movement (1872–1901)* (Kolkata: Seagull Books, 2002); S. P. Sinha, *Life and Times of Birsa Bhagwan*, 2nd edition (Ranchi: Bihar Tribal Research Institute, 1997). For a more recent attempt at capturing Birsa's life within Indian history, see Sunil Khilnani, *Incarnations: India in 50 Lives* (London: Allen Lane, 2016).

6   For example, Kumar Suresh Singh, *Birsa Munda and His Movement*. Also, S. C. Roy, *The Mundas and Their Country* (Calcutta: Kuntaline Press, 1912).

7   Uday Chandra, 'Flaming Fields and Forest Fires: Agrarian Transformations and the Making of Birsa Munda's Rebellion', *Indian Economic and Social History Review* 53, no. 1 (2016): 1–30, p. 28, https://doi.org/10.1177/0019464615619540 (accessed on 17 February 2017).

8   Prakash Kashwan and Rahul Ranjan outline the specific formulation of this emergent framework by using several case studies. See Prakash Kashwan and Rahul Ranjan, 'Introduction' (Special Issue: Echoes from the Woods: At the Crossroads of Forest Struggles and Human Rights in Postcolonial India), *International Journal of Human Rights* 25, no. 7 (2021): 1089–93.

9   The term 'political elites' refers to representatives of the various national and regional parties.

10   Taiaiake Alfred and Jeff Corntassel, 'Being Indigenous: Resurgences against Contemporary Colonialism', *Government and Opposition* 40, no. 4 (2005): 597–614.

11   In doing so, the book draws attention to the recent focus of Partha Chatterjee on the 'after' of subaltern studies. See Partha Chatterjee, 'After Subaltern Studies', *Economic and Political Weekly* 47, no. 39 (2012): 44–49.

12   Ashis Nandy, *The Intimate Enemy: Loss and Recovery of Self under Colonialism* (New Delhi: Oxford University Press, 1983), p. 14.

13   Alfred and Corntassel, 'Being Indigenous', p. 598.

14 Aimé Césaire, *Discourse on Colonialism*, trans. Joan Pinkham (New York: Monthly Review Press, 2000), p. 42.

15 Pheng Cheah, *Spectral Nationality: Passages of Freedom from Kant to Postcolonial Literatures of Liberation* (New York: Columbia University Press, 2003), p. 3.

16 See Priyamvada Gopal, *Insurgent Empire: Anticolonial Resistance and British Dissent* (London: Verso, 2019), p. 23.

17 Ibid.

18 Rangimarie Mahuika, 'Kaupapa Māori Theory Is Critical and Anti-colonial', *MAI Review* 3 (2008): 1–16, p. 4.

19 The concept of affect has various meanings. For instance, it can be 'descriptions of how emotions occur in everyday life, understood as the richly expressive/aesthetic feeling-cum-behaviour of continual becoming that is provided chiefly by bodily states and processes (and which is understood as constitutive of affect)'. See Nigel Thrift, 'Intensities of Feeling: Towards a Spatial Politics of Affect', *Geografiska Annaler* 86, no. 1 (2004): 57–78, p. 60. I use 'affect' as both feeling and emotion interchangeably. Although there is a difference between emotion and affect (as shown by Thrift), the book borrows the idea from the work of Tim Ingold. He writes: 'Affect is simply the way I respond to things or am affected by them in the world. So it is pretty close to feeling and I like feeling too because it is something you do with things rather than something inside you that you express.' See Claire Vionnet, 'From Experience to Language towards an Affected and Affective Writing: A Conversation with Tim Ingold', *TSANTSA* 23 (2018): 82–90, p. 84.

20 The book borrows the term 'everyday politics' from the groundbreaking work of James Scott. See James C. Scott, 'Everyday Forms of Resistance', *Copenhagen Journal of Asian Studies* 4, no. 1 (24 November 2017): 33–62, p. 33, DOI: 10.22439/cjas.v4i1.1765.

21 Tadhg O'Keeffe uses 'landscape-as-power' as a conceptual idea to explain the effects of power landscape. See Tadhg O'Keeffe, 'Landscape and Memory: Historiography, Theory, Methodology', in *Heritage, Memory and the Politics of Identity: New Perspectives on the Cultural Landscape*, ed. Yvonne Whelan and Niamh Moore (Hampshire: Ashgate Publishing Limited, 2007).

22 A series of works have envisioned such a possibility. See Prathama Banerjee, 'Writing the Adivasi: Some Historiographical Notes', *Indian Economic and Social History Review* 53, no. 1 (2016): 131–53; Sangeeta Dasgupta and Daniel J. Rycroft, *The Politics of Belonging in India: Becoming Adivasi* (New Delhi: Routledge, 2011); Uday Chandra, 'Towards Adivasi Studies: New Perspectives on "Tribal" Margins of Modern India', *Studies in History* 31, no. 1 (2015): 122–27, https://doi.org/10.1177/0257643014558479 (accessed on 27 February 2017). Alf Nilsen has done a far more extensive study of Adivasis within the central Indian states to show the contradictions of the post-colonial state (see the theoretical discussion) to highlight the tension of law, subalternity and dispossession. Alf Gunvald Nilsen, *Politics from Below: Essays on Subalternity and Resistance in India* (New Delhi: Aakar Books, 2017); Srila Roy and Alf Gunvald Nilsen, *New Subaltern Politics: Reconceptualizing Hegemony and Resistance in Contemporary India* (New Delhi: Oxford University Press, 2015).

23 The dispute on the date and place of birth is variously discussed in the literature. For instance, in the accounts of Sinha, the place of Birsa's birth is disputed as being between Chalkad and Ulihatu.
24 K. S. Singh, *Birsa Munda and His Movement*, p. 37.
25 Ibid., p. 38; Samar Bosu Mullick, 'Preface', in *Adi-Dharam: Religious Beliefs of the Adivasis of India*, ed. Ram Dayal Munda, pp. 7–12 (Calcutta: Adivaani, 2014).
26 K. S. Singh, *Birsa Munda and His Movement*, p. 38.
27 Steeped in the caste system, Brahmins and upper-caste Hindus wear a white sacred thread called *janeu*. However, it is not restricted and now widely worn amongst other castes. Men receive it as a rite of passage called *upnayana* (initiation into the life of a student).
28 See Steve Derne, 'Religious Movement as Rite of Passage: An Anlaysis of Birsa Movement', *Contributions to Indian Sociology* 19, no. 2 (1985): 251–68 (emphasis mine).
29 K. S. Singh, *Birsa Munda and His Movement*, p. 53.
30 Ibid., p. 54.
31 Rev. Fr. J. Hoffman, Catholic Missionary of Sarwada to the Commissioner of the Chota Nagpur Division, shelf mark IOR/L/PJ/6/540, enclosure 4, file 534, 14th January 1900, British Library, London. For the account of Dharti Aba, please see John-Baptist Hoffman, *Encyclopaedia Mundarica*, vol. 1, shelf mark 14178.e.47, British Library, London (emphasis mine).
32 Ibid., p. 567.
33 Michael Adas, *Prophets of Rebellion: Millenarian Protest Movements against the European Colonial Order* (Cambridge: Cambridge University Press, 1979), p. 18.
34 Ibid., p. 23 (emphasis mine).
35 S. C. Roy, *The Oraons of Chota Nagpur: Their History, Economic Life and Social Organisation* (Ranchi: Thacker, Spink and Company, 1915).
36 A *khuntkatti* Munda has the right to use a suitable portion of the jungle and cultivate it for living.
37 Sachichidanda, 'Social Change in Chotanagpur', *Bulletin of the Bihar Tribal Research Institute* 6, no. 2 (1964): 220–39, p. 222.
38 Sangeeta Dasgupta, 'The Journey of an Anthropologist in Chhotanagpur', *Indian Economic and Social History Review* 42, no. 2 (2004): 165–98, DOI: 10.1177/001946460404100203.
39 Sinha, *Life and Times of Birsa Bhagwan*, p. 105.
40 Ibid., p. 1.
41 Ibid., p. 105.
42 Ibid.
43 Ibid., p. 234.
44 Ibid.
45 Ibid.

46 K. S. Singh, *Birsa Munda and His Movement*.
47 Ibid., p. 1.
48 Ibid.
49 *Panchayat* is a local-body self-government that comprises five elected members (*panch* meaning five) from any community and takes decisions on important issues at the village level.
50 K. S. Singh, *Birsa Munda and His Movement*, p. 1.
51 Ibid., p. 24.
52 Ibid., p. 233.
53 Ibid., p. 232 (emphasis mine).
54 Adas, *Prophets of Rebellion*.
55 Ranajit Guha, *Dominance without Hegemony: History and Power in Colonial India* (Cambridge, MA: Harvard University Press, 1997).
56 Ranajit Guha, *Elementary Aspects of Peasant Insurgency in Colonial India* (Durham, NC: Duke University Press, 1999), p. 9.
57 Ibid.
58 Ibid., p. 13.
59 Ibid., p. 2.
60 Ibid.
61 Ibid., p. 3.
62 Guha, *Dominance without Hegemony*, p. 4. See Eric Hobsbawm, *Primitive Rebels* (Manchester: University of Manchester Press, 1959).
63 Guha, *Dominance without Hegemony* (emphasis mine).
64 Ibid., pp. 123–24.
65 Adas, *Prophets of Rebellion*.
66 Gyan Prakash, 'The Impossibility of Subaltern History', *Nepantla: Views from South* 1, no. 2 (2000): 287–94, p. 287.
67 Ibid., p. 288.
68 Ibid.
69 H. H. Risley, *The Tribes and Castes of Bengal: Ethnographic Glossary*, vol. 1 (Calcutta: Bengal Secretariat Press, 1891). Also see Robert Vane Russell, *The Tribes and Castes of the Central Provinces of India* (London: Macmillan, 1916).
70 André Béteille, 'The Concept of Tribe with Special Reference to India', *European Journal of Sociology* 27, no. 2 (1986): 297–318, p. 311.
71 Meena Radhakrishna (ed.), *First Citizens: Studies on Adivasis, Tribals, and Indigenous People in India* (New Delhi: Oxford University Press, 2016).
72 See the provocative work of Sharmila Rege, who outlines the violent structure of caste realities in Indian society. Sharmila Rege, *Against the Madness of Manu* (New Delhi: Navayana, 2013).
73 Jens Lerche and Alpa Shah, 'Conjugated Oppression within Contemporary Capitalism: Class, Caste, Tribe and Agrarian Change in India', *Journal of Peasant*

Introduction

Studies 45, nos. 5–6 (19 September 2018): 927–49, p. 933, https://doi.org/10.1080/03066150.2018.1463217 (accessed on 30 June 2019).

74 Ibid. Also see Radhakrishna (ed.), *First Citizens*.

75 Virginius Xaxa, 'Formation of Adivasi/Indigenous Peoples' Identity in India', in *First Citizens: Studies on Adivasis, Tribals, and Indigenous People in India*, ed. Meena Radhakrishna, pp. 33–52 (New Delhi: Oxford University Press, 2016), p. 35.

76 Ibid.; Romila Thapar, 'Early Indian History and the Legacy of DD Kosambi', Economic and Political Weekly 43, no. 30 (25 July 2008): 43–51.

77 See Vinita Damodaran, 'Colonial Constructions of the 'Tribe' in India: The Case of Chotanagpur', *Indian Historical Review* 33, no. 1 (2006): 44–75, p. 46, DOI: 10.1177/037698360603300104.

78 Ibid.

79 Béteille, 'The Concept of Tribe with Special Reference to India', p. 317 (emphasis mine).

80 Sanjukta Das Gupta, 'Rethinking Adivasi Identity: The Chota Nagpur Tenancy Act (1908) and Its Aftermath among the Hos of Singhbhum', in *Adivasi in Colonial India: Survival, Resistance and Negotiation*, ed. Biswamoy Pati, pp. 88–111 (New Delhi: Orient Blackswan, 2011).

81 Ibid., p. 91.

82 Ibid.

83 Ibid., p. 108.

84 Gupta, 'Rethinking Adivasi Identity', p. 109.

85 David Hardiman, *The Coming of the Devi: Adivasi Assertion in Western India* (Oxford: Oxford University Press, 1987), pp. 10–13

86 Jai Pal Singh Munda was born into an Adivasi family in Ranchi. He went to a missionary school. After obtaining his degree from the University of Oxford, he proclaimed his role as a politician from the region. As a graduate student at St John's College in Oxford, he led the team from India at the 1928 Olympics in Amsterdam, Netherlands. Upon his return to Chota Nagpur, he began to work on the development of the region by forming his own party, the Jharkhand Party. The party won the majority of seats in the 1951 elections in independent India. However, it subsequently merged with the Congress party, which led to its decline. For an elaborate description of Jai Pal Singh's life, see his biography by Santosh Kiro, *The Life And Times of Jaipal Singh Munda* (Ranchi: Prabhat Publications, 2018).

87 L. N. Rana in his essay investigates Jai Pal Singh's role as a political leader and writes: 'Under his leadership the movement received a new momentum which it had never achieved before. In his presidential address, he frankly admitted that the separation movement had the support of the Muslims, the Christian Missions and the *Bangalis* along with the sympathies of the British officials. He evoked the primordial sentiments of the Adivasis to unite them and declared that the Muslims and Bengalis as genuine Adivasis should get their moral and material support.' See L. N. Rana, 'The Adivasi Mahasabha (1938–1949): Launching Pad of the Jharkhand Movement', *Proceedings of the Indian History Congress* 53, no. 3 (1992): 397–405.

88 Presidential Speech to the All India Adivasi Mahasabha at Ranchi, 28 February 1948. The speech has been reproduced in many places. See Jai Pal Singh, 'Jai Jharkhand! Jai Adivasi! Jai Hind!', in *Jharkhand Movement: Indigenous Peoples' Struggle for Autonomy in India*, ed. R. D. Munda and Samar Bosu Mullick, pp. 2–14 (Copenhagen: International Work Group for Indigenous Affairs, 2003).

89 'Memorandum Submitted by the Chhotanagpur Improvement Society', *Report of the Indian Statutory Commission: Selections from Memoranda and Oral Evidence by Non-officials*, part 1 (Calcutta: Government Printing, 1930), p. 447, cited in Joseph Bara, 'Alien Construct and Tribal Contestation in Colonial Chhotanagpur: The Medium of Christianity', *Economic and Political Weekly* 44, no. 52 (2009): 90–96, p. 91.

90 Despite the prejudice associated with the term 'tribal/tribe', it continues to be used too in the north-eastern states of India. The word 'tribe' is closely tied to the flow of Adivasi migrants from Chota Nagpur in the late 19th and 20th centuries, and hence the term *adivasi* has been received more as a phrase to denote outsiders in north-east India. See Xaxa, 'Formation of Adivasi/Indigenous Peoples' Identity in India'. In the north-eastern states, the term 'tribe' acquires a new meaning, 'politically reconfigured to represent a collective identity like Adivasi' in eastern India. See Bengt G. Karlsson and T. B. Subha, *Indigeneity in India* (New York: Columbia University Press, 2006), p. 4.

91 Alpa Shah, '"Keeping the State Away": Democracy, Politics, and the State in India', *Journal of the Royal Anthropological Institute* 13, no. 1 (2007): 129–45.

92 Alpa Shah, 'Religion and the Secular Left: Subaltern Studies, Birsa Munda and Maoists', *Anthropology of This Century* 9 (2014): 1–12, http://aotcpress.com/author/alpa-shah (accessed on 20 July 2017).

93 Alpa Shah, 'The Agrarian Question in a Maoist Guerrilla Zone: Land, Labour and Capital in the Forests and Hills of Jharkhand, India', *Journal of Agrarian Change* 13, no. 3 (2013): 424–50, p. 428, https://doi.org/10.1111/joac.12027 (accessed on 20 July 2017).

94 Shah, 'Religion and the Secular Left'.
95 Ibid.
96 Ibid.
97 Ibid.
98 Ibid. Shiv *charcha* is a religious gathering of devotees who pray to the Hindu god Shiva.
99 Ibid.
100 Ibid.
101 Ibid.
102 Shah, 'Religion and the Secular Left'.
103 Chandra, 'Flaming Fields and Forest Fires', p. 3.
104 Ibid., p. 4.
105 Ibid.
106 Ibid.

107 For the archival source, refer to H. I. S. Cotton to C. W. Bolton, Foreign Proceedings B, 14 September 1895, National Archives of India (hereafter NAI). See Chandra, 'Flaming Fields and Forest Fires', p. 23 (emphasis mine).

108 Sherry B. Ortner, 'Resistance and the Problem of Ethnographic Refusal', *Comparative Studies in Society and History* 37, no. 1. (1995): 173–93, p. 174.

109 Daniel J. Rycroft, 'Anthropological Archives and "Chiasmic" Time in Modern India', *Irish Journal of Anthropology* 19, no. 2 (Autumn–Winter 2016): 46–68 (emphasis mine).

110 Ibid., p. 46.

111 Ibid., p. 49.

112 Daniel J. Rycroft, 'Locating Adivasi Politics: Aspects of "Indian" Anthropology After Birsa Munda', *Anglistica AION* 19, no. 1 (2015): 133–46.

113 See Gopal, *Insurgent Empire*.

114 Partha Chatterjee, *The Nation and Its Fragments: Colonial and Postcolonial Histories* (Princeton, NJ: Princeton University Press, 1993), p. 4.

115 James Chiriyankandath, 'Colonialism and Post-Colonial Development', in *Politics in the Developing World*, ed. Peter Burnell, Vicky Randall and Lise Rakner, pp. 29–43 (Oxford: Oxford University Press, 2017), p. 34.

116 J. P. Singh, 'Jai Jharkhand! Jai Adivasi! Jai Hind!' (emphasis on *jungli* mine to highlight the significant use of the term).

117 Pooja Parmar, 'Undoing Historical Wrongs: Law and Indigeneity in India', *Osgoode Hall Law Journal* 49, no. 3 (2012): 491–525.

118 Ibid.

119 Colin Samson and Carlos Gigoux, *Indigenous Peoples and Colonialism: Global Perspectives* (Cambridge: Polity Press, 2017), p. 1 (emphasis mine).

120 Nirmal Sengupta, *Fourth World Dynamics: Jharkhand* (Kolkata: Authors Guild Publications, 1984). Sengupta believes that 'one feature common to all these revolts (Santhal and Birsa)—they were all directed specifically against outsiders'.

121 In fact, the Unnati Sabha divided further into small factions. The Kisa Sabha was one of such groups led by two members of Unnati Sabha, namely Paul Dayal and Thebel Oraon. See Gautam Kumar Bera, *The Unrest Axle: Ethno-Social Movements in Eastern India* (Kolkata: Mittal Publications, 2008).

122 R. D. Munda and Samar Bosu Mullick (eds.), *Jharkhand Movement: Indigenous Peoples' Struggle for Autonomy in India* (Copenhagen: International Work Group for Indigenous Affairs, 2003), p. 4.

123 Rana, 'The Adivasi Mahasabha (1938–1949)', p. 398.

124 Ibid., p. 399.

125 Ibid., p. 400.

126 Rana, 'The Adivasi Mahasabha (1938–1949)', p. 400.

127 R. D. Munda and B. P. Keshari, 'Recent Developments in the Jharkhand Movement', *India International Centre Quarterly* 19, no. 3 (1992): 71–89, p. 74.

128 A. S., 'Containing the Jharkhand Movement', *Economic and Political Weekly* 14, no. 14 (1979): 648–50.

129 Amit Prakash, *Jharkhand: Politics of Development and Identity* (New Delhi: Orient Blackswan, 2001), p. 122.
130 Ibid.
131 Sanjay Kumar and Praveen Rai, 'Shrinking Political Space for the Jharkhand Mukti Morcha', *Economic and Political Weekly* 44, no. 33 (2009): 24–29.
132 Louise Tillin, *Remapping India: New States and Their Political Origins* (New Delhi: Oxford University Press, 2013), p. 73.
133 A. Prakash, *Jharkhand*, p. 123.
134 Ibid., p. 83.
135 Vinita Damodaran, 'Environment, Ethnicity and History in Chotanagpur, India, 1850–1970', *Environment and History* 3, no. 3 (1997): 273–98, p. 273, https://doi.org/10.3197/096734097779555854 (accessed on 30 September 2019).
136 Ibid.
137 Ibid., p. 73.
138 In 2017, Meghnath, a leading documentary maker and an established public intellectual in the region, made a movie on his life. It is a great resource for research on R. D. Munda as a key Adivasi public intellectual. For the documentary, see AKHRA Ranchi, 'Naachi Se Baanchi: Film on Ram Dayal Munda (2017)', YouTube video, 2:04, 12 March 2018, https://www.youtube.com/watch?v=dGPuFcbGVns (accessed on 10 March 2019).
139 Munda and Keshari, 'Recent Developments in the Jharkhand Movement'. Munda and Mullick (eds.), *Jharkhand Movement*.
140 Tillin, *Remapping India*.
141 Rycroft, 'Locating Adivasi Politics'.
142 Munda and Mullick (eds.), *Jharkhand Movement*, p. 6 (emphasis mine).
143 Tillin, *Remapping India*, p. 85.
144 Corinne Lennox and Damien Short (eds.), *Handbook of Indigenous Peoples' Rights* (London: Routledge, 2016), p. 4.
145 Ibid., p. 8.
146 For the nationalist writings, refer to Govind Sadashiv Ghuyre, *The Scheduled Tribes: The Aborigines So-Called and Their Future* (Bombay: Ramdas Bhatkal for Popular Prakashan, 1963). However, there were also advocates of Adivasi isolationism, such as the anthropologist Verrier Elwin (1902–64). He was a key figure in working towards instituting a protectionist policy for Adivasis to save them from onslaught of the modernity. Indeed, this debate posed a binary that Shah calls 'to protect or assimilate'. See Alpa Shah, *In the Shadows of the State: Indigenous Politics, Environmentalism and Insurgency in Jharkhand, India* (New Delhi: Oxford University Press, 2011), p. 16.
147 Munda and Keshari, 'Recent Developments in the Jharkhand Movement', p. 79.
148 Ministry of Home Affairs, 'The Bihar Reorganisation Act, 2000', https://www.indiacode.nic.in/bitstream/123456789/2001/1/200030.pdf (accessed on 20 June 2020).

149 Munda and Mullick (eds.), *Jharkhand Movement*, p. 16.
150 See Nuala Johnson, 'Cast in Stone: Monuments, Geography, and Nationalism', *Environment and Planning D: Society and Space* 13, no. 1 (12 October 2006): 51–65, https://doi.org/10.1068/d130051; Planning Commission, Government of India, 'Scheduled Tribe', http://planningcommission.nic.nic.in/data/datable/data_2312/databook.pdf (accessed on 15 June 2018). In addition, the Constitution of India categorically defines Adivasis under the rubric of 'Scheduled Tribe'. The Constitution recognizes the population under the category of Scheduled Tribe defined in Clause 25 of Article 366 of the Constitution. For a historical understanding of migration in Chota Nagpur, see Myron Weiner, *Sons of the Soil: Migration and Ethnic Conflict in India* (Princeton, NJ: Princeton University Press, 1978).
151 Under Article 365 of the Constitution of India, the governor has power to suspend the state government and impose the central government in its place.
152 Rahul Ranjan, 'Unravelling the Narratives of Adivasi Dispossession: A Case Study of Land Acquisition in Nagri Village, Jharkhand'. *Development* 60, nos. 3–4 (2017): 227–34, https://doi.org/https://doi.org/10.1057/s41301-018-0171-8 (accessed on 20 August 2019).
153 Gayatri Chakravorty Spivak, 'Can the Subaltern Speak?', in *Marxism and the Interpretation of Culture*, ed. Cary Nelson and Lawrence Grossberg, pp. 271–313 (Chicago: University of Illinois Press, 1988). This definition moved away from the more loosely defined idea of subaltern by Guha, where he perceived subalternity as a form of opposition to elites. Ranajit Guha (ed.), *Subaltern Studies*, vol. 1: *Writings on South Asian History and Society* (Delhi: Oxford University Press, 1982). However, the book shows the capricious nature of subalternity that is mobilized far more widely from below than just identity—in fact, sometimes as class.
154 Jodi A. Byrd and Michael Rothberg, 'Between Subalternity and Indigeneity', *Interventions* 13, no. 1 (2011): 1–12, p. 3. Gyanendra Pandey has also attempted to situate the debate between the indigenous and the subaltern under the aegis of citizen framework. Gyanendra Pandey, 'Subaltern Citizens and Their Histories', *Interventions* 10, no. 3 (2008): 271–84.
155 Guha, *Elementary Aspects*.
156 Guha, *Dominance without Hegemony*, pp. 64–65.
157 See Ranajit Guha, 'On Some Aspects of the Historiography of Colonial India', in *Subaltern Studies*, vol. 1, ed. Guha, pp. 37–44.
158 Dipesh Chakrabarty, 'Subaltern Studies and Postcolonial Historiography', *Nepantla: Views from South* 1, no. 1 (2000): 9–32, p. 9.
159 See David Ludden, *Reading Subaltern Studies: Critical History, Contested Meaning and the Globalization of South Asia* (London: Anthem Press, 2001), p. 12.
160 Dipesh Chakrabarty, 'A Small History of Subaltern Studies', in *A Companion to Postcolonial Studies*, ed. Henry Schwarz and Sangeeta Ray, pp. 467–85 (Oxford: Blackwell Publishing, 2007).
161 Pandey, 'Subaltern Citizens and Their Histories', pp. 273–74.

162 Partha Chatterjee, *The Politics of the Governed: Reflections on Popular Politics in Most of the World* (New York: Columbia University Press, 2004).
163 Ibid., p. 41.
164 See Robert J. C. Young, 'Postcolonial Remains', *New Literary History* 43, no. 1 (2012): 19–42, p. 20.
165 Ibid.
166 Vivek Chibber in his book reclaimed his reading of Marxism to denounce the credentials of post-colonial and subaltern studies as the domain of culture and a literary attempt that does not offer a cohesive critique of the question of capital and class. See Vivek Chibber, *Postcolonial Theory and the Spectre of Capital* (New York: Verso Books, 2013); Subir Sinha and Rashmi Verma, 'Marxism and Postcolonial Theory: What's Left of the Debate?', *Critical Sociology* 43, nos. 4–5 (2015): 545–58, p. 553.
167 Ibid.
168 Ibid.
169 Ibid., p. 3.
170 Ibid., p. 1.
171 Ibid., p. 5.
172 Uday Chandra, 'Marxism, Postcolonialism and the Spectre of Universalism', *Critical Sociology* 43, nos. 4–5 (2015): 599–610.
173 Gayatri Chakravorty Spivak, 'The New Subaltern: A Silent Interview', in *Mapping Subaltern Studies and the Postcolonial*, ed. Vinayak Chaturvedi, pp. 324–45 (London: Verso, 2000), p. 324.
174 Roy and Nilsen, *New Subaltern Politics*.
175 Spivak, 'Can the Subaltern Speak?'.
176 'Lifeworld' is a broad term. Used in different contexts, the term has gained currency to explain the social experiences and local knowledge of the community and the individual.
177 Alf Gunvald Nilsen, *Adivasis and the State: Subalternity and Citizenship in India's Bhil Heartland* (Cambridge: Cambridge University Press, 2018), p. 20.
178 Philip Zehmisch, *Mini-India: The Politics of Migration and Subalternity in the Andamans Islands* (New Delhi: Oxford University Press, 2017), p. 14.
179 Robert Yazzie, 'Indigenous Peoples and Postcolonial Colonialism', in *Reclaiming Indigenous Voice and Vision*, ed. Marie Ann Battiste, pp. 39-49 (Vancouver: University of British Columbia, 2000).
180 Ibid.; Byrd and Rothberg, 'Between Subalternity and Indigeneity'.

Part II

'Historical Memory'

Chapter 2

Claiming the Munda *Raj* from the Margins

Land, Missionaries and the Making of the Birsa Ulgulan *in Chota Nagpur (1845–1900)*

Yet another Hul
Of Sido-Kanhu
Clutching the iron railings
Of the Bhagnadih enclosure
Squirms to break free once more?
While a rebellion of brave Birsa Munda
Slips and rolls down the slope
Of the Dombari Hill, over and over.

—Jacinta Kerketta[1]

The history of eastern India in the 19th century is dotted with resistance movements led by Adivasi groups.[2] Clear political articulation and goals drove the movements forwards. However, they do not necessarily emerge as 'watersheds' or 'great history' within either nationalist or colonialist writings. For instance, Anil Seal foregrounds his claims about the mass movements during independent struggles as a camouflage by noting: 'Programmes proclaimed from above were at odds with the way politicians worked lower down.'[3] What held in one part of India was not true in another. It is no longer credible to write about a movement grounded in common aims. In this way, Seal suggests, the focus should move to imperialism as it regulates the administrative functions of the country. He dismisses the possibility of the movement led by the subalterns by laying emphasis on economic determinism.[4] However, this claim failed to envision the role of subaltern subjects. In turn, the subaltern historiography reclaimed the protagonist of history not as a docile, passive aggressor but as an active political agent and, importantly, the writer of his or her own history.[5]

This chapter emplaces the importance of subaltern history by focusing on Birsa Munda and his *ulgulan*: a rebellion that was a culmination of an agrarian conflict infamously called Sardari *ladai*.[6] The Sardari *ladai* was a group led primarily by peasants whose land rights were diluted under the new legislative framework introduced at the end of the 18th century. There were land settlements that took place by the late 19th century, generating extreme anger among Adivasis in the region. So far a few works on Birsa and his rebellion provide a glimpse of a historical account of the movement.[7] These works, using primarily archival materials, illustrate the trajectory of groups interlaced with the agrarian conflict and wider political temper in this region.

The purpose of this chapter is to show how key groups such as the missionaries and *zamindar*s, the agrarian conflict (the Sardari *ladai*) and historical memory (Munda *raj*) contributed to the making of the Birsa movement. In exploring these variables, I make two specific inquiries. First, I investigate *new* sources to understand the role of the missionaries from 1845 to 1900 in Chota Nagpur. I use the category of the missionary to represent the restricted group of people who travelled from parts of Europe to Chota Nagpur. This chapter therefore does not reflect on any other groups who worked in other parts of the country. Each missionary group, I must note, represents a unique trajectory in missionary work, and the missionaries are hence irreducible to a general form of analysis. The analysis in the chapter is limited by access to records that I have chosen to examine.[8] These sources help in situating the movement within the broader political and agrarian history of the region that continues to underscore the temper of resistance in the region. Second, I emphasize the role of historical memory in the movement: the Munda *raj* (rule). As a trope of nostalgia about the past, the Munda *raj* shows the significance of *subaltern memory* in shaping the identity of Adivasis and the history of the region.

The chapter underscores how the dearth of sources makes an interesting case of the political use of Birsa's memory. This book lays out the larger problem with the narrow and atypical historical records available to construct a narrative of memory. Reflecting on this problem magnifies the significance of the Birsa movement within the purview of historical memory, which is a recurrent theme in contemporary political discourse, as is shown in subsequent chapters. In pursuing this problem, I argue that Birsa was a visionary who used his messianic characteristic as a political method—confronting the changing dynamics of law and society in this region. Reworking practices of magical healing became a medium for him to appropriate the sentiments of the Mundas. He invoked the Munda *raj*, which was to be achieved by liberation from *diku*s (outsiders). Munda *raj* was employed as a trope to mobilize and awaken political consciousness in the communities. Reference to the nostalgia of the past may appear tangential in the historical framing, but it functioned as a political tool—resting on the imagination of land that is stolen. In this way, Birsa mobilized nostalgia not as a fragmentary idea about the past often steeped in mythical return but rather as a rebellion 'against the modern idea of time and progress' to attain support for political mobilization.[9] He offered an alternative imagination foregrounded in the intergenerational collective memory of *adivasidom*.

To situate the movement within the broader field of subaltern history, I draw on Edward Said's idea of cultural imperialism—one where conversion becomes a form of 'overlapping territories'.[10] These territories are marked with 'ripples and currents that interrupt, retard, reverse or accelerate what would be an undistributed flow of history'.[11] The idea helps us in analysing the role of missionaries that is part of the 'interweaving and disentangling' of Adivasi identity as the two worlds unravel.[12] It also demonstrates a peculiar contradiction where, at once, we see how place-based values of missionaries were used as *moral alibis* to extend the 'civilizing mission', at least in the formative years after their arrival. However, this did not prohibit them from lending political agency to the converts.[13] Harald Tambs-Lyche and Marine Carrin have extensively explored the former theme in their work by distilling periods and groups, and their conflicts and roles, among Santhals in this region.[14] In other words, cultural imperialism recognizes the 'informal network of imperial power' that sought control outside of formalized political framework of imperial rule—in this case, missionaries.[15] A much broader view of this can also be felt from Thomas Babington Macaulay's infamous pronouncement on English education—a defining colonial project of the 19th century.[16]

Cultural imperialism, then, offers a descriptive modality for tracing the effects of colonialism and conversion on the cultural milieu—a fabric of human history fraught with emotive and affective encounters.[17] It maps the textural changes in the social order and makes conversion not 'a coercive ideology that erases the existing identities' but rather a site to mark nodal points of departure, differences and exchanges within the community.[18] These interactions come forth sometimes as violent ruptures and other times as new forms of consciousness evolving from the gradual processes of interactions. It shows us not only a shift in the convert's doctrine but also 'points of overlap and convergence'.[19] This reverberates in the cultural folds of Adivasi society even today.

A caveat, however, is necessary here. This chapter is a limited representation of the missionary narrative based on specific records. There are several contradictions and disputes that form the history of missionaries in this area. It is far from being a simplistic narrative of conversion and is entrenched in the complex articulation of ideas and struggles. Missionaries' archives are indispensable to understanding the vibrant and fraught landscape of Chota Nagpur.

Searching for the 'Heathen Soul'[20]: Adivasis, Missions, and Their History in Chota Nagpur

The history of Chota Nagpur is defined by resistance and resilience. It is marked by emigration and immigration on a remarkable scale, by ruptures and continuities. It offers unique insight into understanding history through a series of acts, events and memories. In showing glimpses of this, I have organized the chapter around two nodal points. First is the historical passage of missionaries in the region that significantly shaped the political landscape. Second are the influences and challenges that the social and political landscape brought to the uprising of Birsa Munda. These factors are evaluated by presenting new material that situates the understanding of the movement within both agrarian and sociocultural transformations driven by external factors.

Chota Nagpur—whose name consists of two words, *chutia* (little) and *nagpur* (diamond)—was taken over by the British dominion in 1765 from the *nawab* (governor) of the *dewani* (powerful government) of Bihar, Bengal and Orissa (present-day Odisha). Captain Camac became the first British officer to come to the Chota Nagpur region in 1769.[21] However, the region witnessed some dramatic events throughout the 19th century. Three of the most remarkable rebellions that shook the region were the Kol uprising (1829), the Santhal rebellion, or Sidhu Kanhu (1855) and a full-blown culmination with the Birsa *ulgulan* (1899).[22] These movements reflected on the systemic exploitation of *jal, jungle aur jameen* by *dikus*. Starting from the Kol uprising that demonstrated 'the necessity of radical reforms in the administration ... giving out several villages to Sikhs, Mohamedans, and others over the heads of the rightful owners, the Mankis and Mundas', numerous legislative measures flooded the region as forms of the emergent rule of law.[23] None of these measures could grasp or attend to the intensity and complex nature of land polity in this region.

Soon after, the Chota Nagpur division became a part of southern Bihar, which consisted of five districts, namely Ranchi, Hazaribagh, Dhanbad, Singhbhum and Palamau.[24] The earliest attempts to ascertain its population date to the early 19th century. For instance, the Kolhan Settlement Act of 1867, submitted by E. W. Collin, reports a rapid increase in population from 11,821 in 1867 to 237,320 in 1897.[25] Inhabited by the Ho Adivasi group, it registered a spectacular resistance—described famously as the 'bloodshed' event, where Hos stood and fought against the *zamindars*.[26] It led to the Kolhan settlement—exempting Hos from paying tribute to the *zamindars*.[27] However, a primal point of conflict here as well was the invasion by foreigners, *dikus*, who were not completely removed even after the settlement and, in fact, were partially recognized by the government, leading to an increase in their number from 1,579 (in 1867) to 10,112 in less than 30 years.[28] As I offer a detailed analysis here, it must be noted that there is not a singular idea of 'tribe' on which we can estimate the different groups. Each group—Hos and Mundas, among others—has its specific sociological nature based on its clans and kinship. Adivasis establish their claims as groups, for instance, in Jharkhand through a process of founding villages around their kinship.[29]

Chota Nagpur had been a homeland to Kols, who traditionally survived on cultivation and landed occupations. The area of Chota Nagpur consists of Kols, who occupied different parts: Those who lived in the northeast were called Oraons, while those who lived in the south and east were called Mundas.[30]

Table 2.1 The census of 1901 in the Chota Nagpur region

Name of race or tribe	Number	Total population (per cent)
Uraons	279,235	23.51
Mundas	236,600	19.91
Kharias	40,737	3.42
Asurs	2,701	0.23
Korwas	1,551	0.13
Gonds	7,007	0.59
Binjhias	3,902	0.33
Kaurs	1,886	0.15
Birhors	586	0.05
Total	574,205	48.33

Source: Commissioned by J. Reid in 1901.

Broadly, the term 'Kol' or 'Cole' is used widely in the missionary and partly in the administrative colonial accounts to denote Munda, Oraon, Kharia and Ho communities in Chota Nagpur. A report describes Kol, or Cole, as the following:

> A non-Aryan tract of Manbhum, Singhbhum and Western Bengal, classed by Dalton and others, mainly on linguistic grounds, as Kolarian.... The general name Kol, which is applied to both Mundas and Oraons, is interpreted by Herr Jellinghaus to man pig-killer, but the better opinion seems to be that it is a variant of horo, the Mundari for man. The change of h into k, we may cite hon, the Mundari for 'child' which is korwa, becomes kon and koro, the Muasi for horo, 'a man'. It may be added that the Kharias of Chota Nagpur call the Munda, Kora, a name closely approaching Kol.[31]

Categorized as 'animists' in the census record, the total population of the so-called animists was estimated to be 45.9 per cent in the region.[32] In particular, the population estimates in the late 19th century confirm that nearly 500,000 Uraons and 279,000 Mundas lived mostly in the northeast.[33]

The traditional system of land ownership was maintained for generations through oral sources. The land was a legally codified subject following the introduction of the Permanent Settlement Act that transformed the eastern region, including the fluvial landscape.[34] In fact, J. C. Jha, in his analysis of customary rights, noted: 'The customary rights date back to as early as the 6th century. Until the middle of the century, there was no *raja* and hence, *para* (which consisted of 15–25 villages) held the land. The local Mundas ruled it.'[35]

In the face of continual attacks on the land, the Kols took refuge in the Christian mission—an act deemed as a political stance by *zamindar*s. This also marked a turning point in the political and social history of this region. Their refusal of Hindu social order and colonial legislative measures displays the fierce history of resistance in the region. The following section shows how the evolution of the mission in Chota Nagpur offers a complex process of social and political negotiation within the broader history of the region and shapes the Birsa movement.

Heathen Souls: The Mission and Kols

In 1813, the Charter Bill was passed, allowing the establishment of bishoprics in India. But it was not until 1845 that the missionaries in Chota Nagpur arrived and recognized the Kols.[36] Four different missions came to Chota Nagpur over 50 years. These were:

1. Gossner Evangelical Lutheran[37]
2. Society for Propagation of the Gospel in Foreign Parts[38]
3. Roman Catholics (Belgium)[39]
4. Dublin Mission[40]

Each group was unique in its vision and contribution to the region, and, therefore, any attempt to lump the groups together would be an oversimplification. On 9 June 1850, four Oraons named Kasu, Bandhu, Gurha and Nawin Porin became the first natives to be baptized at Ranchi.[41] They were baptized by the German Lutheran Agency missionaries sent by Reverend Johannes Evangelista Gossner of Berlin.[42] The Lutherans arrived in Calcutta (present-day Kolkata) in 1844; they became the first missionaries and perhaps the most politically engaged group to come to Chota Nagpur in 1845.[43] Reverends Messis Schatz, Batsch, Brandt and Fanckle performed the baptism.[44] Unable to draw many converts, missionaries began working closely on the translation of the Bible, which was initially received with some suspicion. However, missionaries remained convinced that 'Kols are on the *skirts of civilization* and are in a position which will be improved by the spread of Christianity to an extent immeasurable, both in a temporal and spiritual point of view'.[45] This moral projection of the Adivasis as subjects lacking the inheritance of civilizational value informed the missionaries, at least in the formative period. However, this is not unusual as there are striking parallels to this to be found in the Hindu texts as well. For instance, Asoka Kumar Sen, in his work on the Adivasi landscape, has shown how the 'Sanskrit texts make both tacit and candid admission of the nativity of the "black aborigines" and their politico-cultural advance'.[46]

However, soon after the arrival of missionaries, the great revolt of 1857 took place—also known as the 'Indian Mutiny' in Britain. Emerging as the 'memorial history' by discontented *sepoy* regiments (Indian soldiers) against the British Empire, the mutiny targeted missionaries on a large scale too.[47] The 1857 revolt came to define the work of missionaries not only in this region but also across the country, especially on the northern plains of colonial India.

Mutiny and the Missionaries

The effects of the mutiny dissipated at different rates across Chota Nagpur. For instances, in the neighbourhood of Doranda, which hosted the Ramgarh battalion in the region, the jail was stormed and burnt. In particular, the German Mission Church and the house of European officials in the region witnessed an attack by 'six-pounder guns, evidently with the intention of demolishing the edifice'.[48]

Notably, the most unfortunate loss in the warfare was suffered by the archive, where 'many valuable documents, relating to the history of estates and tenures and the administration, have been irretrievably lost'.[49] The fire ignited by the vandalism engulfed 'a great portion of the vernacular record', making it difficult to recover the historical memory of the region.[50] Scholars since have used varied sources to corroborate and narrate the story.

An interesting report recounts the mutiny as follows: 'From 1850 to 1857, the truth continued to spread silently and surely, so that just before the *mutiny*, the converts numbered more than 700. Since that time, progress has rapidly grown. At the close of 1860, there were 1400 baptised.'[51] In subsequent years, from 1861 to 1867, the number of converts per year rose from 522 to 1,024.[52] In fact, at a congregation at Hazareebagh (Ranchi) in 1868, the numbers had risen to '10,000 baptized besides catechumens'.[53] The increase in the numbers demonstrates that the mutiny of 1857 targeting the white population did not necessarily reduce the number of converts. The mutiny did, however, raise 'the whole question of the relationship between religion and government and led to the abolition of the East India Company and the re-establishment of direct British rule under the Crown, with its promise of strict religious neutrality'.[54]

Nevertheless, missionaries continued to work with 'everyday uncertainties and experiences in the mission field as they encountered, interacted with, and sought to understand the heathen Kols of Chhotanagpur'.[55] They travelled from far-flung places, Gas Frykenberg writes, '[a]ccurately communicating the gospel, ... spreading it to the far end of the world'.[56] One of the missionaries who was confronted with effects of the mutiny wrote:

> April 12 (1859), day by day I have been seeking for a quiet home but could not find it.... I am fully occupied with instructing the candidates for baptism. Christ's work here has lost nothing by the mutiny, and in the midst of our distress, we have joy. To God alone belongs the glory.[57]

Despite the distress, they continued to 'sow the seed without the fruit'.[58]

Theologically speaking, it shows the motivation of the Christian missionaries that had an imperative to take 'the continuous, ongoing, and still unfinished work of God within ... the culture of every people'.[59] Such stances in this part of the region came with a responsibility for political participation in the agrarian crisis and land disputes—a duty that missionaries, especially the German Lutherans, performed well (Figure 2.1).

Figure 2.1 Gossner Evangelical Lutheran Church, Ranchi
Source: Photograph by the author.

Kols, Missions and the Spectre of Cultural Imperialism

Otherwise also known as *dhangar* to the upper-caste Hindus, a group of Kols who performed a range of 'skilled' work were often separated from other Kols.[60] Trained in a specialized form of work, they manually served the functioning of the colonial state at the provincial level as it expanded across the eastern region. But their contribution of labour failed to grant them social recognition; they remained subservient to upper-caste Hindus. However, missionaries received them with a rather sympathetic gesture—or at least some semblance of how we imagine sympathy, one that was denied to the Adivasis by the *zamindar*s and the British.

Conversely, the missionaries also saw in them their naïve subjects of conversion. For instance, mission reports describe them as follows: 'These *dhangars* have long been a despised race, they are usually very poor and *ignorant*, but they are not wanting in good common sense, judgment, or *manliness*, and (as two of the committee can testify) when the Gospel is preached, they hear it gladly'.[61] This depicts the body of *dhangars* whereby their identity is marked by the spectre of the oriental gaze, fraught with degrading characterization ('ignorant'), lacking thereof 'manliness'. The discourse of civility in this stance was a far-fetched ambition.

Notably, it also demonstrates a reflection of Eurocentric cultural values—also a standpoint to explain the peculiar characteristic of cultural imperialism: an imposition of foreign worldviews not with physical power but with the 'imposition of power in everyday life'.[62] Furthermore, such an illustration of imperialism becomes clearer when Missionaries note that 'our converts are not civilised Bengalis, but *rude barbarians*, just as my ancestors in Germany may have been when God, in his mercy sent among them to Irish missionaries (Figure 2.2) to win them to Christ. They were not ashamed of their rude converts.'[63] In describing the *rude barbarian* Kols against those of the *civilised Bengalis,* the missionaries' initial observations about the social fabric weaved them closely into ideas of the caste system—one that was based on purity and pollution.[64] Their descriptions complimented the existing social norms and hierarchies that defined the colonial

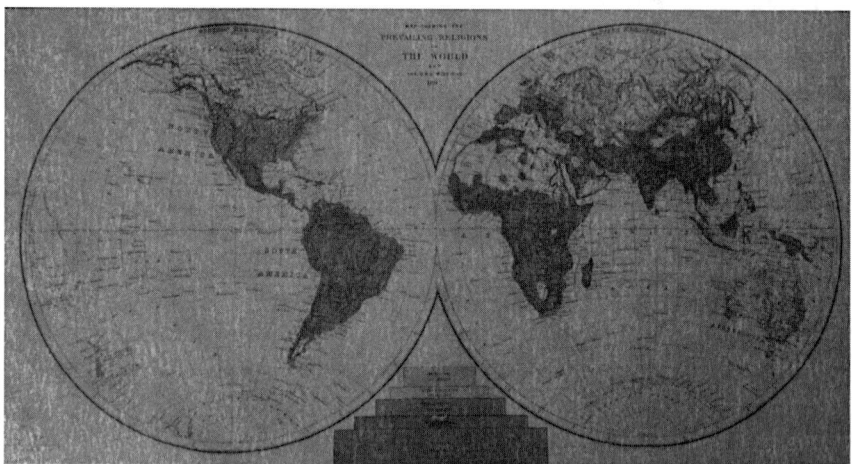

Figure 2.2 A map depicting the representation of religions of the world, where the 'heathens' are singled out, used by missionaries in the 19th century

Source: The Church Missionary Society (CMS) archive, University of Birmingham.

dispositions. Under the influence of such ideas, they frowned upon the worldview of the 'heathens'. This becomes more perceptible, for instance, in the reports of the Society for the Propagation of the Gospel (SPG):

> Men and women as soon as they become candidates for baptism, discard their *excessive ornamentation of the body* to which the Kols are much addicted; they cease to frequent the village dancing-place, which is the *sense of immorality*; they give up drinking their intoxicating liquor and other *evil practices* which are of the daily occurrence among the heathen and not tolerated among Christians.... A man had been excommunicated for his immoral conduct but had left his evils way and apparently repented.[65]

Here, Kols emerges as the embodiment of 'immoral' practices, failing to find a place or a vocabulary within the Christian worldview. In the missionary worldview, cultural practices such as wearing ornaments and dancing were a marker of *excess* that reflected a 'sense of immorality'. While making notes on the behaviour and cultural patterns of Adivasi society, the missionaries produced an assemblage of documents I would call the *empire of ethnography*. It helped classify and naturalize the cultural differences as a way of life, establishing the privilege of European social context. Such an ethnographic collection of data was conducive to the missionaries making sense of the everyday lives of their converts. In turn, it reflected the moral alibi for the civilizing mission that provides for the passage of British colonialism in the South Asian region.[66]

Mission, School and English Education

Missions also made considerable efforts to awaken political consciousness amongst Kols. Education was a key tool in shaping this process of epistemic infrastructure, which empowered Adivasis to pursue the legal battle in this region. Joseph Bara, in his analysis of Western education in Chota Nagpur, claims that 'the tribals gave in seeing that the religious principles of Christianity in substance were not different from their own beliefs, and rather missionaries being white men like British officials, were a potential ally in their struggles for rights'.[67] He rightly points out that the tribals sought shelter in the missionaries, offering to cultivate a political space to fight against the legal regime. But perhaps the reference to religious principles deserves more attention. Amongst others, the fundamental pursuit of the missionaries lay in drawing people to read the gospel, a medium that allowed the transformation of 'heathen' souls to Christianity. In this process, education became a critical tool.

It is a hasty assessment of education to undermine the potential of epistemic changes that it brings to choices, including political ones. The changes in language transform the worldview of an individual. As Ngũgĩ wa Thiong'o says, language is central to 'people's definition of themselves in relation to their natural and social environment, indeed in relation to the entire environment'.[68] Especially in a region such as Chota Nagpur, which was riddled with unsettling experiences of foreign invasion and land disputes, the cultural reformation introduced by education brought a new dimension of social cohesion to the community.

Bara suggests that the historical records and revision of stereotypes continue to inform the debate on Christianity and its close association with Adivasis. He argues that 'underneath the ostensibly exceptional "homogenisation" of evangelical and colonial ideas and certain grounds of consensus between the two camps as regards the goals of colonial policy in India, mission–state conflict was ingrained'.[69] While it is a useful perspective to highlight the homogenization of both camps, the claim here portrays a rather schematic description of the relationship between church and state—one which excludes any material that reveals the overlaps.

Interestingly, it offers an approach to the subject of conversion by emphasizing the Adivasis' receptiveness to Christianity in Chota Nagpur; not otherwise. Of course, the historical register of the missionary suggests that their arrival in Chota Nagpur and a sustainable effort allowed the Adivasis to commence a political awakening. He calls the process of interaction between both as a 'dialogical process', borrowing from the study conducted by Eugene F. Irschick in South India.[70] However, his work hesitates in offering a distinction between the colonial state and the missionary. The colonial epistemic structure that led to the formations of categories such as 'tribe' highlights the same. This epistemic structure—school and ethnocentric European values—enabled a new modality of governance that allowed the colonial state to draw upon the work of missionaries. Sangeeta Dasgupta, in her account, gives a fascinating insight to complicate this subject. She argues:

> Administrators and ethnographers drew upon the writings of missionaries working in their distant mission fields in order to learn from their *everyday experiences*; they consulted them for information on the basis of their recognized contact with the 'natives' amongst whom they lived. And thus they contributed to the making of the ethnographic and anthropological understandings of the tribe.[71]

This illustrates the work produced by the missionaries, which, in turn, complemented the colonial state. Far from serving as a theosophical rumination of experiences in the margins of the *raj*, the ethnographic records supported the claims about the social structure and their insertion into the legal framework. These records reflected on the changing nature of the colonial state by 'officialising procedures that established and expanded their capacity in many areas'.[72]

In addition to this, the colonial state also drew knowledge from the pre-existing Hindu scripts.[73] The state corroborated the Hindu scripts with the ethnographic writings of the missionaries to deal with their anxieties in this region. Effectively, these writings enabled a mode of governance, producing a variety of legislations to control, categorize and regulate the community. Here, Nicholas Dirk reminds us of how keen the colonial state was on the production of material: anthropological documents that prepared grounds for the making of effective governance. The construction of the Adivasis as a 'tribe' emerged from the anthropological surveys and records.[74] Therefore, Bara's reflection is useful as a caveat to situate the use of education within a broader problem with homogenization, but it fails to recognize the political implication and cultural effects that it has on the community. His analysis seemingly deflects or at least refuses to engage with sources as shown in this chapter and those that exist in the record, especially mission reports, which clearly show the cultural and moral imperatives of the missionaries—their Eurocentric values.

Useful to this analysis is Jean and John Comaroff's work on the mission in Africa, where they show 'not only cultural implications of the mission' but also 'inquire how they might be related to the sphere of the manifest political process'.[75] They explore various facets of Christianity that are internally heterogeneous. They argue that 'disparate facets of the practical mission-agricultural reform, the *reconstruction of personhood* and social space, and the abstraction of time and the word all reinforced each other, regrouping on native soil to form an analogue of their European parent culture'.[76] The role of the mission is limited not only to material changes, however construed, but also to an internal reorientation of the individual. The reorientation here is mimetic of the European cultural context, which is not merely incidental but rather detrimental in negating the existing indigenous form of knowledge. In fact, the cultural context of Europe defines the basis of conversion: a practice that is absent in the recipient's context. It allows perpetuating the image of Kols as a passive figure who is a 'simple-minded ignorant'.[77]

The school as a site of secular benefit is crucial to illustrate both social and political implications. In 1869, the Chota Nagpur mission report maintained that Kols 'are quite ignorant, and only acquainted with their mother tongue …

they rarely know a letter. [They] understand and speak Hindi well, they must be able to read the Bible and copy them on their slates.'[78] The training in a foreign language had twofold implications. On one level, it refused to recognize any merit in the mother tongue of the community, finding it ill-equipped to make sense of modernizing forces, namely mission-led education. On another level, the use of Hindi, the language of *dikus*, was promoted for reading the gospel and administrative affairs. Such insistence on a non-native language was not merely functional in the wider schema of how language shapes communities. In fact, the introduction of foreign languages worked as a powerful tool to colonize the plains of the imagination structured in the native language. It profoundly impacted the cosmovision shaped by the vernacular language. We find the reverberating impression of this strain of thought as a telling critique that resonates with the larger body of post-colonial literature.[79] Language, in this sense, served as tool to civilize the Adivasis, as seen here.

> The number of scholars attending the village-school is very small, only 219. There is a large Central Boarding School at Ranchi, which, though carried on at a very great expense, is a most essential institution because from it we must always draw our teachers and readers. Because it is a principal means of elevating and *civilizing the people in the villages*, as each boy and girl educated in this school becomes in a small way a *centre of civilization*.[80]

Laying out the structural need for education, the report clearly indicates how missionaries sought to assimilate Kols into the mainstream of the so-called civilized society. In turn, they (the Kols) became part of the civilization by forcefully renouncing their native lingual worlds. In this description, missions not only restrict the articulation of the community language but also denigrate it. It leaves little space for the articulation of identity of the community that is located at the margins of the British Raj.

The mystified image of education that seeks to elevate people from the community, in turn, colonizes them. It colonizes them through the depiction of their knowledge system as subservient to the civilized context, Europe. The system of knowledge (mission) renders itself visible through a universal model—some sort of ideational way of making sense. It relegates the indigenous system as inadequate for achieving strength on its own. The colonizing tendencies were equally prevalent in their orientation towards the indigenous religion—heathenism—which illustrates the spiritual conflict. This is evident in the report of Reverend John Cave-Browne, who noted:

> These tribes are almost *destitute of religion*, for although they believe in the existence of a supreme being to whom they ascribe some attributes of Divinity, yet they think it unnecessary to worship Him, because he does them no injury, which they would wish to avert. [The] language of both the Uraons, and Mundas are unwritten. The few that can read have learnt Hindi. These remarks will be sufficient to show that the Kols are on the very *outskirts of the civilization*, and are in a position, which will be *improved by the spread of Christianity* to an extent immeasurable, both in a temporal and *spiritual point of view*.[81]

This passage insinuates a remarkable contradiction in the approach of the mission. On the one hand, missions promoted the idea of education amongst Kols to free them from the chains of exploitation and enable them to file petitions in courts. On the other hand, they render the oral cultural and historical ethos of the Kols as marginal. Importantly, the denigration of the Kols' cosmic structure and religious beliefs as subservient to Christianity is perhaps a reflection of the early expansion of ethnocentric values of the European missionaries.

Moreover, the SPG[82] enjoyed the patronage of the British government in Chota Nagpur, which in turn validated the work and views of the missions.[83] It was at the same time that Chota Nagpur also witnessed the creation of a diocese.[84] The patronage received by the British Raj encouraged the missionaries to propagate the gospel to the native heathens.[85] The benefits that churches drew from the Raj in terms of necessary support established a common place for the cultural context of both—Europe. For instance, a letter written by Reverend H. Onasch clearly illustrates the contribution of the British government to the church:

> A duty dedicated to us by our love towards our work, it is not less a duty imposed upon us by a feeling of gratitude which we entertain towards the government of Her Majesty the Queen. We do not only possess the kind of sympathy of many English residents and Government officials here, but are also in many ways supported by pecuniary help on the part of the Government itself, and since more than a quarter of a century our Mission enjoys the protection of the law of her Majesty. Whilst we endeavor *to educate our Kolhs so as to enable them to become in time a Christian nation*, we try at the same time to instil into their hearts love for their *sovereign fatherlands*, principles of rectitude and justice, *obedience to the law*, and all those virtues which tend to advance the national prosperity and the welfare of the state.[86]

Replete with the imagining of the *Christian nation*, the cultural context between the church and the British Raj worked as the unifying principle to undertake the spiritual transformation of the community. With modern ideals of nation-making defined by physical, moral and spiritual undertakings, the colonial state and missionaries drew massively from their own 'imagined communities'.[87] Education for Kols in this sense was imagined as attaining the frontier of religious nation-making—imbuing in them the values of a new class of citizenry that could be effectively used for the Raj. These factors enabled conditions for leaders such as Birsa Munda to envision their opponents with sharp clarity: the missionaries, the Raj and the *zamindars*—*dikus* who left a deep impression on the fabric of the Adivasi community.

Any account of missionaries must also admit to their great work towards the political awakening of Adivasis in their reclamation of their rights. In fact, it is erroneous to make a hasty assessment about the missionaries based on their work of conversion in isolation from the wider political condition in Chota Nagpur. There is therefore huge merit in the process of tracing the modes of expansion and evolution of Christianity in this region that claimed Christian universal values through 'encounters that gave it a new reflection—by both missionaries and the missionized—on the universal and the particular'.[88] These encounters shaped both.

Mission, Political Awakening and Petitioning in the Raj

Contrary to the cultural trope of imperialism shown earlier, the missionaries also played a significant political role in the region. They assisted the Kols not only in taking the issue to the courts, a frighteningly new order, but also in the everyday rigmarole of legal paperwork. Their role, for instance, encompassed assistance in filing petitions in the courts, which were almost unapproachable and often cost a fortune, with cultivators being made to pay a fee as high as 40–50 rupees (half a dollar) in the mid-19th century.[89] The process of litigation seemed ruinous, and any help from missionaries proved a massive help.

> The litigation coincided with civil strife that emerged from the immigration of the foreigners [the *dikus*] in this region. It was estimated that the total emigration outnumbered immigration in the region. Mr. Gait, the Superintendent of the Census of 1901, noted that 'the balance of emigration was heavily against the district in 1891, ... Emigrants now outnumber immigrants by 243,195, compared to 220,517 ten years ago ... the vast majority of emigrants belong to the aboriginal races—Mundas, Uraons and Kharias'.[90] Inevitably, these problems compelled the missionaries to participate more actively in the everyday lives of the Kols.

Consequently, it also led to conflicts within the missions, often in the form of a disagreement over a political subject, and sometimes for seniority within the church. Missionaries presented a range of submissions to the 'Elder Brethren' about the ongoing crisis. In one report it was noted:

> About sixty other Kols converts, apparently at their suggestion of the 'young brethren', applied for an interview, which was granted. They presented two petitions; one of an entirely political character, asking the Bishop to interfere for the relief of a prisoner, and begging of him a general interference in the *land question*; with this, of course, the Bishop declined to meddle saying it was purely case for the Magistrate's cutcherry.[91]

The conflict between the younger and the elder brethren marked a difference between them and the limitations that influenced the mission's goal and aims.[92] It represented a great rift emerging from the political conditions and a desire to be involved in not only the spiritual but also the material lives of their converts. The framing of these intensely political questions of land sometimes required missionaries to risk their own commitments to the Raj. More importantly, this help was construed as immediate forms of resistance towards *zamindars* who were taking control of property. In fact, the series of petitions concerning the land question took a political character—placing the mission's intervention in the existing legal framework at the cornerstone. In this context, British official J. Reid writes:

> Several of the Christians had successfully asserted their rights in the Courts before that year. They were becoming a powerful and organised society, and the aboriginal Christians, backed by the moral and sometimes by the financial support of the European missionaries, were very different persons whether in the court or in the villages to the aboriginal of the primitive village community. An impression rapidly gained ground in consequences that to become Christian was the best means of successfully shaking off the oppression of the landlords.[93]

The contribution of the missionaries in assisting the Kols to reclaim their rights in everyday bureaucracy is remarkable and establishes the complex nature of conversion. It situates the conversion as the space of exchange and communication; relevant to this context is political support. It is widely noted in the historiography of the missionaries (which remains scanty on Chota Nagpur) that it was the help offered by missionaries which enabled the Adivasi community to file petitions against the *thikeddars* (contractors and farmers) and *zamindars*.[94] Kumar Suresh Singh maintained that 'there was a massive rise in the numbers of converts, who claimed to be 14,000 in number and have filed petitions'.[95] These petitions, in turn, turned the *zamindar*s against the missionaries due to their fear of losing caste control in the region. They were aware that Adivasis would have never filed petitions without their support.

Petitioning as a form of processual accountability went beyond this region and was evidently seen as containing disruptive potential. Bhavani Raman, in her work, provides a fascinating insight into how the colonial administration and governance emerged through writing practices—leading to the advent of a new 'textual polity that represented a new disposition to writing'.[96] The petition as a form of written reclamation shook the Raj and, in its limited scope, proved advantageous to the Adivasis too.

Making of the Dharti Aba: Agrarian Crisis and Anti-colonialism

Behind Chota Nagpur's complex sociopolitical conditions, an Adivasi leader rose. Birsa Munda found his way out of Christianity at an early stage. Several reasons led to his renunciation of Christianity. Based on the earlier assessment (the first section), it is possible to suggest that Christians, at least in their initial phase in this region, held problematic views about the 'heathens'. Singh notes that Birsa not only criticized the missionaries and their education system, which devalued the Munda system, but also once remarked that 'Saheb, sahib ek topi hai' (All whites, the British and the missionaries, wear the same cap).[97] He was often to be found protesting against the school system that devalued the Adivasi community.

Birsa struggled to find a method to reassert his lost Munda *raj*. Nostalgia for the past and the political dispensation that favoured the *diku*s shaped his political awakening. The nostalgia for lost land shaped the 'relationship between individual biography and the biography of groups or nations, between personal and collective memory'.[98] This nostalgia for regaining control of the kingdom lost to the hands of the missionaries, the colonial state and the *zamindar*s became the source of his inspiration. As a young adult, he developed associations that drew the question of land from the political struggle in the region. These movements shaped the 19th-century rebellions. The Sardar *ladai*, a defining movement in the region, was one such movement that inspired Birsa Munda.

Land Legislations, Struggles and the Political Life of Birsa

At the appearance of the police force Birsa from the rooftop of his house declared, '*Do not be afraid, the Queen's kingdom has come to an end and my kingdom has begun.'* ... The government, the missionaries and the zamindars all were equally interested in arresting Birsa. The *latter two* gave all possible help to the government in getting hold of Birsa.

—R. D. Munda and Norman Zide [99]

At the time when Birsa moved to Chaibasa, the Sardar movement was brewing in Chota Nagpur. It aimed to attack the system of rent appropriation by the *zamindars*—a casual similarity to this can also be felt in the French Revolution.[100] The movement emerged from the Adivasis' discontent with own their land, as well as the wide-scale changes to the law on the land system. Nitin Sinha, quoting Joh-Baptist Hoffman, writes that the Sadari *ladai* 'was political agitation of Mundas to recover their ancient rights and be put under the direct administration of the British Officers'.[101] However, the movement began to broaden the scope of its resistance against the *zamindars* towards the end of 1879.[102] Sardars 'persuaded not only the ordinary members but also the head or the leaders of the village such as Munda (the civil head of the Munda village) or the *khunt pahan* (the religious head) of the locality, to refuse all payments due to the superior landlord'.[103] The social base of the Sardar movement was wide and consisted of members from different communities—an umbrella of subaltern groups that mobilized each other against systemic exploitation. It insisted on accommodating the grievances of the people (Kols) who believed 'Hindu succeeds in establishing legal claims in the *pati* upon *pati* as soon as ever profitable extents of rice-fields have been created in them by the Mundas'.[104] To the Sardaris, *ladai* therefore became a defining point in the larger agrarian history of the region.

Birsa found it a place to realize his political life and expand his political influence. In doing so, he led groups of peasants to Chaibasa to petition for the remission of forest dues. The petitions concerning the 'Enforcement of the Indian Forest Act of 1878 had resulted in the taking over of the wasteland subject of the cultivator's existing rights by the government'.[105] On the one hand, the colonial state was expanding its economic frontiers into the deep forests to extract resources; on the other, the *zamindars*' share of landholdings increased. Forests that were once spaces of cohabitation and easy access for Adivasis emerged as what Savyasaachi calls 'the regime for primitive accumulation'.[106] Declaring forests as 'reserves of nature', forest dwellers, especially Adivasis, were rendered as an outsider.

In this process, Adivasis became *pariah* (the outcaste—Dalits) who were structurally eliminated from access to their land. Rupa Vishwanath, in her work, shows how 'any threat to the Pariah labourers was a threat to the system of production, the surpluses of which filled colonial coffers, and this control rested on the enforced landlessness'.[107] This meant that their servitude allowed the system of exploitation to work, and therefore the 'unfreedom of Pariah' is important.[108] Although the term *pariah* is anachronistic and holds different historical meanings, it is provocative as an idea to express the forms of exploitation, humiliation and marginalization that impacted Adivasis.

In this view, the Sardar movement was a starting point for a concerted attack on systemic exploitation primarily concerned with land. It drew Birsa in, and he began to engage and organize his people against the rising oppression of the property owners and the colonial state. A peculiar feature of Birsa's campaigning was to target institutions such as the colonial state, *zamindar* holdings and missionaries that posed a threat to the 'social whole' and not necessarily individual interests.[109]

The CNTA and the Bhuinhari Survey
The Sardari Ladai *and the Spectre of Surveys*

The Sardar movement revealed that there was a great disquiet amongst the *zamindars*, the *raiyats* and the administration about the land dispute. A *raiyat* is a person who has the right to hold a property for cultivation purposes. In the CNTA, the definition of the word *raiyat* is as follows: 'A person shall not be deemed to be Raiyat unless he holds the land either immediately under a proprietor or immediately under a tenure-holder or immediately under a Mundari Khuntkattidar.'[110] Considering the situation, the government appointed Lal Lokanath Shahi, a local upper-caste *zamindar*, as an assistant commissioner to conduct the Bhuinhari survey, with Major Hannington having previously mooted it. He commenced operations in 'August 1859 and took up altogether 576 villages in different *pergunah*s (fiscal units of administration), completed his work in 429 and partially in 143 villages'.[111] The special commissioners noted that 'the survey demarcated the privileged lands of tenants (*bhuinhari*) and the landlords (*Manjhihas*) supervised the act'.[112] The survey led to a series of disputes and considerably supported the interests of the landlords. The government felt the need to introduce legislation. In 1869, a major piece of legislation called the Chota Nagpur Tenure Act II was introduced. The aims and scope of the act note:

> The Chota Nagpur Tenure Act of 1869 provided for the survey and record-of-rights of certain privileged tenures locally known as *bhuinhars* and other similar tenures locally known as *Bhutkheta, Dalikatari, Pahnai and Mahatoai* and also known as *Manjhihas*. These tenures were the subject of much dispute, and hence it was considered advisable that they should be defined and the rights and liabilities attaching to them

recorded. The survey and record which extended only to parts of Ranchi district were completed in 1880 and a register was prepared showing all incidents of the tenures.[113]

For many, the upper-caste *zamindar* 'Shahi proved worthy of his salt'.[114] However, it brought a massive change in the existing rules that governed Adivasi land rights for generations. The colonial state argued that the Act was the product of an extensive survey of Chota Nagpur. The report contained

> 2,482 villages in Ranchi district and the total cost amounted to Rs. 2,66,887.… The operations undertaken under the Act, though successful to some extent in the areas in which they were carried out, were a mere palliative of the disorders which prevailed throughout the district as a whole.[115]

The report suggested that the survey had failed to mention the accuracy and extent to which it had covered tenures and believed it to be defective.[116] Not comprehending that the nature of the Munda community had a significant bearing on their *bhuinhari* system contributed confusion to the survey. Reid categorically pointed to two prominent failures: the understanding of the existing meaning of the land system and the inability to reach an agreed definition for the land entitlements.[117] He opined:

> There was no further definition. It is also difficult to determine from the report on the operations what criterion was applied by the officers themselves to the determination of the question what constituted *bhuinhari*, and as matter of fact, the decisions were in some cases at least of an arbitrary character, and consequently somewhat unsatisfactory.[118]

This aggravated the discontent amongst Mundas, who seemed to have suffered most due to the survey. In turn, it meant that the Act also failed to address the agrarian discontent, with a partial legislative framework that ensured the violation of land rights. Furthermore, Reid conceded: 'The operations carried out by Mr Slacke were successful in the areas to which they extended; but throughout the rest of the district, the antagonism between the landlords and tenants continued to be strong as ever.'[119] The Act encouraged Kols to file a suit for the land that they had lost. The special commissioner filed the suit on their behalf.

However, the attempts at ascertaining the land tenure did not bring substantial changes. The Act was hesitant to specify and define the constitution of the land: meaning and traditional usages. It did not consider the rampant migration that had occurred in the previous hundred years. Therefore, such lapses in the survey and the Act not only generated dissatisfaction among the cultivating class of Kols but also rather strengthened the *mulkai ladai*, or the Sardar movement.

Essentially, there are three kinds of land tenures in the Chota Nagpur region: (*a*) *bhuinhari* land, held on the condition of rendering certain labour services, (*b*) *rughu* land, held by rent-paying tenants and (*c*) *mujhu* land, held by those that are at the absolute disposal of the *zamindar*s. Lokenath Sahee restricted his 1860 study to *bhuinhari* land and did not account for *rughu* and *mujhu* land tenure. The *bhuinhari* tenure caused various conflicts. H. D. Dampier, officiating secretary to the government of Bengal, noted: 'The present movement is a struggle [*sardari*] between the Bhooinhars and the *thekedars* and *jageerdars* of the Maharajahs, the object of the latter being to annex to the rent-paying lands those which have been held and are claimed as bhooinhars and rent-free.'[120]

Table 2.2 Land assessment report led by Lall Lokenath Sahee during 1859, 1860 and 1861[121]

Name of *pergunah*	Villages measured: Measured	Villages measured: Completed	Villages measured: Incomplete	Remarks on land/village
Ludma	61	59	2a	In these two no lands were registered.
Khookra	105	5	100b	14 villages were registered, and the opinion of the officer was duly recorded, and *theekedar*s did not bear the signature and seal of the officer. Six villages were registered, but no signature either of the officer or of the parties; eight villages were registered and signed by the *illakadar*s, but neither by the officer nor by *bhooinhar*s; two villagers were registered but no signature.

Odeypore	103	80	25c	All registered; five villages signed only *bhooinhars*, 13 villages signed by both parties, but no seal and signature of the officer.
Sonepore	285	285		Five ditto, without signature of the officer.
Doesa	6		6d	Khusra is not only prepared, no opinion is recorded and no lands are registered.
Korambey	9		9e	Khusra is only prepared, no opinion is recorded and no lands are registered.
Bussea	2		2f	Ditto
Belkudee	1		1g	Ditto
Total	572	429	143	

Source: Explanations by Colonel E. T. Dalton, Commissioner of Chota Nagpore, with reference to the action of the local authorities in his Division during the late famine, IOR/L/PJ/3/1102 No.177: Aug 1867–Sep 1867.

Historically, Chota Nagpur witnessed a massive migration of Kols within different parts. Internal migration within the plateau was caused by the increasing pressure from and extortion by the *jagirdars*.[122] The *jagirdars* were a class of people who essentially hoarded the land of Mundas and Oraons by imposing '*rakumats* and cesses as they acquired *jagirdari* rights'.[123] These *jagirdars* enjoyed special privileges and occupied huge tracts—perhaps the finest share of land. Not admitting to internal migration, the Act failed to make a hasty assessment of the cause. While defining the meaning of 'land' in the Act, the distinction and similarities between the *bhuinhari* and *khuntkhatti* were not maintained.

As mentioned earlier, *bhuinhari* broadly refers to the ancestral property inherited by the Kols in Chota Nagpur, whereas *khuntkhatti* is the property occupied by the Kols through the process of clearing forests and cultivating the land. Originally, all the property at Kols' disposal was in the form of *khuntkhatti*. Over the years, when *zamindars* began to take control of the land, the Kols were deprived of the *khuntkhatti* and were made to pay rent for property that was commonly used for generations. There is a difference between *khuntkhattidar* and Mundari *khuntkhattidar*. The latter refers to

> [a] Mundari who has acquired a right to hold jungle for the purpose of bringing suitable portion thereof under the cultivation by himself or by male members of his family. The heir's male in the male line of any such Mundari, when they are in possession of such land or have any subsisting title thereto. Any portions of such land that has remained continuously in the possession of any such Mundari and his descendants in the male line.[124]

The *bhuinhari* in some sense then became a system by which Kols could only hold their original clearance. The Act anchored the limited definition of the land, and hence it generated discontent amongst the Kols.

Meanwhile, the Kols organized their land system into a new form with migration. A group of villages, popularly known as *manki pattis*, constituted the new system. Those who continued to live in the same region and not migrate were known as *bhuinhari pattis*. In both cases, the *raja* continued to receive contributions in different forms, including gifts and tributes. Therefore, 19th-century Chota Nagpur witnessed a massive restructuring of the traditional forms of the land system that were also closely tied to the cultural memory and sociopolitical structure of the communities.

In this process, the *rajas* emerged as the central figures in the land history of the plateau. They not only formed the basis for the distribution of property but also actively defined boundaries of occupation. They introduced a new class of *dikus* who came from outside the plateau and began to play a significant role in maintaining the status quo of dispossession. *Rajas* in the 19th century were *zamindars*, and they perpetuated the systemic form of land alienation. The English law (the CNTA) was a medium that extended the status quo of the traditional exploitative system of landlordism, only more vocally and arbitrarily. Upon close analysis of the Act, it is evident that it did not sufficiently grapple with historical contingencies such as migration and made an assessment with far less bearing on the historical register of the region. The failure of the Act, however, cannot be attributed to just the problems associated with the definitions.

The problem lay on several levels of understanding the communities who had historically suffered at the hands of *zamindars* and *jagirdars* and now under the Raj. The idea that the law could be instrumental to undertaking reparation of the lost land was myopic. This was primarily because it assumed the availability of land records of communities that survived on the oral tradition and collective community ownership. The lack of knowledge was widely reflected in the 'difficulty of understanding the language'.[125]

This reflects a methodological flaw in ascertaining property through written records and individual titles of ownership. Claims, as Pooja Parmar writes, 'arise in particular legal cultures and are articulated in the languages of those specific cultures'.[126] Claims as made by Adivasis found no place in the Anglo-European legal system primarily because a European system is based on individual property ownership, something broadly uncommon in Kol society. Also, the Act had been introduced at a later stage. Inadvertently, it meant that the continuing process of dispossession had already lessened the reclamation of the land due to the high rate of migration.[127] The distrust between the Kols and the British administration grew disproportionately and generated colossal mistrust. The Kols believed that the British government continued to favour the interests of the landed classes. The *zamindar*s materialized this mistrust between the Kols and the government to widen the gap in the process of land-rights reclamation.

Hoffman noted that the *zamindar*s had spread a rumour across the region during the survey. The rumour was that the intent behind ascertaining the proportion of the *bhuinhari* land was to charge heavier taxes.[128] This rumour, as Shahid Amin observes, functioned as a form of social affect that mobilizes the people and is often a sign of an impending clash.[129] It served its purpose, and the Kols did not disclose their properties. This led to the formulation of a land law that was ineffective and underestimated most of the land primarily belonging to Kols. Kols were further marginalized through land demarcations, and *zamindar*s were able to introduce their monopoly.

The introduction of the new law by the British government reflected poorly on its own understanding of the communities and their social and historical ties to the land. Hoffman described it as 'the general inability of two entirely different civilizations to understand each other'.[130] The result that emerged from the *bhuinhari* settlement aroused resentment amongst the Kols as it disproportionately supported the landowners. All property hitherto unclaimed was declared as property of the *zamindar*s. Such results convinced the Mundas to organize themselves in opposition to this move. They started to use petitions in the courts for the reclamation of their rights. These petitions later came to characterize the Sardar movement.

Nevertheless, the turbulence did not end; it instead took another form—the 1882 Indian Forest Act VII, which jeopardized common rights.[131] It was an Act that contained an 'environmental trope of otherness' to justify a European model. Vinita Damodaran argues that with the Birsa rebellion, 'the protection of forest rights ensued. As forests were increasingly recognized as a revenue resource by the district administration the clash between the foresters and administrators became more apparent.'[132]

The Forest Act was also a specific product of a deep-seated understanding about the jungles that emerged from various colonial administrative practices and botanical knowledge in 19th-century Britain. In his research, K. Sivaramakrishnan demonstrates that British governance perceived forested areas of Bengal as a 'zone of anomaly'.[133] He argues: 'The British embarked upon a political strategy that sought to "break up the unstable concentrations of power on the fringes of the arable." Goals of political control and economic profits were pursued in conjunction with each other, and forest clearing appeared to serve both purposes well.'[134]

The Forest Act gave away a large proportion of wasteland to the government and marked the limitation of the forest. Historically, Adivasis had access to the land inside the forest. The new Act completely overlooked such use value and instead 'villages in forests were marked off in blocks of convenient size consisting not only of village sites but also cultivable and wastelands insufficient for the needs of the *khuntkatti* villages'.[135]

Significantly, these institutional measures and acts failed to address the demands of Adivasis and Mundas in particular. It had led to various uprisings in the past, where Adivasi leaders such as Sidhu and Kanhu led rebellions against the British revenue system that brought massive changes to the Adivasi community.[136] It allowed *dikus*—the colonial state, the *zamindars* and the missionaries—to colonize their land and value system.

Notably, Birsa emerged against the background of such wide-ranging administrative and political changes in the region. He organized his people and launched public attacks on the centres of power. In the process of arousing political consciousness amongst his people, Birsa used multiple guises such as prophet, healer and messiah. One excerpt from the colonial record displays the effective use of nostalgia and memory as a medium to assert the political will. In his account, Reid recounts the following:

> In 1886, however, a petition was presented to the Government of India on behalf of the Mundas, in which the memorialists advanced

> the most extravagant claims, based on theory that the Mundas were the aborigines of the country, that they were *not subject to revenue laws*, and their title was not invalidated by law or prescription. The memorial was, of course, rejected. From evidence collected at the time, it appeared that the agitation was being artificially fostered by self-interested persons in Calcutta. The leaders were certain Munda Sardars, who had abandoned Christianity. These people diligently spread the report that they had obtained *a 'decree' for the restoration of the Munda 'Raj'* and proceeded to levy subscriptions throughout the country, under the pretence of paying the expenses of its execution.[137]

The passage illustrates the political vision of Birsa and how well he understood Munda society. He was aware of the social dynamics and political realities of his people. He creatively placed the problems within an emotive framework: the lost Munda *raj*. It dovetailed the historical alienation from the land and discontentment with existing alternatives such as the Forest Act. His public reach widened, especially after his arrest in 1895.

Gatherings, pilgrimages and chanting surfaced as the most socially acceptable forms of preaching Birsa's political ideas. Birsa displayed his craft to draw people into his fold of political ambition: the Munda *raj*. Such congregations mobilized the Munda *raj* as a viable alternative. In his memoir, Hoffman offered a detailed account of a massive rally led by Birsa and his followers:

> I distinctly remember how the known sardars were urging the common people to go on the pilgrimage to 'Birsa Bhagwan'. At first, I took no notice of what I considered for some weeks as mere acts of semi-savage foolishness. However, the large crowds I soon saw arriving from all parts on their way to Chalkads and the activity of the sardars aroused my suspicion. Rumours of miraculous cures and the resuscitation of dead men were diligently spread … Crowds of the Mundas, especially of the known sardari villages, were constantly going armed. I got certain news, too, that the *religious colouring of Chalkad* was fading more and more, and that the real *political aims* were coming out clearer as chalkad was getting more and more crowded with armed men, permanently settled there with provisions for many a day.[138]

Hoffman's recollection is vivid and detailed. It attests to the political aims of Birsa. Hoffman was one of the very few who could understand the political strategy that was drawn out through the rallies and pilgrimages. These protests displayed Birsa's political ambitions imbued with *religious colouring* and *real political aims*.[139] Birsa soon began to face the consequences of his political choice, primarily in the form of repeated arrests. These arrests and public demonstrations transformed his potential as a promising leader. He was not only deemed as a healer—a *bhagwan*—but also posed as a spearhead for the cause of the Mundas. A semi-official letter from a British functionary marked his appearance as a political threat to the Raj. It notes: 'In 1895, the agitation was greatly fanned by a young man named Birsa Munda, then only 20 years of age ... he announced himself a prophet, foretold the destruction of all except those in his immediate neighbourhood.'[140]

Upon Birsa's arrest on 24 October 1895, a huge crowd of people followed him to the police station, where he faced public trial.[141] Mundas gathered to pay homage to Birsa and publicly announce their acceptance of him as their god. It was advantageous for the *zamindar*s to misinterpret the situation to the police commissioner, who did not understand the Mundari language.[142] This particular arrest occurred quite dramatically as the turning point in the history of what later became known as the Birsa *ulgulan*. A. Forbes wrote an account of an attempt to arrest Birsa:

> It is fully agreed that the present movement is in continuation of the *Sardari agitation*, the history of which government is aware, the leader of which is the notorious *Birsa Bhagwan*. It will be remembered [that] Birsa was sentenced to three [terms of] imprisonment some five years ago in connection with this agitation, his release, on [the] expiration of [the] sentences, dating from January 1898. During the time that Birsa was in jail the agitation subsided, but directly he was released, it was again taken up by the Mundari Sardars, headed by Birsa, against whom an unexecuted warrant is still in force on a charge of rioting and desecrating the *Chutia temple* (in March 1898).[143]

The *ulgulan* began with what Singh calls an 'epidemic of burning and arrow-shooting' on the Christmas Eve of 1899.[144] It was shaped by accumulated frustration, denial and loss. The Birsaites rose in the full blaze of light and targets were shot at. Hoffman was also at the gathering but managed to miss an arrow that was aimed at him.[145] The attacks led to an official order for the arrest of Birsa and his followers. The search took place at different locations, including his house and gathering points.

Arrest

> The Big River is in flood, the dust-storm is brewing,
> O Maina, run, run away,
> The forest is filled with fire and smoke,
> O Maina ...
> Your father is floating away,
> O Maina....
>
> —Kumar Suresh Singh[146]

I found an interesting correspondence—buried beneath colonial judicial files—between a British official and those in charge of Birsa's arrest in the final moments of the rebellion. On 10 January 1900, a copy of a letter by Captain H. J. Roche arrived at camp Burju. Roche gave a detailed description of the arrest of Birsa and his followers, and the death of a few of them in the process.[147] Roche claimed to have left for the search for Birsa and the Bhagwanis (followers of Birsa) who had come together for a meeting at the Sail Rakab hill.[148] Roche was accompanied by the chief commissioner of Chota Nagpur, Streatfield, and 15 armed police.[149] As soon as they approached the hill, Roche and others took shelter around its foot. Nothing happened that night. With the dawn, however, the information about the large gathering of Bhagwanis reached them. They used techniques to seize these, who, as Roche noted, were 'endeavouring to conceal our approach as much as possible by moving through the jungle and along *nullah*'.[150] Streatfield joined him. They eventually began to fan out the police officers. They arrived at the top of the hill by 1 p.m. and claimed to have spotted people hiding behind the stones and trees waving swords and axes and shouting.[151] He furthermore writes that he 'regrets to inform that the bodies of 3 women were found in the jungle having evidently been shot in the pursuit'.[152]

On 25 January 1900, Forbes wrote a letter to J. P. Hewlett contesting the version of the incident reported by Roche.[153] Forbes began his letter by referring to Roche's report as a 'mistaken' piece of information and adding that it was, in fact, reported to Roche by his *subedar* or *hawaldar* (person in charge at a police station).[154] The letter appears to have revised most of the facts from Roche's report. Forbes concluded that the 'native officer's information was incorrect'. He claimed that the report failed to mention about '4 instead of 2 injured people'. Forbes took a sub-inspector with him to the site to corroborate the evidence.[155] The number of causalities remains obscure as different accounts offer different figures.[156] Birsa, however, did manage to escape the site.

The violent crackdown at Sail Rakab was a signal to Birsa to call for an end to the British Raj, the missionaries and the *zamindars*. The Sail Rakab incident marked a sharp and clear disapproval of any form of oppression. However, there is a dispute regarding this incident. Some considered it the 'beginning of the end',[157] while others did not think that the crackdown had shaken 'the recklessly stubborn' Mundas.[158]

In my assessment, which I provide in Chapter 4, Sail Rakab left a deep impression on this region and created a cultural milieu shaped by the historical memory of the incident. It is interesting to note that all these events of arrests and encounters within Birsa's movement have left huge cultural imprints in the collective memory of Adivasis.

End of the Rebellion

Sail Rakab triggered a serious administrative response. On 8 February 1900, the colonial state judicial files minuted the arrest of 'Birsa and his principal adherents'.[159] On the day of the arrest, Hewlett also wrote a personal telegram stating that 'Birsa, the ringleader of Mundas, and most of his adherents have been captured'.[160] In June of the same year, Birsa died in jail, leaving his legacy and teachings. His death emerged as a watershed moment in the history of Adivasi rebellion in the late 19th century.

It marked, I believe, a unique vantage point in history to think more carefully about the voices of the people at the margins of the Raj. The rebellion not only refused to accept the emergent regime of the law but also forced us to reimagine the past of the Munda community. R. D. Munda and Norman Zide, in their essay, give an interesting impression of the movement:

> In spite of its apparent defeat, the movement Birsa led was a triumph (however partial it was) after his death. The government realized that Birsa's stand had reasons (ambitious though it looked in demanding a separate 'kingdom' outside the British Empire). She realized that the agrarian disorders were at the root of the unrest, and Birsa's revolt was the climax of the earlier—Sardar and yet previously little-known—uprisings. A series of agrarian measures began with Survey and Settlement Operations in 1902 ending in the provision for a Tenancy Act.[161]

The invocation of the glorious past as the trope of nostalgia articulated the historic angst of Mundas against the *diku*s. Birsa's rebellion displayed an unwavering potential using the political consciousness—consolidating all forms of methodical strategies towards attaining the rights and reclamation of memory. He emerged as the canon in the register of the resistance movement.

Summary

The chapter provided a glimpse into the historical context of the book as well as the analysis of key themes within the movement. It presented Birsa as a canon who offered an alternative political possibility to the Mundas and placed the core tension at the heart of the Raj. It situated the contribution of the missionaries as the primary interlocutors for the movement within broader agrarian history in two ways. First, the missionary archives contain some of the most significant resources for writing a much wider history of the movement and the region. This chapter captured only a glimpse of what remains a great reserve. Second, it allowed me to explain the shift in the legislative measures and agrarian practices in the region. These components lay out the foundation for the struggle of *jal, jungle aur jameen* that continues to shape the political discourse in independent Jharkhand.

Notably, the fragmented voices of subaltern history revealed in this chapter surface in tangential sources such as missionary records. The chapter demonstrates the limitation and atypical nature of the historical records to characterize the Birsa movement primarily as 'anti-colonial'. This, indeed, gives an interesting reflection on the *small histories* of resistance—regional icons whose rebellion either becomes part of the nation-making narrative or remains submerged under the hegemonic narrative of the elite that dominates the historiography of the Indian colonial experience.[162]

Moving further, the following chapters show how the historical memory of the movement, which clearly accounts for wider political and sociocultural concerns, is often removed from the context. The implication of this is that the proliferation of memory-making that emerges as a new form of *doing* politics often presents anti-colonial ideas as sedimented forms of historical events—effectively drawn out from its potential to cause disruption to the nascent category of memory politics in the present. It shifts the attention to new kinds of political imagination and material. It uses the trope of rebellion to incorporate the demands of post-colonial capitalism through memorialization (see Chapter 4).[163] In effect, it makes memory a tool of politics to mobilize the regional figure through symbolic representation.

Hereafter, each chapter of the book consists of a particular denomination of memory: statue, memorial and resistance memory. It demonstrates how the state and other agencies can control, produce and mobilize memory to garner political support from the targeted constituencies. Therefore, the following chapters offer narratives from the contemporary political landscape and the process of memorialization that weaves history and memory into politics.

Notes

1 Jacinta Kerketta, *Angor* (Kolkata: Adivaani, 2016), p. 97.
2 Ranajit Guha, *Elementary Aspects of Peasant Insurgency in Colonial India* (Durham, NC: Duke University Press, 1999).
3 See Anil Seal, *Locality, Province and Nation: Essays on Indian Politics 1870 to 1940* (Cambridge: Cambridge University Press, 1973).
4 Ibid. In identifying nationalist history, Dipesh Chakrabarty noted that it was more about the 'moral battle between colonialism and nationalism'. This is a useful point to underline the recognition and role of subaltern agency within the literature of the subaltern studies collective. It focused neither on colonial nor on nationalist historiography. See Dipesh Chakrabarty, 'A Small History of Subaltern Studies', in *A Companion to Postcolonial Studies*, ed. Henry Schwarz and Sangeeta Ray, pp. 467–85 (Oxford: Blackwell Publishing, 2007).
5 Ranajit Guha, 'On Some Aspects of the Historiography of Colonial India', in *Subaltern Studies*, vol. 1: *Writings on South Asian History and Society*, ed. Ranajit Guha, pp. 37–44 (Delhi: Oxford University Press, 1982).
6 Vinita Damodaran, 'Environment, Ethnicity and History in Chota Nagpur, India, 1850–1970', *Environment and History* 3, no. 3 (1997): 273–98. Such disturbing tendencies generated an active impulse of resistance amongst the Mundas, and they began to organize themselves actively. They also started to use petitions in the courts to reclaim their rights. These petitions later came to be known as the 'Sardar movement'. Birsa also supported the Sardar movement in the early phase of his life. See Fidelis de Sa, *Crisis in Chota Nagpur, with Special Reference to Judicial Conflict between Jesuit Missionaries and British Government Officials, November 1889–March 1890* (Bangalore: Redemptorist Publication, 1975), p. 66. Classified land records documented by the Raj through the land survey in 1902–10 and later in the years 1927–28 became the official sources. See R. N. Pandey Roy, *Manual of Chhotanagpur Tenancy Laws*, vol. 2 (Allahabad: Rajpal and Company, 2001).
7 Kumar Suresh Singh, *Birsa Munda and His Movement (1872–1901)* (Kolkata: Seagull Books, 2002). Mahasweta Devi, *Chotti Munda and His Arrow* (New Delhi: Blackwell Publication, 2003). Also see Daniel J. Rycroft, 'Looking Beyond the Present: The Historical Dynamics of Adivasi (Indigenous and Tribal) Assertions in India–Part II: Indian Confederation of Indigenous and Tribal Peoples', *Journal of Adivasi and Indigenous Studies (JAIS)* 2, no. 1 (2015): 1–10.
8 For a comprehensive history of Christian missionary work in the region, see S. J. Peter Tete, *A Missionary Social Worker in India: J.B. Hoffman, The Chota Nagpur Tenancy Act and the Catholic Co-operatives 1893–1928* (Roma: Universita Gregoriana Editrice, 1984).
9 Svetlana Boym, 'Nostalgia and Its Discontents', *Hedgehog Review* 9, no. 2 (Summer 2007): 7–18.

10 Edward Said, *Orientalism* (London: Routledge & Kegan Paul Ltd, 1978).

11 Gauri Viswanathan, *Outside the Fold: Conversion, Modernity, and Belief* (Princeton, NJ: Princeton University Press, 1998), p. 4.

12 Ibid.

13 Jean Comaroff and John Comaroff, *Of Revelation and Revolution: Christianity, Colonialism and Consciousness in South Africa*, 2nd edition (Chicago: University of Chicago Press, 1991). The words 'civilizing mission' are kept in quotations for two reasons: First, they are borrowed from a document that is used later in the section on missionaries and schools. Second, the colonial state also used them in the context of English education.

14 Marine Carrin and Harald Tambs-Lyche, *An Encounter of Peripheries: Santals, Missionaries, and Their Changing Worlds, 1867–1900* (New Delhi: Manohar Publication, 2008).

15 Andrew Porter, *European Imperialism, 1860–1814 (Studies in European History)* (London: Macmillan Press, 1994), p. 7.

16 To draw Indians into the British system, Thomas Babington Macaulay proposed that Indians be educated in English. His infamous quote goes as follows: 'We must at present do our best to form a class who may be interpreters between us and the millions whom we govern; a class of persons, Indian in blood and colour, but English in taste, in opinions, in morals, and in intellect.' Thomas Babington Macaulay, 'Minute of 2 February 1835 on Indian Education', in *Macaulay, Prose and Poetry*, selected by G. M. Young, pp. 721–24 (Cambridge, MA: Harvard University Press, 1957), p. 729.

17 For example, Arun Shourie's work, which claims to treat Christianity as an invading institution, takes the form of a neo-Hindu critique. It fails to consider the nuances within the process of conversion. It offers convoluted accounts of the convert's agency and corrupts the possibility of thinking across the experiences. See Arun Shourie, *Missionaries in India: Continuities, Changes, Dilemmas* (New Delhi: ASA Publications, 1994).

18 Viswanathan, *Outside the Fold*, p. 76.

19 Ibid., p. 185.

20 The word 'heathen' is in quotes to indicate that it is a terminology used for a group of people or community that do not subscribe to Abrahamic religions in the register of missionaries. 'Pagan' is another popular term used to denigrate such people or communities. In this chapter, I have used 'heathens' on multiple occasions to describe the religion of Adivasis as maintained in the missionary records. I have used it to underscore the political implication of the term and depict the evolutionary schema that was prevalent within the work of missionaries in this region. Amongst others, see 'The Chota Nagpore Mission: A Brief Statement of the Circumstances under which the Society for the Propagation of the Gospel in Foreign Parts', Shelfmark number: Tr. 206 (o), British Library, London. Also see Sangeeta Dasgupta, 'Heathen Aboriginals, Christian Tribes and Animistic Races: Missionary Narratives on Oraons of Chotanagpur in Colonial India', *Modern South Asian Studies* 50, no. 2 (2016): 437–78.

21 'Final Report on the Survey and Settlement Operations in the District of Ranchi 1902–1910 by J. Reid', Shelfmark IOR V/27/314/103, British Library, London.

22 For a discussion on the Kol uprising, see Jagdish Chandra Jha, 'The Kol Rising of Chotanagpur (1831–33): Its Causes', *Proceedings of the Indian History Congress* 21 (1958): 440–46.

23 Ibid., p. 33.

24 William Wilson Hunter, James Sutherland Cotton, Sir Richard Burn, William Meyer and Great Britain India Office, *The Imperial Gazetteer of India*, vol. 21 (Oxford: Oxford Publication, 1908), p. 197; William Wilson Hunter, *The Imperial Gazette of India* (Oxford: Oxford University Press, 1881).

25 *Final Report on the Settlement of the Kolhan Government Estate in District Sighbhum* (Calcutta: Bengal Secretariat Press, 1898).

26 Ibid., p. 1.

27 Ibid.

28 Ibid., p. 3.

29 For a detailed difference, see Sanjukta Das Gupta, 'Rethinking Adivasi Identity: The Chota Nagpur Tenancy Act (1908) and Its Aftermath among the Hos of Singhbhum', in *Adivasi in Colonial India: Survival, Resistance and Negotiation*, ed. Biswamoy Pati, pp. 88–111 (New Delhi: Orient Blackswan, 2011), p. 93.

30 'Report of the Chota Nagpur Mission with S.P.G (1869–1870)', File No Tr. 158 (r), British Library, London.

31 See H. H. Risley, 1903, *Census of India 1901*, vol. 1, Ethnographic Appendices, IOR/V/15/60, British Library, London. Also see Eyre Chatterton, *The Story of Fifty Years Mission in Chotanagpur*, cited in S. Mahato, *A Hundred Years of Christian Missions in Chotanagpur since* 1845 (Ranchi: Chotanagpur Christian Publishing House, 1971).

32 Ibid. 'Final Report on the Survey and Settlement Operations'.

33 Ibid.

34 Nitin Sinha, 'Fluvial Landscape and the State: Property and the Gangetic Diaras in Colonial India, 1790s–1890s', *Environment and History* 20, no. 2 (May 2014): 209–37.

35 Division to Owsley, 29 August 1839, para. 3, no. 247, Misc. Dispatch Book, G.S. Agent's office, Patna Archives, para. 2, cited in Jagdish Chandra Jha, *The Tribal Revolt of Chota Nagpur (1831–1832)* (Patna: Kashi Prasad Jayaswal Research Institute, 1987).

36 Mission stations were established at Ranchi (1845); at Domba, nine miles south-west of Ranchi (1864); at Lohardaga, 48 miles to the west of Ranchi (1848); and at Govindpur, 30 miles to the west of Ranchi. These were the first converts made in Chota Nagpur by the German Evangelical Mission sent out to India by Pastor John Evangelist Gossner of Berlin. On 26 October 1851, Rev. Mr Schatz baptized Sadho Munda of village Balalong. See S. C. Roy, *The Mundas and Their Country* (Calcutta: Kuntaline Press, 1912).

37 The Gossner Evangelical Lutheran church missionary came from Germany. Lutherans worked extensively in the region. They not only supported the Kols in political affairs but also produced useful documents that work as an archive for the community today.
38 The SPG sought affiliation to the Church of England.
39 The Roman Catholics arrived in India from Belgium in 1859. They made a big impression on the area. Father Lievens became the most popular priest in the entire region. Joh-Baptist Hoffman also belonged to the same church. He was the leading figure in the making of the CNTA. See S. J. Peter Tete (ed.), *Constant Lievens and the Catholic Church in Chotanagpur* (Ranchi: Archbishop's House, 1993).
40 Interestingly, the Dublin Mission led by the Dublin University consisted of students who worked extensively in the field of medicine, studying disease in the region.
41 *Goßner's Mission unter den Kols in Britisch Ostindien, 1845–1895 Eine Festschrift*, Berlin, 1895, p. 4, as cited in Sa, *Crisis in Chota Nagpur*, p. 76.
42 'The Petition of the Society for the Propagation of the Gospel in Foreign Parts Sheweth', Shelfmark number: IOR/L/PJ/190, J&P 986, British Library, London.
43 'The Chota Nagpore Mission'.
44 Ibid.
45 Ibid (emphasis mine).
46 Asoka Kumar Sen, *Indigeneity, Landscape and History: Adivasi Self-fashioning in India* (New Delhi: Routledge, 2018). p.17
47 Astrid Erll, 'Re-Writing as Re-Visioning Modes of Representing the "Indian Mutiny" in British Novels, 1857 to 2000', *European Journal of English Studies* 10, no.2 (2006): 163–85. For further work on 1857, see Crispin Bates (ed.), *Mutiny at the Margins: New Perspectives on the Indian Uprising of 1857* (New Delhi: SAGE Publications, 2013). Crispin Bates and Alpa Shah, *Savage Attack: Tribal Insurgency in India* (New Delhi: Social Science Press, 2014).
48 Ibid.; 'Final Report on the Survey and Settlement Operations', p. 33.
49 Ibid.
50 Ibid.
51 'Report of the Chota Nagpore Mission Ranchi for the Year 1867', Shelf mark: Tr. 158(p), British Library, London (emphasis mine).
52 Ibid.
53 Ibid.; 'The Petition of the Society for the Propagation of the Gospel in Foreign Parts Sheweth'.
54 Church Missionary Society Archive, 'Section 4: Missions to India', in *Parts 5–6: North India Mission, 1817–1880* (Marlborough: Adam Mathew Publications, 2007), p. 9.
55 Dasgupta, 'Heathen Aboriginals, Christian Tribes and Animistic Races', p. 438.
56 Robert Eric Frykenberg, 'Introduction: Dealing with Contested Definitions and Controversial Perspectives', in *Christians and Missionaries in India: Cross-Cultural*

Communication since 1500, ed. Robert Eric Frykenberg, pp. 1–33 (Michigan: William B. Eerdmans Publishing Company, 2003), p. 2.

57 'Report of the Bhaugulpore Mission, in Connexion with the Church Missionary Society, from October 1, 1858 to September 30, 1859', Shelfmark number: Tr. 158(ee), British Library, London.

58 Ibid.; 'Report of the Chota Nagpore Mission Ranchi'.

59 Ibid.

60 See Edward Tuite Dalton, 'Descriptive Ethnology of Bengal 1872', Shelfmark number: General Reference Collection DRT Digital Store 10007.y.1, British Library, London.

61 Ibid.; 'Report of the Chota Nagpur Mission' (emphasis mine).

62 Ibid.; Said, *Orientalism*.

63 Ibid (emphasis mine).

64 Ibid.; 'Report of the Chota Nagpur Mission'.

65 Ibid.; 'The Chota Nagpore Mission' (emphasis mine).

66 James Mill, in his description of the Indian as having the 'rude and weakest state of human mind', justifies colonialism as a civilizing tool for India. It is possible to draw similarities between the English mission and the Christian mission. Though they operated as separate enterprises and came to India with varying interests, it is noticeable that the lens of European cultural imperialism primarily guided their approach towards the natives. See the work of Javed Majeed who worked extensively on Mill's liberal imagining. Javed Majeed, *Ungoverned Imaginings: James Mill's 'The History of British India and Orientalism'* (London: Clarendon Press, 1992).

67 Joseph Bara, 'Western Education and Rise of New Identity Mundas and Oraons of Chotanagpur, 1839–1939', *Economic and Political Weekly* 32, no. 15 (1997): 785–90.

68 Ngũgĩ wa Thiong'o, *Decolonising the Mind: The Politics of Language in African Literature* (Nairobi: East African Publishing House, 1981), p. 4.

69 Joseph Bara, 'Colonialism, Christianity and the Tribes of Chhotanagpur in East India, 1845–1890', *South Asia: Journal of South Asia Studies* 30, no. 2 (2007): 195–222.

70 Ibid.

71 Dasgupta, 'Heathen Aboriginals, Christian Tribes and Animistic Races', p. 440 (emphasis mine).

72 Bernard S. Cohn, 'Representing Authority in Victorian India', in *The Invention of Tradition*, ed. Eric Hobsbawm and Terry Ranger, pp. 165–211 (Cambridge: Cambridge University Press, 1983).

73 Vinita Damodaran, 'Colonial Constructions of the "Tribe" in India: The Case of Chotangapur', *Indian Historical Review* 33, no. 1 (2006): 44–75.

74 See Nicholas Dirks, *Castes of Mind: Colonialism and the Making of Modern India* (Princeton, NJ: Princeton University Press, 2001).

75 Jean Comaroff and John Comaroff, 'Christianity and Colonialism in South Africa', *American Ethnologist* 13, no. 1 (February 1986): 1–22, p. 1.
76 Ibid. (emphasis mine).
77 Ibid.; 'The Chota Nagpore Mission'.
78 'The Chota Nagpore Mission', p. 4.
79 See Thiong'o, *Decolonising the Mind*.
80 'The Chota Nagpore Mission Report' (emphasis mine).
81 See John Cave-Browne, *The Mission Report*, File No Tr. 158 (r), P-5, British Library, London (emphasis mine).
82 On 21 June 1869, under the SPG mission, Reverend J. C. Whitley arrived at Ranchi. In 1890, under Whitley as the first bishop, Whitley formed a separate diocese in Chota Nagpur. He devoted himself to the mission and worked towards understanding the social fabric of the communities.
83 Singh, *Birsa Munda and His Movement*, p. 13.
84 Ibid.
85 The English mission of Chota Nagpur under the auspices of the SPG was established in 1873.
86 Emphasis mine. See Revd. H. Onasch and 15 others to His Honour the Lieutenant, Governor of Bengal, 17 May 1876, 'Outbreak of Mundas in the Ranchi District', IOR J&P 1900, British Library, London. Also see S. P. Sinha, *Conflict and Tension in Tribal Society* (New Delhi: Concept Publication Company, 1994), p. 240.
87 Benedict Anderson, *Imagined Communities: Reflections on the Origin and Spread of Nationalism* (revised edition) (London: Verso Publication, 2006 [1983]).
88 David Mosse, *The Saint in the Banyan Tree* (California: University of California Press, 2012), p. 3.
89 'Final Report on the Survey and Settlement Operations in the District of Ranchi 1902–10'.
90 Ibid., p. 10.
91 Ibid.; Cave-Browne, *The Mission Report*. In addition, a brief statement was released on the circumstances under which 'the Society for Propagation of the Gospel in Foreign parts … were induced to take charge of the missions of the Kols in Chota Nagpur' (emphasis mine).
92 Ibid.; 'The Petition of the Society for the Propagation of the Gospel in Foreign Parts Sheweth'.
93 Ibid.; 'Final Report on the Survey and Settlement Operations', p. 34.
94 Singh, *Birsa Munda and His Movement*. Also see Uday Chandra, 'Millenarian Dreams, Modern Aspirations: Tribal Community-Making and Contentious Politics in Colonial Chotanagpur', Working Papers WP 14-01, ISSN 2192-2357, Max Planck Institute for the Study of Religious and Ethnic Diversity, Göttingen, Germany, April 2014, https://www.mmg.mpg.de/60983/wp-14-01 (accessed on 15 November 2019).

95 Singh, *Birsa Munda and His Movement*, p. 25.
96 Bhavani Raman, *Document Raj: Writing and Scribes in Early Colonial India* (South Asia across the Disciplines) (Chicago: University of Chicago Press, 2012).
97 Singh, *Birsa Munda and His Movement*, p. 37.
98 Boym, 'Nostalgia and Its Discontents'.
99 R. D. Munda and Norman Zide, 'Revolutionary Birsa and Songs Related to Him', *Journal of Social Research* 12, no. 2 (1969): 26, Christian Missionary Society Collection at the Cadbury Research Library, University of Birmingham (emphasis mine).
100 The word *sardar* could also possibly emerge from the *ghatwali* system, the leading executive unit of which is the *sardar*, or head of the subordinate *ghatwal*s (*tabidar*s) of a village. See Risley, *Census of India 1901*, vol. 1.
101 S. P. Sinha, *Life and Times of Birsa Bhagwan*, 2nd edition (Ranchi: Bihar Tribal Research Institute, 1997), p. 36.
102 Roy, *The Mundas and Their Country*.
103 Ibid.
104 Hoffman to Commissioner of the Chota Nagpur Division, 4 January 1900, Enclosure 4, File no 543, British Library, London.
105 Munda and Zide, 'Revolutionary Birsa and Songs Related to Him', p. 39.
106 Savyasaachi, 'Primitive Accumulation, Labour, and the Making of "Scheduled Tribe", "Indigenous", and Adivasi Sensibility', in *First Citizens: Studies on Adivasis, Tribals, and Indigenous Peoples in India*, ed. Meena Radhakrishna, pp. 53–73 (New Delhi: Oxford University Press, 2016), p. 35.
107 *Pariah* is term used to refer to a specific outcaste group in Tamil Nadu and Kerala. The work of Rupa Vishwanath is used to illustrate the wider spectrum of violence and caste system that exists in the subcontinent. Rupa Vishwanath, *The Pariah Problem: Caste, Religion and the Social in Modern India* (New York: Columbia University Press, 2014), p. 4.
108 Ibid.
109 Louis Dumont uses the idea of social hierarchy as a form of superiority over all forms of the individual. However, it reflects the peculiarity of each individual. The idea reflects the value system predominant in the non-west. See Louis Dumont, *Essays on Individualism: Modern Ideology in Anthropological Perspective* (Chicago: University of Chicago Press, 1986).
110 See 'The Chota Nagpur Tenancy Act being Act 6 of 1908 with notes and judicial rulings framed under the act by J. Reid', Shelfmark: T 7377, British Library, London.
111 Babu Rakhal Das Haldar, Special Commissioner to the Deputy Commissioner, Loharduaga, Shelfmark IOR/L/PJ/6/540, No. 11, Judicial files 1900, J&P 869, 22nd May 1880, British Library, London.
112 Sinha, *Life and Times of Birsa Bhagwan*, p. 73.
113 Ibid.; 'The Chota Nagpur Tenancy Act being Act 6 of 1908', p. 9.

114 Babu Rakhal Das Haldar, Special Commissioner under the Chota Nagpore Tenancy to the Deputy Commissioner, Loharduaga, Ranchi, 22nd May 1880, Judicial files: 1900, British Library, London.
115 'Final Report on the Survey and Settlement Operations'. Also see Singh, *Birsa Munda and His Movement*, p. 25.
116 Ibid.; 'Final Report on the Survey and Settlement Operations'.
117 Ibid., p. 35.
118 Ibid., pp. 35–36.
119 Ibid., p. 41.
120 'Papers relating to Chota Nagpore agrarian disputes', H. D. Dampier, Esq, officiating secretary to the government of Bengal to the secretary to the government of India, Home Department, shelf mark no. W 560, no. 1613, dated 26th May 1868, British Library, London.
121 Ibid.; A letter from Mr H. L. Oliphant, Esq, Deputy Commissioner of Lohardega to the Commissioner of the Chota Nagpore Division, 1867, p. 14.
122 In a letter a colonial officer based at Chota Nagpur noted: 'Jagirdars were no other than the predecessors of the Nagvanshi, Rajput, Rantia, Bhraman, and Bhiman, illaquadars of the present day. […] The Nagpore jagirdars had lived among the Kols for many generation pasts; their interests were not utterly deprived of common sense or common humanity could scarcely fail to see the great usefulness of the aboriginal cultivators.' See Babu Rakhal Das Haldar, Special Commissioner under the Chota Nagpore Tenancy Act to the Deputy Commissioner, Loharduaga, Ranchi, 22nd May 1880, judicial files, J&P 11, British Library, London, p. 83.
123 Damodaran, 'Colonial Constructions of the "Tribe" in India', p. 57.
124 Ibid. 'The Chota Nagpur Tenancy Act being Act 6 of 1908'.
125 Sa, *Crisis in Chota Nagpur*, p. 63.
126 Pooja Parmar, *Indigeneity and Legal Pluralism in India: Claims, Histories, Meanings* (New Delhi: Cambridge University Press, 2016), p. 10.
127 Myron Weiner, in his study, notes that at the end of the 19th century, 179,000 people in Chota Nagpur and Santhal Pargana emigrated to Assam. Myron Weiner, *Sons of the Soil: Migration and Ethnic Conflict in India* (Princeton, NJ: Princeton University Press, 1978), p. 161.
128 John-Baptist Hoffman, *Mundarica Encyclopedia*, vol. 2 (New Delhi: Gian Publishing House, 1912), p. 276.
129 Shahid Amin believes that 'in Indian villages even printed texts often revert to their oral characteristics in the very process of communication. It has been noted that newspapers, pamphlets, etc. are made intelligible to the illiterate population in the countryside by reading aloud, paraphrasing the text in the rustic dialect and commenting on it.' See Shahid Amin, 'Gandhi as Mahatma: Gorakhpur District, Eastern UP 1921-2', in *Selected Subaltern Studies*, ed. Ranajit Guha and Spivak Gayatri Chakravorty, pp. 335–39 (New Delhi: Oxford University Press, 1988).

130 Hoffman, *Mundarica Encyclopedia*, vol. 2, p. 53, as cited in Sa, *Crisis in Chota Nagpur*, p. 67.

131 Damodaran, 'Environment, Ethnicity and History in Chotanagpur, India, 1850–1970'.

132 Vinita Damodaran, 'Indigenous Agency: Customary Rights and Tribal Protection in Eastern India, 1830–1930', *History Workshop Journal* 76, no. 1 (October 2013): 85–110, pp. 94–96.

133 K Sivaramakrishnan, *Modern Forests: Statemaking and Environmental Changes in Colonial Eastern India* (California: Standford University Press, 1999), p. 36.

134 Ibid.

135 Please see Ahmed Raza, *Chotnagpur Tenancy Act: A Handbook on Tenancy Law in Jharkhand* (New Delhi: Human Rights Law Network, 2015), p. 14.

136 Daniel Rycroft offers a compelling account of the movement. See Daniel J. Rycroft, *Representing Rebellion: Visual Aspects of Counter-Insurgency in Colonial India* (New Delhi: Oxford University Press, 2006).

137 'Final Report on the Survey and Settlement Operations in the District of Ranchi 1902–1910', p. 42 (emphasis mine).

138 Hoffman to Forbes, Jan 1900, Progs No. 336, August 1900, Home Dept. N.A.I., British Library, London, quoted in, Singh, *Birsa Munda and His Movement* (emphasis mine).

139 Ibid.

140 C. W. Bolton (chief secy. to the Govt. of Bengal) to the Secretary to the Government of India, Judicial files 1900, File no: J&P 226, British Library, London.

141 Ibid.

142 Ibid. Also see Tete, *A Missionary Social Worker in India*.

143 From A. Forbes, Commissioner of Chota Nagpur Division to the Chief Secretary of Bengal, 20 January 1900, (J&P 268), India Office Records, British Library, London.

144 Singh, *Birsa Munda and His Movement*, p. 112.

145 Ibid., p. 113.

146 Ibid., pp. 94–95.

147 A copy of Letter from the Captain from H. J. Roche, to the officer commanding 6th Jats, Camp Burju, 9 January 1900, J & P, Judicial Files (1900), British Library, London.

148 The letter did not describe the word *bhagwani*. I use the term to refer to the supporters of Birsa, otherwise known as Birsaites. Ibid. Also see Singh, *Birsa Munda and His Movement*, p. 124.

149 Ibid.

150 Ibid.

151 Ibid.

152 Ibid.
153 A Demi-official Letter from Mr A. Forbes, O.S.I, Commissioner of Chota Nagpur, 25 January 1900, J & P, Judicial Files (1900), British Library, London. J. P. Hewlett was Secretary to the Government of India, Indian Home Department.
154 Ibid..
155 Ibid.
156 Ibid.
157 Ibid., p. 130.
158 Cited in Singh, *Birsa Munda and His Movement*.
159 Munda rising in the Chota Nagpur, Department of Revenue and Agriculture (Judicial and Public Paper), 8 February 1900, Reference No IOR/L/PJ/6/531, File No 224, British Library, London.
160 Mr J. P. Hewlett to Sir Arthur Godley, Home Department India, 1 February 1900, File No J & P W 304-314, British Library, London.
161 Munda and Zide, 'Revolutionary Birsa and Songs Related to Him', p. 47.
162 Guha, *Elementary Aspects of Peasant Insurgency in Colonial India*.
163 Kalyan Sanyal, *Rethinking Capitalist Development: Primitive Accumulation, Governmentality and Postcolonial Capitalism* (New Delhi: Routledge, 2007).

Part III

Ethnography of Memory, Objects and Resistance

CHAPTER 3

Memories Set in Stone
Political Aesthetics and the Statue of Birsa Munda in Post-colonial Jharkhand

> In any community, remembering the dead is filtered through techniques of memorializing, sometimes at the behest of the dead themselves. These techniques often focus on material substitutes for the absent person. Their design and their very materiality seem intended to defy forgetting by solidifying the deceased, as if they have not gone and our relationship with them has not been changed by their departure. Though these objects help us remember, they also help us forget, by selectively controlling 'how' we remember and forget. Yet, ultimately, even the most interactive object is relatively passive: it may have agency, but how far can it argue, negotiate, or be persuaded to change its mind?
>
> —Piers Vitebsky[1]

Drawing on the historical background of the Birsa movement, this chapter traces the making of Birsa Munda's statue in contemporary Jharkhand. It makes this leap from the previous chapter—anachronistic in nature to distil the reproduction of Birsa's persona through emergent forms of memory politics. The chapter construes history as not merely a scale of time defined by ruptures but rather an unfolding process, each co-constituting the other. In this schema, the Birsa rebellion becomes not *only* an event of the past. In doing so, it draws on Reinhart Koselleck's idea of history that is characterized by different notions of temporal and spatial existence. These temporal modalities include the process of remembering—the memory of the past as one of the key features. It does not approach the past in an 'objective and disinterested manner in order to construct a picture of historical reality by which to measure the falsity of various ideological constructions thereof'. Rather, it treats history as an image of the past that has not ruptured from one moment to another but is instead unfolding.[2] But it also spills over—making slippages and continuing 'traces' through imprints of memory of people, communities and the institutions.[3] Memory becomes an image of the past that resists the emergence of the historical. It flattens the time in which modernity is imagined.[4]

In other words, as Prathama Banerjee in her work has shown, 'the internal presence of the "primitive"', the non-modern, inspires the imagination of temporality as chronology—that is, as an abstract numerical series. Consequently, it can be argued that it is the presence of the '"primitive" which makes historicality possible in the first instance'.[5] This instantiation of the 'primitive' within the historical imagination helps the chapter to locate the urgency of thinking about memory as a form of resistance against time or history.

Sometimes, such images of the past are replicated in the objects that *help us remember* and *selectively control how we remember and forget*.[6] Memory expresses itself through tangible and intangible facets such as statues. It mediates our sensibilities to experience the past through objects. The contesting narratives embodied in the statue of Birsa Munda situate the use of objects as both resistance to and representation of the past. In this chapter, it emerges primarily in the form of ethnographic material: interviews and visuals-as-speech. These narratives contain speech and visuals; they are contrasted and compared to illustrate how the popular representation cast by the dominant group often occludes the social, material and moral lifeworld of Adivasis.

Examining the representation of subaltern speech as forms of aesthetic objects inscribed in statues is not merely a 'correct theoretical practice'; rather, it personifies statues of icons such as B. R. Ambedkar, Kanshi Ram and Birsa Munda. As I show, at the same time these objects also emerge as forms of 'dialogical object' that disrupt the hegemonic structure of representation engrained in caste affinities and allegiances.[7] I argue that the statue of Birsa Munda is a political text that offers mediation between the past and the present. On one level, the materiality of the object (statue) negotiates with history to capture a specific version of the subject (Birsa) of the representation. Variously, it also constitutes public memory as the built environment of remembrance.

As a political text, the aesthetic display of Birsa's body allows the landscape to acquire a field of interaction between competing claims of representation, forging a new identity through ordinary everyday encounters. Such practices of memorialization are widespread within Jharkhand, and semblances of the same are global, in general, transforming the forgotten rebellion and unsung heroes into icons of the past within a milieu I call *material memory*.

In approaching material memory politics, this chapter employs three approaches. First, it uses the template of *material memory* to examine the statue of Birsa Munda as a 'site of memory'.[8] It explores the contrasting material silhouette of subalternity against symbolic representation. Particularly, it examines three statues located in Ranchi and Ulihatu and stitches them together with field narratives and visuals. Material memory, such as statues, permeates and limits the scope of subaltern identity within discursive practices of representation. In other words, it shows how statues as material objects only encapsulate a fragmented, often selective version of what constitutes much wider histories of subaltern struggle.[9] In an attempt at such representation, it enforces amnesia, a forceful forgetting at a scale that is resistant to realizing the full potential of the emerging narrative of historical memory. Birsa Munda's statue therefore highlights the prevalence of memorialization as a symbolic politics in different contexts—often commemorating icons and contexts as events.[10]

Second, the chapter analyses the making of the statue as part of the wider creation of the built environment as spaces of mediation. In his work, Sigurd Bergman extends this line of argument about the built environment within sacred spaces to demonstrate the effects and influence of religion on the infrastructure. He suggests that

> the negotiation of power takes place in religious semiotics, where architecture materializes religious codes such as the encounter between the above, and below, heaven and earth, the interplay of centre and periphery, inside and outside, hierarchies of height (represented in plateaus, thresholds and territorialization of exclusion where only the initiated are permitted to enter sacred areas, and much more).[11]

It is interesting to note that Birsa is also widely perceived as 'Birsa Bhagwan', a god, and incarnations of such popular images are replicated in the statues to extend the affective appeal of the built environment. This incarnation as a Hindu god sits at the heart of tension in Jharkhand. It typecasts the entire community as Hindu, a prototype nationalist fervour at 'assimilating' the Adivasis in the fold.[12] Aesthetic display in this chapter underlines the tension prominently.

Furthermore, the chapter shows how these statues enable the state and the political elites to produce, control and distribute this memory. In effect, the burgeoning representation of Birsa Munda within the new built environment in urban and rural areas reflects a complicated relationship between aesthetics, the sacred and the political.[13] Specifically, as a tool of political mobilization, statues ossify a selective segment from a vast schema of past events. Such selective representations as a narrative of the past disavow people's collective and individual memory and history. When it takes the form of an object in 'extrabodily form', it requires a set of ritual orders through which we remember—and forget—our past.[14] It is a site that produces the materiality of the object.[15] Statues take the form of memory of the past through liturgical practices, where 'the fundamental goal is, precisely, to revivify the past and make it live in the present, to fuse past and present, chanter and hearer, priest and observer, into a single collective entity'—and often in this recitation as formulae to remember, a vast schema of everydayness, emergent tensions are either sublimated or excluded.[16]

Finally, the last section of this chapter contrasts the statue of Birsa Munda with Dalit icons to illustrate the conflicting nature of memory and social values of the symbolic in public. It examines memory from the vantage point of social time, where bodies of Dalit icons (statues), for instance, reclaim the linear time dominated by the built environment of the upper castes—an immense possibility to learn radical politics. It illustrates how Dalit and Adivasi bodies, which are requisite for the survival of violent caste order, also pose a threat by their presence. It shows how and why Dalit icons pose challenges to the echelon of public space dominated by upper caste, while the Adivasi icons are increasingly absorbed into the dominant nationalist framework or defined as Hindu god (Birsa Bhagwan, for instance).

In elaborating all these, I firmly defend the need for greater public representation of these subaltern icons in order to radically break or make obsolete the idea of the public aesthetic in India that remains steeped in structures of graded inequalities and caste. I advocate for the proliferation of statues—in varied forms—of narratives and stories told by the oppressed communities to delegitimize the moral overtone and often superficial requirement for offering economic benefits. Statues of subaltern icons situate the absolute need to bear witness to their history of oppression.

In the following section, I outline the theoretical framework of material memory. I set out the possibility of explaining the non-speech and affective forms to understand subaltern memory politics.

Towards Material Memory Culture

Memory takes multiple forms. An individual or a society can remember an object for various reasons, and this process of remembering is generative of the *materiality* of the object.[17] The object does not in itself store memory or produce it. It is the act of affective *encounter* that produces the meaning of the object.[18] Using a personalized collective and individual *image of the past*, it is transformed into a site of memory. This materiality of the object forms the memory distributed amongst members of the community.

I craft two significant strands of material memory that are useful to elaborate the case studies. First, it provides a scope of understanding the material of the object as a form of social and political text that represents the past of the community. In this, the community collectively engages with material form and projects its identity onto it through various routinized rituals and practices. These practices then allow the generation of an image of the past in the object. Second, it offers political opportunity. The state, civil society and community inscribe their political ideology (content) through the aesthetic (form) concerns.

This brings the chapter to establishing the intimate relationship between memory and material. Significant to the definition is the work of Andrew Jones, where he explains material memory as

> the term memory in relation to objects, buildings and such as a way of re-addressing the relationship between the people and objects in the activity of remembering. If we take on board the point that people and objects are conjoined through practices and that causations (the seat of action) are distributed between people and objects, then both people and objects are engaged in the process of remembering. This is not to say that objects *experience*, *contain*, or *store* memory; it is simply that objects provide ground for humans to experience memory.[19]

Jones poses a certain value in objects that is generative of relationships between people and the community. People give meanings to objects by associating them with their lived *experiences*. These experiences allow the community to remember and forget. Normatively, the material object, as indicated earlier, does not possess the capacity to mobilize people. This explains the association of an object with the representational or symbolic values. The *materie* (physical form) is immobile, static and often (a)historic if it hesitates to display a symbolic meaning. Material is useful but remains 'external' to our world. Perhaps it should be considered that material objects outside the fold of our body (a range of relational experiences) function as *indexes* or *reminders*, as Jones suggests.[20] In this way we do not simply create a binary between the human and the object, an analogue that continues to focus on the anthropocentric as *prima facie*.

The change of function associated with objects opens ways of thinking about the relationship between memory and material. When we examine the role of material in a statue, there are certain notable characteristics even in its display as an installation in public places. For instance, it functions as an open, vague and abstract entity that remains significantly visible with its obscure characteristics and purpose. Therefore, the memory of the dead is commemorated not only as a material formation (statue) to signify their importance, but it also functions as a site of 'creative process constituted by performance, material, culture, place, and landscape'.[21] The term 'memory' also shifts with the changes in creative practices of the subject of representation (individuals, events and icons). This suggests that memory and material culture pose a more complex relationship than may first appear in the wider built environment.

Such consideration is often excluded from the political discourse. In fact, the study of politics as an objective examination with an emphasis on empirical data not only discounts the merit in exploring the representation of the fact but also derides anything non-empirical or objective as 'merely cultural'.[22] Judith Butler addresses this trend by examining new forms of social movements that are deemed *merely cultural* and primarily typecast as 'identity-based, factionalizing and particularistic'.[23] Significantly, this underscores how the material reality of any society finds a voice in the cultural politics of the same. Therefore, the idea that cultural politics (read: statue politics here) is supplementary or oppositional to material struggle defeats the purpose of examining the shadow of the state—often found in symbolic representation, mobilized by the engaged affective politics.

Memory, as with other contours of representation, has received inconsistent critique from historians and perhaps the most inadequate response from political scientists.[24] The motive of studying memory—sometimes as a method, sometimes as a theory—ends in finding coherence within the description rather than exploring the possible tool that it lends to analyse the structural problem in the discourse of representation.

Political performance associated with memorial practices displays this irony. In the context of Jharkhand, for instance, it lends opportunities to the political elites to use various forms of commemoration and memorial practices as a place to widen political and social base of their ideologies. This often overlooks the Adivasi struggles and lifeworld. Therefore, the chapter shows how subaltern Adivasis mobilize memory to display the classic question of the political consciousness that is not simply a *transient* triumph of memory over the material.[25] In fact, the material ('class' in strict Marxist terms) and the symbolic (memory, culture) are not necessarily oppositional but complimentary ideas. To extend Glen Sean Coulthard's argument, we can use memory as an approach to cast insights into 'the cycles of colonial domination and resistance that characterise the relationship between settler states [read: post-colonial here] and indigenous peoples'.[26] It helps us engage with emergent forms of capitalist expansion, colonialism and entanglements with memory. This chapter captures the tension between both in Jharkhand.

Resistance against the institutional practices of memorialization does not erase the articulation of the class question. Gayatri Chakravorty Spivak in her work makes an attempt to understand the idea of speech—voice and gestures, amongst others—and has identified the possibilities of listening to voices within the network of power that radically obstruct it.[27] In explaining such a conceptual problem with the idea of the representation, she breaks the conceptual edifice thus:

> Two senses of representation are being run together: representation as 're-presentation', as in politics, and representation as 're-presentation', as in art or philosophy. Since theory is also only 'action', the theoretician does not represent (speak for) the oppressed group. Indeed, the subject is not seen as representative consciousness (one representing reality adequately). These two senses of representation—within the state formation and the law, on the one hand, and in subject-prediction on other—are related but irreducibly discontinuous.... Are those who act and *struggle* mute, as opposed to those who act and *speak*? These immense problems are buried in the difference between the same words.[28]

The creative tension here highlights the problem with the simplification of representation as *merely* an impression of the subject. It reveals the difficulties of finding subjectivity within the representation discourse. In other words, individual consciousness cannot be represented in a network of power that continually obstructs the entry of voices and, in this case, the subaltern. The assumption that the subaltern, a 'dislocated class subject', finds a voice through representation, sometimes in the form of material objects (such as statues), within memory representation politics overlooks the unequal position of individuals in a society.[29] It is this impossibility, entanglements, absences and death, in the case of the historical character in Spivak's text, which define the limits of representation. As Rajeswari Sunder Rajan notes: 'Subaltern death, or the death of subaltern, poses questions about the manner of death but also about the meaning of death.'[30]

Variously, the idea of subaltern speech poses various stakes—written, non-written and gesture. Margery Sabin, in her work, explores the same tension: 'Anyone attempting to transpose the unwritten subaltern consciousness into written form proposes to cross a great divide and does so by interpreting a variety of signs: if not speech, then faces, or actions, or legal certificates, or other documents.'[31] It is on this incommensurable plain that representation takes a complicated turn. It becomes a methodological insistence that foregrounds emergent forms of memory politics through objects, often when the subject of representation is claimed for political requirements.

In the following sections, I reflect on this entanglement of representation with objects. Each section seeks to construe the use of material memory (statues) as a political tool within an overarching discussion on the possibility of the representation.

Mapping the Mammoth Memory: The Making of Birsa's Statues

Historically, India's administrative culture of memorialization became more widespread with the arrival of the British. Colonial India burgeoned with memorials, statues and friezes. These memorials captured *eventful* memories and figures who made remarkable contributions. Some memorials, as time passed, were also renamed and designated different characters than those assigned at the beginning. For instance, the Victoria Memorial in Lucknow was built in 1901 as a park with a bronze statue to memorialize Queen Victoria. In 1962, the park was renamed as Begum Hazrat Mahal Park after the wife of Wajid Ali Shah, the last nawab of Awadh, who had fought the British in the Indian rebellion of 1857.[32] The renaming of the memorial was based on her contribution to the uprising as well as the belief that Queen Victoria (whose statue was removed) simply betrayed the spirit of independent, anti-colonial India. This is a wide-ranging practice, sometimes neatly tied to anti-imperial or colonial characteristics.

Various works have highlighted the use of memorials that were institutionalized in post-colonial India. However, these institutional affiliations were more clearly directed towards restoring colonial 'nostalgia', with the cemeteries of those British (Europeans more broadly) who died for the cause of the Raj being one example.[33] Gradually, the change in the ruling dispensation and political need shifted the objects of material memory and memorial landscape (including statues). Nevertheless, the shifting nature of the memorial landscape is a characteristic feature in India.

A Note on Statues

Amongst the wide body of material memory studies, statues have attracted little scholarship. As has been seen globally, statues, in particular, have stirred similar debates about the contested nature of representations of the past and the canonization of figures who have inherited legacies of violence. The statue is a material object that is generally made with stone, bronze or cement to display an individual whose heroic contributions are defining to collective memory. This representation can also contain skewed ideas and insular doctrines, lending support to those who occupied positions of power. A statue freezes time into an artefact of memory to articulate a selectively curated and strategically positioned narrative. Erected in public places, most commonly at intersections and on throughfares and sometimes inside museums, the shape, size and colour aim to represent multiple facets of the subject.

Statues as public artefacts are also bold and often political in nature.[34] As Rahul Rao writes: '[S]tatues are vulnerable, typically standing alone, unguarded … simultaneously, aggressive and insecure,'[35] Statues represent the vulnerability of the subject in the eye of the public, withstanding possible damage and resistance against it—for example, the episode of the Rhodes Must Fall protest in South Africa and the desecration of Mahatma Gandhi's statue in Ghana in the recent past.[36] These incidents reflect the effect of statues within the public memory and their political implications.

Birsa and His Statue

Significantly, the making of Birsa Munda's statue in post-colonial Jharkhand opens a case for aesthetic concerns and political mobilization.[37] Ever since the formation of Jharkhand, the statues have become remarkably ubiquitous. Over the period, the state witnessed a booming culture of popular forms of representation. Several initiatives such as 'Momentum Jharkhand' have opened the gates for business and industrial houses, extending their base and access to forests and minerals. A symbolic impression of this, for instance, can be seen in the flying elephant mascot, symbolizing the utilization of the state's rich reserve (forest, mountains and animals) to make industrial gains. At the superficial level, the mascot is not only aesthetically unpleasing and quite unreal, since an elephant is depicted as flying, but at another level, it demonstrates the possibility of the actual disappearance of elephants from the forest, which will be cleared and replaced with extractive industries. The changes were apparent and also manifested in the aesthetic appeal of the state, shifting the meaning of nature into a potential reserve for development.

What follows hereafter is a descriptive analysis and visual reading of a specific case study of the Ulgulan Foundation. The section demonstrates how material memory works as a tool to reproduce and mobilize the past through affective sites such as the statue of Birsa Munda. The use of first-person narrative situates both the approach and the tension of working as a researcher, outsider, *sadan* and non-Adivasis. It locates the tension, which is a part of the book's ethnographic method.[38] This tension highlights the texture of memory that has become a new way of *doing* politics in post-colonial Jharkhand.

Architecture of Memory: Mammoth Statue, Regional Political Elite and Fieldnotes

October 2018, Police line, Ranchi

Seated on a white chair in an open veranda of a bungalow overlooking the vast swathes of green gardens with a parking area for cars, I was asked to move inside. I had arrived an hour early to meet a member of the legislative assembly (MLA)[39], Sudesh Mahto, who had stood for an election from the Silli region's Vidhan Sabha constituency in Jharkhand for the AJSU Party.[40] Popular amongst his electorate and in the state of Jharkhand as a youth leader, Mahto had a political career as deputy chief minister under the leadership of Arjun Munda, who had won the election in 2009 under the right-wing BJP.[41] There was an alliance between both the parties again during the 2014 elections for the legislative assembly. This seemingly uncomfortable alliance at the ideological level eventually broke down. The alliance in the two periods reflected the BJP's clear stance for Adivasi rights in which 'development' was used as a catchword in the elections, seeking to draw benefits from mineral resources for the state.[42] Mahto's ideology remains indistinct, if not unclear and opportunist. He failed to establish a stable ideological standpoint both within the alliance and outside it, in his own party. Nevertheless, over the years, he seemed to have made some efforts to appropriate issues that concerned the public of Jharkhand. For instance, he organized *mahila panchayat* (women's meetings) to woo his female voters by invoking the slogan 'Maa aur maati' (Mother and soil).[43] The *mahila panchayat* had great appeal amongst poor Adivasis and was given a massive turnout for the meeting.[44]

Slogans such as 'Maa aur maati' suggest the apparent political appropriation of electorates. Seemingly, it transforms women's bodies into a territory to fight battles against poverty. It imagines the gendered body as a site to identify the existing lack thereof caused by material inequalities. In doing so, it appoints and mobilizes the masculine trope of development to overcome the gap. That said, Mahto had conducted some work that had led to the 'constitution of hundreds of women's self-help group [being] assigned departmental projects, thus making them financially independent'.[45] Grassroots-level support is crucial to elections across India. Grassroots-level mobilization is a precondition of governance in a state such as Jharkhand, where a majority of the population reside in rural areas. *Gram panchayats* (rural grassroots-level institutions) strengthen the spirit of Indian electoral democracy, and it is incumbent on *gram panchayat* leaders to conduct impartial elections in order to keep institutions alive. In a recent work on *gram sabhas* (village assemblies) and *panchayats*, Paromita Sanyal and Vijayendra Rao write:

> Deliberative institutions, like the gram sabha, are becoming increasingly important in the world as forums to allocate resources to the poor. By moving decision-making power from government bureaucracies to villages and neighbourhoods, these institutions have been viewed to wrest power from elites. They are ways of making the implementation of development interventions more efficient and improving the equity and transparency of allocations. 'Citizen Engagement' of this kind is seen as the key to accountability.[46]

Gram sabhas help politicians simplify their political ambitions for electorates at the grassroots level. These ambitions are otherwise tied to the goals of the national parties—often distilling their ideological fronts through a complex network of negotiation or the use of excessive power. Mahto's recent past suggests an interesting turn towards the concerns of Adivasis for the obvious political gain that comes from the iconography of anti-colonial figures.

Mahto has commissioned a forum called Ulgulan Foundation, named after the Birsa Munda rebellion.[47] This foundation aims to build a statue of historical importance. The processes involved in constituting the foundation to erect a statue of Birsa tell a fascinating story. The proposed site is National Highway 33 (Ranchi–Jamshedpur), where it promises to be 150 feet tall in stature, 'giving an aerial glimpse to those who fly down to the historic landscape of Jharkhand', as noted by Mayank, a Delhi University graduate.[48] During the process of allotting a site for the statue, Mahto devised a popular slogan: 'Har ghar se pathar, har ghar se sahyog' (A stone from each home, a helping hand from each home). The slogan invokes a sense of solidarity in erecting the statue and suggests, in Mahto's words, 'the collective will of the people'. It is noteworthy that 'the will' of Adivasis is always invariably voiced in India by non-Adivasis—for the former remain and are conditioned to function as recipients. As Mahto's political ideology struggles to gain a firm foothold on Adivasi issues, the attempt to build a statue cannot be discerned. This becomes clear as he begins to offer his justification for it.

As soon as he arrived at his office, I was asked to join him in another room inside, which was embellished with objects of antiquity so that it looked like more of a museum. I found a non-descript way to introduce myself since, given my subject location in a foreign university, there was an assumption of roles being played. I note this as an underlining feature that underscores the rest of the description. The interviewer's background often influences the content, accessibility and mode of the interview. It sets out not only the terms of the conversation but also introduces vague assumptions about their background.

The room, as it turned out, had vaulted ceilings typical of colonial design, making the long spell of summer bearable. This room was supposedly the official corner for conversations, limited in access and hosting only a select few. It was followed by another gateway to the outside that conjoined a long hall with a round table for discussion with the *jan*, the people who had been lining up since morning. This series of rooms, each with a low-lying table containing stacks of dust-laden files, were designed for meetings that also reflected Indian bureaucracy and, figuratively, the movement of red files.[49] The rooms' lurking features of delay and slow motion had also affected the dispensation of justice. Any chance of quickening the process is usually contingent on the applicant's background and power to influence this system.

In this room, the warmth of the *sarkari*, the bureaucratic aesthetic, was vivid in one place: the long wooden desk held high, covered with double-sheet glass and decorated with a slightly skewed Indian flag stand and numerous files awaiting attention. As Mahto appeared in the room to take his elaborate seat, a ticking clock became a reminder of his two-hour delay. However, he settled down to give an interview while a few people huddled behind a glass door to watch the clock for he was scheduled for many more such meetings. Upon being asked to shed some light on what he thinks about Birsa Munda, he candidly said: 'He [Birsa] was a legend and continues to remain so. Birsa and the likes [presumably other Adivasi leaders] had an idea of *nature* which remained at the core of their struggles.'[50] There was an unusual rush—a sort of premonition he had about this conversation. As time seemed limited, I stopped myself from sharpening my questions.

Memories Set in Stone

Birsa Munda, said Mahto, 'continues to remain a story of a legendary hero who displayed his courage and fought against the Raj'. The legendary characterization of Birsa here is woven into a narrative that emphasizes the importance of 'nature' in struggles led by the Adivasis in general. Nature, however, vaguely defined, remains at the cornerstone of the Adivasi movement and often becomes instrumental for political elites' mobilizing of the issues to create new political space in their constituencies and at the national level. Furthermore, he illustrated the significance of nature when he said:

> In contemporary times, the kind of national or international policies that we see for the Scheduled Areas is highly destructive. It unsettles and uproots the everyday lives of the poorest. A kind of policy that we were able to fend off even while we were under British rule and not the elected government that we have now. A group of people who sit in New Delhi, a political influence to decide for people here. If they fail to understand the situation, it can have multiple damages [*sic*] on the people's lives here in different forms.[51]

Vague references to national and international policies readily rebuffed the opportunity to specify the political actions taken by parties that have an impact on 'nature' and people. In distancing himself from blame by pointing to national policy, he seemed to be placing the scale and implication of his work outside the political fold. The vagueness of the reference obscured his political position against statements extending empathy towards natural resources and people.

Moreover, the reference to New Delhi is worth underlining. The federal state of Jharkhand has two historic pieces of legislation regarding Adivasi land rights. At least one of these emerged due to the Birsa movement: the CNTA. There are three major laws—the CNTA (1908), the Santhal Parganas Act (1949) and the Bihar Land Reforms Act (1950)—that are fundamental to understanding the land history of the state. Together, these legislations served the *manki munda* (village headman and the priest) village administrative system.[52] These laws, in turn, require that the state carefully assesses the nature of land, identifies the beneficiaries and imposes limits on transferability and saleability, amongst others.

Mahto cogently shifted these nuances of the legislations and ensuing legal obligations to New Delhi, while most cases of violations of the CNTA receive support or at least implicate the engagement of regional political leaders in favour of industrial interests.[53] In fact, political actors play a significant role in determining the scale and impact of the violation of land rights. In a journal article I note that in the recent episode of land-rights violation in Nagri, Jharkhand, associated with land acquisition, the state and political actors (Adivasi leaders, ironically) were found to be at odds with the rights of the *raiyat*s and extended limited support.[54] Following several demonstrations that had led to the large-scale preventative detention of students and activists who were against the proposed amendments to the CNTA, the BJP had to withdraw the clause and restore the original provisions.[55] Therefore, the reference to the New Delhi problem simply suspends any engagement with specific issues that lead to extractivism in Jharkhand.

Against the background of rising tensions in the state, Mahto, on the contrary, felt compelled to reassert the legacy of Birsa Munda—awakening public consciousness to the contribution of iconic Adivasi leaders. He marshalled the Ulgulan Foundation and assembled a blueprint (pamphlet) for the installation of what would be India's second-largest statue. The tallest statue in India is currently the 'Statue of Unity' representing the nationalist politician Sardar Vallabhai Patel (who fought alongside Gandhi), built by Larsen & Toubro, a major conglomerate, and sculpted by Ram V. Sutar. It cost up to 420 million dollars.[56] The statue stands on the Narmada River in Gujrat, known for the historic anti-dam movement Narmada Bachao Andolan (NBA).[57]

The Patel statue represents a profound irony. It stands as one of the 'world's biggest statues' and can be apparently seen from space, while it overlooks the most immediate, historically contentious problem associated with Adivasis, who were dispossessed in the process of the construction of the dam. In fact, the inauguration of Patel's statue was met with resistance far away in the villages, where hundreds of Adivasis were detained to avoid any problems with the inauguration.[58] This is not an isolated event regarding statues, but it does inform us about the specific nature of memorialization that reflects the insidious workings of symbolic power.

What emerges as an aesthetic display of a historical past and site of remembrance can also present an account of forgetting. Effectively, it shows how material display can reflect on the depth of memory politics. However, Mahto's attempt to install a 150-feet tall statue of Birsa Munda exhibits an interesting and, perhaps, more nuanced representation of the past. In the following discussion, I argue that Mahto's attempt to install the statue offers an opportunity to understand *memory as politics*. It describes a narrative in which Birsa Munda seemingly becomes a figure whose ubiquitous presence is indelible and, sometimes, far removed from material reality in the service of aesthetic concerns. In this process, he comes to occupy an empty signifier—essentially appropriated by the political spectrum, which removes the historical perspective or represents a dimension that is useful to mobilization.

Nationalizing Memory: A Brief Background

As a background to the making of the statue of Birsa, before the Ulgulan Foundation was established, the Birsa Munda Statue Committee in Rourkela (in Odisha, now a neighbouring state) installed a bronze statue in 1982. This was also a moment of resurgence for Birsa's memory in the wake of the Jharkhand movement. Following the erection of the statue, the government of India took decisive steps that marked remarkable steps towards commemorating the memory at the national level.

Starting with the launch of a postal stamp featuring Birsa's image in 1988, a portrait of Birsa was unveiled in the Indian parliament in 1989.[59] The portrait was an impressive move and historically significant as it was the first portrait of an Adivasi leader to be hung in the parliament. In fact, Jai Pal Singh Munda, who represented the Adivasis in the constituent assembly debates, finds no portraits at all in the gallery of this hall of democracy—making canonization an inherently political project. Subsequently, the Central Jail also installed a statue and observed the centenary of his martyrdom, construing this as processual work by inviting various members from the community. Later, the neighbouring state of Odisha set up a research centre widely known as 'Birsa Maidan' in Rourkela.

The burgeoning of these artefacts, statues and portraits led to the emergence of the national memory of Birsa Munda, framing him in the popular imagination and within the list of heroic icons who often have anti-colonial legacies. However, it also underlines the fact that Birsa Munda was not given any considerable degree of attention until Kumar Suresh Singh wrote the most comprehensive and detailed account of his life. Singh's book, *The Dust-Storm and the Hanging Mist: A Study of Birsa Munda and His Movement in Chhotanagpur, 1874–1901*, was first published in 1966. The book led to literary responses to the persona of Birsa Munda, later including Mahasweta Devi's book *Aranya Adhikar* and Surendra Prasad Sinha's *Life and Time of Birsa Bhagwan*. These works became instrumental in situating the importance of Birsa's story within literary and academic circles, most widely popularized when Devi received the Sahitya Akademi Award, the country's foremost literary honour, in 1979. The circulation and production of Birsa's image, centred around the theme of resistance, allowed him to occupy a crucial position within national remembrance.

If there has been widespread reception of Birsa's persona in the literary and political space, what compelled Mahto to come up with a 150-feet statue? What is there to spell out about Birsa that remains implicit in his story? How far can an object designed to cater to aesthetic appeal—in this case a statue—emerge politically? These questions seek to draw our attention to the process that might explain it.

Narration and Design of the Statue

Returning to the conversation, Mahto assumingly pulled out a book—the Hindi edition of Kumar Suresh Singh's work—from the shelf of his glass-sheeted table. Having assumed its broader readership, he hesitantly suggested: 'Everything is written down in text. Nevertheless, it remains silent or limited to writings. An expansion of his [Birsa's] ideas is important. What I intend to do is to layout the history to the public in the form of the statue.'[60]

This statement may seem compelling as it promises to elaborate the scope of understanding history through the built environment—an architectural display of historical memory. As I understood it, history, for Mahto, is not fixated in simply the sources within a textbook but sometimes exists or needs to be illustrated in the built environment. He firmly believed that a 'reliable' source of history should always be readily available and displayed in public—sometimes in the form of a statue. He referred to this as *etihaas se mulaquat* (encountering history). Such representation amplifies people's capacity to consume history—giving them a visual memory embedded in inanimate objects. This suggests that Mahto clearly believes that there is a selective version of history as against the whole of it on public display.

A belief that visual material displayed through the built environment opens the text to the public is perhaps great in theory. However, the execution of the plan and the process of thinking through the subject have been rather complex. Mahto has appointed two political assistants to present his commitments and political standpoint to urban English-speaking visitors. I was drawn to, if not distracted by, their presence as they huddled behind the door. Upon their arrival in the room at the end of my interview, they insisted on knowing more about the project. During this conversation, Mayank, the Delhi University graduate previously mentioned, offered a pamphlet with a detailed report on the structure, location, aesthetics and economics of the statue. It is notable that the plan for the construction of the statue has been well structured in consultation with architects and government offices—appealing to popular sensibilities through the representation of Birsa (Figure 3.1).

Mahto's effort to woo middle-class sensibilities is captured by comparing the height of the statue to that of a building. 'The statue will attract tourists', making this display a 'mela [festival],' Mahto claims. His self-proclaimed intent is to pay homage to Birsa, and he imagines that this will help spread 'Birsawaad' (the teachings of Birsa)—no matter how discreet or unexplained the teachings remain

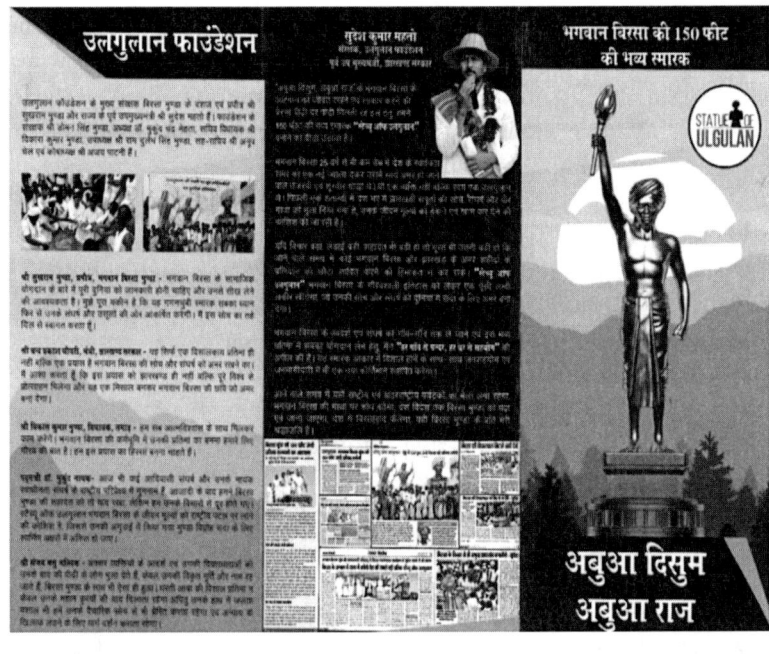
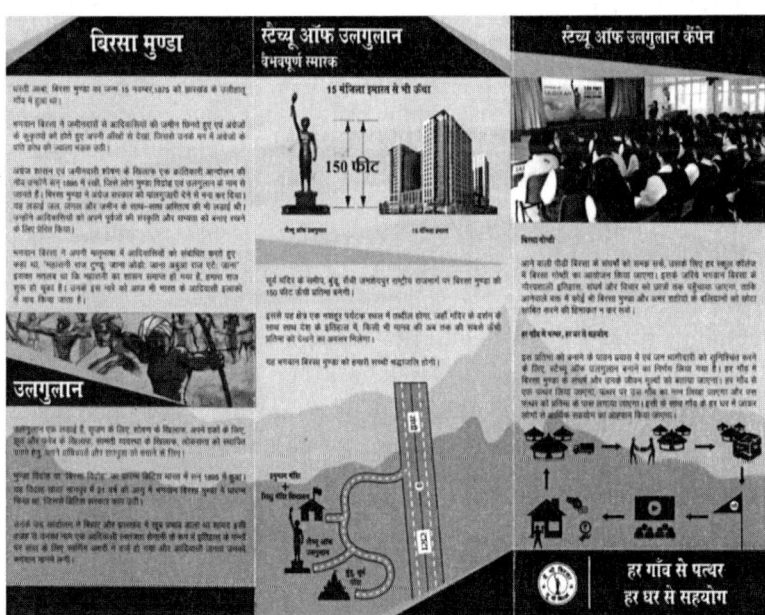

Figure 3.1 Ulgulan Foundation pamphlet

Source: Author's copy of the pamphlet received at Sudesh Mahto's office.

for his own understanding. This, of course, drew the spotlight of the media, staging Mahto as a politician attempting to resurrect the historical memory of the region. Claiming to appoint Sukhram Munda, the great-grandson of Birsa, as the leader of the project, Mahto is shown in a traditional hat at what appears to be a public gathering, with the pamphlet quoting Mahto as saying:

> We must not let the sacrifice of our martyr be in vain. The Statue of Ulgulan will draw a historical line that will display the contribution of Birsa, not only at the regional level but also on the world stage. It will be a promising history to view and read for people from around the world, and this would be my homage to his memory.

The display of such strong convictions in installing the statue also suggests its broader political purpose as a tool to shape the public discourse on icons. The pamphlet also essentializes the contribution of Birsa to society as a *martyr* who fought against the Raj. This recognition dovetails the topical formulation of martyrdom with the national imaginary of the freedom struggle. It is not at variance with the ambition of Birsa's vision. However, it restricts the mobility of his political vision, the focus of which was not limited *only* to the imperial forces but rather a vast swathe of people, the *diku*s, who dispossessed the Adivasis. In fact, the foregrounding of martyrdom reduces the scope to understand the political space of sub-national polity that continues to dominate the state as I show in Chapter 5. It prefigures Birsa as serving the imagination of the nation state—one in which he is conveniently dislocated from his primal political objective of *abua disum, abua raj* (my village, my rule).

Interestingly, the bottom half of the second page in the pamphlet is laid out in three paragraphs that contain some biographical information. They set out the meaning of *ulgulan* and its historical relevance, stressing the features of the movement as an exclusively 'anti-colonial' one. This is a significant point to show the contradiction and shift in the image of Birsa within various forms of the memorial landscape for two reasons. First, the dominant display of his memory accentuates the point of reference as exclusively the anti-colonial one. Second, it contradicts Mahto's proposal that he would be casting Birsa in a different light, as I show in the following section.

In addition, the pamphlet also presents Birsa's popular rallying cry during the rebellion: 'Maharani raj tundu jaana auro abua raj etee jaana' (We call an end to the maharani [queen] kingdom; we will now have our own kingdom, our own land). This is located beside a depiction of the statue that compares it to a multi-storey building. The reference to the 'queen' simply suspends any engagement with what is found in the historical record: 'abua disum, abua raj', a slogan that echoes through several movement today about land rights. This is supplemented with pictorial depiction showing the construction of the statue through the support of people: 'each household donating a stone containing their name on it'. This was quite overwhelming to imagine as we moved past the tentative date for the completion of construction (November 2018). But the temper of political rhetoric runs high. Almost invariably, regional leaders fashion their slogans as paeans to prime minister Narendra Modi, often vacuous and far removed from any substantive efforts towards addressing the rights of the Adivasis.

Narrations of Memory: Shift in Symbolism

In the pamphlet, the design of the statue is impressive. Unlike most of the statues that are widely seen across Jharkhand, this one displays unique features by emphasizing posture and using symbolism. The proposed *ulgulan* statue has a miniature form installed near the Jonha Falls, Ranchi, symbolizing Birsa as a social reformer—a segment of his personality and his teachings that stems from Vaishnavism. The symbolic use of the torch signifies the importance of light for the community, marking a shift in the aesthetic orientation and affective message within projects in the built environment. Unlike the depiction of his personality in statues across the state with an aggressive face, rebellious posture and other physical attributes, this statue is consciously designed to make a different appeal to the public. It focuses on laying out a message folded in his teaching—a sort of biographical information that is 'not so *political*', as Sanjay Bosu Mullick, a popular activist in the Adivasi struggle for identity, autonomy and rights to resources, said.[61]

Delving into this new version of Birsa as a social reformer, Mullick offered an impressive account of processes in the making of the miniature statue. Mullick has been an academic and activist in Jharkhand for over four decades.[62] In fact, along with R. D. Munda, he was one of the few interlocutors to attend various sessions on the Indigenous Peoples group of the UNWGIP in Geneva, Switzerland. Bosu shared an anecdote about the process of sculpting the miniature statue. This anecdote illustrates how modernity is lived as a political reality in everyday lives within post-colonial spaces, in which the Adivasis and their bodies are either prefigured as relics of the past or superimposed with popular imaginaries of icons. Drawing on his anecdote, Bosu said: 'We have only two photographs [of Birsa]. Those are not good pictures. Nevertheless, you can imagine his bodily structure: short height, thin person, but his face I cannot ascertain.'

Meanwhile, he paused to attend to someone who visited his office, and I glanced at my notes to find out cues for subsequent questions. Most people, especially researchers, pay at least one visit to Bosu's office, which offers a huge reserve of data on forest and land rights. Returning to the conversation, he said:

> I was given a responsibility by the AJSU Party to help the sculptors make Birsa's statue.... I had to go and sit with the artists in Delhi. Subsequently, I was angry to see what he [the artist] produced—a face of a Rajput fighter, with a sharp nose and round face. It was a Rajput reincarnation. I had to then teach him that when you sculpt a face, you think of the person's background and then sculpt.

He continued his story, noting:

> Based on two photographs, I began to imagine him [Birsa]. Now I must say that he is a Munda person, and I will have to see the ideal-typical face is there. You cannot superimpose a sharp nose; you will have to give the specific key features such as eyes, where the upper eyelid is dominating the lower eyelid. However, in the case of Mundas, they are on the same front. They [Mundas] have no beard and little hair on the face. He [Birsa] is from a hardworking family, and therefore it must be reflected in his body. All of this had to be taught to the sculptor. He had to change the whole thing. There are many pieces of the sculpture already in place. A miniature form of the sculpture was inaugurated on 9 September 2018. I am not happy with the sculptor. Sculpting as an art has been highly subordinated to technology. This mechanised process is forming a historical figure. There is no imagination in it.[63]

Mullick's story unveils the complex process of producing Birsa's persona. His insights on imagining Birsa in the form of a sculpture are intriguing in terms of understanding the wide reception of Birsa outside the state as much as within it. A broad characterization of an Adivasi body accentuated through his use of the word 'typical' also exposes manifold biases or, at least, a shorthand use of racialization. This, of course, has little or no bearing on his work, which has mainstreamed Adivasi land rights. But it impinges on rather systemic normalization of vocabularies that allow middle-class Indians at large to describe Adivasis. Solidarity often, as I mentioned in the preface, is extended as forms of patronage—the microcosm of which sits in these moments.

Regimes of Historicity: Birsa as Memory and Heritage

There is a noticeable trend in not only portraying Birsa as the 'memory' of the past but also positing it as 'heritage', especially to those who are non-Adivasis. Mahto and Mullick radiate an impulse towards drawing out Birsa from the confines of history by using the trope of heritage—one that results in a context that is frozen in time. It radically transforms the past, from being a taxonomic indicator of history, into heritage. François Hartog's sophisticated account of time explains this shift. Hartog presents time as an experiential category in which individuals and society relate to time—'here and elsewhere, yesterday and tomorrow, making it being in time'.[64]

Apparent in both Mahto and Bosu were a concern about replicating the legacy of Birsa from the forms that they had received (history and photographs) into an extended version of their political imaginaries. They do not consider the possibilities in rupturing the status quo of political discourse on Birsa and incorporating an alternative vision that reflects on new forms of extractivist economic exploitation. For them, 'there is enough of that'—a point I find troublesome since, during several years as a *sadan* and researcher there, I failed to find a statue or broader aesthetic design that attends to, listens and allows subaltern Adivasis to make their own history (read: statue). On the contrary, Mahto and Bosu were invested in highlighting the *sahadat*, the martyr or social reformer.

It occurred to me that we are remembering to forget, for there remains a saga of Birsa we have never insisted on pursuing. This is not to discern the definitive nature of photographs that are used as a template to reproduce Birsa's image, but it is evident that in the contemporary landscape, Birsa acquires multiple temporalities—as a rebel for the Maoists and as a *bhagwan* for the Birsaites, as I discuss in subsequent chapters. The selective reproduction and wide circulation of Birsa as an exclusive 'anti-colonial movement' accentuates him as the subaltern icon in the nationalist movement. There is a unitary attempt across the spectrum (civil society and politicians) to manufacture their visions through material memory representation. Such a discursive shift in the representation also reflects the changing nature of regional politics that uses the trope of heritage now.

The nodal point for explaining this phenomenon—a massive shift to new forms of representation—is driven by the need to develop a heritage culture of Birsa. In the context of France during the 1980s, for instance, the state actively participated in curating national history in different forms, including the construction of museums, often shifting history into memory and heritage. Hartog suggests that 'heritage becomes the memory of history, and as such, a symbol of identity. Memory, heritage, history, identity, and nation are united in the polished style of the legislator.'[65] He foregrounds his claims by considering heritage within a wide range of requirements (conservation, renovation)—features that emerge routinely in all the chapters of this book. Amongst others, commemoration, he believed, is added to the 'duty of memory'—a point that I explore more widely in the next chapter.[66]

An impression of heritage as a place for the concretion of identity is a defining characteristic of the Ulgulan Foundation too. The foundation not only acts as a space for the political theatrics of representation for Adivasi constituencies but also caters to a broader appeal to nationalism through aesthetic concerns. I give an impression of this in the following account that contests the unitary representation in Mahto's account. It moves away from the trope of nostalgia for Birsa that restricts the articulation of his subalternity in the 'realm of memory'.[67]

Memory as Politics: Listening to the Voice of Resistance, Dayamani Barla

> *Adivasi aakrosh, ulgulan ka aakrosh, hul ka aakrosh, aaj bhi waise hi hai* (The angst of Adivasis, the *ulgulan* and the *hul* is still the same). The fire is still burning. One hundred years ago, Birsa Munda spoke, and today, I repeat it. Therefore, it is erroneous to believe that Birsa had died.[68]

Against the ceremonial performance of civil society, Dayamani Barla emerges as an unusual figure in the political landscape of Jharkhand. For several decades now, Barla has found herself in a struggle against the extractivist agendas of influential industrial projects. In this schema of thinking, coal, for instance, has left the largest footprint of extractivism in the region. Dispossession in this process is intertwined—for coal mining requires the land of the Adivasis. Kuntala Lahiri-Dutt, Radhika Balakrishnan and Nesar Ahmad have shown how 'tribal land acquisition for captive coal mining demonstrates the "violence" of mining and reveals the formal and informal tactics deployed by the state and private companies to dispossess the poor'.[69] Barla routinely engages in working with huge groups, extending her solidarity to resistance movements against the development-induced dispossession. Amongst others, she was a quite central figure within the Koel-Karo and Nagri movements.[70] A number of charges have been raised against her, and she is subjected to constant intimidation, but her political standpoint remains uncompromising. She is, I must acknowledge, an admirably helpful person who agreed to an interview without tossing around the issues—an experience I share with many who have interviewed her previously.

Barla called the meeting at her teashop. It was 5.30 p.m., and the streets of the city were slowly being reclaimed by cars and bicycles. The streetlights had begun to blink on amid the usual evening bustle along this road, which offers a syncretic fold of modernity and tradition. On the one side were mushrooming aspirational private coaching classes for engineering and medicine students, crammed into a multi-storey building; on the other, a view to a missionary college established by the Gossner (Lutheran) Church that sat on the edges of a lake. In contrast, Barla's teashop seemed to occupy a tiny space to pass the time. The shop housed a few seats, especially for working-class customers to find some rest as they sipped their chai and looked on as the city rushed past them. The place is known amongst its patrons for piping hot samosa and chai and faces a middle-class restaurant serving continental dishes. By dusk the shelves of the teashop had been emptied and restocked.

Barla, walking barefoot through the narrow passage by the busy road, emerged draped in a green cotton saree with a *jhola* on her sleeves, a common feature of many political activists in India. *Jhola*, a side sleeve bag, is popularly understood as a symbol of a person who believes in so-called communist ideas.[71] While she does not identify with communism, her unfailing resistance stands firm against the visceral expansion of capitalist extraction in this region. As we took our seats in the teashop, she seemed to gloss over the bookshelves containing printed material on displacement and conversion, now coated in the dust blowing into the shop from the road.

Barla had offered her support in the past, a rare quality for the circle of people who work on Adivasi issues, especially political elites. Barla finds herself as 'one among equals', a phrase she and some other Adivasi colleagues use for Birsa. An anecdotal rumination on this emerged in a conversation with a group of women during a visit to Ulihatu: They regularly used *usko* ('he' without an adjective) but *aap* (respectful way of saying 'you') when in conversation with me. The usage of different vocabularies reflect the personification of Birsa as a member of the Adivasi community. As we settled down, I asked Barla to consider the relevance of Birsa in the contemporary political landscape. She looked out from her seat facing the road and took a moment to reflect. She then replied in firm voice:

> At that moment [colonial rule], when Birsa fought against the empire, we, then, had one East India Company [EIC]. The EIC against which Birsa rose to seek independence for his river, forest, land, language. In fact, before Birsa, history is evident in how there was a presence of self-governance, and people gradually developed their lives and regulated according to *khuntkhatti* rights. In that village, the question of *khuntkhatti* was pursued by Birsa to seek self-control and regulation against foreign invasion and establish the *khuntkhatti*. He reiterated the centrality of the Adivasi village, and the importance of the self-ruling mechanism that defines it as a unique institution. However, in today's time, everything that we had fought since Sidhu Kano, Birsa Munda, their lives and sacrifices and their dreams have been trampled on. In independent India, and now 18 years into new Jharkhand, there is an attack from all quarters. There was one EIC, and now we have many.

Significant to this response is the invocation of the 'empire' (implying the Raj), which faced resistance by Birsa, to explain the continual forms of violence. Barla compressed the history of centuries into a single line: *We then had one empire*. Interestingly, Barla did not seem to distinguish between the EIC, the Raj and post-colonial Jharkhand. The EIC becomes a metaphor to expose the processual extraction—one that was prevalent in the British Raj as much as it is in contemporary Jharkhand.

I think this sought to establish a relationship between the capital, empire (read Raj too) and the land. Barla's use of the EIC expands the scope of tracing the changing nature of regimes supported by capital-intensive industries that project Adivasis as participants, who in turn reproduce what is called 'adverse inclusion'.[72] In a sense, she laid out the serious contradiction that has now emerged in post-colonial Jharkhand where projects to support expansion are met with frequent resistance—resistance that mobilizes the historical memory of the region: the *ulgulan*. Instead of referring to some sort of schematic description of the past, as seen in Mahto's interview, Barla seeks to underline a specific formation that explains the tension by drawing our attention to the struggle of *jal, jungle aur jameen*.

Historically, *jal, jungle aur jameen* was the cornerstone of political movements in the state, as discussed in the introduction. It is now confronted with the newer kinds of oppression and extraction that dispossess Adivasis of their land and heritage, making the resistance multifaceted against the *dikus*. This oppressive structure is cleaved into various segments such as industrial groups, their benefits steeped in land, and a whole gamut of politicians. This has jeopardised the primacy of institutions of village self-rule; the *parha* system, for instance, had played a prominent role in shaping Adivasi society.

Antonio Negri and Michael Hardt make an interesting observation about similar tendencies that have come about with the advent of modern capitalism, where 'it is decentred and deterritorializing apparatus of rule that progressively incorporates the entire global realm within its open, expanding frontiers'.[73] Negri and Hardt argue that the form of empire has shifted from the traditional idea of singular institutions to now managing 'hybrid identities, flexible hierarchies, and plural exchanges through modulating networks of command'.[74]

The articulation of material deprivation and exclusion of Adivasi from their resources paves the way for an emergent form of memory politics more effectively here. When Barla reflects on imperial rule, she also intimately ties it to the ongoing crisis and struggles. Her constant drift from the memories of the past to the present significantly marks the use of memory as a trope that defines the struggle of communities. Memory transforms the event of the past into the act of the present. It offers a space to lay out the various fragmentary histories into continuous form in the present through a series of negotiations.

However, what seemed to be an event of rebellion, which unsettled the colonial order of Chota Nagpur, now emerges as the *minority history* within the local and national memory of independence—for instance, Mahto's initiative to install a statue not to *stage a protest* against the newer forms of oppression but rather to cement the positioning of *minority history* into the national frame of a martyr. Birsa's act of rebellion is characterized by his martyrdom for the cause of the nation. This singularity drives Mahto's own political ambition.

As Dipesh Chakrabarty says, 'the transformation of once-oppositional, minority histories into "good" histories illustrate how the mechanism of incorporation works in the discipline of history'.[75] Against the limited archival records and research on the scope of Birsa's rebellion, the defining feature was isolated from a much larger land struggle. Minority history therefore limits the scope of the wider articulation of the struggle as it is framed by Mahto.

However, Barla underscores the relevance of the past by offering new semblances—the *many EICs* in the new Jharkhand. Minority history only serves to give a space for the political appropriation of Birsa as a crucial figure within the limits of the nationalist imagination. Subsequently, it also functions to perform the symbolic recognition of Adivasi contribution to nation-making, even though their own lived experiences, fraught with relentless material challenges, are sacrificed.

Barla's use of 'many EICs' as a metaphor prompted me to follow up with a more specific question on memory. I was keen to seek the relevance of a statue for Birsa's legacy in today's Jharkhand. Barla replied:

> If you look at the politics of the statue, it reflects something interesting. The making of a statue in Jharkhand produces a symbolic discourse and lip service to camouflage the extraction business that will receive a gateway through their villages. It is entirely for the politics of vote banks. Adivasi's own *sarana, masna, hargari* [ritual sites including burials], which is one part of history, is under attack from all quarters. According to the constitution, every individual is entitled to practice the religion of his or her choice. The new anti-conversion rule overrules this freedom. The government announced that those who converted would not have any further access to SC or ST act, nor can they fall under the ambit of the CNTA. This is a violation of Schedule 5. The rights that are entitled to us have been diluted over the years. Birsa Munda's dreams are being trampled on.

This highlights the intersectional scope of memory that emerges within the full range of cultural practices to constitute the identity of Adivasis—and must be seen in relationship to the wider environment. The use of intersectional memory in an object such as a statue, considering it as a template, opens up a range of political questions. The statue of Birsa is being used to camouflage the extractive industry. Far from considering the ethical imperative to mainstream the political necessity of symbolic discourse that lays out the material aspirations and needs of the Adivasis, the built environment in Jharkhand stands as an empty signifier.

Barla invokes the practice of *sarna* (religion), which has come under attack in the recent past by the BJP during the leadership of Raghuvar Das as chief minister. Adivasi community observes *sarna* through various rituals and festivals such as Sarhul that signify the importance of forest and land within the community. Adivasis celebrate this collectively, performing rituals in large groups at the *akhra* with a series of songs and rituals.[76]

The following section illustrates the significance of this mainstreaming of the role of environment. Emerging in the broader context of environmentalism, politics and memory in Jharkhand, I situate a specific festival, Sarhul, and its ritual, to underscore the importance of the environment (not nature) as the co-constitutive component in the lifeworld of Adivasis. I distinguish between 'environment' and 'nature'. Fundamentally, the use of the term 'environment' widens the scope of understanding 'nature' within the broader context of relationships between humans and non-humans. 'Nature' suggests a particularly geological dimension, whereas 'environment' illustrates the significance, meaning-making and co-dependence between humans and non-humans.[77]

Sarhul: A Cultural Description of the Political

Sarna is associated with the grove of the *sal* tree (*Shorea robusta*). Traditionally, the *sal* tree occupies a place of worship and a site where rituals are observed. *Sarna* is described in the work of Carmina Peñarrocha Giménez as follows:

> a grove of sal trees where the tribal worshipped on a certain occasion, but this word has over the years acquired additional meanings too. Now this refers to their deity, it is also used to refer to the people who are non-Christian tribals. Besides, it has acquired political overtones too in the context of Jharkhand.[78]

Another popular festival is Buru Bonga (*buru* meaning 'hill' and *bonga* meaning 'god'), during which Santhals remember their god through a 'process of worship'.[79] Hansda Sowvendra Shekhar notes that these are similar to Hindu festivals (such as Pahar Puja), drawing our attention to 'an amalgamation of the Hindu and Sarna faiths'.[80] This stems from Shekhar's perception of lived religious traditions that, he says, leads to 'cultural intertextualities [that] transcend theological specificities'.[81] While Shekhar projects cultural transcendence as a way to salvage religious appropriation and, indeed, offers an elaborate description of the transfiguration of Adivasi pantheons into Hindu gods, I must also remark how dangerous any slippages in the viscerally insular and rampant Hinduization of Adivasis in Jharkhand could be.

A recent attempt at diluting the theosophical space is felt through the Pathalgadi movement, when a group from the Sati Pati cult had attempted to deviate from the traditional practices and Hinduize it. Sarhul, as an Adivasi festival, declares this political urgency to recognize it as a distinct practice—one that presents the intertwining of environmental concerns and theological spaces, illuminating a perspective that dovetails *bonga*, land and the lived experience.

During my fieldwork, I observed two consecutive Sarhul festivals. Drawing on an elaborate process of prayers, *pahan*s (village priests) took rounds of a *sal* tree, chanting hymns while holding a few leaves of the tree in their hand. They were followed by two women draped in traditional *khanria*, a white saree with broad red borders, also singing the song of the *singbonga* (the spirit of the sun, an Adivasi god), while the *pahan*s wore white *karia* (a long white cotton cloth draped around the waist) (Figure 3.2). After a few rounds, the *pahan*s sat down to perform an elaborate ritual, gripping their hands around the stems of the tree rooted in a pot (Figure 3.3). The guests and I were warmly welcomed with a piece of new stem, *phool khonsi*, clipping them around our ear to mark the celebration, and were invited to participate in the music with traditional dance.

This festival is significant in unifying the environmental imaginaries into everyday lives of the Adivasis. On one level, it displayed the contingent organization of the relationship shared between the Adivasi community and the much wider existence of the natural worlds. In other words, as Shekhar cogently writes: 'Adivasis are nature worshippers and have been known to worship monoliths.'[82] This monolith worship encompasses a composite whole, containing elements of the natural world sewn together with lived experiences. On another level, it marks the departure of Adi Dharma from organized religion drawn on textual dictums and formal strictures. This draws us close to a compelling account by R.D. Munda on the question of Adivasi dignity, where he explains Adivasi religion:

Figure 3.2 *Pahan*s wearing white *karia* and women draped in traditional *khanria* performing the rituals of Sarhul around a *sal* tree

Source: Photograph by the author.

Figure 3.3 A *pahan* performing an elaborate ritual with stems of *sal*

Source: Photograph by the author.

> *Adi-dhorom*, in my understanding, is the core form of religion to Adivasi within Indian landscape. It is variously described as 'primitivism', 'aboriginal religion', 'Sarnaism', 'Bongaism', amongst others. Within our constitution, Adivasi have received considerable recognition for the cultural entity. However, as a religious group, they are subsumed under the mainstream religion; namely, Hindu, Muslim among others and, if none of them identifies the following, then they are marked as others.[83]

Munda locates the primacy of Adi Dharma, which has ceased to exist under the category of 'others' within the Indian census.[84] Adi Dharma organizes the lifeworld of the Adivasis —one in which the environmental landscape—*jal, jungle aur jameen*—constitutes the very meaning of their existence. *Bonga* (spirit) becomes ubiquitous in this description and is adorned by ritual practices, placing the natural world at the heart of it. Reverberating evidence that emerged in the missionary records from the late 19th century attests to this sentiment, as John-Baptist Hoffman recalls:

> The being conceived by the Mundas as the originator and ruler of the universe and the master of all other spirits, is by them supposed to have

its abode in the sun, and therefore goes by in the name of *singbonga*, from *singi*, the sun. Hence, in the Munda mind the term *bonga* denotes any being endowed with intelligence and free will, which is independent of matter, either by or because of death.[85]

Evidently, *bonga*s unify the identity of Adivasis with various forms of living entities. *Bonga*s form their notion of *being* and their relationship to the environment—*the landscape of memory*.[86] The rendering of this vibrant and cultural co-dependence became prominent as I watched the Sarhul unfold with rituals centring on a composite braiding of cultural practices rooted in the natural world. As the day progressed, several artists took to performances demonstrating the use of myth and stories, while drumming began in the background. These stories and myths constitute the core lifeworld of Adivasis, who now face the forces of extractive industry on one side and symbolic lip service to their icons on the other.

Hence, Barla underlines the most significant component of Adivasi politics—that is, *jal, jungle aur jameen*. This struggle is jeopardized in the process of symbolic gestures that targets votes from Adivasi constituencies. To explain the importance of symbolic practices, the next section locates a dispute regarding the statue of Birsa Munda at a major intersection in the city of Ranchi. It shows how symbolism plays a significant role in shaping the collective memory of the past. It also emphasizes how the aesthetic becomes the medium in politics, profoundly affecting the course of memory.

Birsa in Shackles: Casting Negative Images or Framing Historical Struggle

In 2016, the BJP government announced the removal of the shackles, or handcuffs, from the Birsa Munda statue installed at Birsa Chowk in Ranchi (Figure 3.4). The government argued: 'After Independence, statues of freedom fighters with handcuffs or in chains does not give the right message to society.'[87] Upon my insistence on hearing her views on the battle over such symbolic politics, an unsettling feeling seemed to surface on Barla's face. Barla took a while to think and said,

> Unleashing the handcuff, I felt was unsolicited. His *jangir* [handcuff] was a symbol of our struggle.... When we as Adivasi used to look at the handcuff, we used to feel inspired that we need to fight the new form of slavery, a new mode of oppression under the ambit of the global market.[88]

Memories Set in Stone 123

Figure 3.4 Birsa Munda's statue showing him in shackles at Birsa Chowk, Ranchi

Source: Raj Kumar, 'Birsa Loses Cuffs sans Ceremony', *The Telegraph* (online edition), 16 July 2016, https://www.telegraphindia.com/jharkhand/birsa-loses-cuffs-sans-ceremony/cid/1328597 (accessed on 18 February 2019).

I was attentive to the brewing tension in her voice, resisting the politeness of conduct expected during an interview. Far from feeling passive, or impartial—encouraged by the formal set-up for the interview—it is this anger, an affective response emerging from accumulated tension, that I believed needed to be heard. Pausing to think, she elaborated on this move:

> We need to break the chains that tie us into *anyaay ke changul* [the spectre of injustice]. I said it then against those who advocated for the unchaining of the shackles—if you really wish to take away the handcuffs, it must be attained by *mull adhikaar ki azaadi*, the material form of independence.

Casting away any hesitation in elucidating the relationship of the state that supports the needs of industry, while at the same time performing a symbolic gesture, Barla said compellingly that

> the material independence lay in implementing Schedule 5, CNTA, SPTA [Santhal Pargana Tenancy Act], as per the Constitution of India. The symbolic gesture of unshackling the chains is not beneficial at all. It serves the politics of appeasement. Respecting Schedule 5 is important to everyone who lives under the *gram sabha*, irrespective of his or her caste, class and gender.

Her clarity of ideas exceeds the limits of historical understanding and advocates for an anachronistic insight into politics. She made references to the past by dovetailing it to the present when she claimed: 'It is our right that predates the Constitution.' This is a point about the dilution of traditional village autonomy that Asoka Kumar Sen construes as 'the loss of control of lived and forested landscape [that] put the Adivasi in a double bind'.[89] This double bind is profound, as Barla also explained: 'All new laws that dispossess the peasantry should be erased to begin the process of independence if it is meant. You cannot change history. Histories that reflect were written with oppression and subjugation. The symbolic act of taking off handcuff is futile. Our frustration is bottled up.'

By drawing an analogy between the chains in the statue and the modern forms of slavery, Barla insinuated the nefarious power of symbolism. She identified the *jangir* as a metaphor tied to emergent forms of oppression against Adivasis specific to the nature of the post-colonial condition. Such a symbolic gesture explains the continuity of the past in the present, defying any claims associated with reformist visions and aesthetic appeals, as shown earlier. The statue therefore continually transforms into various imaginaries—land, law, legislation—forming an assemblage of entanglements. Effectively, such entanglements with the statue also shift the meaning and function of a symbolic artefact into the material manifestation of inequalities. The material object becomes a medium to reflect a conflicting aesthetic narrative that changes the use and performance of the symbolism.

In other words, it is crucial to understand that a cultural artefact is not an object isolated from the social and political contexts. Here, I emphasize the culture as a code folded into the contemporaneous history of Adivasis, which has political stakes, even as the removal of handcuffs was motivated by an alleged desire to right 'the historical wrong' for the present. The political stakes in Birsa's history are now manifold, as Barla says. The simplistic, naive critique of the Raj must be placed within the threats of the present—the violations of Adivasi rights, mining and coercive land legislations that are often buried by symbolic commemoration of Adivasi icons.

The symbolic must reflect reality in the form of radical engagements with redistributive and substantive need for justice—putting land tension at the heart of the crisis. Such radical engagements can be placed in dialogue with the material manifestation, where, as James Clifford writes, 'once cultures are no longer prefigured visually—objects, theatre, texts—it becomes possible to think of a cultural poetics that is an interplay of voices, of positioned utterances' and therefore dissenting voices of the subaltern, their memory and heritage as 'a cultural poetics' allows 'situating' the role of histories from below.[90] This process not only challenges the dominant modalities of representation but also insists on writing *culture* (read: memory) as *politics*.

Barla's sentiment about the act of removal as being symbolic echoed with others too. In an interview at the time, Soma Munda, a Munda chieftain, said: 'It is a symbolic gesture. His [Birsa's] statue might be free, but his tribal land is still under threat. *Abhi bhi zameen ki ladai hai* (Still, there is a fight for land).' 'While earlier the exploiters were Britishers,' he says, 'now it is the state, and the fight is to protect *jal, jungle aur zameen.*'[91] Mahto's reaction to this strong stance on symbolism brought annoyance to his face, and he said: 'People have their own logic. Some people fight amongst themselves based on their limited understanding. For me, personally, it does not matter.'[92] However, Barla held a contradictory view in spelling out the symbolism of the chains. She said: 'Two years ago, on the same day, 22 October 2016, the government had to barricade villages to stop people from organizing marches and agitations. However, they could not stop it.' She finds this formidable resistance resulting from sedimented forms of Adivasi *aaakrosh* (angst). Here, *aakrosh* is a microcosm of structural violence faced by Adivasis. Barla fascinatingly ties it to the view that 'ulgulan ka aakrosh, hul ka aakrosh, aaj bhi waise hi hai' (the angst of Adivasis, the fire of the *ulgulan* and the *hul* is still the same) and claims that 'the fire is still burning. One hundred years ago, Birsa Munda spoke, and today, I repeat it. Therefore, it is erroneous to believe that Birsa had died.'

Barla's contrast with Mahto is a sharp one. She draws on the legacy of Adivasi leaders who have historically forestalled the *diku*s outside their territory. The oppressor and the outsiders' unflinching attack on the territorial sovereignty of Adivasis are remarkably clear and direct in Barla's words. In this moment, subaltern speech negates and defines the resistance not in isolation from the systemic structure—more precisely, the law. In fact, for Barla, resistance is a politics of negotiation with the law or 'judicialization of law', as pointed out by Jean and John Comaroff, where the subaltern population uses the law as an instrument to negotiate their problems and enhance their lives.[93] Underlining the importance of land, Barla foregrounds the agency of Adivasis as not a passive recipient of state policies but active agents who negotiate with the modern nation state in their everyday politics. Subaltern speech is at the heart of resistance. Any refusal to recognize this reflects on our own lack of structures of hearing. The subaltern can and have always spoken.

Santosh Kiro, a biographer of Jai Pal Singh Munda, resounded Barla's resentment against such symbolic displays. He associated the ongoing struggle of Adivasis with the historical injustice that continues to hold meaning in the community. 'While Birsa is a historical figure, his rebellion is not,' he said. The continuous attack on the forest and land, he added, 'philosophically speaking, is an attack on the lifeworld of the Adivasis'.[94] Reflecting upon the philosophical dimension, he asserted: 'Adivasis do not treat the land as private property. It [private property] is a Eurocentric idea based on the biblical notion that humans are supreme and God has submitted everything under his power. The idea of land in the Adivasi world dwells in common ownership and unsaleable entity.'[95] This is illuminating, and I can draw a parallel with several encounters that I had during my stay in different villages in Khunti district. Another instance of this was also to be found while speaking with Koli Munda,[96] a resident in Dombari village in Sail Rakab (a historic site of memory). He reminded me that the 'forest defines the worldview as well as the past and ancestors'. Recalling Birsa as an ordinary *horo* Munda who sought to claim the rights of the Adivasis, he believed that 'Birsa displayed divinely characteristics that mobilized the Adivasi to collectively fight against the outsiders'.

Such a characterization of Birsa also suggests that the rebellion was an outcome—not merely a messianic moment but a response to the historic attack on the 'rights' of Adivasis. The scare quotes for 'rights' highlight the Adivasi struggle that is based on collective assertion of the past. Besides, 'right' is a liberal manifestation. It is both limited and representational. The Adivasi struggle aims to achieve something far more—cosmic unity—in which the natural world and landscape is the primal force. Here, the cosmic also refers to the spiritual memory associated with the past—a history of struggle against the outsiders, definitive of 'the landscape of Jharkhand'.[97]

The spiritual memory contains extraterrestrial meaning associated with the composition of the universe. Adivasis do not see themselves as supreme beings located at the centre of the universe in order to govern and control it. The *singbonga* defines their lifeworld. In the same respect, Hoffman puts it lucidly:

> How do they conceive the nature of this barrier which separates the *nedisumrenko*, those of this world, from the *paromenko*, those of the world across? In what does it consist? Not in anything that be expressible in terms of space, distance, heights or depths; for the *paromenko*, those of the world across, are thought of as living in far-away places, such as popular notion among Christians regarding heaven and hell assigns to them, since they dwell in the huts of their nearest relatives, in streams, rivulets, tanks, ponds, rocks, forests, fields and mountains of their villages, and Singbonga, the lord of them all, is explicitly declared to be *everywhere and see everything*.... Bongas are those living beings, which, though firmly believed in as existing and influencing us for good, or evil, can neither be seen nor heard nor perceived: though fluttering about everywhere, they are, as far as sense perception goes, just as if they were not.[98]

Spiritual memory is formed by exposure to environment and sense perception. It is apparent how the dwelling of spirits in a vast schema of landscape such as rivulets and forests situate the sensorial, material and spiritual world of Adivasis. This dovetails with Barla's assertion that the past of Adivasis must reflect in their material reality in the present. Statues cannot merely function as symbolic acts. Such dialectical attempts in stitching together the narrative of struggle with the past and the present affords an understanding of the complicated relationship between Adivasis and the natural world.

Therefore, it is crucial to treat memory not *only* as a reproduction of the past in the form of the cultural artefact but *also* as an active, negotiated image. Memory, which is a broad spectrum of representation, works as an interstitial space between the past and the present. Any form of representation that claims memory of the past must also demonstrate a perception of it in the present and the negotiation between both. Barla's dismay with the statue suggests the lack of concern amongst the elite who claim to represent the past of Birsa in particular and of Adivasis in general. It must locate the centrality of the struggle in the formation of the object, which is used for public memory. Such ethics display a formidable concern about the community whose past and present are at stake in the process of representation.

The following section contextualizes the struggle of Adivasis in one of the most impoverished villages, which has emerged as a site of political tourism and commemoration. The village, Ulihatu, is an interesting place to explore the relationship between the symbolic and the material. It situates an interplay of memory, commemoration and political symbolism.

When Birsa Came Home: The Statue in Ulihatu Village

13 October 2018, Ulihatu Village

Ulihatu, a small village located amid forest and hills (Figure 3.5) and the birthplace of Birsa Munda, is also infamous as part of the 'red corridor'.[99] Nevertheless, in contemporary Jharkhand, Ulihatu is perceived as Birsa's home and attracts politicians, researchers and new sightseeing tourists. Ulihatu is a small village with a population of 1,126 people living in 196 houses and falls under the Erki block of Khunti district.[100]

I drove through the village on a single-lane road swallowed by the forest at either side of the road. The edges of the road had been reclaimed by people as a space to leave grains out to dry. The road is a convenience for politicians on their visits here and represents a profound irony as we shall soon see. Women and kids who sat on the road to bask in the early winter sun moved aside to make way for vehicles. Some of them were drawn to the noise while others continued their daily chores.

This description portrays a poetic rumination of the village—imagery that Alpa Shah calls the aesthetics of poverty. While explaining the plight of Adivasis in Tapu, Shah suggested that there is 'seductive visual imagery of poverty' that allows the rural elites to legitimize development projects.[101] I was aware of this flattening of image both as a past resident of the state and now as a researcher. Ulihatu offered a similar evocation. Not only has the area received a vast deployment of the military to control the Maoist influence, but as the 'land of the martyr' it has also become a political destination to commemorate the memory of Birsa.

Figure 3.5 Landscape of Ulihatu, Khunti district—an unending patch of forest and hills

Source: Photograph by the author.

The celebration of martyrdom quite simply has brought nothing except some seasonal politicians and increased policing. The village is one of the most impoverished in India, with only one school run by a missionary, and suffers from inadequate supply of electricity. However, it hosts two prominent tourist destinations: a statue and the house where Birsa was born. The house is now taken care of by his brother's great-grandson, Sukhram Munda, who has also become the face of Birsa's heritage. This process of heritagization attracts political parties here to promulgate a variety of schemes promising to 'uplift' the impoverished.

Ulihatu is also a flashpoint to locate the irony of symbolism that seeks to promote a change in the lives of the people without showing any material change. Multiple billboards and a prominent statue serve an extensive display of symbolism. For instance, a billboard in front of Birsa's place of birth displays the prime minister of India, Narendra Modi, and the then chief minister of Jharkhand, Raghubar Das (both from the same party), promoting a scheme (Figure 3.6). Also widely known as the National Health Promotion Scheme, the the Ayushman Bharat

Figure 3.6 Billboard displaying the prime minister of India, Narendra Modi (*left*), and the then chief minister of Jharkhand, Raghubar Das (*right*), from the right-wing Bharatiya Janata Party (BJP) government, promoting the Ayushman Bharat scheme that seeks to offer 'free health service to 57 lac [5.7 million] families for up to 5 lac [half a million] cost'

Source: Photograph by the author.

scheme claims to offer free healthcare up to half-a-million rupees. The scheme will also subsume the existing scheme, Rashtriya Swasthya Bima Yojana, introduced by the UPA (United Progressive Alliance) government in 2008. The scheme provides secondary health services and does not offer any primary healthcare.[102] The inauguration of the scheme took place in Jharkhand in 2018 at a public park in Ranchi, where the prime minister began his speech in Mundari while wearing a so-called 'tribal' jacket in a performance of indigeneity—an aesthetic appeal that he uses notoriously as political campaign mushrooms across the country.

Despite a range of programmes and displays of promises on billboards, the Adivasis in Ulihatu lead precarious lives in which performances regarding nationalism and progress can be heard in two distinct forms—that is, political tourism and the Maoist insurgency. This description of Ulihatu illustrates the lives of the inhabitants:

> Situated deep inside the Naxal district of Khunti, Ulihatu retains its rustic charm, but by default and neglect. Most of the houses are made

of stone and are in dire need of repair; electric poles are present but electricity is conspicuously absent; a medical dispensary can be located but not the doctor; a government residential school runs out of a dilapidated building but classes are mostly empty; a Central Bank of India signboard can be seen in the village, but the branch functions from a dingy grocery shop ...[103]

Schemes displayed on the billboards are symbols of the contrast. It brings the state closest to people in terms of the imagined citizen. Donal Cruise O'Brien invokes the concept of 'symbolic confrontation' to understand the state and its relationship with defined social groups. He construes symbolic confrontation as a tool in the form of pedagogy that, in turn, politicizes the issues related to groups.[104] It is a symbolic contrast because Ulihatu is home to some of India's poorest Adivasis who have historically failed to receive any political support to combat high mortality due to illness and poor health services.

Moreover, the village's association with commemorations of Birsa's birth comfortably overlooks its material reality. A prominent journalist articulated such a perception in a meeting that took place in Ranchi upon my return from a field trip. Asking to remain anonymous, he drew a map for me to outline the prospective plan that would give a new face lift to Birsa's heritage. After drawing a circular pathway on a piece of paper, he elaborated that for any visitors to Ranchi, their trip begins from the Birsa Munda Airport. Having been received by a person from the proposed hotel located at the heart of the city, guests will visit Dombari Hill the next morning. Driven along an upcoming six-lane highway through the *wilderness* of the forest, visitors can attain the feeling of *ulgulan*. After that, it would follow the same highway to Ulihatu, where visitors could go inside Birsa's home and feel the warmth of his village. On the way back, they will visit the statue nearby. The trip will give a glimpse of history, or what one might call *memory*. The beaming smile on his face following this explanation seemed sardonic.

His description brought out the aspirations of the urban dwellers who seek to transform the state into an industrial corridor. It is an imagination that seeks to legitimize the narrative of development. The changing form of aesthetic appeal, such as the statue and the mascot for the state (the flying elephant), validates such aspirations. In this process, symbolism plays a significant role in shaping the aesthetic of the state and political propaganda. In Ulihatu, the house and statue of Birsa represent material memory. It draws people to *experience* his life and remember his contributions. It is a house, perhaps the only one in the entire village, which has a tiled courtyard and mural on the wall. It is taken care of by his brother's great-grandson, who lives in a tiny room beside the house.

Birsa's home is a new spot for political tourism (Figures 3.7a and 3.7b). Politicians pay routine visits and make promises to lift the village out of poverty. Sukhram, living in a small house beside Birsa's, recalls the names of prominent

Figure 3.7a The main gate of Birsa Munda's house extended by a courtyard used by women to dry grains

Source: Photograph by the author.

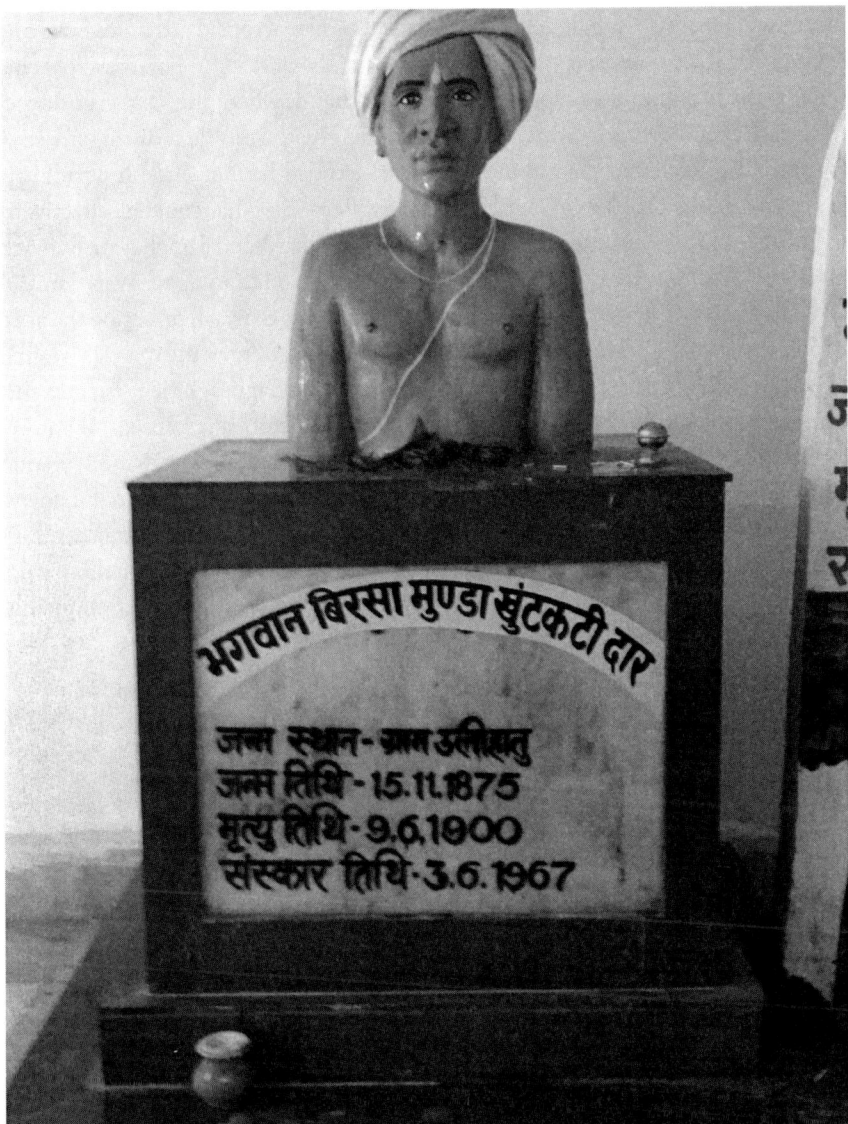

Figure 3.7b A statue of Birsa Munda inside a room of Birsa's house depicting the timeline of his life

Source: Photograph by the author.

politicians who have made their appearances in the recent past—Atal Bihari Vajpayee, Jairam Ramesh and Babulal Marandi, amongst others.[105] In an interview with *The Hindu*, he noted an absence of some of the most basic needs and said:

'Because there is no water here, we can't grow too many crops. I grow rice but only enough for the house to eat. I also grow a little dal and some potatoes.'[106] The water crisis is defining to regions such as Jharkhand, where the vast majority of Adivasis depend on agriculture. I was confronted by the problem during my stay as summer peaked and the groundwater level receded further. Videsh Upadhyay has discussed the problem of ownership over waterbodies that could be effectively used for multiple purposes. He maintains: 'The Jharkhand Panchayati Raj Act 2001 vests the right of ownership over minor waterbodies in Panchayati Samitis and Zila Parishad. However, it is the state government that will prescribe the area within this right.'[107] The problem is a glaring example of how the material reality of the area does not reflect the political use of Birsa (Figure 3.8). It isolates the competing claims over livelihood issues that have historically caused migration in the area. Often, quite jokingly, Amit, a boy who helped me navigate Ulihatu, said: 'We die of mosquitos more often than bullets of Maoists.' The statement profoundly impacted my own experiences here. It generated in me huge discomfort at my own complicity as an academic whose writing circulates to serve those who do not live as well as at the honest admission of this horrendous situation by this young person.

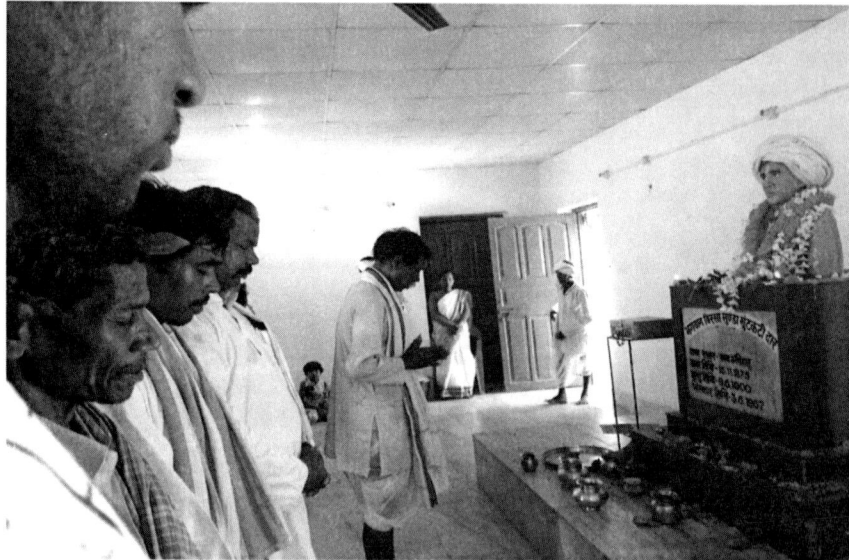

Figure 3.8   People gathered at Birsa Munda's house to observe his death anniversary, 9 June 2018

Source: Photograph by the author.

Most people, including Sukhram's son, have become a subject of the mass migration to other states in search of employment. Those who continue to live in the village have to struggle with poverty, the state and the Maoists. During my stay in Jharkhand, I frequently witnessed crowds of women and men who line up at the edge of the road early in the morning for informal employment as *reja*, unskilled labourers in an informal economy.

Vasavi Kiro, while ruminating on her solidarity and participation in various movements in Jharkhand, said: 'Ulihatu is a glaring example of the failure of the modern state of Jharkhand.'[108] She added: 'On the one hand, we continually celebrate and commemorate Birsa's life, while on the other we see a massive rate of dropout of children from the school, deaths due to illness, land problem.'[109] 'The statue or other kinds of symbolic politics cannot be meaningful,' she continued, 'if we do not address the severe problems in the village.'[110]

Similarly, the statue of Birsa in Ulihatu is a remarkable display of memory that can be a ploy, a political campaign tool and a site of living history or archive. It is a ploy because it gives an opportunity to various political parties to define or promote a version of Birsa's life that serves their own political ideologies. It is a political tool to mobilize Birsa's memory within Adivasi constituencies, at least symbolically, to demonstrate respectability and commitment towards appropriating Adivasi leaders as 'martyrs'. This portrayal suspends any possibility of questioning more significant concerns of Adivasi livelihoods that face continued deterioration, especially after the creation of Jharkhand. The statue of Birsa in Ulihatu becomes an ornamental display, a contrast to the reality experienced by people who live in the same village.

The statue is painted gold, ironically holding the iconic Adivasi bow and arrow in the middle of a small field that offers space for parking (Figure 3.9). The field has a cascading staircase on one end that offers seating space for people to hear speeches by politicians. When the political drama draws to a close, children in the village use it as a playground. Interestingly, as I took a round of this place one day, a man approached me. Wary of my background, I was asked where I was from and the reasons for the visit. This brief exchange with him turned into a prolonged conversation, and I realized that the statue is encircled by an army camp, which was installed there a long time ago. Perhaps the intensity of the Maoist insurgency in the area made it inevitable. As a researcher based abroad, I occupied territory in this region and in the minds of state officials as a 'critical person', and he ended his conversation with me.

This is an important point in underlining the visibility of the military stationed in such a remote landscape for people who live in the city nearby. The visibility of

Figure 3.9 The main statue of Birsa Munda in Ulihatu, Khunti district

Source: Photograph by the author.

the military shares a contingent relationship with rising militancy. The Adivasis, unfortunately, are on the receiving end of the violence from both sides. Some reports highlight the false framing of cases against young Adivasis as Maoists, which in turn leads to the rise in insurgency.[111] Ulihatu is one of the most affected areas in the region. In the recent past, the region has witnessed a massive upsurge.

Ulihatu has become a political epithet that demonstrates the use of Adivasis for national and regional identity formation. On the one hand, we see the theatrical performance of politicians who regularly come to commemorate Birsa Munda and his legacy—often selectively appropriating narratives that suit the nationalist vision and characterize him as a martyr. On the other hand, the area continues to witness spikes in poverty, illness and unemployment.

Over the years, the rise in militancy by Maoists, protests against land-grabs and resistance movements have brought the area into media focus. A cornerstone in the village—the house of Birsa and the statue—has undergone considerable change. For instance, after the formation of the state of Jharkhand, Birsa's house and the statue were renovated in 2002 as a part of *saundariyakaran*, the beautification project, under the leadership of Ramesh Singh Munda.[112] Before the renovation project, the statue did not have a bow and arrow. It was painted in brown, perhaps more aesthetically appeasing and human than the golden paint that covers Birsa's body today. The statue bears a resemblance to Birsa's photos recovered from missionary accounts and S. C. Roy's work. However, it is more emblematic of a material installation that caters to a political class and, more prominently, the anti-colonial narrative.

What I found interesting in the narratives about the symbolic memory of Birsa Munda and his legacy underscores a need to widen the scope of understanding the canon. The anti-colonial framework serves as an empty signifier, an easily dispensable framework with which to suspend the ethical responsibility required in the present. The removal of handcuffs, the construction of statues and the burgeoning schemes directed towards Adivasi constituencies fail to address the struggle for *jal, jungle aur jameen* that remain at the heart of their precarity. It camouflages material conditions in order to seek entry into the mineral-rich Adivasi region by transforming the role of memory into a useful tool of politics.

The following section concludes the chapter by giving an illustration of different Dalit icons and their statues within the scope of the discussion on memory as politics. In doing so, it shows how two different formulations of subaltern history—that is, the Adivasis and the Dalits—produce a distinct notion of political space and time through mediums of representation in material memory. It illustrates how displaying Birsa's statue is likely to remain politically unhinged against the glaring reality of poverty and forceful occupation that defines the everyday lives of Adivasis, whereas Dalit statues clearly explain their political plight by asserting their identities. This provides a broad spectrum of memory politics through which to understand the intra-subaltern identity, their similarities and their differences.

Meaningful Disruptions and Memory: Dalits Icons and Statue Politics

By using the phrase *meaningful disruption*, I wish to mainstream statues of Dalit icons as a source of intervention in the existing echelon of public space defined by social segregation based on caste. This disruption, as I construe it, reimagines the spatial-temporal dimension of Indian society based on a violent and historically unjust caste order. Therefore, the canonization of Dalit icons in the form of aesthetic display challenges the social construction of caste, thereby giving meaning to the disruption by expressing Dalit subjectivity. In effect, the aesthetic display confronts the Brahmanical occupation of space and time.

It is useful to understand the differences and similarities produced by the installation of statues associated with Dalit and Adivasi icons. It provides significant insight and contrast to consider figures such as B. R. Ambedkar, Mayawati and Birsa Munda who emerge on the broader spectrum of subaltern history. There are various statues commissioned across the country, most prominently in the heart of North India's Hindi belt centred on Lucknow. This is not to suggest that statues in other states are insignificant, but the region has a contentious response to the scale of production of statues. However, in the recent past, the statues of Ambedkar and Mayawati have evoked radical responses in various forms—such as desecration and removal.[113] These responses draw me to explain the tension at the core of Dalit identity to explain memory politics.[114]

There seems to exist a discomfort in accepting the material memory of the Dalit Bahujan Samaj Party leader, Kanshi Ram, and his successor, Mayawati who was several times chief minister of India's most populous state, Uttar Pradesh, as Dalit figures. As a chief minister, Mayawati made concerted efforts to install numerous bronze friezes, statues and memorials of herself across Uttar Pradesh in general and in Lucknow in particular. Often placing herself in the lineage of Dalit political representation alongside Ambedkar and Kanshi Ram, Mayawati, the 'Dalit queen', has raised the visibility of Dalitness across the country.

What is interesting in such installations of material memory is a sense of the political assertion of rights and bodily presence. It seeks to restore the dignity that has been either historically denied to or forcefully snatched from Dalits. It addresses a denial that emerges from a violent history of exclusion, untouchability and enforced inhuman treatment to defined groups—namely Dalits and Adivasis. Significant to this, Malia Belli writes, it is 'not surprising that the territorial claiming of physical space and marking it with Dalit historical figures—thereby visually demanding that they are recognized—is an integral component of Mayawati's radical brand of Dalit assertion'.[115]

Time and Memory: Dalit Statues in Retrospect

The assertion of subaltern bodies through statue challenges the historically denied agency of Dalits and reallocates their presence in the public space. It also effectively lays out the order of time, as we understand it, as a linear progression of events into primarily forms of subjective experience—flattening the vertical hierarchies. In this, the historical denial of time as a subjective experience, folded into acts such as intimate access to the place and body, defeats the linear movement that progressed outside the Dalits' lifeworld. In fact, the time that occurred outside the Dalit experience, in a series of linear progressions, upwardly, suggesting mobility and growth, remained inaccessible to them. As an affective site, statues and memorials of Dalits and Adivasis disrupt this universal category of time experienced and enjoyed by upper castes.

Subalterns experience time in the most personal and perhaps violent ways—bearing witness to exclusion, recognized as pollution and, importantly, as the invention of modernity.[116] Denied the background of the most basic humanity, Dalits and Adivasis stand as the inverse of time with bodies bearing witness to memory. Therefore, the standard definition of time defined by caste hubris and linear progression cannot be used for the construction subaltern subjecthood. Koselleck offers a fascinating notion of time that is relevant to explaining this tension. He writes:

> Historical times can be identified if we direct our view to where time itself occurs or is subjectively enacted in humans as historical beings: in the relationship between past and future, which always constitutes an elusive present. The compulsion to coordinate past and future so as to be able to live it all is inherent in any human being. Put more concretely, on the one hand, every human being and every human community has a space of experience in which one acts, in which past things are present or can be remembered, and, on the other, one always acts with reference to specific horizons of expectations.... That historical time occurs within the difference between these two temporal dimensions can already be shown by the fact that the difference between experience and expectation itself changes—that is, it is specifically historical.[117]

Historical time is socially produced by negotiating the experience and expectation. In other words, based on human experience, we draw out time into a standardized format, representing an abstraction of experience and expectation. However, a standardized form of time could also emerge from the dominant structures and experience and therefore assume a universality of form. Dalit and Adivasi experiences were, in similar ways, either coercively subtracted by segregation or written out in the process of the standardized idea of historical time in which everything else has progressed in a linear fashion.

Arguably, Dalit leaders have used statues as a medium to challenge this naturalization of time by articulating their specific experiences of caste-based exclusion and visceral violence. The insertion of these experiences into the statues forms the basis for interpenetration of their identities within the milieu of public space defined by echelons of caste and gendered norms. Therefore, the statues provide a scope to evince any anti-caste assertions that are historically unavailable in the socio-habitus based on brahmanical values. Significantly, this also represents the political consciousness of Dalits as the *new* visible body in this time and forms of affective assertion of the caste through statues.

These assertions through material memory constitute the reclamation of internally segregated public space, which is made available unequally and displayed aesthetically, allowing subaltern groups to reclaim the collective memory from below. The aesthetic expression of Dalits in the city of Lucknow, for instance, through Dalit memorials, friezes, and statues displaces the spatial segregation. It positions the notion of excluded subjecthood at the centre of a conflict that adds political texture to architecture. Belli explains architecture as a site of power and memory in the same context, with which I mostly agree:

> For centuries in India, Dalits have been denied a presence in space and time, both literally and symbolically. This spatial and historical exclusion then perpetuates Dalit social marginalization, inside and outside the community. It is therefore not surprising that the territorial claiming of physical space and marking it with Dalit historical figures—thereby visually demanding that they are recognized—is an integral component of Mayawati's radical brand of Dalit assertion.[118]

In turn, as mentioned earlier, these built environments give a meaningful definition and lead to the concretization of the Dalit identity to unify them into an 'imagined community'.[119] The imagined community derives a source of constant political assertion from such inanimate objects, which imply the importance of Dalit identity and their reclamation of historical injustice.

On the one hand, this emerges in forms of veneration of such beliefs, which can be routinely felt throughout the streets of India as Dalits gather to commemorate the memory of their iconic leaders. Colossal processions lead these commemorations and drive massive demonstrations to monumentalize their importance. On the other, these objects, as the built environment, also weave the physical manifestation of identity into the core of mainstream politics—causing a stir and generating pushback against these developments, often leading to facile arguments questioning the economic utility of the objects.

However, unlike the statues of Ambedkar and Mayawati, Birsa does not seem to pose an immediate challenge to the hegemony of political parties in the battle for competing memories. Birsa Munda becomes malleable to parties: They can manipulate and appropriate his image while designing policies that structurally damage the community, whereas Ambedkar's statue poses a political threat and a living reminder of the centuries-long historical injustice suffered by Dalits. Ambedkar's statue offers a space for the symbolic demonstration of the reclamation of rights, fought on the constitutional terms and in the most modernist fashion.

In other words, the symbolic means become a political tool. Much as in the case of Birsa, however, there have been attempts to appropriate Ambedkar by insinuating gestures associated with Hindus. Nevertheless, Dalit activists have actively resisted such misappropriation. In his work on the iconography of Ambedkar, Nicolas Jaoul notes that 'this iconography, which represents Ambedkar as a man of international stature, rather than in traditional Indian dress ... has attracted a wide range of critics from different political backgrounds, from Marxists to Gandhians and nationalist Hindus, all of them sharing a concern for cultural authenticity'.[120] The iconography referred to here is Ambedkar's statue in a blue suit with a book and shoes. The conservative Hindus and Gandhians did not find this 'Indian' enough for nationalist politics.

Perhaps such resistance against the established narratives of nationalism and the caste Hindu order makes Dalit politics a *living threat* to the status quo of Hindu nationalism. It also reflects how material reality has roots in symbolic means. It clearly sets out from the generic illustration offered by Mahto, whereby the statue serves as a reminder of the past dislocated from its relevance in the present. The symbolic claims are central to the political definition of Dalit identity. Furthermore, in the same context, Jaoul writes: 'Symbolic claims were thus given equal footing with material ones. Symbolic assertion had become a major feature of Dalit political culture, and the political efficacy of such skills was soon to be demonstrated.'[121]

This also highlights the existing challenges of contemporary India that the symbolic politics of Adivasis and Dalits face. Each requires an investigation based on their historical trajectories. However, they are both unequivocally defined by subaltern marginalization and historical injustice. They come together to forge a broad umbrella of struggle that requires specificity—ethics, as I would call it—that ensures the representation of the subaltern voice. In other words, the memory of Birsa Munda cannot be understood in isolation from the contemporary forms of demonstration. The decoupling of Birsa Munda and his statue from the unified struggle of Adivasis—that is *jal, jungle aur jameen*—is politically ineffective. While Birsa occupies multiple temporalities, prominent amongst them remains resistance against the *diku*s and the striving for *abua disum, abua raj*. The narrative of such resistance requires a place in the symbolic articulation of the past in the region.

Summary

This chapter used statue as a template to show the symbolic and material conflict for the role of subaltern memory. These statues are strictly controlled and produced by state actors, governments and political elites to characterize Birsa, considering their political ideologies. Often this dislocates him from the historical unity of the movement—more importantly from its recurring relevance to the present. The critical aspect of the statue lay in a mediated representation of the memory (of Birsa) with an unusual blend of party politics that occludes the ongoing struggle of Adivasis.

I have shown how the state controls domains of statue governance, often by casting the image of Birsa as an empty signifier. The state plays a decisive role in controlling and distributing the memory of the past—for instance, the Birsa Chowk incident showed how chains were removed from the statue tactically, at midnight, to avoid any resistance. It was a decision proposed by the Art and Culture Ministry of the state and endorsed by a non-Adivasi chief minister. The incident suggests how the privilege of writing subaltern history in the form of the built environment is withdrawn or negotiated out of the hands of the subalterns by the state. The Birsa Chowk statue was *not merely* a cultural artefact; it was also emblematic of Adivasi resistance against imperial forces that continue to remain influential in the state.

As is shown in Barla's interview, the removal of chains from the statue is symbolic—far removed from the material realities that define Adivasi lives in today's Jharkhand. Here, the symbolism functioned to conceal the complex nature of representation that is intertwined with the narrative of development. In this process, it seeks to draw the subjects of representation as external participants in their own memory. It permeates the possibility for the state to enter the areas that are conflicted with the past and present in a new fashion.

For instance, Ulihatu emerged as a place for political tourism, targeting the Adivasi constituency as a potential vote bank by commemorating the village's statue of Birsa. This presents a double bind. While on the one hand the state and the political elites commemorate the memory of Birsa, this plays a significant role in recognizing the importance of small histories within national memory. It does not change the Adivasi status quo as a people who are reeling from massive poverty and violence in their everyday lives. The symbolic tales of heroism that the state promotes do not substantially address the material conditions of the subaltern. This is perhaps the reason for Barla's resistance. She believes that symbolism is beneficial when it reflects reality.

However, the case of Dalit statues, which seek to represent political challenges for the accommodation of their memory, reconfigures the symbolism. Dalit statues did not identify with the politics of memorialization offered by the state. In fact, the statues constitute their own temporality. The processes posed challenges to the historical segregation of public space and time as imagined by the upper castes.

Despite the historical denial and injustice perpetrated by the Hindu caste order, Dalits consistently struggled to make political claims from within the structure using constitutional language. Such modernist intervention is evident in the approach taken by Ambedkar, who used adult franchise and universal laws as the language to assert Dalit rights. Mayawati also raised claims of access to and injustice towards a statue in another sense. In fact, Dalits were part of the same thread of historical time struggling against the caste order.

However, Adivasis were 'invented' as the subjects of modernity. They were recognized in a given template of bourgeois politics that did not allow their active participation and often portrayed them as docile subjects of governance. They became subjects of governance animated into policies that recognized them as a 'Scheduled Tribe'. Even as Birsa rose to fight against the *dikus*, the nationalization of his memory almost perversely refuses to accept the conditions of the Adivasis in contemporary Jharkhand. Importantly, the Adivasi politics in my understanding demands a different register—one that exceeds the constitutional limits of accommodation. This register is a demand not simply for political space but also territorial power of self-governance, an imagination that remains steeped in Jai Pal Singh Munda's iconic speech as laid out in the introduction. In other words, there is a textural difference between Dalits and Adivasis in so far as the demands for political space are concerned. But they are unified, as with many other struggles led by LGBTQI+ and feminist groups that confront the brahmanical patriarchy.

Notes

1   Piers Vitebsky, 'Loving and Forgetting: Moments of Inarticulacy in Tribal India', in *The Scheduled Tribes and Their India: Politics, Identities, Policies, and Work*, ed. Nandini Sundar, pp. 168–95 (New Delhi: Oxford University Press, 2016), pp. 171–72.

2   See Reinhart Koselleck, *The Practice of Conceptual History: Timing History, Spacing Concepts*, trans. Hayden White (Stanford: Stanford University Press, 2002), p. 10.

3   The chapter uses 'trace' as an idea that always remains more than an event within the chronology of time. 'Trace' emerges as a methodological tool to investigate the presence of what Jacques Derrida calls the 'excess' in a text. Similarly, the Birsa movement is not defined by a point in time; it rather expresses itself in various forms of cultural artefacts and memorial displays. Harold Bloom, De Paul Man, Jacques Deridda, Geoffrey H. Hartman and J. Hillis Miller, *Deconstruction and Criticism* (London: Routledge and Kegan Paul, 1979).

4   See Prathama Banerjee, *Politics of Time: 'Primitives' and History-Writing in a Colonial Society* (New Delhi: Oxford University Press, 2006).

5   Ibid., p. 2.

6   Ibid.

7   Tariq Jazeel, 'Subaltern Geographies: Geographical Knowledge and Postcolonial Strategy', *Singapore Journal of Tropical Geography* 35, no. 1 (2014): 88–103. For the 'dialogical object', see Quentin Stevens, Karen A. Franck and Ruth Fazakerley, 'Counter-Monuments: The Anti-Monumental and the Dialogic', *Journal of Architecture* 17, no. 6 (2012): 951–72.

8   Pierre Nora, 'Between Memory and History: Les Lieux de Mémoire', *Representations* 26 (Spring 1989): 7–24.

9   Richard E. Lee, 'Lessons of the Longue Durée: The Legacy of Fernand Braudel', *Historia Crítica* 69 (July–September 2018): 69–77.

10 Sometimes, the commemoration is evident in the context of the post-colonial reading of the World Wars. For example, Michele Barrett's study examined the role of commemoration commission in inscribing 'race and creed' in the principle of commission as a repeated form in the materials. His analysis of the graves of soldiers marked differently as 'white graves' and 'the native' suggest an intimate relationship between the commemoration and the practices of remembrance. See Michele Barrett, 'Subalterns at War', *Can the Subaltern Speak? Reflections on the History of an Idea*, ed. Rosalind C. Morris, pp. 156–78 (New York: Columbia University Press, 2010).

11 See Sigurd Bergmann, 'Religion in the Built Environment: Aesth/Ethics, Rituals, and Memory In Lived Urban Space', in *The Sacred in The City*, ed. Liliana Gómez and Walter Van Herck, pp. 73–95 (London: Bloomsbury Press, 2012).

12 Govind Sadashiv Ghuyre, *The Scheduled Tribes: The Aborigines So-Called and Their Future* (Bombay: Ramdas Bhatkal for Popular Prakashan, 1963).

13 See Bergmann, 'Religion in the Built Environment'.

14 Andrew Jones, *Memory and Material Culture* (Cambridge: Cambridge University Press, 2007). Jones's work is one of the most exciting in the field of material memory. It offers a lucid and detailed analysis of the relationship between community and objects.

15 'Materiality' is a term popularly used to describe material things, or 'the material beings of the world in general'. It shares a complicated relationship with culture.

See Stuart McLean, 'Materiality and Culture', in *International Encyclopedia of the Social and Behavioral Sciences*, 2nd edition, ed. James D. Wright, pp. 765–71 (Amsterdam: Elsevier, 2015), https://doi.org/10.1016/B978-0-08-097086-8.12207-X (accessed on 9 August 2022).

16 Gabrielle M. Spiegel, 'Memory and History: Liturgical Time and Historical Time', *History and Theory* 41, no. 2 (2018): 149–62.

17 Jones, *Memory and Material Culture*.

18 See Claire Vionnet, 'From Experience to Language towards an Affected and Affective Writing: A Conversation with Tim Ingold', *TSANTSA* 23 (2018): 82–90. 'Encounter' is a useful way of thinking about both the object and mobility. On one level, the encounter in an anthropological sense creates a moment for the recipient of an object to feel the occupation of it, while on the other it gives a glimpse of the historical background to it. I mobilize encounter as an affective not only in the sense of discovering the object but also as a site to capture the sensorial relationship at that moment.

19 Jones, *Memory and Material Culture*, p. 22 (emphasis mine).

20 Ibid., p. 26.

21 Howard Williams, 'Death, Memory, and Material Culture: Catalytic Commemoration and the Cremated Dead', in *The Oxford Handbook of the Archaeology of Death and Burial*, ed. S. Tarlow and L. Nilsson Stutz, pp. 195–208 (Oxford: Oxford University Press, 2013), p. 1.

22 Judith Butler, 'Merely Cultural', *Social Text* 52–53 (Autumn–Winter 1997): 265–77.

23 Ibid.

24 Marcus Ohlström, Marco Solinas and Olivier Voirol, 'On Nancy Fraser and Axel Honneth's Redistribution or Recognition? A Political-Philosophical Exchange', *Iris* 3, no. 5 (2011): 205–21.

25 Butler, 'Merely Cultural', p. 35.

26 Glen Sean Coulthard, *Red Skin White Masks: Rejecting the Colonial Politics of Recognition* (Minneapolis, MN: University of Minnesota Press, 2014).

27 Gayatri Chakravorty Spivak, 'Can the Subaltern Speak?', in *Colonial Discourses and Post-Colonial Theory: A Reader*, ed. Patrick Williams and Laura Chrisman, pp. 66–111 (New York: Columbia University Press, 1994).

28 Rosalind C. Morris (ed.), *Can the Subaltern Speak? Reflections on the History of an Idea* (New York: Columbia University Press, 2010), p. 28 (emphasis original).

29 Ibid.

30 Rajeswari Sunder Rajan, 'Death and the Subaltern', in *Can the Subaltern Speak? Reflections on the History of an Idea*, ed. Rosalind C. Morris, pp. 117–38 (New York: Columbia University Press, 2010), p. 117.

31 Margery Sabin, 'In Search of Subaltern Consciousness', *Prose Studies* 30, no. 2 (2008): 177–200.

32 Amita Sinha, 'Colonial and Post-Colonial Memorial Parks in Lucknow, India: Shifting Ideologies and Changing Aesthetics', *Journal on Landscape Architecture* 50 no. 2 (Autumn 2010): 60–71, p. 62.

33 For an elaborate discussion on the use of cemeteries and the making of the British Association for Cemeteries in South Asia (BACSA), see Elizabeth Buettner, 'Cemeteries, Public Memory and Raj Nostalgia in Postcolonial Britain and India', *History and Memory* 18, no. 1 (2006): 5–42.

34 Rahul Rao, 'What Do We Mean When We Talk about Statues?' 10th Africa Day Memorial Lecture, 2018 edited by Patrick Williams and Laura Chrisman, https://www.ufs.ac.za/docs/default-source/ufs-news-list/read-lectures-here.pdf (accessed in September 2022).

35 Ibid., p. 4.

36 It was a movement led by students at the University of Ghana.

37 There is unfortunately no record of a Birsa statue that was built before the making of Jharkhand as a separate state. Unlike Ambedkar, who had a statue installed in the 1960s in Bombay, there is a bronze statue installed in Odisha, which emerges as the only piece of information about Birsa's statue before 2001. This is quite interesting as it highlights the neglect of Adivasi history within the mainstream writings on art history and the political need for Birsa's statue in contemporary times. For the visual history of Ambedkar's statue in particular and of Dalits in general, see Gary Michael Tartako, *Dalit Art and Visual Imagery* (New Delhi: Oxford University Press, 2012).

38 Piers Vitebsky, in his research, explores the tension of being the outsider: 'The tension is part of our method (ethnographic). In scholarship, one cites previous documentation as evidence. But in a discipline so deeply rooted in fieldwork (Anthropology), the documents eventually run out and the trail ends in direct experience. We know what we know through human interaction, so there can be no anthropological account of a society that does not derive from an anthropologist's relation with local people.' Piers Vitebsky, *Living Without the Dead* (Noida: HarperCollins Publishers, 2018), p. 2.

39 The MLA sits in the Vidhan Sabha, the state legislative assembly.

40 The AJSU Party is different from the AJSU (All Jharkhand Student Union). The AJSU is a product of the Jharkhand movement that joined the struggle much earlier than the AJSU Party.

41 The BJP is a right-wing party. Historically the party is rooted in the Bharatiya Jana Sangh founded by Shyama Prasad Mukherjee in 1951. The Jana Sangh merged with several other parties to form Janata Party and won the election for the first time in 1977 in the aftermath of the Emergency (1975) imposed by Indira Gandhi, the leader of the Congress Party. The Janata Party, however, was dissolved, and Jana Sangh was ousted again until it began to gain momentum through the Ram *janambhoomi* (birthplace) movement at the end of the 1980s. In 1998, the BJP came to power by forging an alliance under the umbrella of the National Democratic Alliance (NDA). At present, after a massive growth in vote share during the 2014

general election, the BJP forms its government under Narendra Modi. For an elaborate discussion on the history and politics of the BJP, see Christophe Jaffrelot, *The Hindu Nationalist Movement and Indian Politics (1925–1990)* (London: C. Hurst & Co. Publishers, 1996). For a contemporary discussion, see Edward Anderson and Christophe Jaffrelot, 'Hindu Nationalism and the "Saffronisation of the Public Sphere": An Interview with Christophe Jaffrelot', *Contemporary South Asia* 26, no. 4 (2 October 2018): 468–82.

42 See *Economic Times*, 'BJP Manifesto a Blueprint for Jharkhand's Development: Raghuvar Das', 12 November 2014, https://economictimes.indiatimes.com/news/politics-and-nation/bjp-manifesto-a-blue-print-for-jharkhands-development-raghuvar-das/articleshow/45127602.cms (accessed on 9 August 2022).

43 See Amitabh Srivastava, 'Sudesh Mahto Borrows Nitish's, Mamta's Slogans to Woo Women Electorate in Jharkhand', *India Today*, 29 March 2013, https://www.indiatoday.in/india/north/story/sudesh-mahto-jharkhand-women-electorate-mahila-panchayat-all-women-rally-157194-2013-03-29 (accessed on 9 August 2022).

44 *Panchayat* literally means a body of governance consisting of *panch*—that is, five— members that function as the village council in many regions of South Asia. A grassroots-level institution ensures the democratic strength of electoral politics in India. It should not be confused with Khap Panchayat, which is a social body.

45 Srivastava, 'Sudesh Mahto Borrows Nitish's, Mamta's Slogans'.

46 See Paromita Sanyal and Vijayendra Rao, *Oral Democracy* (Cambridge: Cambridge University Press, 2018), p. 5.

47 Ulgulan Foundation was formed by Mahto to make a 150-foot-tall statue of Birsa Munda.

48 Mayank, in a personal interview with the author, Ranchi, 16 October 2018. The announcement was widely reported and captured by the media. See Inextlive, 'बिरसा मुंडा 150 फीट ऊंची प्रतिमा लगाएंगे', 16 November 2016, https://inextlive.jagran.com/150-feet-statue-of-birsa-munda-142413 (accessed on 9 August 2022).

49 Akhil Gupta authored an interesting study of the red files to explain the working of Indian bureaucracy. It gives an exemplary account of the relationship between poverty and bureaucracy in Uttar Pradesh through ethnographic inquiry. See Akhil Gupta, *Red Tape: Bureaucracy, Structural Violence, and Poverty in India* (Durham, NC: Duke University Press, 2012).

50 Sudesh Mahto, in a personal interview with the author, Ranchi, 16 October 2018 (emphasis mine).

51 Ibid.

52 Judicial Academy Jharkhand, *Handbook on Land Law* (Ranchi: Judicial Academy Jharkhand, n.d.), p. 11, https://jajharkhand.in/wp/wp-content/uploads/2019/08/06_handbook_on_land_law.pdf (accessed on 9 August 2022).

53 For an elaborate discussion on the CNTA, see Sanjukta Das Gupta, 'Rethinking Adivasi Identity: The Chota Nagpur Tenancy Act (1908) and Its Aftermath among the Hos of Singhbhum', in *Adivasi in Colonial India: Survival, Resistance*

      and Negotiation, ed. Biswamoy Pati, pp. 88–111. New Delhi: Orient Blackswan, 2011.

54   Rahul Ranjan, 'Unravelling the Narratives of Adivasi Dispossession: A Case Study of Land Acquisition in Nagri Village, Jharkhand'. *Development* 60, nos. 3–4 (2017): 227–34, DOI: 10.1057/s41301-018-0171-8. Since the year 2000 the state of Jharkhand has signed more than 70 memoranda of understanding (MOUs) allowing the disproportionate expansion of industrialization in the areas marked by protective legislations.

55   See Prashant Pandey, 'Jharkhand Govt Approves Freedom of Religion Bill', *Indian Express* (online edition), 6 September 2017, https://indianexpress.com/article/india/jharkhand-guv-approves-freedom-of-religion-bill-land-act-bjp-welcomes-move/ (accessed on 20 January 2019). Also see Alok Raja, 'Tribal Communities Protest Changes in Jharkhand Land Laws', *Scroll*, 5 April 2017, https://thewire.in/rights/local-tribes-protest-changes-jharkhand-land-laws (accessed on 8 February 2019).

56   The project is funded by the state and central governments under the Sardar Vallabhai Patel Rashtriya Ekta Trust (SVPRET). For a detailed report on the specific component of the statue, see *Business Line*, 'All You Need to Know about the Statue of Unity', 31 October 2018, https://www.thehindubusinessline.com/news/national/all-you-need-to-know-about-the-statue-of-unity/article25378713.ece (accessed on 8 February 2019). The size of investment for the construction has generated debate both inside and outside the country.

57   For further discussion of the NBA movement, see Amita Baviskar, *In the Belly of the River: Tribal Conflicts over Development in the Narmada Valley* (New Delhi: Oxford University Press, 1997).

58   See Aarefa Johari, 'Statue of Unity', *Scroll.in*, 1 November 2018, https://scroll.in/article/900473/drowned-dreams-why-nearly-300-adivasis-were-detained-before-modi-could-unveil-the-statue-of-unity (accessed on 9 February 2019).

59   In his study of iconography, Daniel J. Rycroft shows that the circulation of Birsa's image began with the publication of S. C. Roy's work, and finally the *ulgulan* photograph was released by the Jharkhand Autonomous Council. Rycroft has meticulously shown how the reproduction of photographs also demonstrated the politicization and de-politicization of Birsa. See Daniel J. Rycroft, 'Capturing Birsa Munda: The Virtuality of a Colonial-Era Photograph', *Indian Folklore Research Journal* 1, no. 4 (2004): 53–67.

60   Sudesh Mahto, in a personal interview with the author, Ranchi, 16 October 2018.

61   Sanjay Bosu Mullick is known formally as Samar Bosu Mullick. I refer to him as Mullick throughout the book.

62   Sanjay Bosu Mullick, in a personal interview with the author, Ranchi, 18 August 2018. I wish to highlight that Mullick is one of the key interlocutors of my access to the elite interview conducted with Mahto. He is known not only for his years of contribution in the Jharkhand movement but also as a person with great humility who helps researchers to find sources to work in the region. I am deeply thankful for his support.

63 Sanjay Bosu Mullick, in a personal interview with the author, Ranchi, 18 August 2018. The Rajputs are an upper-caste group classed as warriors in the *varna* social system. Rajputs belong to the warrior class within the caste arrangement. Historically, they are also perceived as a class that has displayed masculine power to guard the borderline of the caste order.

64 François Hartog, 'Time and Heritage', *Museum International* 57, no. 3 (2005): 7–18, p. 8.

65 Ibid.

66 Ibid., p. 10.

67 Pierre Nora, 'Between Memory and History: Les Lieux de Mémoire', *Representations* 26 (Spring 1989): 7–24.

68 Dayamani Barla, in a personal interview with the author, Ranchi, 22 October 2018.

69 Kuntala Lahiri-Dutt, Radhika Krishnan and Nesar Ahmad, 'Land Acquisition and Dispossession: Private Coal Companies in Jharkhand', *Economic and Political Weekly* 47, no. 6 (2012): 39–45, p. 40.

70 Ranjan, 'Unravelling the Narratives of Adivasi Dispossession'.

71 Yogendra Yadav wrote an exciting response to such an association within popular media. 'Left is Dead, Long Live the Left', *The Tribune*, 12 March 2018, https://www.tribuneindia.com/news/comment/left-is-dead-long-live-the-left/557395.html (accessed on 21 February 2019).

72 Dev Nathan and Virginius Xaxa, *Social Exclusion and Adverse Inclusion: Development and Deprivation of Adivasis in India* (New Delhi: Oxford University Press, 2012).

73 See Antonio Negri and Michael Hardt, *Empire* (Cambridge, MA: Harvard University Press, 2000), pp. 12–13.

74 Ibid.

75 Dipesh Chakrabarty, 'Minority Histories, Subaltern Pasts', *Postcolonial Studies* 1, no. 1 (1998): 15–29.

76 An *akhra* is space of sociality in Adivasi community. People use it for various purposes such as festivals and meetings, amongst others. The word has gained a renewed currency in the recent past. Various organizations use it as a name for collective initiatives.

77 I refer to the work of Timothy Morton to understand the difference. See Timothy Morton, *Ecology without Nature: Rethinking Environmental Aesthetics* (Cambridge, MA: Harvard University Press, 2007).

78 Cited in Carmina Peñarrocha Giménez, 'Rescuing the Identity of the Adivasis from Their Invisibility: The Encounter between Jesuits and the Indigenous Peoples of India', PhD dissertation, Doctoral Programme 14003, Development Cooperation, Universitat Jaume, Castellón de la Plana, Spain, 2017, p. 42.

79 Hansda Sowvendra Shekhar, 'Sarna-Hindu Theology: A Study of Some Cults, Gods and Worship in Jharkhand', *The Apollonian* 4, nos. 1–2 (2017): 94–106.

80 Ibid., p. 96.

81 Ibid., p. 105.
82 Ibid.
83 R. D. Munda, *Adivasi Astitva aur Jharkhandi Asmita ke Sawaal*, 2nd edition (Ranchi: Rumbul, 2018), p. 66.
84 For example, in the census report of 2011, the total population of people defined as 'Addi Bassi'—86,877—was concentrated mainly in Jharkhand, Madhya Pradesh and Maharashtra. Some 4,957,467 people were recognized under the category of 'Sarna' in Bihar, Chhattisgarh, Jharkhand, Odisha and West Bengal. Similarly, there are various groups such as Gonds, who are known for their religion of the same name as that of their community. They all invariably fall under the umbrella category of 'Other Religions and Persuasions' and are not acknowledged by their unique identity. The total number of people identified under the 'Other' religion in the state of Jharkhand in 2011 is 4,235,786, which is equal to 12.84 per cent of the population, with Hindus being the highest percentage (67.83 per cent). See Government of Jharkhand, *Census Report of Jharkhand, 2011*, https://www.census2011.co.in/census/state/jharkhand.html (accessed on 16 February 2019).
85 John-Baptist Hoffman, *Encyclopedia Mundarica*, vol. 1, 1914, shelf mark 14178.e.47, British Library, London.
86 Chapter 5 broadly discusses the significance of *the landscape of memory*.
87 Raj Kumar, 'Birsa Loses Cuffs sans Ceremony', *The Telegraph* (online edition), 16 July 2016, https://www.telegraphindia.com/jharkhand/birsa-loses-cuffs-sans-ceremony/cid/1328597 (accessed on 18 February 2019).
88 Dayamani Barla, in a personal interview with the author, Ranchi, 22 October 2018.
89 Asoka Kumar Sen, *Indigeneity, Landscape and History: Adivasi Self-fashioning in India India* (New Delhi: Routeldge, 2018), p. 123.
90 Ibid.
91 See Rajiv Singh, 'India at 70: Why Freedom Fighter Birsa Munda's Village in Jharkhand Is Still in Fetters', Kractivist, 14 August 2017, https://kractivist.org/india-at-70-why-freedom-fighter-birsa-mundas-village-in-jharkhand-is-still-in-fetters (accessed on 15 July 2018).
92 Sudesh Mahto, in a personal interview with the author, Ranchi, 16 October 2018.
93 Jean Comaroff and John Comaroff, *Law and Disorder in the Postcolony* (Chicago: University of Chicago Press, 2006).
94 Santosh Kiro, in a personal interview with the author, Firayal Chowk, Ranchi, 26 October 2018.
95 Ibid.
96 I have given a fictitious name to anonymize the identity of the respondent as he does not wish to be identified.
97 Vinita Damodaran, 'History, Landscape, and Indigeneity in Chotanagpur, 1850–1980'. *South Asia: Journal of South Asia Studies* 25, no. 2 (2002): 77–110.

98   Hoffman, *Encyclopaedia Mundarica*, vol. 1, p. 612 (emphasis mine).

99   'Red corridor' is a euphemism used to describe the country's eastern and central regions, along with parts of southern India, which have a high intensity of left-wing insurgencies. It is where an ultra-left-wing group of the Communist Party of India (Maoist) use armed struggle against the state. In addition, these areas suffer from high levels of unemployment and disproportionate inequality of wealth. For a riveting account of Maoist lifeworld and journey across the eastern part of Jharkhand, see Alpa Shah, *Nightmarch: Among India's Revolutionary Guerrillas* (London: Hurst Publications, 2018). It is disputable, as we learn in K. S. Singh's account where he suggested that the birthplace in the popular folk songs refers to different places. Singh, in fact, believes that Birsa was born in a field and by the river in Bamba village. See Kumar Suresh Singh, *Birsa Munda and His Movement (1872–1901)* (Kolkata: Seagull Books, 2002).

100   See Government of Jharkhand, *Census Report of Jharkhand, 2011*.

101   Alpa Shah, *In the Shadows of the State: Indigenous Politics, Environmentalism and Insurgency in Jharkhand, India* (New Delhi: Oxford University Press, 2011), p. 69.

102   For a commentary on the Ayushman Bharat scheme, see *Indian Express*, 'Amartya Sen: Ayushman Bharat Neglects Primary Healthcare, Sector Needs Radical Change', 28 February 2019, https://indianexpress.com/article/business/amartya-sen-ayushman-bharat-neglects-primary-healthcare-sector-needs-radical-change-5603964 (accessed on 20th November 2019).

103   See R. Singh, 'Why Freedom Fighter Birsa Munda's Village in Jharkhand Is Still in Fetters'.

104   For a comprehensive understanding, see Donal Cruise O'Brien, *Symbolic Confrontations: Muslims Imagining the State in Africa* (London: Palgrave Macmillan, 2003).

105   These are prominent leaders from national and regional parties. Atal Bihari Vajpayee served as the BJP prime minister of the country. Jairam Ramesh of the Indian National Congress served as the Minister of Mineral Resources, while Babulal Marandi, then in the BJP, served the first Chief Minister of Jharkhand.

106   For an elaborate interview of Sukhram and reporting on Ulihatu, see Rukmini S., 'In Search of Another Saviour', *The Hindu*, 16 April 2014, https://www.thehindu.com/opinion/op-ed/in-search-of-another-saviour/article5916044.ece (accessed on 11 November 2019).

107   Videh Upadhyay, 'Water Law and the Poor', in *Legal Grounds: Natural Resources, Identity, and the Law in Jharkhand*, ed. Nandini Sundar, pp. 132–56 (New Delhi: Oxford University Press, 2009), pp. 142–43.

108   Vasavi Kiro, in a personal interview with the author, Patratu and Ranchi, 25 October 2019.

109   Ibid.

110   Ibid.

111   Bagaicha Research Team, 'A Study of Undertrials in Jharkhand'. Sanhati, 2 February 2016, http://sanhati.com/excerpted/16044/ (accessed on 24 February 2019).

112 Ramesh Singh Munda served as an MLA from the Janata Dal (United). The Maoists allegedly shot him down in 2008. He was amongst many other politicians who fell victim to Maoist insurgency.

113 Ashish Tripathi, 'Mayawati's Statue "Beheaded" in Lucknow, Police Call it Sacrilege', *Times of India*, 26 July 2012, https://timesofindia.indiatimes.com/city/lucknow/Mayawatis-statue-beheaded-in-Lucknow-police-call-it-sacrilege/articleshow/15161969.cms (accessed on 11 December 2019).

114 *Dalit*, a word that emerges from Sanskrit and Marathi (spoken in the western state of Maharashtra), literally means 'broken' or 'scattered'. It denotes the hierarchical caste system of Hindu society. At the same time it is a conscious replacement of terms such as 'Untouchables' or, as proposed by Gandhi, 'Harijans'.

115 Malia Belli, 'Monumental Pride Mayawati's Memorials in Lucknow', *Ars Orientalis* 44 (2014): 85–109.

116 In particular, the idea of the invention of modernity is relevant to Adivasis. This is primarily due to the approach of the colonial and post-colonial governmentality of Adivasis as the subjects of the modern nation state. Adivasis have been primarily received through the sociality with the traditional culture that echoes the idea of the past. In some sense Adivasis remain as the historical subject within the contemporary formulation of subjecthood. See Crispin Bates, 'Race, Caste and Tribe in Central India: The Early Origins of Indian Anthropometry', *Edinburgh Papers in South Asian Studies* 3, no. 3 (1995): 2–35.

117 Koselleck, *The Practice of Conceptual History*, p. 111.

118 Belli, 'Monumental Pride', p. 86.

119 See Benedict Anderson, *Imagined Communities: Reflections on the Origin and Spread of Nationalism* (London: Verso Publication, 2006 [1983]).

120 See Nicolas Jaoul, 'Learning the Use of Symbolic Means: Dalits, Ambedkar Statues and the State in Uttar Pradesh', *Contributions to Indian Sociology* 40, no. 2 (2006): 175–207.

121 Ibid., p. 193.

Chapter 4

'Burying the Dead, Creating the Past'*
The Making of Memorials, Stone Slabs and Birsa Munda in Jharkhand

> Committing history is a form of externalization: by committing sublime historical deeds, by doing things that are at odds with our identity, we place history outside ourselves. Committing history thus is a kind of burial: we take leave of ourselves as we have come to know ourselves and become what we as yet do not know. In the process we come to see what is lost forever: what we are no longer.
>
> —Eelco Runia[1]

Drawing on the previous enquiry on statues, this chapter is invested in discussing the significance of *samadhi sthal*s (mausoleum sites) and stone slabs, often used in burials, in Jharkhand. These sites offer a unique intersection between material-memory culture and the rituals of nationalism. While Birsa Munda's *samadhi sthal* is located in the urban industrial settlement of Ranchi, a memorial pillar is located at the top of Dombari Hill amidst a village surrounded by a forest in Khunti district. They present an account of a concerted effort by the state and political elites to build a 'site of memory' and, with it, political tourism.[2] Contrary to statues, they represent a unique *affective turn* by dovetailing both material memory and commemorative practice.[3] That is to say, they allow us to move away from treating the material installation as a merely aesthetic display and

---

* The title of the chapter draws inspiration from Eelco Runia's groundbreaking essay on the practice of burial. See Eelco Runia, 'Burying the Dead, Creating the Past', *History and Theory* 46, no. 3 (2007): 313–25.

instead treat them as sites of emotion. In such a rendering, the representation of Birsa Munda becomes a tool of memory for political mobilization.

In this chapter, I argue that the relationship of the state with the past of Adivasis vis-à-vis the production of capital provides a new lens to understand the politics of commemoration. I illustrate the processes involved in making the space for remembrance of the dead by using two gripping case studies that are tied with field narratives, political discourse and popular representation. These materials highlight the muzzling of the voices of subaltern Adivasis in the mainstream representation of Adivasi icons by political elites and the state. I also show the changing notion of *Adivasiness* within the urban political spectrum. That is to say, the architectural design and spatial arrangements shape the textures of commemoration. Together they create conditions for political mobilization in the state that now rests in unthinkable possibilities.

The chapter offers competing notions of commemoration and asks how far material objects succeed in attaining glimpses of the past and allowing the subaltern Adivasis to reimagine their belonging. I show this in two ways. First, I situate the different stories about the making of the *samadhi sthal*, which functions *prima facie* as Birsa's burial ground. I highlight how state-led commemoration of Birsa overlooks the complicated process of memorialization of the dead amongst Adivasis in Jharkhand. Second, I examine how the memorial pillar at Dombari reveals an intimate relationship between memory and post-colonial capital. I illustrate the importance of landscape, the performance of rituals and political ideologies that ritually emphasize the memory of Birsa Munda.

In order to undertake this task, I delineate a specific theoretical foundation of commemoration in the following section. It highlights the key characteristics of the concept, the background and the use of the idea in the chapter. This also helps to contextualize the differences and similarities between memorializing Birsa Munda using material memory.

Commemoration: Theorizing the Past of the Present

In the *Oxford English Dictionary*, the word 'commemoration' finds its root in the 16th-century Latin word *commemoratio*, meaning 'brought to remembrance', from the verb *commemorare*, which is a portmanteau of *com-* (meaning 'altogether') and *memorare* (meaning 'relate' from *memor*, or 'mindful').[4] This suggests that the word 'commemoration' refers to a conscious effort to remember the past. In doing so, an external agent of representation places the past as the present. The object therefore compresses time into the form of object and creates a temporality of its own. These objects take various forms that produce a range of emotions amongst people from the community whose members they represent. A commemoration is an instrument for society to *remember* the past. It is a tool of remembering by using a vast schema of mnemonic practices. It is 'affect-laden', transforming 'historical knowledge' into 'collective memory' and displaying a range of emotions that tie peoples' pasts into the present.[5]

Unlike other mnemonic practices, commemoration offers an intimate recalling of the past. Sometimes it is in the form of an enclaved space; at other times, an open public space. In other words, while being part of the built environment, it personalizes the space into a community-specific site of remembrance. It emerges from personal or collective experience to 'account for unimaginable events caused by human beings'.[6] Therefore, commemoration is also a 'retroactive' representation of the past.[7] Such a function allows commemoration sites to acquire multiple temporalities and identify human emotion in a range of expressions.

Commemoration is the act of personalizing the grand physical object that plays a significant role in shaping public memory. It is often performed for major events and for deceased persons who have made a remarkable impression on history. Commemoration creates a rendering of specific historical events in ordinary time and space using objects. It effectively draws out people's collective and individual memory through a set of rituals and practices involved in observing and remembering the dead. As an affective site, it allows people to identify with, belong to and relate themselves with the representation of the dead or deceased. Alternatively, as argued in a ground-breaking essay by Eelco Runia, it is 'a straightforward manifestation of our desires to commemorate'.[8]

Runia defines commemoration as a 'prime historical phenomenon of our time'.[9] He suggests that the historians long denied their own desire to commemorate and, instead, dismissed it as an ephemeral public showcase. However, it is evident in their writings that commemoration has routinely 'taken over' as phenomena that they themselves do not understand. Keeping aside the binary opposition between 'history' and 'memory' proposed by Pierre Nora, Runia proposes several theses in which the poles of opposition are 'history' and 'commemoration'. He considers history as a 'botanizing' discipline that 'contributes to the ever more truthful biography of a nation'.[10] Therefore, commemoration is 'self-exploration—typically the fruit of an era obsessed with therapeutic and spiritual welfare'.[11] Understanding commemoration as 'sublime' events produced by 'acts of the people', an epistemological question primarily changes our 'worldview'.[12] Furthermore, he argues that sometimes 'scarcity of memory' as ontological homesickness to regain the 'blessed state' produces an urge for commemoration.[13] In turn, this homesickness manifests in the form of 'nostalgia' that allows us to reconstruct a home that has been lost.[14]

Similarly, Andrew Jones explores the relationship between the people and artefacts that process memory.[15] He argues: 'As physical materials, artefacts provide an authentic link to the past and as such can be re-experienced.'[16] Furthermore, he claims: 'History can no longer simply treat objects as symbolic media; rather the *materiality of object* is best seen as impinging on people sensually and physically at a fundamental level.... Objects can act as physical traces of past events which are amenable to the process of reading.'[17] The materiality of the objects creates a sensorial experience to the community which belong to the subject of representation. It lends them an 'extra-terrestrial' quality and works as an 'index' of the past.[18]

This materiality is a useful tool in analysing the abstract domain of death and its representation through an object. For instance, objects that display the dead at mausoleum sites are not merely external agents that remain meaningless without human interaction. We create them. In the process of creating such sites, we are co-constituted. Jones stresses this point by showing a shift from memory to commemoration. He writes: 'Things provide people with the capacity to act and through actions things and people endure. Things make people exist, and people make things exist.'[19] This instantiation configures the materiality of the object as the core function of it.

In other words, it is in the constant interaction between objects and humans that memory survives. Memory on its own does not exist. This is particularly interesting in the context of the chapter for the case study. The mausoleum sites that draw a range of politicians to display performative commemorations of Birsa Munda show concerted efforts in preserving his memory. On any other day, the mausoleum site remains in a vacuum, without memory. Similarly, Emma Blake asserts that 'memory and tradition alone do not preserve an object's identity; it is the ongoing incorporation of that object into routinized practices that generates meaning'.[20] The ritual and routinized performative functions associated with commemoration sites make a living agent of the memory. In this context, Jones draws upon commemoration:

> A commemoration is paradigmatic of the kind of *connective practices*, which tie together people and things. Precisely because of participation and immersion both with other people and with external objects, places, and texts, the commemoration is ultimately a connective process.[21]

'Burying the Dead, Creating the Past'

In imagining commemoration as a participatory framework, we can perhaps extend this argument to identify the role of agent and subject of representation. The case study in this chapter shows that the state plays a significant role in shaping the material culture of commemoration. It makes the mausoleum sites that represent icons in restricted and often-contradictory spaces of memory.

Commemoration as Political Project: Stakeholders and Architecture

The chapter focuses on physical objects that drew imagination and architecture through a series of conflicting ideas in order to make commemoration a site to remember the canon. The need for a remembrance site emerges from the political elites, who are part of civil society. Partha Chatterjee uses civil and political society as conceptual categories to explain politics in India. He writes:

> Most of the inhabitants of India are only tenuously, and even then, ambiguously and contextually, rights-bearing citizens in the sense imagined by the constitution. They are not, therefore, proper members of civil society and are not regarded as such by the institutions of the state. However, it is not as though they are outside the reach of the state or even excluded from the domain of politics. As populations within the territorial jurisdiction of the state, they have to be both looked after and controlled by various governmental agencies. These activities bring these populations into a certain political relationship with the state.[22]

Chatterjee's illustration of political and civil society suggests the differential treatment of 'citizens' based on their access to the state. The state defines, regulates and governs the citizens in terms of their location within the structures of power—that is, civil and political society. Therefore, the state, constituted by political elites in post-colonial space, has a complicated relationship with the formal category of citizens as borrowed from the European framework.

In the same way as the state controls and defines 'territorial jurisdiction', it also controls the production of memory and the process of memorialization. It actively engages with civil society to devise models of memorializing the past. It builds sites of memories through the wide-scale built environment, often located in urban centres.

However, in the recent past, the ruling dispensation, the BJP, was keen to recover the subaltern memory—to assimilate the rural canon into the manifold of nationalism. Amongst others, Birsa Munda has acquired a new currency in the national memorialization process.[23] This has allowed the state to enter an Adivasi constituency that is on the frontline of a war between the state and the Maoists. The process of memorializing also offers the state an opportunity to exercise its power inside the most democratic systems of governance, such as *parha* (local priest decision-making system).[24] Legislation such as the Panchayats (Extension to the Scheduled Areas) (PESA) Act from 1996 establishes such a model.[25] These models display an attempt through the collective effort of the people to negotiate democratically with the state. Despite the existence of such protective legislation, the areas continue to witness the violation of the rights of Adivasis across India.

Significant to commemoration is also the structure, shape, emplacement and embodiment of sites of remembrance. Unlike statues that are present in three dimensions within public space, visible from the distance, a mausoleum site is usually constructed in an enclosed space, displaying burial pits (sometimes symbolically placed at a different location) and the grave mound in different ways. It invokes practices that shift the role of memory from memorializing to commemorating. It invites a specific set of rituals such as rites of passage, pilgrimage and extended chanting, amongst others, whereby a particular historical past becomes a relic in some cases and a remembrance site in others.[26] The following section contextualizes the use of the aforementioned theoretical discussion. It locates the process of the commemoration of Birsa Munda by investigating the process of making the *samadhi sthal* in Ranchi.

Setting the Context: Commemorating Birsa Munda and His *Ulgulan*

A mausoleum is, according to the *Cambridge Dictionary*, 'a stately or impressive building housing a tomb or group of tombs'.[27] However, the meaning has evolved with new forms of remembering. It is interesting to note that some of the cultures that also use remembrance sites through the construction of impressive architecture do not necessarily find translations in English. This chapter discusses the remembrance site for Birsa Munda—the *samadhi sthal*.

Samadhi, originally a Sanskrit word, means a yogic state in which one attains or meets with the divine. This suggests that the divine has a form, even in abstraction, as a power. For example, Islam and Christianity have a form of God—an Abrahamic one. However, within the cosmic world of Adivasis, the idea of the divine is formless and monotheistic. Adivasis believe in formless spirits: *bongas*. Interestingly, the word *bonga* finds explicit mention in 19th-century documents (both land records and personal papers). For instance, John-Baptist Hoffman writes:

> Bonga is any spirit conceived as wielding influence for good or evil over men and their affairs. The specification is generic names of places in which the various spirits are supposed to have their adobe: burubonga (the mountain spirit), ikirbonga (the spirit of a tank or pond), orabongake (the spirits dwelling in men's houses).[28]

This offers a useful description of the idea of the spirit. The *bonga* appears here as a formless spirit. The cosmic world of Adivasis recognizes that the *bonga* resides in our perceptual experience for their existence. Hoffman illustrates it thus:

> According to Mundas, *sense perception* is the only bar between us from them. Bongas are those living beings, which, though firmly believed in as existing and influencing us for good, or evil, can neither be seen nor heard nor perceived: though fluttering about everywhere, they are, so far as sense perception goes, just as if they were not.[29]

This restates that *sense perception* plays a significant role in assessing the form of the spirit. Importantly, it emphasizes that the presence of spirits is heterogenous—*fluttering about everywhere*. In that sense, commemoration through an architectural form of a *samadhi sthal* highlights an existing gap between the popular culture of commemoration and existing alternatives amongst the community. On the one hand, architecture defines the dead through material formation, while on the other it allows the institutional forces of the state to manufacture a site for collective social grief and ritual performance to highlight the significance of specific icons.

The following section broadly discusses the *samadhi sthal*. For now, practices of commemoration are an essential template to understand the politics of memory and the various forms that it takes within shifting cultural contexts. Importantly, such shifts define the unique characteristics of material culture. The uses of material for the curation of memory in the form of statues and mausoleum sites are quite different from each other. Therefore, it is crucial to understand the theoretical basis of the shift in meaning, use and practices associated with material-memory culture. Commemoration as a process to curate or represent memory through material installation invokes an affective reaction. What follows hereafter is a section on *samadhi sthal* that shows the use of material culture in the process of memory-making in Jharkhand. Effectively, it displays a narrative that emanates from the state.

Samadhi Sthal: Grieving the Dead to Remember and Forget

> Memorials to the dead are certainly as old as human history. They correspond to a fundamental state of being, given to human beings, in which death and life intertwine in whatever ways they are referred to one another.
>
> —Reinhart Koselleck[30]

Erected as a burial mound, sheathed in black marble, with a few steps and beneath a canopy structure held aloft by eight pillars, and covering an area of 1,200 square feet, the *samadhi sthal* of Birsa Munda is open to the public (Figure 4.1). The structure was built in 2012 by the Department of Art, Culture, Sports and Tourism at a cost of approximately 34 lakh (3.4 million) rupees.[31] It was inaugurated by Sudesh Mahto (see Chapter 3). However, the foundation stone for the construction was installed in 1993. Halen Kujur brought together a group of people, identified the location and performed rituals before installing the foundation stone.

Figure 4.1 Birsa Munda's *samadhi sthal* located at Kokar distillery, Ranchi

Source: Photograph by the author.

'Burying the Dead, Creating the Past'

A stone slab seated next to the *samadhi* and a mural provide a 'historical timeline' of the making of this site. The slab details the people who have contributed towards setting up the place for commemoration while giving limited information about Birsa Munda and his contribution (Figures 4.2 and 4.3). The list of names on the stone does not suggest their whereabouts—except for the politicians who have paid visits and donated for the renovation of the place, which were initiated in 2004 and 2012.

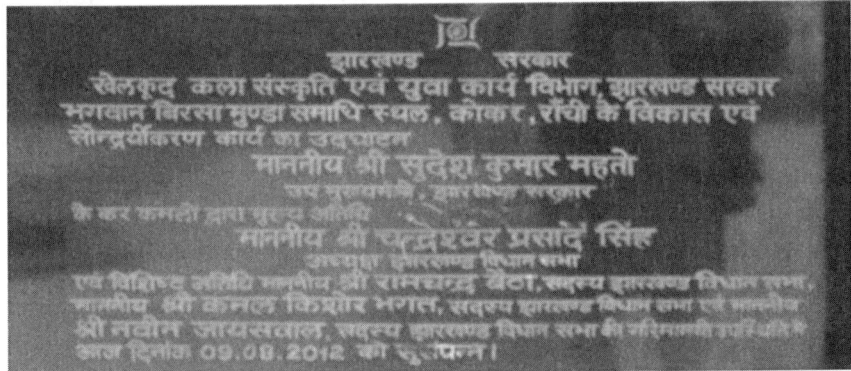

Figure 4.2 A stone slab acknowledging Sudesh Mahto's contribution to the construction of Birsa Munda's *samadhi sthal*

Source: Photograph by the author.

Figure 4.3 A stone slab at Birsa Munda's *samadhi sthal*, with information on the members who built it

Source: Photograph by the author.

Located at Kokar distillery in Ranchi, the neighbourhood is surrounded by industrial houses, a bustling market and a busy road. The memorial was built at the edge of the distillery's *talab* (pond) towards which several drains from around the city run, radiating a pungent odour, which is challenging to endure.[32] Despite undergoing a series of renovations, the dust from the road and the odour of the drain overwhelm the area. The road hosted various makeshift shops of informal chicken and vegetable vendors. The working Adivasi women who are part of India's huge informal sector sat by the road to sell their *tendu patta* (leaves of the Coromandel ebony tree, *Diospyros melonoxylon*) throughout the day, at least during early summer. These women travel from distant villages, many of them from as far as Bero block, taking rides on a tempo (autorickshaw) while carrying stacks of *patta* in their arms and on their heads. As I visited this gathering, many of them told me that they have to take their place assiduously, if at all, inside the tempos as the drivers often accept more passengers than the vehicles reasonably allow. In my memory of growing up in this town as a young adult, these remarkable journeys spark recollections of the state's glaring inequalities. Far from simplistic ethnographic descriptions, the experiences of these women, structurally reduced to the underpaid informal sector, resemble what Jens Lerche and Alpa Shah call 'conjugated oppression', in which the social oppression of the Adivasis is co-constituted by their class location and identity.[33] This, in turn, further entrenches them at the 'bottom of social and economic hierarchies'.[34] The role of the informal labour force is colossal but, in the grand narratives of development, often remains unwritten. Travelling from far-flung places in order to earn a basic income not only helps us understand the nature of their work but also explains the varying stories of migration. While this migration is often forced upon them, sometimes it is embarked upon in order to 'gain independence from parents or live out prohibited amorous relationships' that structure the moral lives of migrants—making migration a fraught story.[35] Through the metaphor of the jackfruit, Dolly Kikon presents an ethnographic account of labourers who draw themselves to the memory of their homeland.[36] She argues that narratives of 'Adivasi articulations about belonging and memories inform us about political experiences'.[37] Frustration, anger and persistent alienation fold the working of capital with the labour force as not a 'thing' but a 'set of social relations'.[38] In these moments of alienation, Adivasi icons such as Birsa Munda emerge as what Duncan Bell calls 'mythscape', a process through which the nation's memory is selectively narrated and dramatized to (re)construct its past.[39] In the failure to recognize the plight of Adivasis and the appropriation of their past lies an inherent contradiction of Indian decolonization story.

'Burying the Dead, Creating the Past'   163

Bindrai, a 69-year-old woman (Figure 4.4), angrily describes her dissatisfaction at sitting along this bustling road only to return home in dismay about the falling rate of *tendu* consumption as it is being increasingly replaced by plastic plates.[40] She is impatient to finish her task since she finds the stench from the *talab* and the chicken vendor on the other side so immensely difficult to bear. Throughout our conversation, both of us were subject to bouts of dirt gushing into our faces from the road. An encounter of this sort is a microcosm of Adivasi lives—the dust in the lungs of Adivasis across the state. Their labour has historically been seen by the state as dispensable, easy to use and move. Adivasis like Bindrai, who were sitting along this street, are a reminder of heritage and the past; the Birsa memorial fails to reflect stories from her own life.

Theatrics and Emotions

In the meantime, the renovation programme undertaken by the Municipal Corporation of Ranchi had made Birsa's *samadhi sthal* a place for commemoration. This place is embellished with floral decorations and draped with billboards featuring *sahadat*s (prose of martyrs) on the anniversary of Birsa's death. The ritual visits by politicians, sometimes followed by a group of Birsaites, add texture to the process of this memory-making of Birsa in Ranchi. During my stay I attended two such functions, which attracted a sizeable number of people to the memorial. Most who attended had vague or schematic ideas about Birsa. Some told me he was a

Figure 4.4   Bindrai and her friend displaying their *tendu patta* bowls

Source: Photograph by the author.

'freedom fighter', while others conceived of him as *bhagwan ke avatar* (incarnation of god); meanwhile, history rests in waiting. I attended the functions with several days of visits to the *sthal*, where I ordinarily witnessed a massive spell of forgetting, if not the dust-laden floors yearning for another occasion.

I attended one of the processions headed by Mahto. He had made efforts to have Birsaites included in the procession. Along with the masses I huddled along the Kokar–Lalpur road, coming to a standstill as military personnel managed the crowd entering the memorial. The atmosphere in the space appeared more concerned with security than with remembering Birsa's death. It is difficult to control any group of people moving as part of a procession in any part of the country. However, unlike the festive mood that is generally felt in political processions, the mood here was one of bereavement—commemorative mediation through hymns, chanting and songs. The memory of Birsa as it crystalized in this procession was 'travelling' in nature—as it wandered through 'multifaceted media, contents, forms and practices of memory'.[41] Political theatrics had taken over, attracting groups of politicians assigned to perform commemoration rituals. In this public display of emotive gesticulation surrounded by media screens, an ordinary Adivasi can barely find space to breathe and enter the site; acts of remembrance remain on another tangent. This is not to suggest that grieving, mourning and remembering are contingent on spatial-temporal factors such as a quiet place or enigmatic infrastructure. The collective and individual grief that emerges from affective sites such as *samadhi sthal*s produces emotions. It also allows the personalization of individual and collective memory.

The Birsaites who participated in this procession were bussed into the city on a journey of three hours or more from the remote forested areas of Khunti (Figure 4.5). Such travelling, entailing the displacement of everydayness in order to observe a commemoration, is telling of organized forms of remembrance activities. Commemorations almost always entail an extraordinary scale of investment, guided by the importance of the events being commemorated, as is often evident at national commemorations of war.[42] Michèle Barrett, for instance, explores the politics of naming subaltern troops from South Asia and Africa that served the British Empire in the First World War. She suggests that 'the military experiences were connected to political economy', and the 'memorials of First World War sites reflect their importance in terms of national affect'.[43] Memorialization at national and international scales remains a contentious question due to its contentious nature, form and structure. Similarly, the scale of defining the remembrance day of Birsa as designed by the state is far less realized by subaltern Adivasis than by the state's own perception and use of this event.

Figure 4.5 A newspaper reporting the procession of Birsaites with Mahto and the police, a day after Birsa Munda's birth anniversary and Jharkhand Foundation Day (15 November)

Source: *Prabhat Khabar*, 16 November 2018.

Birsa's *samadhi sthal* emerges at the confluence of political interests, the notion of Adivasiness eulogized by Adivasi leaders and the changing nature of the state. It builds political promise on the archaeology of death (*samadhi sthal*) that situates the focus of Birsa in the unified structure of a mound (Figure 4.6). The archaeology of death, then, transforms the representation of the icon engraved in the material structure in order to occupy and produce a value that remains unperishable. Sarah Tarlow defines the archaeology of death as 'a class of evidence, gravestones are history and archaeology, text and artefact. They are both deliberately communicative and unintentionally revealing'.[44] I would argue that sites such as gravestones or *samadhi sthals* are also sites of affective politics. They lend a space for the mobilization as an icon of the deceased into the active public sphere of political representation. It allows the state, the political elites and the civil society to appropriate and reimagine the icon.

Figure 4.6 The statue of Birsa Munda inside his *samadhi sthal*, Ranchi

Source: Photograph by the author.

Similarly, the *samadhi sthal* bolsters efforts to characterize Birsa Munda as *shaheed*, a martyr (Figure 4.7). The problem does not emerge from the use of the word per se, which is a Quranic Arabic word that originally meant 'witness' and was later also used to denote a martyr; it emerges instead from the language used by Adivasis—here, notably, the Mundari word *darenjaan*.[45] The word consists of two equals: *dareen* meaning 'to sacrifice oneself' and *jaan* meaning 'the one'. *Darenjaan* is an adjective that defines the sacrificial attributes of an individual, meaning thereby that it does not necessarily presuppose a sacrificial cause, such as the nation or kingdom.

However, the state uses the word *shaheed* as an adjective in commemoration sites; it has a definitive meaning and nature. The object of representation becomes an illustration, as in the case of the *samadhi sthal* of Birsa Munda. The image is of an episodic contribution made by an individual striving for national independence. Effectively, the use of the built environment and iconographic display of Birsa's imagery as being aimed exclusively against the Raj eulogizes the selective anti-

Figure 4.7 A mural of Birsa Munda's *ulgulan*—sculpted by Amitav Mukherjee on the wall of Birsa's *samadhi sthal*—depicting a scene of hideout under the cave of Sail Rakab, Khunti district

Source: Photograph by the author.

colonial narrative. The cartographic imagery disseminates the unified identity through the powerful use of visuals in widespread circulation and often reflected in statues, as shown in the last chapter. The iconography, along with the linguistic articulation of heroism, holds the image together for political representation (see Figure 4.10). Tanika Sarkar, in an essay, addresses the characterization of women as nationalist through the use of iconography. She writes:

> Against the broad, though somewhat shadowy, backdrop of a freedom movement often visualised as constructive Swadeshi, a major subplot is that of a more intimate struggle within the household/local rural community.... Traditional social ideology and practices were regarded by most shades of nationalists as the one domain that was unmediated by foreign rule, the one independent space. Women and peasant, the only people yet unpolluted by western education, could preserve the purity of that domain.[46]

Such cartographic imagination is a recurrent theme within nationalist fetishization of the 'inner world', the nation against the 'outer' world, the West. Likewise, the circulation of Birsa and his followers' imagery, restricted by the historical record, emerges in an anti-colonial form to such an extent that it supports nationalism. However, it is indisputable that he fought against the British officials, amongst others, and lost his life to the cause.[47]

Interestingly, the people who struggled to curate Birsa's memory in the early years of the Jharkhand movement imagined the *samadhi sthal* in a different light. The following section explores those alternative imaginations about the model of remembrance that could have existed in a different form. It introduces a few key members of civil society who have done extensive work on Birsa Munda. I have chosen to focus on two interlocuters. Their contribution to the field of memorialization offers an overview of the *samadhi sthal*—the process, contestations and alternative imagination about the place.

Architecture of Memorial: Contesting Narrative of Remembrance

October 2018, Bariatu (Ranchi)

The passage that led to Anurag's house sliced through the area from the main road overlooking what we in Ranchi call 'Tagore Hill', famous amongst the city's youths as a place for romance. From the hilltop escarpment, one can take in a rapidly changing aerial view of the city. Coughing mildly from one corner of his red velvet sofa, Anurag insisted I should have a cup of tea.

Anurag Faisal is a journalist and has worked in the state for more than three decades. He worked closely with Kumar Suresh Singh in translating his book on Birsa. Over the past few years, he has captured some of the most dramatic events in state politics, with a particularly keen interest in Birsa Munda. He is also a driving force behind the making of the memorial. I accepted the offer of tea while Anurag had a word with a guest who had arrived before me. As the guest left his house, he asked that we move to another end of the room to a reclining sofa with some chairs arranged around it. Uninhibited by my voice recorder, he insisted that I start the interview. He put his faith in the project's ambitions.

As I began to talk about Birsa Munda, an eagerness drew over his face, and he moved the voice recorder closer. This was clearly not an occasion for an interview, where Birsa required an introduction. Upon my enquiring as to his understanding of Birsa, he promptly replied:

> Birsa can be understood in three folds within the contemporary landscape. First, the group of Adivasis who do not have any political affiliations; second is a group of people from the RSS [Rashtriya Swayamsevak Sangh] and the BJP; and the third is revolutionary forces [Maoists and the CPI]. There is another group of Jharkhandi political parties such as the JMM, the AJSU and other parties—they also have their own concept of Birsa.[48]

Classification of this sort was unusual but reaffirmed months of research data. He continued:

> We can see this as a phenomenon that explains the variety of political and non-political relevance of Birsa, as he was the first leader to have understood the roots of exploitation. He cornered a range of exploiters such as *zamindars*, the British, the insider British, and identified them as encroachers. For ordinary Adivasis whose land has not come under attack, they perceive Birsa Munda as a symbol of resistance who fought, when needed, against the outsiders.

An underlying theme was explaining how Birsa remains significant in how he is used politically. Emphasizing the role of the RSS, a Hindu voluntary organization that works at the grassroots level to promote the idea of a Hindu *rashtra* (nation state), is crucial. The organization is notorious for being linked to various cases such as the assassination of Mahatma Gandhi.[49] It has also been banned multiple times since independence. Christophe Jaffrelot's account of the RSS has influenced South Asian scholars' understanding of the organization to a significant extent. He claims that it was 'Hindu nationalism's thick layers of ideological and institutional entrenchment, cultivated over many decades by cadres across the country, that enabled the proliferation of Hindutva and its efforts to establish India as a Hindu *Rashtra*'.[50]

Anurag's emphasis on the RSS is a telling clue to the transformation of Birsa Munda into 'Birsa Bhagwan' across the state. Furthermore, he asserts that

> now the narrative of RSS is also interesting, especially in understanding the portrayal of Birsa as a Hindu, by framing his ideas as entirely anti-missionary and not anti-British. The same portrayal is in resurgence today. Birsa is reincarnated as a Hindu symbol by the RSS. He is not Hindu. Adivasi are not Hindu.[51]

The previous chapter laid out a similar discussion. However, the transformation of Adivasi culture and its incorporation into the Hinduized and Christianized ways of life raises serious concerns in the state and beyond. In the recent past, the practice of religious conversion had been discussed extensively by state politicians.

In 2017, the Jharkhand legislative assembly under the leadership of the BJP had passed a legislation entitled 'Religious Freedom Act'.[52] The Act makes forced and induced conversion a punishable and non-bailable offence, and has led to disputes across the political spectrum. While the BJP supported it to highlight the rise in the number of Christian converts, the opposition argued that there is an existing provision in the Constitution addressing forced conversion.[53] In this discussion, the voice of Adivasis, who are both the victims and the beneficiaries of conversion, is muffled. The politicians not only obscure the voice of subaltern Adivasis but also design models of governance for them. The discussion on religious freedom overlooks the question of Adivasi identity and the Adi Dharma. This is primarily due to the discomfort in addressing the historical reason behind the history of conversion in the state. Here, the struggle is not perhaps between the state and the church. It is, according to Gundal Munda, between the 'communist within the church and the state'.[54] He adds that the 'church is not a unified institution and has internally differentiated characteristics', which is also broadly analysed in Chapter 2.

In fact, the church has evolved as the state has been made: 'It tried to give itself a tribal face and have accepted Birsa as a tribal leader'.[55] Furthermore, as Gunjal added, 'a generation ago as told to me by my elders the church was opposed to singing and dancing culture amongst Adivasis until as late as the 1980s'.[56] The 'communist in the Church' is a reference to those who fought for Adivasi land rights against the *zamindar*s. Besides, the conversion is also a result of other forms of developments that have taken place, primarily in the form of education—the expansion of Ashram Schools formed under the Tribal Sub-Plan to 'increase education among the Schedule Tribes including the PVTGs [Particularly Vulnerable Tribal Groups]', for instance.[57] This provides free residential schools in the areas most affected by the Maoist insurgency. Despite considerable efforts to expand the schools, the dropout rate is 22 per cent higher than the national average.[58] The Standing Committee report on the working of Ashram Schools in tribal areas suggests one of the reasons for this is the language of instruction.[59]

Some activists and scholars have raised serious concerns about the expansion of the schools. Drawing on a Survival International report, Gladson Dungdung claimed that practices cultivated by the residential schools in tribal areas such as a ban on traditional ornaments, short hair and giving pupils Hindu names make it a site of 'cultural genocide'.[60] Calling these burgeoning schools sinister, he points out that the mining companies that dispossess Adivasis are now funding schools such as Adani Vidya Mandir, which was established and is financed by the Adani corporate group.[61]

This lays out the complex nature of the political space in the state. However, as Gunjal notes, there remains a tendency to distance the 'Adivasi cultural entity'. The question remains: What is the cultural identity of Adivasis? Does it operate in modalities of representation that we tend to see in the ever-changing indigenous politics led by 'middle-class activists' and the political elites, who further marginalize Adivasis through their 'class-based politics'?[62] How is the cultural identity of Adivasis displayed in memorial practices and commemorations?

The following section examines an alternative model of memorialization in which I argue that the cultural identity of Adivasis is folded into the religious, social and economic structures of society. To understand this cultural identity and modes of remembering, it is crucial to explore the epistemic category of the Adivasi lifeworld. To demonstrate the alternative or existing mnemonic practices that allow 'concretion of identity' of Adivasis, I also analyse a folk song to unravel the cosmic values associated with the place and the process of remembering.[63]

Memorial: A Site of Adivasi Cultural Laboratory and Munda Cosmic Structure

> There is a fetish in finding heroes. Unlike the manifold of Hindu icons, Birsa was one amongst equals. He had a vision, a leadership spark, but it was a collective effort that disrupted the order. I am personally worried about the way we seek heroes. It may render invisible other stories and the equality that distinguishes Adivasi society.
>
> —Meghnath[64]

Meghnath, who runs a small collective called *akhra*, seemed dismayed by the resurgence of Birsa's memory. For Meghnath, the worrying developments regarding Birsa lie in the appropriation of history. Having worked in the state of Jharkhand for more than three decades, he thinks that in Birsa politicians have found a political currency. He considers Adivasi leaders (including Birsa) as 'non-aggressors': those who took up arms to protect themselves. 'He [Birsa] should be remembered as a hero who fought for humanity,' Megnath said.⁶⁵ Referring to the resurgence of jingoism in the recent past and the depiction of Birsa as a soldier, he claimed: 'Birsa cannot be identified as a virile, aggressive person, who used the militant technique to sabotage anyone. He fought to defend.'⁶⁶

People are seeking an 'umbrella of memories to seek patronage from their identity', claims Meghnath. The recognition often grants them access to gaining personal popularity. It also allows individual clients to claim benefits from political parties that mobilize Birsa's memory (Figure 4.8). This is an interesting observation and is also relevant to the *samadhi sthal*. The use of memory as a political ploy complements the propaganda of elites who represent Adivasi icons.

Narratives of Memorialization: Individual and Collective Memory

After a brief discussion on political parties, I returned to seek Anurag's view on the memorialization of Birsa in the changing context of the built environment. He smiled and said: 'My cancer has shortened my memory to recall events.'⁶⁷ A strange stillness descended upon the room. I pleaded with him to pause the interview, but he insisted on continuing. He said that memory 'is not always an easily forgettable

Figure 4.8 A billboard—erected on the eve of Independence Day at Harmu Chowk in Ranchi, 2018—illustrating the aesthetic vision of nationalism in which Birsa Munda is equated to Indian soldiers to demonstrate his contribution to the nation

Source: Photograph by the author.

thing.... I remember we were a group of people. I remember Sardar Ji, who was the one to find out the place of Birsa's burial.' Drawing on a pattern of interconnected imagery, he attempted to verify the recalled memory, an idea that Yadin Dudai and Micah G. Edelson call 'personal memory'.[68] Personal memory works as a 'node in a highly distributed multi-dimensional memory space, in which the contribution of the individual is only part of an informational syncytium that transcends the personal'.[69] Of his recollection of the event, Anurag said:

> At the initial stage, we thought of his [Birsa's] memorial site as a place for 'Adivasi cultural laboratory'. We had hoped to make his presence through the memorial highlight the cause of his struggle. It would have signified a perspective of democracy, the fight for *jal, jungle aur jameen* in the light of a new state called Jharkhand. We wished to portray different quotes and excerpts from researched materials by historians, folk singers, that could serve as 'public memory' or as I would call 'folk memory'. However, I still believe that we must have a cultural laboratory for Birsa Munda, roughly imagined as *hor mitan* [meeting place], where tribals and their non-tribal friends meet. As long as we do not abandon the corporate mentality, we cannot fulfil this dream.[70]

Anurag and his colleague conceptualized the Adivasi cultural laboratory at the time when the Jharkhand movement was seeking inspiration. The idea was publicized in newspapers, and it became part of the political party agenda: to build the *samadhi sthal*. Contrary to this, the alternative imagination for the memorial would have inserted a consciousness of *hor mitan*—a place to curate Birsa's memory through dialogue with Adivasis. Drawing upon what Anurag calls 'folk memory', the memorial would have transcended the physical boundaries of its design and offered a place to produce a new cultural milieu, archive and memory for generations to come. 'Folk memory'—reflective of nostalgia, which 'dwells on the ambivalence of human longings and does not shy away from contradictions of modernity'—would have allowed an imaginative space of remembering.[71] In a sense, the *hor mitan* at the *samadhi sthal* would have transposed subaltern consciousness through constant recognition and rendering of the same power that structures the history of the 'other'. It would have exposed the fact that any form of remembering is an act of privileging the power of the dominant —it fails to represent the subject of representation. In other words, as Margery Sabin puts it in the context of writing about the subaltern consciousness, 'reading and writing about society's Other is always a mediated, partial, and imaginative construction. Accepting this truth makes interpretation more dramatic, more speculative ... allows for ... imagination, and uncertainty in the search for knowledge of society's Other.'[72]

Any commitment towards forging a collaborative and independent foundation in the state to build scholarship on Birsa Munda is negligible. An *akhra*, a group of civil society activists—Bosu, Anurag and other individuals such as Gunjal and Dayamani—try to address not only Birsa but also the broader Adivasi cultural milieu. This is also a moment to acknowledge the grit Anurag showed at a time in Jharkhand when members of the civil society faced abuse and were framed in charges of heinous crimes.[73] Such individual efforts uphold the memory of Birsa whose impression on the state is indelible.

The idea behind the social laboratory suggested an attempt at imagining the subaltern memory through collaborative efforts. It would have been a space that offered what Peter Berger calls a 'symbolic universe', where people bind themselves together with their experience and expectation to forge a new space of culture in a universe.[74] For the political elites, this idea did not seem to appeal to their ideological standpoint, and hence the memorial transmogrified into a *samadhi sthal*. It is undoubtedly a form of commemoration, but it removes the possibility to imagine the robust use of Birsa's political ideas. It was Birsa's vision to restore the Mundadom. The aspiration to break away from the colonizing forces, visible today in the form of starvation and landlessness, fails his ideas.[75] Now, unfortunately, on an ordinary day, the memorial is covered in dust, poorly painted and sits beside a *talab*. Remembrance is an occasion now. The memorial becomes relevant when it is about an event, a date in the calendar.

Does this suggest that in daily lives, memorials, as the *archaeology of the dead*, do not serve any purpose? How do we imagine a memorial as a site of memory in the specific context of Adivasis? In the case of Birsa, as an Adivasi who fought against the *diku*s, his memorial operates as a place of commemoration for political purposes and not for the sociality of emotions and memories. Today, the space reflects the 'scarcity of memory' as ontological homesickness to regain the 'blessed state'.[76] It results in a nostalgia that is uninformed about the past. These commemoration sites provide an opportunity neither for the community nor for individuals to draw an organic relationship between the past and the present. They remain relics in the museum of memory.

The following section analyses an adjunct site of commemoration related to Birsa and his *ulgulan* to illustrate the archaeology of the dead and address the question of commemoration. The site is known as Dombari Buru (also known as Sail Rakab). I argue that Dombari Buru is a site of memory that remains significant in shaping the historical memory of Birsa and his *ulgulan*. It dovetails the past seated in the collective memory of Adivasis into a new form of temporality that locates the relevance of Birsa in contemporaneous time. I pursue this temporality as a source under the idea of the landscape. The landscape as memory reorients the temporal form of physical space as material value. It adds to it a cosmic value that operates within an Adivasi worldview. It reiterates that these sites are not 'merely cultural' but instead offer an imagination where the material and spiritual cohabit.

Stone Slabs as *Aide Mémoire*: Dombari Hill, a Landscape of Rebellion and Remembrance

> Chota Nagpore is a land without a written history, and records are few of all that occurred more than a hundred years ago. Legends only have passed down from generation to generation, gathering additions as they went, and obvious fables have been invented to account for the causes of those things that baffle the limited native intelligence and defy authentic explanation. It is a land of mystery, witchcraft, and spirits, mostly evil and malign that cause the ignorant, shrinking native to pass his whole life in fear and dread and unceasing attempts at propitiation.
>
> —Francis Bradley Bradley-Birt[77]

Written in 1903 and based on his excursion in the region, this excerpt from Bradley's work portrays a classical frame for imagining the Orient. Such descriptions of the 'tribes' who dwell in a darkness devoid of history were rather common in the ethnographic studies conducted in this region. The British officials, ethnographers and upper-caste Hindus perceived the 'tribals' in Chota Nagpur as examples of 'savage men' who belonged to 'barbaric civilization' and were often viewed as 'non-Aryan' racialized subjects.[78] These descriptions supplemented the process of rendering the oral and non-written records as non-history or 'mystery'.[79]

However, the region is fraught with what I would call *counter-memory*. Not only had the populace in this region confront the Raj, but they also actively negotiated with it as a historical agent. Therefore, I build on the effective use of a specific historical landscape (Dombari Buru) to demonstrate the role of memory in the Adivasi community. In doing so, I offer an analysis of archival material from the 19th century, combined with field notes, to present the contemporaneous nature of memory that makes Dombari Buru an *aide mémoire*, a reminder of the past in the present.

Dombari Buru: The History

Dombari Buru is significant for the Adivasi community—a landscape of historical memory. It is a hilltop that is part of the village of Sail Rakab and stands as a monumental site of memory in the Chota Nagpur region. The site evokes a range of historical emotions and allows people to remember the past: a place where Birsaites fought against the British troops to assert 'Raj is ours, not theirs and that [we] intend to fight for it and get it'—an idea that echoes through the sprawling resistance movements in Jharkhand today.[80] A. Forbes, the commissioner of Chota Nagpur, noted:

> At 8 pm, I received [a message] from Dr Nottrott, head of the German Lutheran Mission to the Koles.... I found that Dr Notrott, fully impressed with the seriousness of the situation and the great danger, in the existing state of the revolt of the followers of Birsa, to the Christian community generally, and especially to the European members of the different staffs.[81]

Dr Notrott, a teacher who taught in a missionary school where Birsa Munda notably rebelled against Christianity for the first time, reports the trouble caused by Birsa and his followers to the establishment embodied by *saheb lok* (white Europeans and *zamindar*s). The threat emerged against the backdrop of alienation from the land but more sporadically as a reaction against the repression of Mundas in Chota Nagpur. Birsa Munda and his followers led the Mundas' struggle to assert their territorial claims and fend off the outsiders. Sail Rakab was one of the significant sites of the uprising. It witnessed the bloodshed of those who not only believed in Birsa's political teachings but also organized themselves to wage resistance as a militant outfit against the *diku*s. The confrontation between the troops and the Mundas cited in the record illustrates the importance of the encounter. Forbes wrote:

> Captain Rooke and I now called the men together, as we saw that there was no chance of their overtaking any of the fugitives, and we were apprehensive of their using their firearms indiscriminately in their excited state. We found four dead and three wounded, and I deeply regret to say that, in the jungle behind the insurgents' position, we also found three dead bodies of women and one dead boy and a little child badly injured ... on further search, however, we found that these misguided people had, in many instance brought their whole families with them; apparently thinking the position a perfectly safe and impregnable retreat;

and two old men, one young man, and as many as twenty women, and eight children were discovered hiding in caves and concealed in the jungle amidst rocks.[82]

This lays out a plan and manoeuvre by British officials to deal with the Mundas. It is particularly interesting to emphasize the role of British officials, who understood the rebels as 'fugitives' in their own homeland and found them in their 'excited state'. It was their historical alienation from their land through a series of new processes such as the *bhuinhari* tenures that had caused this 'excitement'.[83] Missionaries and *zamindar*s assisted the officials in arresting the rebels. These rebels were ordinary residents of the homeland, the Munda *raj*, an identity that continues to shape their claims on the region. For Mundas, the excitement emerged from the searing effects of deprivation caused by the prolonged attack on their land. The officials stationed in the area also realized this. H. C. Streatfield foresaw the possibility of a rebellion in a letter dated 4 January 1900 in which he characterized the uprising in the following terms:

> These outrages are the outcomes of years of sedition and agitation among the Mundas, though it would be absurd to represent them as amounting agitation to a rebellion or rising among the Mundas. There can be no doubt whatever they amount to an organized attempt to terrorise the district by a series of 'moonlight' murders, attempts at murder, and acts of incendiarism, into accepting Birsaite religion and the Birsaite Raj.[84]

The passage highlights a great sense of identity drawn on their own vision of kingdom as against the usage of *raj* as a category to define British rule.[85] Mundas identify the Munda *raj* as their homeland. Therefore, the dismissal of the Mundas' attachment to their land cannot be seen from the universal category of property such as law that defines rights to land. Specifically, the introduction of new laws attempted to disentangle the culture of belonging from the land in an area where the past (ancestors) speaks to the present through the medium of the land—memories that are crafted through intergenerational knowledge in folklores, stories and collective memory. For Adivasis, the land was not a legal subject or even a place subject to definition by the law. The land was not a property; it was and remains a landscape of memory. Any form of aggression against their land was an aggression against their identity as Adivasi.

The indigenous notion of land amongst Mundas has preconditions of ancestral lineage sustained by a variety of mediums, such as *sasandiri* (burial graveyard). A graveyard stone defines the notion of belonging that establishes the relationship

Figure 4.9 A stone slab in the middle of a field representing the *sasandiri* practice in Sail Rakab village, Khunti district

Source: Photograph by the author.

between the dead and the living—an interstitial space is mediated by cosmovision for which there is no place in law (Figure 4.9). Before the arrival of the British, and under the helm of the local *raja*, the 'dispossession of tribals from their ancestral land was minimal' and therefore did not cause significant disruption.[86] This raises a significant point of difference that exists in the way Europeans and the indigenous peoples understood physical entities such as land. This draws our attention to similar tensions that arose in other places across the globe. In the context of Aboriginals in Australia, Nichole Graham notes a similar conflict of meaning:

> The placelessness or atopia of law was the ideological condition of the colonisation of the world and the imposition of alien regimes of property. The absence of place is the condition of the possibility of a universal and universalising law that can extend across the globe, like a coinage reducing all things to a common measure.[87]

This conception of law as universalizing force is useful in explaining the formidable resistance led by the Munda agitation. The resistance organized by the Mundas at Sail Rakab was not merely a demonstration of an excited state—a temperamental attitude or messianic belief in Birsa Munda and his religion—but rather solidarity forged by mounting anxiety due to the consistent failure to protect the land. Therefore, in the Munda *raj*, the land is not merely property that is produced by the 'absence' of place and culture.[88] The land in the Munda *raj* is a constellation of cultural memory and cosmovision sustained and interlaced with the physical entity (material) that defines the 'connective structure' of the society in its 'social-temporal' relation to the past.[89]

The next section illustrates how it became the plot for sub-national politics in the region. In that process, Sail Rakab came to acquire an imaginary of remembrance—an Adivasi memoryscape. Birsaites visit the place to this day to observe the tragic loss of lives. The commemoration is not observed by the 'scarcity of memory' to regain the 'blessed state' but rather works as a continuous reminder or 'index' of the Munda struggle.[90]

Sail Rakab is a village in Khunti district (Figure 4.10). Created as the 23rd district in the state of Jharkhand in 2007 and situated 40 kilometres away from the state capital, Khunti was known for the Maoist movement in the recent past and forms a part of the red corridor.[91] The ongoing disruption caused by the warfare between the state and the Maoists meant that the villages barely experienced any growth or access to government schemes. In fact, it is the district in both the state and the country most affected by the warfare.

Dombari Buru: The Memory

Despite the newly constructed highway nearby being widened to six lanes, the village reflects the glaring presence of poverty. Sail Rakab is sparsely populated. It is possible to reach the village by vehicle on a single-lane road assembled from

Figure 4.10 The constellation of hills surrounding the lush green landscape of Sail Rakab, Khunti district

Source: Photograph by the author.

uneven patches of asphalt and concrete. The isolated route from the highway to the village cuts through a broad swathe of forest. One is likely to spot military vehicles and flags of different colours and affiliations—forming a unique array of confrontations and symbolism.

However, what distinguishes Sail Rakab is its extensive process of memorializing Birsa Munda. Initiatives such as the Archaeological Survey of India's (ASI) facelift programme and the Shaheed Gram Vikas Yojana (Rural Martyr Development Scheme), amongst others, are rapidly transforming the landscape.[92] The government of Jharkhand launched the Shaheed Gram Vikas Yogjana to 'uplift the tribal areas'. It aims to bring development to areas of the rural martyr, Birsa, who fought against the British. BJP president, Amit Shah, and the then chief minister, Raghuvar Das, launched the programme in Birsa Munda's hometown of Ulihatu. Responding to the programme, Birsa's grandson said: 'They come to us once in a while. Things are spruced up. Then things remain the same. They are coming again now. We hope that this time the assurance becomes a reality.' Specifically, the initiative to develop Dombari Hill as a new tourism venue suggests two significant points. First, it explains the production of post-colonial capital. Second, it suggests the nature and use of collective memory. The latter situate how the collective memory is 'excessively biased in transmitting the historical episode into the present'.[93] However, there is varied use of collective memory. On the one hand, it is a mnemonic tool for any community to remember the past. On the other hand, it can also become a political tool to seek an entry into historically significant places such as Dombari.

Dombari Buru as Pan-ethnic Memory: Mistrust and the Field

The making of Dombari Buru as a historic landscape in contemporary Khunti is crucial to the extension of tension that exists between the narrative of development and the people. The memory-making of Dombari represents a twofold process. First, the process involves the significance of Dombari within the cultural milieu of the Adivasi lifeworld, popularly articulated through the medium of folk songs (R. D. Munda's work) and Birsaites' performance of rituals in order to commemorate Birsa. Every year, a group of Adivasis leads a procession up to the hilltop, singing and chanting Birsa *bhajans* (hymns). In the Adivasi cultural milieu, Dombari reflects a deep sense of loss and invokes historical bereavement, but it also emerges as a 'pan-ethnic' memory, primarily anchored through songs.[94] Second, the state has sought to develop it as a site of memory. This has entailed the installation of a stone slab on top of Dombari Hill (Figure 4.11). However, the uneven terrain with its canopy of trees, recent resistance movements and Maoist influence make the area sensitive.

Figure 4.11 A stone slab on Dombari Hill bearing the names of people who were killed on 9 January 1900

Source: Photograph by the author.

On frequent visits during my somewhat interrupted stay in this area, the use of a camera and notebook and, importantly, my non-Adivasi background, raised concerns. This reflects an interesting insight into *deep* subaltern constituencies within the shadow of the state. I use *deep* as a way of explaining an entangled visual description. This foremost reflects the indisputable tension between the state and the people (including the Maoists). It variously explains difficulties in conducting any work in the region, which is shaped by unequal relationships, based on exceptional mistrust towards *diku*s as well as *sadan*s. Against such a backdrop, any negotiation emerges from a continuous display of solidarity—a place that defines my position in writing, thinking and living in the region.

Otherwise undervalued in the narratives of fieldwork, mistrust, as an idea and lived experience, defines the scope of any research on memory. The continual apathy of the state towards the Adivasi community has strengthened the narrative of mistrust. Any valiant attempt to bridge the gap begins by forging friendship at any possibility. Matthew Carey's compelling ethnographic account of *mistrust* defines the possibility of friendship as follows:

> [F]riendships ... are not about disclosure and the blurring of personal or moral boundaries, but [they] recognize and embrace the alterity of others as both a source of risk and pleasure. Mistrust at the heart of human relations also affects collective activity and political practice. It is the fundamental unreliability and untrustworthiness of others that gives rise to a political sphere predicated on ephemerality and contingency, one that is oriented toward the concrete and eschews abstract concepts of the good.[95]

The precarious state of the Adivasi community shapes their relationship with the state. *Unreliability* and *untrustworthiness* become watchwords in dealing with anything or anyone from outside the community. The state's renewed interest in Birsa's heritage enables a mode of entry into the village that has no bearing on any structural change within the constituency. Any development concerning heritage-making confronts the material reality of the region—visceral poverty. Therefore, mistrust takes the central stage in defining relationships.

Bearing Witness: Visual Narrative

In popular memory—such as that of my participant, who I will call Bharmi Munda—Dombari Hill offers an inexplicable sense of collective memory.

While on the one hand it reflects grief and mourning for lives lost, on the other it is a site of pride and honour.[96] The association of grief with the site emerges against the background of long-standing *mulki ladai*, the struggle to restore the Mundadom. However, this grief also transforms into a sense of pride in realizing the defeat of systemic violence that had historically denied Adivasis from reclaiming their territory. Therefore, the landscape of Dombari is significant as a site of collective memory amongst the Adivasi community. The place acquires a metaphorical meaning in the making of the landscape. It becomes a metaphor of *ulgulan*—the rebellion. As shown in Figure 4.14, the memorial pillar bears the names of those who lost their lives in the battle. It works as a form of memory against forgetting.

The pillar stands as a marker of collective memory. As a material object (stone), it acquires contemporaneous characteristics to constitute a collective identity of Adivasis crystallized by the memory of the past. The history of Dombari, Bharmi says, is the 'present in the past'—emerging as forms of multiple temporalities. It does not limit the scope of defining the importance of the hill only as *a relic of the past* but rather functions as an *aide-mémoire*.

As part of the sensorial experience, I understood how the visual pillar becomes part of the ethnographic description to illustrate the texture of memory. In fact, the visual images are as 'inevitable as sounds, smells, textures and tastes, words or any other aspect of culture and society'.[97] In effect, the pillar marks the memory and attracts a congregation of Birsaites on 9 January every year to commemorate people who lost their lives. In doing so, it situates the symbolic importance of remembering for Adivasis. The congregation is an elaborate process that involves various rituals including the chanting and singing of hymns for those sacrificed for the Mundadom. Therefore, each segment of memory—stone slab, songs and hymns—constitutes the materiality of the same (Figures 4.12 and 4.13). It highlights the role of commemoration within the Adivasi community that harvests the memory through various indexes and reminders.

Narratives of Landscape and Memory
September 2018, Sail Rakab

My friend and members of the civil society based in Ranchi initially turned down my request to visit the Dombari Buru, the primary reason being the massive presence of Maoist groups and the rise of the Pathalgadi movement in the region.[98] However, upon subsequent meetings, two collaborators, Puri and Rabi Munda, decided to visit the area and arrange for the stay.[99] We drove to Dombari early

Figure 4.12 Birsaites gathered at Dombari Hill to commemorate the memory of their ancestors, 9 January 2017

Source: Photograph by Rupesh.

Figure 4.13 Birsaites on their way to the Dombari hilltop in Sail Rakab, Khunti district

Source: Photograph by Rupesh.

in the morning. Khunti district is 40 kilometres away from Ranchi, with the expected growth of the mineral business in the area leading to the construction of a highway. National Highway 20, which runs to Dombari from Ranchi city, is broad, smooth and expected to be widened. Hundreds of heavy trucks transporting the masses of red soil and coal that characterize the uniqueness of Jharkhand as a mineral-reserve state frequent the highway. The red soil and sand are crucial to the state economy.[100]

As we drove past the last point on the Ranchi city limits, Birsa Mrig Vihar (a forest reserve for deer) and a billboard welcomed travellers to the area. A long line of trees on either side formed a canopy over the road. As the soil often spills from the overfilled trucks, the road had become muddied. The growing number of shops that had sprung up along the highway, selling everything from bottled water to Mughlai food, offered a familiar tableau of capitalist expansion in rural belts. My stay in this region coincided with the Pathalgadi movement to which I return at length in the next chapter. The stones became visible as we took a turn from the highway and towards the village. The stone bearing the excerpts of the Constitution of India brought discomfort to the state—a background impression that I drew from popular media. The motorbike we were travelling on suddenly began to cut left and right across the road, avoiding holes left by vanishing asphalt and concrete. The entrance to the village offers a primal glance of how inequalities shape lives. Mud houses began to appear on either side of the road as people seemed to be peeping out at us.

Soon after we parked the motorbike under the tree, Puri and I went to meet an older man, Gaya Munda, who was sitting by the edge of a low wall overseeing his goats. Extending his *johar* (greetings), Puri began his conversation in Mundari. I tried to fit in a few words with my functional knowledge of the language to seek his permission to spend some time in his village—a lesson I learned where a *sadan* (an outsider but not a *diku*) must seek the permission of the *panch* (headmen). Besides, the space and culture that co-constitute the only medium for conversation is perhaps rooted in recognizing one's own position. This recognition as an outsider provides space for people in the community to offer their words of acceptance, intimacy or sometimes refusal to a distant foreigner. Notably, the villages in Chota Nagpur have witnessed waves of migration by outsiders coming to work in industries. The mining companies have damaged not only the 'sacred landscape' of Adivasis but also their cultural milieu and cosmic structure that define their lifeworld.[101] I will return to this later in detail in the next chapter.

Upon our request, Gaya Munda agreed to take us to the top of Dombari Hill (Figure 4.14). The path up to the hill is patchy and uneven. The compound that

Figure 4.14 The memorial pillar on Dombari Hill with a symbol of the sun in the middle

Source: Photograph by the author.

leads to the hill had old white paint on the wall, a running hand pump and a small school nearby. Its gate was open to all visitors. Kids were using it as a playground. Inside the compound there was a statue of Birsa Munda with a stone slab, the *menhir* (Figure 4.15). The statue offered a rather interesting view, almost confusing given its purpose, being placed on a raised plinth but surrounded by a spiral staircase that partially concealed the statue's body. The presence of the staircase casts doubt on its making and purpose as it seemingly hides the presence of Birsa. Gaya said: 'It was built for the convenience of the politicians to garland.'[102] It rendered a reflection of Birsa and his valorous past in a politically convenient form. That is to say, the question of memory does not define the aesthetic design and importance of the icon. Such a design also removes the power of visuality—the posture, colour and size that shapes the public memory.

A Tale of Memory Pilgrimage: The Historical and the Memorial

With this conversation with Gaya, we began to climb the rocky foothills of Dombari. As we climbed our way up and down—Gaya kept looking back for me as I was struggling to walk at his pace. Along the way, as it began to drizzle, we came across young boys and girls taking shelter under the branches of trees. Everyone waiting under their trees watched us as we walked past. They were grazing their cows and goats, while in the distance someone was playing the flute.

'Burying the Dead, Creating the Past'   187

Figure 4.15 The statue of Birsa Munda at the entrance of the Dombari Buru gateway

Source: Photograph by the author.

I could not resist asking Gaya about the importance of this place as we reached the top of the hill. He said: 'Our ancestors have laid their lives here against the outsiders. It is a place of historic memory for us. We mourn and seek inspiration. On 9 January every year Birsaites come here to pray. God, what a great feeling we have that day.'[103]

Disputing the official number from the historical description (see Chapter 3), Gaya said: 'Hundreds of people died here.'[104] I promptly asked him how people perceive the place. He said they saw it as the site of 'death of their people but for a cause'.¹⁰⁵ This description of a higher number of deaths than that given in official accounts foregrounds the role of the actor who writes the history. The official numbers offer what the British officials wished to record, given the nature of the investigation, the dispute over numbers and records prepared by officials. The lives counted by officials certainly act as evidence in colonial records, but they fail to capture the enormity of the trauma, a seeming frustration against outsiders and the collective memory of the movement. The tale of memory as narrated by Gaya for this pilgrimage to the hill represents the collective memory of the Adivasi community when they gather every year to mourn the loss and remember their ancestors. The failure of the official narrative to correspond with lived experience and memory of the community is not unusual. In fact, it situates the continuing *modes of remembrance* that emerge from the cultural milieu and vernacular sources that shape the language of the past in the present.¹⁰⁶

In the following section, I outline an emerging trend in the process of memorialization by using the case study of a stone installation at Dombari Hill. It shows the political use of historical memory and focuses on the institutional measures taken by the state to make it a site of memory. I argue that Dombari Buru offers a unique vantage point to understand the intersection between three different strands: memory, capital and post-colonial. I show that in the process of crystallization, memory sometimes operates within the 'closed horizons of global capital, and it cannot but be affected and animated by the constraints and the compulsions this closure imposes'.¹⁰⁷ At the intersection of these strands lies the possibility of imagining a new form of memory politics. It underscores the potential of capital to seek entry into historical memory through an affective appeal to memorialization that remains occluded from the narrative of development politics. The contradiction that emerges from memory, post-colonial and capital strands seems speculative but merits an investigation. Dombari offers a possible venue to highlight such a contradiction.

Memory as Capital: A Tale of a Memorial Pillar at Dombari

Against the background of collective memory, the state of Jharkhand has made few advances towards memorializing Birsa and his heritage. The memorial pillar on Dombari Hill is one such attempt at memorialization. The memorialization has a seductive appeal that allows the flow of capital in the area, which has historically remained at the margins of development. In other words, as Alan Milward writes, 'the history of memory represents that stage of consumption in which the latest product, ego-history, is the image of the self not only marketed but also consumed by the self'.¹⁰⁸ The renewed interest in recovering the historical memory, thereby consuming the past through tourism, emerges from an excessive desire to commemorate regional heroes. It allows the mobilization of a nationalist vision—the celebration of the martyrdom of Birsa Munda. The problem as such does not lie in the atypical historical records that dispute such claims but within the selective framing of the canon.[109] Essentially, the recovery of memory becomes a tool of forgetting, 'which is constitutive in the formation of a new identity' in the light of anti-colonial canonization.[110] The following description addresses both.

In 2012, the ASI announced a 'sterling facelift' under the supervision of superintending archaeologist N. G. Nikoshey.[111] The 'heritage makeover' emerged as the defining motivation.[112] In this process of heritage-making, the past is carved out of the rocky hills amid a dense forest to allow 'tourists' to visit the historical place. In this respect, it is noteworthy that 10 lakh rupees (14,000 dollars) were earmarked to develop the place as a 'tourist magnet' through the installation of the memorial pillar on the hilltop.[113] Little has been written about the significance of Dombari, but the emerging turn towards the 'historic' heritage-making is already underway for the tourist to change the landscape.

Here, memory becomes a potential site to generate capital. It draws upon the 'memory boom' which reflects on 'widespread identity politics' that is predominant in the West.[114] In post-colonial spaces, it becomes a complex process that allows for the utilization of the past (eventful and episodic memory) as a form of withdrawal from the material condition of the claimants. That is to say, the post-colonial contradiction of the capital that relies on the semi-feudal model defines the scope and scale of memorialization.

The memorial pillar as it remains today in Dombari brought little change to the lives of those whose ancestors have made this a historic landscape. In fact, the school that functions beside the gateway to the hill does not even teach in Mundari. It does not have a secondary or higher secondary programme. Its textbooks do not refer to their ancestral history. The stage next to the statue inside the compound has become a children's playground. Considering the everyday struggles of the village posed by 'adverse inclusion' and increased rate of militancy, memory has become a medium of cultural survival for people, while the state thinks of it as an asset. The language of heritage in this process has transformed the idea of memory.

Post-colonial Capital and Folk Memory

The proposition above poses a few questions. First, how do memory and landscape generate any value to the community and reveal the unique relationship with capital? Second, does it also indicate that memory continues to be treated as non-political capital? The unique characteristic of post-colonial development is relevant in explaining the phenomena of heritagization of Dombari. The conditions of post-colonial development not only explain the necessity of memorialization as a medium to articulate the past but are also those on which memorialization stands today in 'non-capital' spaces such as Dombari. Sanyal offers a formulation that clarifies the role of capital in such spaces:

> The 'other' of capital is now *non-capital*, which articulates itself with capital, and the institution of the market constitutes the space in which the articulation resides. In other words, commodity relations integrate capital and non-capital to form the post-colonial *economic*.... Capitalist development in this scenario means not a structural shift from non-capital to capital, but the development of the entire *capital-non-capital complex*.[115]

The capital–non-capital complex illustrates the complicated role of historical condition as well as of space. Belonging and memory are tropes that explain it. The non-capital notion of Dombari and the importance of the historical landscape offer conditions to transform the heritage as placemaking plan. This new political articulation of heritage placemaking for the audience outside the fold of lived memory or representation complicates the relationship between the community and the state. The latter makes extensive efforts to produce the memory that can effectively incorporate people of non-indigenous background through the rhetoric of heritage.

Significantly, the 'grand narrative of modernity that contains subtexts of forgetting' transforms the historic importance of Dombari as the new site of memory.[116] The primary objective behind the transformation of the place is 'unleashed by the advent of the capitalist world market that tears down feudal and ancestral limitations on a global scale' to accommodate new modes of capital production.[117] The state enforces the ordeal of the past in two ways. On the one hand, it extends its control of 'landscape-as-power', where the existing community is suspended from the duty of ownership and the state takes charge of the asset. On the other, it uses the absence of memory (atypical historical source) as a precondition for the creation of the same in the former case: The state actively designs, reformulates and shapes the route of memory in order for capital to penetrate the territory. While for years the place suffered amnesia, it is now a site of memory shaped by the effective use of political propaganda to make it significant. Infrastructure is one factor (Figure 4.16) amongst many: construction through the call for tenders advertised by the Tourism Department in the name of

'Burying the Dead, Creating the Past' 191

Figure 4.16 The compound that hosts the stage and the statue beside the gateway to Dombari Hill—alternatively used by children who attend the school (the building in the background with shutters)

Source: Photograph by the author.

'Development of Ulihatu and Dombari Buru Hill as Heritage Tourism Destination, in Khunti District'.[118]

In this process, those who have accentuated the importance of the Dombari landscape not as an external agent for the tourist but as sites of 'landscape-construction and so of identity-formation' are written off in this new capital venture.[119] The site becomes a place to attract the external agent to qualify the meaning of memory and transform the nature of the landscape into a form of touristic consumption.

Matt Hodges has argued that in the context of rural France the 'rural heritage tourism co-habits with, and co-opts other "modern" practices of remembering, frequently through local disciplinary programmes pursued by new middle classes comprised of entrepreneurial incomers and some locals'.[120] The fantasy of rural wilderness amongst the urban middle class to catch a glimpse of the historical landscape of Birsa sits at the heart of the contradiction. This contradiction stems from a systematic exclusion of the participants of memory: the Adivasi community and its desire for belonging. Not only does the contradiction reflect strategic planning, a sort of entrepreneurial income as highlighted above by the state to design the past, but it also highlights the specific nature of capital. In fact, it becomes the condition to enable expansion. In other words, the non-capital memory generates profits by lending capital the imagination of heritage.

Broadly, the 'invention of tradition' is a characteristic of a modern nation state.[121] It is precisely the continuing Adivasi community practices such as the procession up the hill and orality (songs) that attach significant value to the site. The modern state builds upon compatible versions of traditions—that is, by retaining and appropriating such 'continuing traditions from social life'.[122] This, in turn, creates the opportunity for capital to co-opt new venues while not radically disrupting the scale of memorialization. In other words, the intimate value of the site that is contained in the folk memory of the community transmogrifies into the notion of property as capital memory. In this process, the figure (Birsa Munda) is transformed from a regional canon to the idea of a national hero. His image becomes the part of the nation that 'commands such profound emotional legitimacy'—paving a way for capital alongside the process of memorialization.[123]

The property now holds a marketable value for tourism and political campaigning. A whole *kasba* (locality) transforms into a historical pilgrimage that invites tourists to take a safari through the past. For Adivasis, the past is now found amidst a busy road frequented by outsiders. Rashmi Varma reflects on this correspondence between the modern and the primitive. She writes: 'Pushing the colonial archive into the postcolonial period requires one to examine how this figure circulates—in the official and bureaucratic policy … as a complex of sedimented images of primitivism and backwardness, insurgency and deprivation—against which "modern" citizens define themselves.'[124]

Certain subjects of the colonial imagination were reified in independent India. Amongst others, the figure of the Adivasi emerged in the most elaborate fashion. 'Primitivism and backwardness' became almost invariably accepted vocabulary with which to speak about Indian modernity. Varma has shown that 'art itself exposes that process of commodification and accumulation on a global scale and offers resistance to it'.[125] This is a critical insight in thinking about the agency of Adivasis in the resistance against the outsiders. However, it fails to consider the role of institutions in containing and redefining the resistance. Notably, in the case of Dombari the state does not resist the social lifeworld of the subaltern; instead, it absorbs it into the symbolic memorialization of the canon—Birsa Munda and his followers.

The state uses various technologies of governance to assist the idea of nationalism. Akhiil Gupta reflects on the complementary role of nationalism and capitalism. He writes: 'Nation and nationalism themselves undergo a transformation during their existence … and capitalist transformations may fundamentally alter not only the modality, but also the content of nationalism and what it means to be a nation.'[126] In turn, this suggests that capital exploits the Adivasi memory to expand the frontier of control and production of value.

In other words, the existence of 'native memory' here is a precondition for the entry of the capital. The landscape of Dombari therefore offers a narrative of anti-colonial legacy and now of capital-induced nationalism. It isolates the historical possibilities to understand the scope of Birsa and his movement in the light of sub-national polity. In fact, it folds the scenic beauty of the forested area into nationalism by enforcing this amnesia on both the visitors and the residents of the village. This leads us to ask a few questions. First, do we have an alternative imagination for the commemoration of Birsa? What are the alternative mediums through which *the subalterns speak and remember* in this context? How can we use the Adivasi cultural milieu and knowledge system to learn about the landscape of memory? The next section explores these questions.

Memory as Culture: Alternative Imagination of Ulgulan *in Folk Songs*

As opposed to the idea of 'landscape construction' that illustrates the authoritative role of the state, Dombari also emerges as a site for collective memory for the community. Dombari Hill is where Adivasis graze their cattle and play their flutes, asserting their landscape of memory. On any ordinary day it is a place comprising lush, green, forested meadows and a quiet hilltop. Therefore, within the cultural milieu that evokes practices shared by the community in the process of remembering, Dombari is also 'landscape construction as identity'. As Sumit Sarkar writes, this is the place where Birsa gave his clarion call: 'Katong baba Katong. Saheb Katong. Rari Katong Katong …' (O father, kill the Europeans, kill the other castes, O kill, kill …).[127]

To situate the significance of cultural milieu as non-capital memory, it is essential to locate the sources that are not necessarily official accounts but continue to emerge as cultural history. Here, Dombari can be understood in two ways. One dominant form of representation as accentuated by the state is the drive towards capital memory that has no bearing on the collective participation of the community and produces steering effects through tourism. At another level, the landscape continues to remain the site of memory within the community through cultural practices. The latter suffers from a lack of analysis due to its nature and unavailability of sources.

Unlike Dalits, who have increasingly developed their archives drawn out of 'life-writing as a repository of facts about Dalit lives', Adivasi historiography remains thin and often has to rely on sources that are mainly defined by colonial bureaucracy or supplemented with 'self-reflexive forms of field-work and anthropological writing'.[128] This book combines both. It has proven to be more difficult in the recent past, given the military confrontation between the state and the Maoists. The history of Adivasi is woven from the cultural sources that contain affective articulation of the past, seemingly described through oral history, folk songs and material culture, including graveyard practices. However, these practices always emerge in footnotes and appendices. They fail to register the central affect, culture and memory-as-politics.

In what follows, I will analyse a folk song to demonstrate the idea of 'landscape construction' with Adivasi folk songs, whereby songs become the history.[129] The use of folksong to explain the role of memory in Adivasi society is prevalent. Singh famously used songs in his work. However, his work treats folk songs as appendices—suggesting an additional role of memory in constructing a history that is otherwise objective and chronological. In showing the centrality of memory within the context of Dombari, I wish to differ from such an approach. I believe songs are sources in the cultural milieu of Adivasis that define the political structure and unveil the importance of the cosmic value of the land. Evidently, they also become a tool for constructing identity. For instance, the folk song presented here is translated into Hindi from Mundari to situate the significance of Mundari language that is now rarely used in Jharkhand.

डोमबारी बुरु चेतान रे	डोमबारी पहाड़ पर
डोमबारी बुरु चेतार रे	डोमबारी पहाड़ के ऊपर
ओकोए दुमाङ रूतानाको सुसुनताना।	कौन मांदर बजा रहा है, लोग नाच रहे हैं ।
डोमबारी बुरु लातार रे	डोमबारी बुरु लातार रे
चिमाए बिगुल साड़िताानाको सांगिलाकादा ॥	कौन बिगुल बजा रहा है, लोग ऊपर ताक रहे हैं ॥
डोमबारी बुरु चेतार रे	डोमबारी पहाड़ के ऊपर

'Burying the Dead, Creating the Past'

बिरसा दुमाङ रूतानाको सुसुनताना ।	बिरसा मांदर बजा रहा है, लोग नाच रहे हैं ।
डोमबारी बुरु लातार रे	डोमबारी पहाड़ के नीचे
सायोब बिगुल साड़िंतानाको सांगिलाकादा ।।	साहब बिगुल बजा रहा है, लोग ऊपर ताक रहे हैं ।।
जोनोम दिसुम नागेनेगे	जन्म देळा के लिए ही
बिरसा दुमाङ रूतानाको सुसुनताना ।	बिरसा मांदर बजा रहा है, लोग नाच रहे हैं ।
गोली चालाओ नागेनेगे	गोली चलाने के लिए ही
सायोब बिगुल साड़िंतानाको सांगिलाकादा ।।	साहब बिगुल बजा रहा है, लोग ऊपर ताक रहे हैं ।।
गोली बारूद चाबाजाना	गोली बारूद खत्म हुए
बिरसा दुमाङ रूतानाको सुसुनताना ।	बिरसा मांदर बजा रहा है, लोग नाच रहे हैं ।
डोमबारी बुरु चेतान रे	डोमबारी पहाड़ के ऊपर लोग
जोनोम दिसुम आबुआ:को काकालाताना ।।	'जन्म देळा हमारा है' को गूंजित कर रहे हैं ।।[130]

Dulae Chandra Munda originally wrote the song 'डोमबारी बुरु चेतान रे' (Dombari Buru Chetan Re). After that, the song was popularized by the late R. D. Munda, who sang it on various occasions before it came to be recorded.[131] Describing the importance of Dombari Hill, the author begins on an inquisitive note by saying that 'someone is playing the मांदर (*mandar*) at the top of Dombari and people are dancing to the tune'.[132] The *mandar* is a drum-like musical instrument specific to the Adivasis in the region and is used widely in various festivals. Dulae Chandra goes on to say 'डोमबारी पहाड़ के नीचे कौन बिगुल बजा रहा है, लोग ऊपर ताक रहे हैं.ङ्ग बिरसा मांदर बजा रहा है, लोग नाच रहे है' (On the foothills, someone is playing *bigul* [an instrument], and people are looking above … oh, Birsa is playing the *mandar* and people are dancing to it). The use of drumbeats suggests the temper of the moment caught in the certainty of war—explaining the strategic use of mediums for communication.

To set the stage at the top of Dombari, *mandar* is crucial to the congregation and Birsa is playing it. Birsa is playing to call for his people to come together, who are dancing to his tune; meanwhile, someone else is playing the *bigul* in the foothills, and they are all heading up the hill. The *bigul* player is identified with the *saheb*—a word used to denote British officials and characterized in the official record as *saheblok*.[133] The mood of the song also signifies a clear political agenda—to seek liberation from the clutches of outsiders. The recounting of the event in the song situates the political consciousness of the community that characterizes Birsa as its spearhead. In his compilation of work on folk songs about Birsa, R. D. Munda wrote: 'The politician in Birsa had already revived itself with the talking of taking over the "country" by his closest disciples, some of whom were personally involved in the Sardar movement. The serene religious atmosphere was turning into a hot political background.'[134] This accentuates the presence of Birsa as the lead figure within the narrative of the *ulgulan*.

The song ends on a hopeful note—imagining an independent Munda *disom* (village). However, the use of a word such as 'जोनोम दिसुम' (birth of a nation) is slightly unclear. Upon seeking clarification about the word from Gunjal (who teaches endangered languages at the University of Jharkhand), he suggested that the word is contextual and therefore its translation as 'nation' is uncertain and could instead denote 'village'. This is useful in understanding that various allegories and symbols in Adivasi folk songs are open to myriad interpretations. The restricted use of terms can often reduce their contextual meanings. Besides the structure of the song, it is vital to situate the significance of the landscape. The landscape of Dombari functions as a memorial site. The representation of Birsa in the built environment can limit the memory of folk songs that contain the affective gestures and political consciousness of the Adivasi worldview.

As we have seen in the case of the memorial pillar, the intention behind the commemoration emanates from capital's need for expansion, replacing the possibility of addressing the needs of those who continue to live impoverished lives. Significantly, the commemoration site as imagined by the political elites and the state receives Adivasis as passive recipients of their own heritage and memory. In other words, Adivasis, notably those who live with the intergenerational memory of Birsa, including Birsaites, seem to play a marginal role in forming the shape, size and economy of the commemoration. The state occupies a defining role in the process of commemorating the national canon.

Fundamentally, as Meghnath says, 'Birsa, as we come to know today through such massive heroic commemoration virtually in all corners of Jharkhand, and the nation, remains one among equals in Adivasi society'. The culture of hero worship and the cult of icons that we witness in our society are negligible amongst Adivasis. They treat their leaders as 'one among equals'. This was evident also in the way the folk song emplaces the role of the collective in organizing the dissent at the heart of Dombari. Therefore, folk songs not only function to merely support the existing claims of representation but also effectively enable a medium to articulate and locate the agency of the subaltern. They destabilize the hegemonic form of historical imagination that has grown from the official record, and they emphasize the role of the community that bore witness.

Summary

In this chapter, I explored specific sites of commemoration. Firstly, I investigated the case study of the *samadhi sthal*. In doing so, I highlighted the role of political elites and the state. I situated the importance of the built environment, such as memorials as affective sites, and located various components, such as place and economy, that influence it. I also examined the making of Dombari as a landscape of memory. I sought to understand the role of community and the state through different models of power and culture.

The two sites are different but uniquely interconnected models that offered interesting insights into commemoration. The *samadhi sthal* displayed the use of political power as a method to control and regulate the process of remembering or forgetting through organized practices of commemoration. I identified key actors who not only design the model of remembering but also actively use the trope of nationalist nostalgia and eventful memory to invent various fragmented forms of remembering. In addition, the making of Dombari as the landscape of memory highlighted the use of 'memory as heritage'. In this process, I raised a concern about the relationship between memory and capital. This was particularly interesting in the context of the Dombari facelift programme as it offers scope to understand the irony of commemoration that displaces the subject of memory (the Adivasis who live in Sail Rakab) from the project of curation of memory (facelift of Dombari as tourist venture). To situate the other forms of remembering of Birsa, I presented a brief account of a folk song to display an alternative imagination of remembering and commemoration that receives little scholarly attention. Moreover, I stressed the marginal role that folk songs continue to receive in the historiography of the community and of Birsa in particular.

Importantly, I offered a possibility to think about the different notion of historical memory that functions through a close association between the postcolonial state, political elites and capital. Each one of them provides a condition for the other to survive and expand. This process of representing events of the past through affective sites of Birsa Munda jeopardizes the material conditions of Adivasis. Not only does it indicate problems associated with the process of commemoration, where the 'absence of memory' creates conditions for memorialization, but it also effectively removes the participants (Adivasis) from the event and makes them passive recipients enclosed in their own temporalities.[135] In other words, the creation of the memorial does not represent the modes of remembering and memorializing. This is primarily due to the absence of any democratic medium that provides a platform to the Adivasi community to offer its worldview. The memory work—that is, statue and memorials—is invariably defined by the political elite's interest in the votes of specific constituencies or opportunities to extend the state's industrial corridor.

I believe that the problem with commemoration also clearly emerges from the lack of our understanding of Adivasis and their lifeworld. There is a lack of voices to design Adivasi heritage beyond the stewardship of the state. The chapter showed how the experiences are not historically frozen in events, times and archaic models of representation. The model through which we remember, such as memorial landscape, needs to be radically rethought. This would involve a 'thick' understanding of the cosmic structure through which the Adivasis remember their dead and their ancestors, and all of it needs to be defined and driven by them: a new model that not only allows memory to work as a 'moment of recollection that always involves reconstruction of past experiences' but also incorporates everyday lives and struggles.[136] Perhaps there is need to decolonize the epistemological categories through which we represent the past.

Notes

1. Eelco Runia, 'Burying the Dead, Creating the Past', *History and Theory* 46, no. 3 (2007): 313–25, p. 325.
2. Pierre Nora, 'Between Memory and History: Lieux de Memoire', *Representations* 26 (Spring 1989): 7–24.
3. Berber Bevernage, 'Tales of Pastness and Contemporaneity: On the Politics of Time in History and Anthropology', *Rethinking History* 20, no. 3 (2 July 2016): 352–74.
4. Lexico (Oxford English Dictionary), s.v. 'commemoration', https://en.oxforddictionaries.com/definition/commemorate (accessed on 22 April 2019).
5. Hiro Saito, 'From Collective Memory to Commemoration', in *Handbook of Cultural Sociology*, ed. John R. Hall, Laura Grindstaff and Ming-cheng Lo, pp. 629–38 (London: Routledge, 2010), p. 629.
6. Anita Kasabova, 'Memory, Memorials and Commemoration', *History and Theory* 47, no. 3 (2008): 331–50, p. 332
7. Ibid.
8. Runia, 'Burying the Dead, Creating the Past', p. 314.
9. Ibid.
10. Ibid., p. 316.
11. Ibid.
12. Ibid., p. 318.
13. Ibid.

14 Svetlana Boym, 'Nostalgia and Its Discontents', *Hedgehog Review* 9, no. 2 (Summer 2007): 7–18.

15 Andrew Jones, *Memory and Material Culture* (Cambridge: Cambridge University Press, 2007), p. 2.

16 Ibid., p. 3.

17 Ibid., p. 19 (emphasis mine).

18 Ibid., p. 23.

19 Ibid., p. 37.

20 Emma Sardinia Blake, 'Nuraghi: Four Millennia of Becoming', *World Archaeology* 30, no. 1 (1998): 59–71, as cited in Jones, *Memory and Material Culture*, p. 40.

21 Jones, *Memory and Material Culture*, p. 46 (emphasis mine).

22 Partha Chatterjee, *The Politics of the Governed: Reflections on Popular Politics in Most of the World* (New York: Columbia University Press, 2004), p. 38.

23 Daniel Rycroft, 'Capturing Birsa Munda: The Virtuality of a Colonial-Era Photograph', *Indian Folklore Research Journal* 1, no. 4 (2004): 53–67.

24 *Parha* is a 'socio-cultural-political institution of self-governance for the well-being of the Adivasi community'. Vincent Ekka, 'Lessons from the Institution of "Indigenous Self-Governance"', in *Being Adivasi: Existence, Entitlements, Exclusion*, ed. Abhay Xaxa and G. N. Devy, pp. 80–93 (New Delhi: Rupa Publications, 2021), p. 82.

25 Panchayats (Extension to the Schedule Areas) Act, popularly known as PESA, is a mandate under the Ministry of Panchayati Raj. The ministry offers a mandate to implement the Part IX of the Indian Constitution provision regarding the District Planning Committee as per Article 243ZD in Part IXA and PESA. The provision of the PESA Act is extended to 10 fifth-schedule areas, including Jharkhand. 'Under the PESA Act, {section 4 (b)}, a village shall ordinarily consist of a habitation or a group of habitations or a hamlet or a group of hamlets comprising a community and managing its affairs in accordance with traditions and customs.' Besides the guarantee to uphold the power of *gram sabha*, the Act indicates the 'right to mandatory consultation in land acquisition, resettlement and rehabilitation of displaced persons […] prevent land alienation and restore alienated land' amongst other clauses that ensure the rights of Adivasis and the tribal population are not violated. See Ministry of Panchayati Raj (Government of India), 'Mandate of the Ministry of Panchayati Raj', https://pesadarpan.gov.in/en (accessed on 1 May 2019). Also see Paromita Sanyal and Vijayendra Rao, *Oral Democracy* (Cambridge: Cambridge University Press, 2018).

26 The United Nations has made a concerted effort to recognize and protect the mausoleum sites that hold historical importance to human civilization. In China, for example, the United Nations Educational, Scientific and Cultural Organization's (UNESCO) initiative to conserve world heritage has provided a detailed record and history of the mausoleum of the first Qin emperor, which is historic for the country now. For further information, see UNESCO World Heritage Convention,

'Mausoleum of First Qin Emperor' (UNESCO: World Heritage List, Lington Country, Shaanxi Province, 1987), https://whc.unesco.org/en/list/441 (accessed on 1 May 2019).

27 Cambridge Dictionary, 'mausoleum', https://dictionary.cambridge.org/dictionary/english/mausoleum (accessed on 10 September 2019).

28 John-Baptist Hoffman, *Encyclopaedia Mundarica*, vol. 1, shelf mark 14178.e.47, British Library, London, p. 612.

29 Ibid (emphasis mine).

30 Reinhart Koselleck, *The Practice of Conceptual History: Timing History, Spacing Concepts*, trans. Hayden White (Stanford: Stanford University Press, 2002); Reinhart Koselleck, *Future Past: On the Semantics of Historical Time*, trans. Keith Tribe (New York: Columbia University Press, 2004), p. 238.

31 Vijay Deo Jha, 'How Not to Revere a Freedom Fighter', *The Telegraph,* https://www.telegraphindia.com/states/jharkhand/how-not-to-revere-a-freedom-hero/cid/1365672 (accessed on 2 May 2019).

32 The distillery's *talab* is a noted public concern due to the odour that it generates. It has also caused discomfort for many locals to see Birsa's memorial placed adjacent to it. Ibid.

33 Jens Lerche and Alpa Shah, 'Conjugated Oppression within Contemporary Capitalism: Class, Caste, Tribe and Agrarian Change in India', *Journal of Peasant Studies*, 45 nos. 5–6 (2018): 927–49.

34 Ibid.

35 Alpa Shah, 'The Labour of Love: Seasonal Migration from Jharkhand to the Brick Kilns of Other States in India', *Contributions to Indian Sociology* (n.s.) 40, no. 1 (2006): 91–118.

36 Dolly Kikon, 'Jackfruit Seeds from Jharkhand: Being Adivasi in Assam', *Contributions to Indian Sociology* 51, no. 3 (2017): 313–37.

37 Ibid., p. 314.

38 Karl Marx, *Capital,* vol. 1 (New York: Penguin, 1990).

39 Duncan Bell, 'Mythscapes: Memory, Mythology, and National Identity', *British Journal of Sociology* 54, no. 1 (2003): 63–81.

40 Bindrai, in a personal interview with the author, Kokar, 21 September.

41 Astrid Erll, 'Re-Writing as Re-Visioning Modes of Representing the "Indian Mutiny" in British Novels, 1857 to 2000', *European Journal of English Studies* 10, no. 2 (2006): 163–85, p. 11.

42 See Michèle Barrett, 'Subalterns at War', in *Can the Subaltern Speak? Reflections on the History of an Idea,* ed. Rosalind C. Morris, pp. 156–78 (New York: Columbia University Press, 2010).

43 Ibid., p. 156.

44 Sarah Tarlow, *Bereavement and Commemoration: An Archaeology of Mortality* (Oxford: Blackwell Publishers, 1999), p. 2.

45   I learnt the word in personal correspondence with Gunjal Munda during the field visit. Gunjal Munda is an assistant professor of linguistics and has been involved in the project of endangered indigenous languages in Jharkhand. His expertise in the field of language carries forward the legacy of his father, R. D. Munda, who played a significant role in the Jharkhand movement.

46   Tanika Sarkar, 'Nationalist Iconography: Image of Women in 19th Century Bengali Literature', *Economic and Political Weekly* 22, no. 47 (1987): 2011–15, pp. 2012–14

47   Kumar Suresh Singh, *Birsa Munda and His Movement (1872–1901)* (Kolkata: Seagull Books, 2002).

48   Anurag Faisal, in a personal interview with the author, Ranchi, 16 October 2018.

49   For a detailed report and judgement on the case, see G. D. Khosla, *The Murder of the Mahatma* (Mumbai: Jaico Publishing House, 1965).

50   Edward Anderson and Christophe Jaffrelot, 'Hindu Nationalism and the "Saffronisation of the Public Sphere": An Interview with Christophe Jaffrelot', *Contemporary South Asia* 26, no. 4 (2 October 2018): 468–82, p. 469.

51   Anurag Faisal, in a personal interview with the author, Ranchi, 16 October 2018.

52   Harsh Mander, 'Why Jharkhand's Anti-conversion Bill is against Constitution and Not Necessary', *Hindustan Times*, 12 September 2018, https://www.hindustantimes.com/columns/why-jharkhand-s-anti-conversion-bill-is-against-constitution-and-not-necessary/story-FIhGsnxuqIItvniVAoiLQO.html (accessed on 22 April 2019).

53   Ibid.

54   Gunjal Munda, in a personal interview with the author, Ranchi, 18 August 2018.

55   Ibid.

56   Ibid.

57   'Centrally Sponsored Scheme of Establishment of Ashram Schools in Tribal Sub-Plan Areas', New Delhi, 2008, https://www.india.gov.in/scheme-establishment-ashram-schools-tribal-sub-plan-areas (accessed on 19 November 2019).

58   Joyita Ghose, 'Standing Committee Report Summary Working of Ashram Schools in Tribal Areas', New Delhi, 2014, https://www.prsindia.org/sites/default/files/parliament_or_policy_pdfs/1393414764_SCR Summary-Working of Ashram Schools in Tribal Areas.pdf (accessed on 19 November 2019).

59   Ibid.

60   Gladson Dungdung, 'Adivasis on the March: Crisis and Cultural Genocide in Tribal India', Adivasi Hunkar, 14 March 2019, https://www.adivasihunkar.com/2019/03/14/adivasis-on-the-march-crisis-and-cultural-genocide-in-tribal-india.

61   Ibid.

62   Alpa Shah, *In the Shadows of the State: Indigenous Politics, Environmentalism and Insurgency in Jharkhand, India* (New Delhi: Oxford University Press, 2011), p. 31.

63   Jan Assmann, 'Collective Memory and Cultural Identity', *New German Critique* 65 (Spring–Summer 1995): 125–33.

64 Meghnath, in a personal interview with the author, Ranchi, 18 August 2018.
65 Ibid.
66 Ibid.
67 Anurag Faisal, in a personal interview with the author, Ranchi, 16 October 2018.
68 Yadin Dudai and Micah G. Edelson, 'Personal Memory: Is It Personal, Is It Memory?', *Memory Studies* 9, no. 3 (2016): 275–83, p. 275.
69 Ibid.
70 Anurag Faisal, in a personal interview with the author, Ranchi, 16 October 2018.
71 Boym, 'Nostalgia and Its Discontents'.
72 Margery Sabin, 'In Search of Subaltern Consciousness', *Prose Studies* 30, no. 2 (2008): 177–200, p. 179.
73 For instance, when I was in Ranchi in 2018 and began interviewing people, Stan Swamy was charged with involvement in what became an 'urban Maoist' campaign. In the series of arrests that took place in different parts of the country, five prominent people were put behind bars allegedly for undertaking the 'anti-national' activities. In July 2021, he died in hospital because of delayed treatment and menial living conditions in the jail. For a detailed report on Stan Swamy, see Rajendran Narayanan and Debmalya, 'Father Stan Swamy, Children and the Unholy State', *The Wire*, 3 September 2018, https://thewire.in/rights/stan-swamy-jharkhand-adivasis-undertrials-pesa-uapa (accessed on 24 April 2019).
74 Peter L. Berger and Thomas Luckmann, *The Social Construction of Reality* (London: Penguin Books, 1991).
75 See *The Wire*, 'At Least 15 Have Died of Starvation in Jharkhand in Last One Year, Say Activists', 28 September 2018, https://thewire.in/rights/right-to-food-campaign-issues-statement-on-jharkhand-starvation-deaths (accessed on 24 April 2019).
76 Runia, 'Burying the Dead, Creating the Past'.
77 Francis Bradley Bradley-Birt, *Chota Nagpore: A Little Known Province of the Empire* (New Delhi: Asian Educational Services, 1998 [1903]), p. 9.
78 H. H. Risley, 'The Study of Ethnology in India', *Journal of Anthropological Institute of Great Britain and Ireland* 20 (1891): 235–63, pp. 238–39.
79 Bradley-Birt, *Chota Nagpore*.
80 A. Forbes to the Chief Secretary of Bengal, 10th January 1900, J&P 268, shelf mark number IOR: 2/PJ/6/531, British Library, London.
81 Ibid.
82 Ibid.
83 *Bhuinhari* literally means 'the descendants of original clearer of the land'. Loknath Sahi conducted the *bhuinhari* tenure. A Nagvanshi by caste, who owned extensive property in the area, Sahi was considered reliable to assess those who were resisting against property owners and imperial forces. The operation for the survey was conducted in 1869 across 576 villages. For the record, see Babu Rakhal Das Halder

to the Deputy Commissioner of Lohardaga, J&P 268, no. 11, dated Ranchi, the 22nd May 1880, British Library, London.

84 H. C. Streatfield, Deputy Commissioner of Ranchi, 4 January 1900, J&P 224, shelf mark number IOR/L/PJ/6/5320, British Library, London.

85 C. A. Bayly, *Indian Society and the Making of the British Empire* (Cambridge: Cambridge University Press, 1990).

86 Barbara Verado, 'Rebels and Devotees of Jharkhand: Social, Religious and Political Transformation among the Adivasi of Northern India', PhD disseration, London School of Economics and Political Science, University of London, 2003, p. 87. This disruption also contains a caveat. The pre-colonial era did not exist in vacuum or an absolute state of equality. In fact, Hindu *raja*s were also oppressive and often used caste-based differences that relegated Adivasis to subservience. There was a huge economy driven by social norms more broadly across the country.

87 Nicole Graham, *Lawscape: Property, Environment, Law* (New York: Routledge, 2011), p. 8.

88 Ibid.

89 Assmann, 'Collective Memory and Cultural Identity'.

90 Runia, 'Burying the Dead, Creating the Past'. Also see Jones, *Memory and Material Culture*.

91 Government of India, 'Census of India 2011: Jharkhand' (Jharkhand, 2011).

92 *India Today*, 'Shaheed Gram Vikas Yojana Launched: Know about the Tribal Folk Hero Birsa Munda', 19 September 2017, https://www.indiatoday.in/education-today/gk-current-affairs/story/shaheed-gram-vikas-yojana-1047830-2017-09-19 (accessed on 11 August 2019).

93 Assmann, 'Collective Memory and Cultural Identity'.

94 R. D. Munda and B. P. Keshari, 'Recent Developments in the Jharkhand Movement', *India International Centre Quarterly* 19, no. 3 (1992): 71–89.

95 Matthew Carey, *Mistrust: An Ethnographic Theory* (Chicago: HAU Books), p. 107.

96 The name of the interviewee is fictitious to conceal his identity for personal reasons.

97 Sarah Pink, *The Future of Visual Anthropology: Engaging the Senses* (London: Routledge, 2006), p. 21.

98 Apart from Maoist rebellions, there are various groups such as the Tritiya Prastuti Committee and the People's Liberation Front that are active in the region. These groups regularly have close encounters with the military personnel deployed in the area nearby. These encounters shape the popular consensus amongst the people in the urban locality about the Maoists and sometimes Adivasis. See Nabamita Mitra, 'On a Road without a Milestone', *Times of India*, 12 July 2015, https://timesofindia.indiatimes.com/city/ranchi/on-a-road-without-a-milestone/articleshow/48037789.cms (accessed on 1 February 2009). https://timesofindia.indiatimes.com/city/ranchi/On-a-road-without-a-milestone/articleshow/48037789.cms

99 Both Puri and Rabi are fictitious names to conceal the identities of the individuals. I am indebted to them for their help.

100 Historically, the state has suffered at the hands of mafia *raj* (mafia regime). As part of the state of Bihar, the country and this region in particular, Jharkhand saw a rise in organized crime under the behest of the state's bureaucrats, elected politicians and businesspersons.

101 The concept of sacred landscape has been variously used by scholars who have studied indigenous peoples across the world. In the context of this chapter, I refer to Vinita Damodaran, 'Sacred Landscapes: Mining, Globalisation and the Environmental History of Eastern India', Centre for World Environmental History, University of Sussex, http://www.sussex.ac.uk/cweh/research/sacredlandscapes (accessed on 1 May 2019).

102 Bharmi Munda, in a personal interview with the author, Ranchi, 22 October 2018.

103 Ibid.

104 Ibid.

105 Ibid.

106 Erll, 'Travelling Memory', *Parallax* 17, no. 4 (2011): 4–18.

107 Lucy Bond, Stef Craps and Pieter Vermeulen, 'Introduction', in *Memory Unbound: Tracing the Dynamics of Memory Studies*, pp. 1–26 (New York: Berghahn Books, 2017), p. 6.

108 Alan S. Milward, 'Bad Memories', *Times Literary Supplement*, 14 April 2000, p. 8, as cited in Jay Winter, 'The Generation of Memory: Reflections on the "Memory Boom" in Historical Studies', *Archives and Social Studies: A Journal of Interdisciplinary Research* 1 (March 2007): 363–97, p. 378.

109 Uday Chandra, 'Millenarian Dreams, Modern Aspirations: Tribal Community-Making and Contentious Politics in Colonial Chotanagpur', Working Paper WP 14-01, ISSN 2192-2357, Max Planck Institute for the Study of Religious and Ethnic Diversity, Göttingen, Germany, April 2014, https://www.mmg.mpg.de/60983/wp-14-01 (accessed on 15 July 2019).

110 Paul Connerton, 'Seven Types of Forgetting', *Memory Studies* 1, no. 1 (January 2008): 59–71, p. 63.

111 Santosh Kiro, 'A Road to Birsa's Iconic Battle Hill: ASI's Rs 10-Lakh Facelift for Dombari Buru', *The Telegraph*, 17 December 2012, https://www.telegraphindia.com/india/a-road-to-birsas-iconic-battle-hill-asis-rs-10-lakh-facelift-for-dombari-buru/cid/352472 (accessed on 29 April 2019).

112 Ibid. In attempts to reach the ASI office, I failed to find any reports.

113 Ibid.

114 Winter, 'The Generation of Memory'.

115 Kalyan Sanyal, *Rethinking Capitalist Development: Primitive Accumulation, Governmentality and Postcolonial Capitalism* (New Delhi: Routledge, 2007), pp. 41–42 (emphasis mine).

116 Koselleck, *Future Past*.
117 Connerton, 'Seven Types of Forgetting', p. 63.
118 'TD Tenders from Jharkhand Tender Notice – 8798021', Tender Detail, https://www.tenderdetail.com/Indian-Tenders/TenderNotice/8798021/481855ad-27e8-4569-b778-96cf45c9499d$development-of-ulihatu-and-dombari-buru-hill-as-heritage-tourism-destination-khunti-district (accessed on 1 February 2019).
119 Tadhg O'Keeffe, 'Landscape and Memory: Historiography, Theory, Methodology', in *Heritage, Memory and the Politics of Identity*, ed. Niamh Moore and Yvonne Whelan, pp. 3–18 (Hampshire: Ashgate Publishing Limited, 2007).
120 Matt Hodges, 'Reinventing "History"?'. *History and Anthropology* 26, no. 4 (11 September 2015): 515–27, p. 77.
121 Eric Hobsbawm and Terence Ranger, *The Invention of Tradition* (Cambridge: Cambridge University Press, 1983).
122 Ibid., p. 2.
123 Anderson, *Imagined Communities: Reflections on the Origin and Spread of Nationalism* (London: Verso Publication, 2006 [1983]), p. 14.
124 Rashmi Varma, 'Primitive Accumulation', *Third Text* 27, no. 6 (2013): 748–61, pp. 749–50.
125 Ibid., p. 749.
126 Akhil Gupta, 'Imagining Nations', in *Companion to the Anthropology of Politics*, ed. David Nugent and Joan Vincent, pp. 267–81 (Oxford: Blackwell Publishing, 2007), p. 276.
127 Sumit Sarkar, *Modern India 1885–1947* (London: Palgrave Macmillan, 1989), p. 40.
128 Prathama Banerjee, 'Writing the Adivasi: Some Historiographical Notes', *Indian Economic and Social History Review* 53, no. 1 (2016): 131–53, p. 132.
129 O'Keeffe, 'Landscape and Memory'.
130 For this song, I am profoundly indebted to Gunjal Munda, Dulae Chandra Munda and late R. D. Munda. Gunjal has provided the song from his late father's personal collection and has offered his support at various stages during the fieldwork. See the appendix for the translation and transliteration.
131 For the song, see Rashmi Katyayan, 'Dombari Buru Cetanare: Ram Dayal Munda', YouTube video, 5:08, 21 August 2012, https://www.youtube.com/watch?v=rDDhh2COUHU (accessed on 15 November 2019).
132 I have transliterated the text of the song from an already translated version in Hindi. Any discrepancies in the transliteration stem from my unfamiliarity with the language. Mundari does not have a script; it is a spoken language.
133 A. Forbes to the Chief Secretary of Bengal, 10th January 1900, J&P 268, shelf mark number IOR: 2/PJ/6/531, British Library, London.

134 R. D. Munda and Norman Zide, 'Revolutionary Birsa and Songs Related to Him', *Journal of Social Research* 12, no. 2 (1969): 37–60. I accessed it from the Christian Missionary Society Collection at the Cadbury Research Library, University of Birmingham.

135 Runia, 'Burying the Dead, Creating the Past'.

136 Saito, 'From Collective Memory to Commemoration'.

Chapter 5

Echoes from the Graveyard
Pathalgadi, *Birsaites and the Landscape of Memory*

> For both the archaeologist and the native dwellers, the landscape tells—or rather is—a story. It enfolds the lives and times of predecessors who, over the generations, have moved around in it, and played their part in its formation. To perceive the landscape is to carry out an act of remembrance, and remembering is not so much a matter of calling up an internal image, stored in the mind, as of engaging perceptually with an environment that is itself pregnant with the past.
>
> —Tim Ingold[1]

The landscape is not nature. It is not land. It is an imprint of the lifeworld. In his recent work, Asoka Kumar Sen defines Adivasi landscape as *jal, jungle, jameen*, which is a 'constitutive element in forging the Adivasihood'. Similarly, in this chapter, I show that the Adivasi lifeworld is a constellation of lived experiences and knowledge. It is a 'field and flow of living worlds'.[2] Therefore, the landscape also captures the lifeworld of the community—one that is forged through the everyday use of memory. Drawing on previous works on material memory, I aim to delineate a new perspective about the relationship between the landscape and memory. I focus on two nodal points to show functions of memory. In the first section, I investigate the historical importance of stone slabs within the Adivasi community. In the second section, I show how stone slabs are mobilized in the resistance movement, the Pathalgadi. Historically, *pathalgadi* is a custom prevalent amongst Adivasis to 'mark a happy, sad, or significant occasion' by erecting a slab.[3] However, this has taken a political turn and transformed into a massive resistance movement in Jharkhand—a point that is tied to broader implications concerning Birsa Munda and his memory.

Using a variety of sources encompassing reports, visuals and archives, I contextualize the Pathalgadi movement within a broader and more urgent ecological and political standpoint of this region. The descriptions of historical memory are then dovetailed with the contemporary articulation of the movement. I argue that Adivasis mobilize the law, using excerpts from the Constitution of India to assert their rights by drawing on their worldview as it is entangled with landscape—one that is fraught with memory. In other words, I offer an insight into the role of an emergent framework: memory as politics.

Traces of Memory: The Burial Practice of *Sasandiri* in Chota Nagpur

> The burial custom of the Mundas whereby they restrict (with certain exceptions) the privilege of Sasindiri, that is, the placing of flat stones in the graveyards of the village to members of the original killi [sect] which established the village, is practically [an] *infallible test of whether a Mundari claimant* is a member of the original killi which established the village.[4]

While formulating the deed of records in 1908, T. S. Macpherson recognized graveyards as a marker of territory. These graveyards are installed through a burial practice called *sasandiri*—a practice that remains prevalent in Jharkhand today. It consists of two words: *sasan* and *diri*. *Sasan* comes from *sasanmasan*, meaning the 'village of the burial ground of the *khuntkhattidar* or *bhuinhars*', while *diri* means 'the ground'.[5] *Sasandiri* can be construed as a 'dolmen comprised of a capstone placed on four or more stones'.[6] Historically, Mundas are the first community known to have their *sasandiri*.[7] The *sasan* and *sasandiri* remain distinctive features of the Munda community.[8] There are, however, differences in the methods of observing the dead, and the process of designing structures the burial practice within the Adivasi community. An overlap can simplify the crucial role of rituals, which is detrimental to definitions of land ownership.

The *pahans* (customary headmen) lead the procedural aspect of this ceremony. The process entails a settlement amount and a feast before the property is allowed to observe *sasandiri* practice. This emphasizes the importance of land for the memory of the dead. In his study of the archaeology of the burial, Howard William has suggested: 'Grave-goods ... cemeteries ... as well as their landscape contexts and environments ... are arenas of contestation and engagement between archaeologists and present-day communities and publics.'[9] It is an important cursory practice to understand the relationship between death, burials and memory.

Different cultures use death as a site of heritage harnessed by both memory and remains (such as graveyards and burials). The remains allow for 'memorialising the cremated [or buried] dead in traditional commemorative environments, and the choices made over how to dispose of ashes elsewhere, represent the diversification, personalisation and re-sentimentalising of death in a late-modern post-industrial world'.[10] Similarly, the tradition of *sasandiri* constitutes an essential component of the cosmic structure of Adivasi lifeworld that personalizes death. In this process of observing it through the complex structure, 'these emotions are mediated and orchestrated through the careful and selective management of the mourner's multisensory interaction with the corpse at each stage of the funeral', and a landmark is created by the erection of a commemorative stone slab.[11]

The historical evolution of *sasandiri* offers a glimpse into myriad forms of entanglement where the environment also becomes a cultural space. John-Baptist Hoffman noted that each *sasandiri* had a 'peculiar feature' that sets its off from the *bhumij* (Munda people of Chota Nagpur).[12] Only those Mundas who were *khuntkhattidar* buried their ancestors under the stone slabs. In the early 19th century, when the dead were cremated, the remaining bones, or sometimes skulls, were buried under the stone. By the mid-19th century, the practice of cremation began to decline. The shift in the practice and ritual is an interesting point that explains the effects of conversion on the texture of the living and the dead in any society—as elaborated upon in Chapter 2. In an interview recorded by M. Topno in 1955, an older man recalls his *memories of grandparents* who would mention pyre practices rather than burial. It is believed that conversion to Christianity had changed the practice.[13] With the passage of time and the influence of missionaries, as Hoffman noted, the practice of burial became more prevalent.[14]

Not everyone gets a *sasan* after death (Figure 5.1). No burial is granted to those who die unnatural deaths—for instance, death by drowning or being attacked by an animal. The Munda community's outlook towards the human–animal conflict has been undergoing transformation in contemporary Jharkhand.[15] Mundas who do not die a natural death are often 'believed to cause other people to die similar deaths'.[16] Such unnatural deaths are called *ranuda gonoe*, and their shadows *are birjanae* which means they 'become wild or furious'.[17] These rituals have helped to

Figure 5.1 Stone slabs depicting *sasandiri* in Khunti district
Source: Photograph by the author.

ceremonialize the erection of stone slabs and attach social prestige to the material object (Figure 5.2). In turn, they form a cosmological belief structuring the lifeworld of the community—making the landscape a 'cultural process' mediated by memory, experiences and traditional practices.[18] This enables the dead to occupy positions as transcendental figures, capable of acquiring forms and function as intergenerational memory within the community.

Echoes from the Graveyard

Figure 5.2 Members of the Adivasi community in Khunti district performing ceremonial rituals to erect a burial stone

Source: Photograph by Rupesh.

Graveyards to Red Files: Burials as Evidence of Territorial Claims

By the 19th century, the practice of burial emerged as a testimony to historical claims of belonging. It was noted frequently as evidence within colonial law's encounters with the indigenous peoples in Chota Nagpur. For instance, the report of the CNTA (1908) contains an account by the Settlement Officer who notes the burial custom for legal purposes:

> [T]he Settlement Officer, owing to the burial custom of the Mundas can easily ascertain whether the claim to hold certain lands as khuntkatti is true or not. No Mundari can rightly be buried save in the *burial ground* of the village of which his ancestors on the paternal side was the founder.[19]

Once legal considerations of the burial as the form of claim had been established, these grounds were further entrenched in order to testify the truth. In short, the support of community members and their historical roots were required in order to approve burials as the authentic claims on territory. Often, it was determined by the common denomination: 'every killi has its own burial ground'.[20] The CNTA contained the description of the process and requirements for the claims. In the document, Hoffman noted:

> To these burial slabs, therefore, the *highest evidential value* attaches; and hence it is that, when in comparatively recent times written and registered documents came into use as title-deeds to prove propriety or other interests in land, the Mundaris summed up their views on the matter in the saying '*Sasandiriko Horonkokoa pata*' (their burial stones are title-deeds of the Munda race).[21]

This explicitly demonstrates how burials became a marker of territorial sovereignty for the community. Conceptualized as a form of stone, they function as material memory. Moreover, 'graveyards then stand as icons of the sacred relationship between pioneers and the territory' that constitute the landscape of memory for Adivasis. It allows the community to use graveyards to 'objectify pioneering clans and legitimize their land possession'.[22] Furthermore, as a title deed for the rights to the land, this recognition served various functions. On one level, it recognized a piece of such mnemonic material as the surviving objects of remembrance, crystallizing the memory of ancestors in the form of burial; on the other, it emerged as a site of what I would call 'memory law'.[23] The latter explains an interesting story.

I believe it stands as memory law because the colonial state employed legal exceptionalism in order to recognize existing norms and practices. As memory law, it drew upon the customary methods to examine the validity of the claims (such as *killi*). There was, in fact, a concerted effort by the colonial state to negotiate with subjects and mitigate the loss caused by the absence of the written records. However, the attempt to recognize the memory law by the colonial state also suggests the two interrelated motivations that drove it. First, there was a shift in the governance model of the colonial state led by the making of the 'ethnographic state'.[24] Second, it highlighted 'regimes of colonial recognition' as the prerequisite condition for the recognition of title deeds—negating any possibility of imagining the organization of land entitlements based on other forms of customary practices.[25]

The former stance reflects the efficacy of the colonial state to generate data and produce documents. The ethnography, as Nicholas Dirks would argue, was undertaken extensively to situate 'social differences and deference—pervasive features of Indian society'.[26] However, with overlaps between caste and custom, it sank further into confusion. Importantly, it 'shifted old meanings slowly, sometimes imperceptibly, through the colonial control of a range of new institutions' and reinstated inequalities in the social world of the subaltern.[27] However, the latter expands our horizon of understanding memory law and the inherent contradictions in the politics of recognition. Kaushik Ghosh clarifies this:

> Laws are not only the content of *regimes of colonial recognition* but also the concrete signs of some of the most spectacular achievements of nineteenth-century adivasi struggles against colonial capitalist rule. The mechanism of governmental power in adivasi areas and the particular territorial imaginations of indigeneity embedded in it therefore carry significant marks of this historical agency of indigenous populations in India.[28]

The *regimes of colonial recognition* elaborate the relationship between memory and the law. Colonial governance seeks legitimacy by establishing the legal regime to produce new subjects. These subjects emerge not merely as the passive recipients of legal regimes but rather through the 'persistence of revolts'.[29] The Birsa rebellion, for instance, defined the scope for extensive governance models such as the CNTA. In effect, the law introduced an ambit, 'colonial governmentality', where it used templates of memory (*sasandiri*) as a marker for the distinct identity of Adivasis.[30] It allowed the colonial machinery supported by the extensive ethnography of missionaries to generate a new domain of recognition based on 'exclusive governmentality'.[31] Ghosh defines 'exclusive governmentality' as a 'form of relating to a foundational tribal otherness or ethnicity, [where] the principle of recognition is that of exclusion'.[32]

Ghosh's proposition helps us understand the familiarity of the colonial state with the question of ethnicity, identity and governmentality. However, it does not sufficiently address the role of memory in the making of the legal regimes. For instance, the recognition of burial grounds (*sasandiri*) highlights *not only* the politics of recognition but also a moment of legal intervention from below. It disrupts the homogenous definition of land that seeks recognition as a form of material object—one that is weighed and evaluated through the established order of measurements. It seeks to identify the land with something beyond a physical form of property as well as with memory. Memory defines the land. Land without memory is an abstraction. It is memory that dwells as a landscape for land to exist as more than material.

Incidentally, it also suggests that land exists in multiple temporalities. It cannot be reduced to a singular notion that is contingent on its outer mode—the physical property. It is counter-productive to isolate a vast schema of thinking about the land vis-à-vis memory and landscape. In the next section, I will draw attention to the existence of such multiple temporalities through a close reading of the Pathalgadi movement, a contentious contemporary movement formed to assert what I would call *resistance memory*. The idea of resistance memory explains the use of memory as a political tool to articulate temporalities in which land inhabits contemporary Jharkhand. It illustrates an interesting continuum in which 'memory and the past are tied like beads together in a thread', as acts unfolding without the rupture.[33]

On the Continuum of Memory: the Pathalgadi Movement as a Site of Resistance Memory

गाँव छोड़ब नहीं, जंगल छोड़ब नहीं,
माए माटी छोड़ब नहीं, लड़ाई छोड़ब नहीं, ...
जल जंगल जमीन छोड़ी हमीन कहाँ जाए,
विकास के भगवान बता, हम कैसे जान बचाए ...[34]

Clearly articulated in this song is a sense of resentment and angst against the unabated scale of dispossession in Jharkhand.[35] At the same time, it throws light on the vanishing landscape that constitutes the lifeworld of subaltern Adivasis. Bhagawandas Maji, who wrote the song, has been part of the continual agitation against the bauxite companies across the eastern belt in India. Various resistance movements have demonstrated the effects of development borne by the millions of people at the lowest rung of the economy.[36] One such movement that has occasionally captured national headlines is Pathalgadi.

The word *pathalgadi* has two roots: *pathal* (meaning 'stone') and *gadi* (meaning 'installation'). It refers to a process in which people install a stone slab. However, in recent times Adivasis have used stone slabs in distinctive ways. The stone slabs have turned into a form of political resistance, with big stone plaques being erected outside villages across Jharkhand. The plaques bear excerpts from various pieces of legislation and the Constitution. This came to be locally known as the Pathalgadi movement. Soon after, it came to popular attention through an extensive dissemination of information, especially on social media. The name of Birsa Munda was surprisingly brought back into the limelight because the movement began in Khunti and further intensified in villages nearby.[37]

Exploring the outline of this movement, I argue that the use of stone slabs frames the resistance movement in a unique semblance that blends the traditional burial practices (*sasandiri*) with the contemporary articulation of political consciousness. It mobilizes the past as a useful tool of resistance that is not merely an 'opposition to the effects of power' but rather a 'struggle against the privilege of knowledge'.[38]

This resistance, in turn, causes disruption and allows to display the dissent through the *articulation of indigeneity*.[39] In the following section I discuss the background to the movement to show how it was tied to the larger Adivasi struggle of *jal, jungle, aur jameen* and policies that have faced challenges in the recent past.

Forest Democracy: Law, State and the Pathalgadi Movement

In 1996, B. D. Sharma, an Indian Administrative Service (IAS) officer (1981) and a Scheduled Caste and Scheduled Tribes commissioner (1986-91), and Bandi Oraon, a former member of the Indian Administrative and Police Services, installed a stone slab that bore provisions of the PESA. The PESA is a law enacted by the government of India to recognize the power of *gram sabha*s and extend the laws to the Scheduled Areas recognized by the Fifth Schedule of the Constitution. This meant that *gram sabha*s—that is, 'an institution of direct democracy' at the most local level of Indian society—became peoples' forums to air grievances.[40] This, in turn, led to the advocacy of the substantive value of democracy from the below and effectively led 'strategies to connect people to the government'.[41] Besides, the Act introduced strict compliance with the value system of the *gram sabha*. Among other essential features, it stated the following:

1. State legislation on the Panchayats that may be made shall be in consonance with the customary law, social and religious practices and traditional management practices of community resources;

2. Every Gram Sabha shall approve of the plans, programmes and projects for social and economic development before such plans, programmes and projects are taken up for implementation by the Panchayat at the village level.[42]

Having inaugurated the legal foundation of such a principal Act and inscribed it on the stone slab in order to raise the consciousness among people about their rights, the word *pathalgadi* became popular in mainstream media. Soon after, the Act also generated great discomfort for the state as it sought to acquire land for industrial purposes and expansion of companies into the deep forest. This has caused tension between the government of Jharkhand and the Adivasi community. One such tension has manifested itself in the Pathalgadi movement.[43]

Defining the Pathalgadi Movement

Various authors have attempted to define the Pathalgadi movement. In her analysis of the movement, Anjana Singh defines the Pathalgadi as a movement that has 'questioned the very notion of governmentality and development through the meaningful empowerment of the gram sabha as an alternative agency of village governance'.[44] Furthermore, the movement has introduced prohibitions on outsiders in order to make 'gram sabhas the supreme authority' which 'in fact, responds to a reinvented indigenous system of village governance'.[45] Alternatively, Virginius Xaxa, in his essay, conceptualizes the movement as an outcome of 'social mooring'.[46] He believes that the 'imposition of foreign laws' since the colonial times led to 'havoc in tribal areas'.[47] Additionally, protective legislation such as the CNTA and the Santhal Pargana Tenancy Act (SPTA) (1949) have recently come under the attack, as discussed in Chapter 3. This continued process and attempts at violations coupled with new legislative measures have led Adivasis to 'defend themselves from such assault by asserting their constitutional and legal rights emanating from the Fifth Schedule of the Constitution'.[48] This is a useful insight to investigate the broader ambition of the movement—that is, a prohibition on outsiders and the protection of village governance. It also sets out the movement as a peoples' movement for the reclamation of their rights using various mediums such as the practice of *pathalgadi*. In Jharkhand, the movement has created an outstanding spectacle and highlighted unresolved problems.

Mapping the Movement and Its Controversies

On 19 June 2018, a group of five women working for a non-governmental agency went to a village to perform a street play against trafficking. Later, they were abducted and raped in a village in Khunti district.[49] A group of armed men undertook this criminal activity in Kochang jungle. The case was filed in the court, and the Jharkhand High Court convicted all of the accused, handing down life sentences.[50] Following this, on 26 June 2018, armed men in the same district abducted three security personnel who worked for a member of the legislative assembly. Both of these incidents occurred in highly militant Maoist areas and intensified the process of militarization in the region.[51] The series of incidents popularized the alleged involvement of *pathalgadi*s (men involved in the Pathalgadi movement).

Media reports were supplemented with numerous photos of *pathalgadi*. The photos caused deep trouble for the state. Slabs not only contained provisions of the Constitution—Schedule 5 and the PESA—but also asserted the primacy of village rule. It is a sentiment that has historically shaped Adivasi resistance movements against *dikus*. The Pathalgadi movement was simply a testimony to it.

Legislative Measures and Their Violation

A close look at the photo in Figure 5.3 clarifies the stance of the Pathalgadi movement. It has two main objectives: restitution or respect of protective legislation and primacy of *gram sabha*. On the one hand, it invokes Article 244(1) of the Constitution. Now, Article 244(1) establishes a particular area as a Scheduled

Figure 5.3 A *pathalgadi* stone slab displaying Article 244 of the Constitution of India and declaring the area as 'non-judicial'

Source: Photograph by the author.

Area. Two preconditions for identification as a Scheduled Area are 'preponderance of tribal population and economic backwardness of the area as compared to the neighbouring areas'.[52] Each Scheduled Area has a Tribal Advisory Council. It advises the government on the welfare and development of the tribal community. In effect, the president, in consultation with the governor, holds the power to make laws and rescind boundaries for the Scheduled Areas. In other words, 'the Governor may, by public notification, direct that any particular Act of Parliament or the Legislature of the State shall or shall not apply to a SA [Scheduled Area] or any part thereof in the State, subject to such exceptions and modifications, as specified'.[53] On the other hand, however, it situates the primacy of the village assembly, or *gram sabha*, as established by the laws. Therefore, Schedule 5 defines the structures of India's democracy at the lowest level. However, various other legislative arrangements complement Schedule 5 and work towards the decentralization of power and the empowerment of *gram sabha*s in tribal areas.

For instance, the measures established for the Scheduled Areas, the PESA and the Forest Rights Act (FRA) of 2006 that brought significant amendments to the existing framework of governance, are crucial to our understanding of the larger question of the Pathalgadi movement. The FRA in particular sheds light on the concept of forest democracy. Sudha Vasan writes: 'In spirit, it represents a paradigm shift in forests and forest dwellers. It explicitly recognizes the injustices of earlier practices of forest management.'[54] In short, it underscores the importance of community resources: forest, land and water as defined by the community. In recent times forest rights, alongside other laws, have also suffered a major setback. Various conservation groups and government policies, such as the Compensatory Afforestation Fund Management and Planning Authority (CAMPA) and wildlife conservation, have obstructed the rights of Adivasis under the FRA. Over the years, the Supreme Court of India has received a number of petitions regarding conservation and 'appears to favour conservation over peoples' rights'.[55] Forest rights, as with the rising conflicts, are also emerging as a paradigm for understanding human-rights violations. They seemingly complement each other, as Prakash Kashwan and I have discussed in a special-issue article.[56]

These Acts have led to the emergence of ongoing tensions between conservation groups, the courts and the Adivasi community. While each region has its specific guidelines concerning forest rights, these are nonetheless designed to support and ease the claims under the Act. In Jharkhand, the question of forest rights is intimately tied to other forms of legislation, such as the CNTA that safeguards the rights and ensures the non-violability of the land. In the recent past the state government has made a few attempts to dilute the existing safeguards in order to promote development agendas. This has caused large-scale resistance against the government. Failing to find a medium to access the forest, the government has designed new models to support the interests of industrial groups. The new models of land management such as land bank allow the state to nominate the available asset to prospective companies to decide their sites of operation. 'Land bank' is a term used for a portal that manages the transfer of land to industries. It is a way of 'managing land conflicts' for industrial expansion.[57] As maintained in the Jharkhand Industrial Policy document, 2016, the purpose of a land bank is as follows:

> To provide land for the establishment of industrial areas, industrial estates and new industrial units, Industrial Area Development Authorities will strengthen and expand their land bank by identifying barren, *un-irrigated land and unutilized land* of government departments and corporations in their respective areas…. To facilitate the setting up of technical/educational institutions under the private sector, the Govt. proposes to provide land from land banks for such institution to willing investors.[58]

The document lays down the foundational meaning of the term and suggests the functions of the land bank. In doing so, it focuses on the central role of the state in managing and producing an account of 'un-irrigated and unutilized' land for the expansion of the industrial corridor.[59] The record of the land, in turn, is submitted to the land bank portal so that it is easily accessible. In a drive to make it more convenient, the government of Jharkhand has made it an e-portal. Upon surveying the reports published by the state government on the e-portal, I have found certain overlaps that are crucial to the understanding of the land.

The following section outlines the design of the policy and demonstrates how fundamental it was in the formation of the Pathalgadi movement.

Fire in the Forest Democracy: Land Bank and the Rise of Pathalgadi

Forests comprise 2,232 hectares, which is roughly 29 per cent. Of that 29 per cent, 18.58 per cent is reserved forests, 81.2 per cent is protected forests and 0.14 per cent is unclassed forests (Figure 5.4).[60] These classifications have roots in the colonial National Forest Policy introduced in 1894 which narrowly defined the access of Adivasis to the forest. However, the situation became worse with subsequent amendments to the Act in 1952—'rights and privileges given to tribesmen and *sadan* in 1894 were transformed into rights and concessions'.[61]

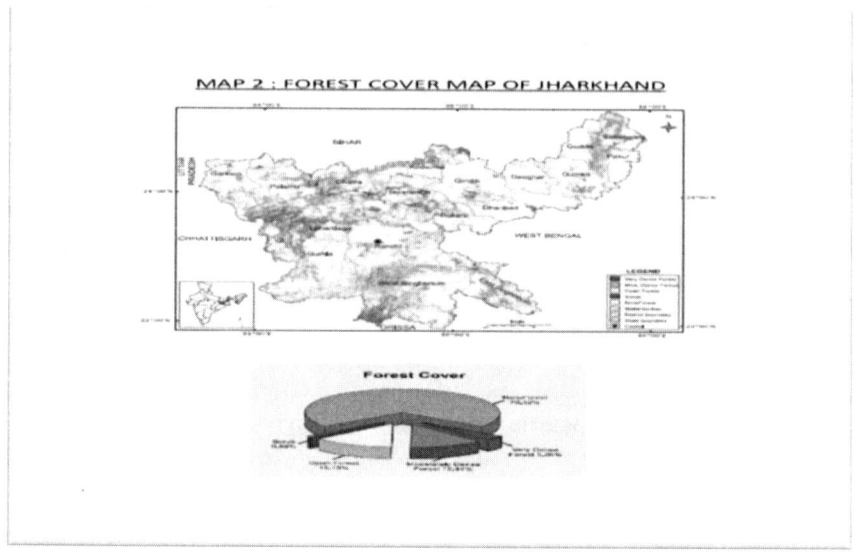

Figure 5.4 Map of Jharkhand's forest cover

Source: Forest Survey of India, cited from *Indian Forest Report*, 2011, Jharkhand.

Furthermore, amendments in 1978 and 1995 introduced several restrictions on people's access to the forests.[62] This suggests that there has been a gradual decline in the Adivasis' access and rights to the forests in the region and at the national level. The Comptroller and Auditor General (CAG) released a report on the management of the Jharkhand state forest in 2017. It stated: 'Though 19.185 lakh hectare was declared as the Protected Forest through preliminary notifications mostly between 1952 and 1967 under the Indian Forest Act, 1927, the Department failed to issue a single final notification in the last 65 years.'[63] In highlighting the need to establish the records, it also noted the failure to ensure alternative livelihoods for affected right holders in the reserve.[64]

The violation of the safeguards enshrined by law, including the CNTA, has been rampant in the state, which led a group of *pathalgadi*s to mount a protest. 'Momentum Jharkhand',[65] held at Ranchi in 2017, was the tipping point for the emergence of the movement.[66] The cover photo for the programme portrayed the mascot, an aesthetically unpleasing elephant with feathers, getting ready to fly to signify the growth of the economy. It promised that the state has 'investment commitments to the tune of over Rupees 3 lakh crore with 210 MoUs (Memorandum of Understandings) being signed' over two days in 2017.[67] Seventy-four proposals were received on the day of Momentum Jharkhand, promising

2,100 crore rupees and 10,000 direct jobs. Besides the promises made at the event, the state had sold a great swathe of land to the Adani Group to produce electricity. This case followed a different trajectory about the immediate response by *pathalgadis*. However, it is constitutive of the more considerable resentment amongst the people. The land acquired by the Adani Group was given legal status, which suggests it had sufficiently fulfilled the conditions of the Social Impact Assessment. Villagers who have lost their land that fell under the SPTA dispute this.[68] In displaying such commitments, the event posed severe threats to land governance in the state. Among others, the land bank and attempts to dilute the CNTA became catalysts for the rise of the movement.

A series of notices released by the government of Jharkhand on the issue of the land bank offer an interesting illustration.[69] They categorize some lands as 'deemed forest' (Figure 5.5).[70] There is no mention of the term in any document on either forest or land policy in the state. However, it is explained as *jungle jhaari, sukhua jungle* (waste and dry forest) in the document in Figure 5.5. This suggests that any land that is not defined as protected or reserved forest can be 'deemed forest'. This is an important point to draw our attention to the use of the land bank because it suggests that the land bank consists of any property that is neither one nor the other. It is also potentially available to the state: 'to facilitate the setting up of technical/educational institutions under private sector the Govt. proposes to provide land from land banks for such institution to willing investors.'[71]

In addition to this, it brings into question the access to forests as guaranteed by the FRA, which was promulgated to correct the historical wrong done to the tribals. Contrary to the dominant narratives of conservation and protection that stemmed from the colonial times and prevailed until now, the FRA established how the relationship between the forest and people is crucial for the coexistence of both. It emphasized the multiple meaning, use and role of the forest in the Adivasi lifeworld (Scheduled Tribe, more broadly), sometimes as 'sacred groves', other times as sources of livelihood.[72] In his recent study, Kashwan demonstrates how parliamentary politics meets subaltern mobilization through the FRA. He suggests that the FRA led to the intertwining of 'popular politics with social mobilization—both of which then shaped the emergence of formal political institutions, including the local government statute—PESA'.[73] There are various cases of rejection of the claims made under the FRA. By 31 January 2019, 42, 29, 230 FRA claims rose to (40,80,842 Individual Forest Rights claims and 1,48,388 Community Forest Rights claims). Most of the individual and collective forest rights allow the community to make claims about their land. In the recent past, a large number of claims have been rejected due to existing discrepancies in the

जिला दण्डाधिकारी एवं उपायुक्त का कार्यालय,
पूर्वी सिंहभूम, जमशेदपुर
(राजस्व शाखा)

अनापत्ति प्रमाण पत्र

पथ प्रमण्डल, जमशेदपुर के अंतर्गत पिपला (एन0एच0–33 पर) घोड़ाबन्धा–गोविन्दपुर–अन्ना चौक तक सड़क निर्माण हेतु इस कार्यालय के ज्ञापांक– 1454/रा0, दिनांक– 25.6.2018 के द्वारा निर्गत अनापत्ति को संशोधित करते हुए जिला स्तरीय वन अधिकार समिति के प्रतिवेदन एवं जिला कल्याण कार्यालय, पूर्वी सिंहभूम, जमशेदपुर के Memo No 1162/2018, dt-26.6.2018 के आधार पर राजस्व एवं भूमि सुधार विभाग के परिपत्र संख्या 1817/रा0, दिनांक– 30.04.2015 के आलोक में "गैर मजरूआ Deemed Forest (जंगल–झाड़ी, सखुआ जंगल इत्यादि) भूमि जो जिला– पूर्वी सिंहभूम, अंचल– जमशेदपुर, मौजा– कस्तुलिया, थाना संख्या– 1206, प्लॉट संख्या– 213, रकबा– 0.217 एकड़ एवं प्लॉट नं0–118, रकबा– 0.718 एकड़, किस्म भूमि– जंगल–झाड़ी में कुल रकबा– 0.935 एकड़ में सन्निहित है, तथा अधिसूचित वन भूमि तथा संरक्षित वन भूमि एवं अन्य वन (Deemed Forest) भूमि से बाहर है, के अपयोजन हेतु माननीय सर्वोच्च न्यायालय द्वारा पारित आदेश के आलोक में प्रयोक्ता एजेन्सी द्वारा वन संरक्षण अधिनियम 1980 के तहत पर्यावरण एवं वन मंत्रालय, भारत सरकार से पूर्वानुमति प्राप्त कर ली जाय। पूर्वानुमति प्राप्त होने के पश्चात् इसके विधिवत् हस्तानांतरण हेतु प्रयोक्ता एजेन्सी द्वारा गैर मजरूआ भूमि के हस्तान्तरण के प्रस्ताव की प्रक्रिया की तरह प्रस्ताव समर्पित किया जायगा। गैर मजरूआ जंगल–झाड़ी (Deemed Forest) भूमि के सशुल्क हस्तान्तरण/लीज बन्दोबस्ती हेतु राजस्व एवं भूमि सुधार विभाग द्वारा राज्यादेश निर्गत किया जायेगा"।

ह0/-

उपायुक्त,
पूर्वी सिंहभूम, जमशेदपुर।

ज्ञापांक –2624/रा0, जमशेदपुर, दिनांक – 01 वीं ~~अक्टूबर~~ नवम्बर 2018 ई0

प्रतिलिपि – कार्यपालक अभियंता, पथ निर्माण विभाग, पथ प्रमण्डल, जमशेदपुर को उनके पत्रांक– 2674, दिनांक– 26.10.2018 के प्रसंग में सूचनार्थ एवं आवश्यक कार्रवाई हेतु प्रेषित।

प्रतिलिपि – वन प्रमण्डल पदाधिकारी, जमशेदपुर को सूचनार्थ एवं आवश्यक कार्रवाई हेतु प्रेषित।

प्रतिलिपि – सचिव, राजस्व, निबंधन एवं भूमि सुधार विभाग, झारखण्ड, राँची को सूचनार्थ एवं आवश्यक कार्रवाई हेतु प्रेषित।

उपायुक्त,
पूर्वी सिंहभूम, जमशेदपुर।

Figure 5.5 A land document outlining the status of 'deemed forest'

Source: Forest, Environment and Climate Change Department, Government of Jharkhand, https://forest.jharkhand.gov.in/About_us/geo_dis.aspx (accessed in September 2022).

methods of the Ministry of Tribal Affairs (MoTA) to produce the updated data.[74] However, the proposal for the FRA in Jharkhand seems to have been a hasty assessment for the land bank.

The state government has acquired '21 lakh acres of *ghair mazurwa* (uncultivated and common)' to woo industries.[75] In doing so, they cancelled various *jamabandi* titles that were assured to Adivasis through an official confirmation in the land records (Khatiyan Part II).[76] Analysing the data (Figure 5.6) that gives away 90 per cent of the specific district to the land bank, Gladson Dungdung asserts:

> This is a gross violation of section 4(1) and (5) of the Forest Rights Act 2006, which recognizes the individual and community rights over the forest and forest land. It has been categorically mentioned in the

Echoes from the Graveyard

Table 2: Forest land in Land Bank

Sl. No.	District	Total Plot	Area of land in Acre	Forest Land In Acre	In %
1	Ranchi	10,327	1,07,677.69	78,256.44	72.68
2	Khunti	5,863	53,387.93	12,888.14	24.14
3	Lohardaga	3,951	14,372.30	9,742.95	67.79
4	Gumla	98,209	1,81,222.78	87,082.74	48.05
5	Simdega	1,10,766	3,58,450.52	2,44,434.50	68.19
6	East Singhbhum	22,151	31,607.71	8,159.21	25.81
7	West Singhbhum	27,041	3,75,662.09	49,922.02	13.29
8	Saraikela	5,609	24,467.66	5,008.71	20.47
9	Bokaro	2,624	21,827.03	19,823.80	90.82
10	Dhanbad	6,504	30,769.46	11,648.14	37.86
11	Ramgarh	574	4,284.94	2,795.72	65.25
12	Kodarma	278	4,128.11	73.38	1.78
13	Hazaribagh	1,973	25,190.21	15,801.12	62.73
14	Chatra	482	6,490.65	5,993.08	92.33
15	Palamu	0	3,005.20	1,668.50	55.52
16	Garhwa	31,319	33,546.72	7,536.10	22.46
17	Latehar	12,508	79,177.25	34,407.49	43.46
18	Dumka	17,308	77,762.05	16,629.96	21.39
19	Pakur	15,460	69,241.36	31,436.90	45.40
20	Deoghar	7,106	43,562.69	15,424.56	35.41
21	Giridih	16,642	4,52,074.26	3,29,539.12	72.89
22	Godda	4,956	23,417.28	5,929.15	25.32
23	Jamtara	9,607	36,086.36	5,803.17	16.08
24	Sahebganj	7,889	39,591.56	16,675.58	42.12
Total		4,19,147	20,97,003.81	10,16,680.48	48.48

Figure 5.6 A land-bank report

Source: 'Land Bank', Department of Land Reform and Revenue, Government of Jharkhand, as cited in Gladson Dungdung's analysis of the land bank.

section 4(5) that no member of a forest dwelling Scheduled Tribe or other traditional forest dweller shall be evicted or removed from forest land under his occupation till the recognition and verification procedure is complete. In fact, the forest rights are denied to the community by enlisting the forest land and community forests in the land Bank.[77]

The land bank emerged as a defining moment for Adivasis to stage their resistance against the historical encroachment that dates back to the making of the modern forest. As K. Sivaramakrishnan writes, 'travelling, surveying, and fighting wild animals, officials of the Company Raj worked to identify, control, and conserve landscapes of production in forests of Bengal', most of which remained prevalent today.[78] Such a colonial idea construed 'forests as a refuge and wild place [laying] the ground for incipient colonial ethnology that would make irreducible differences between caste and tribal society in India'.[79] Significantly, a narrative portraying the *forests as a refuge* in the Raj has now been divided as the protected and reserved forests. The new forms of 'forests as a refuge' is now evident in the remaking of the land bank as a *modern forest*—that which restricts not only the access but also the scope to define land as more than an asset. In that sense, the modern forest is not only emblematic of the 'otherization' of the values of the Adivasi lifeworld but also has become a point that articulates the danger of memorialization. For instance, a key feature of post-colonial Jharkhand, which prides itself on the legacy of Birsa Munda and his anti-colonialism, now supports access to the forest for those who would set up extractive industries. The memorialization becomes *merely symbolic* as a method that situates the present material grievances of Adivasis as inferior to the politics of respecting their past.[80] The image of the past, then, selectively appropriated—as in the case of Birsa Munda—is framed for the national memory of anti-colonialism. Such systematic arrangements of symbolic politics allow the political parties to appease the voters for their specific constituencies. However, in the case of the land bank it has failed to do so: A group of Adivasis organized themselves to confront the state.

The Pathalgadi movement emerged in opposition to the scheme. In displaying their anger, Adivasis used the ancient stone-slab practice. These stone slabs were painted in various colours, predominantly green and white. Each slab bore excerpts from Schedule 5, the PESA and perhaps, most intimidatingly—a signpost for the *dikus* (outsiders) to seek permission for their entry into the village from the *gram sabha*.

In the following section, I examine how the movement took the form of *resistance memory* through visuals and popular representation in the media. In doing so, I argue that memory is an *affective* (affect-as-emotion) tool that Adivasis have used on various occasions to articulate their political consciousness. It offers the complex use of material memory and political mobilization. Importantly, I show that any form of attack on Adivasi land is not merely a form of disruption to their territorial boundaries but *also* an attack on their cosmic structure and worldview.

Landscape of Memory: *Pathalgadi* and the Battle of Cosmologies

On 22 July 2019, an ordinary sultry summer's day, Adivasi groups across India took to the streets to march. As can be seen in Figure 5.7, protestors are holding a banner that says 'Ranchi and Delhi have your rule; my village shall have mine'.[81] The demonstration on the road was against the Supreme Court ruling that directed the state government to evict people from the forest after the failure of their claims under the FRA. This emerged from a hearing on 13 February 2019 regarding a petition by wildlife organizations and retired forest officials against the FRA.[82] However, upon its review of the status on 23 July 2019, the Supreme Court asked for more time to decide.

I invoke this decision and the photo in Figure 5.7 to situate the importance of the forest to Adivasis in India and for indigenous peoples elsewhere in the world. Importantly, the banner that read 'my village, my rule' is reminiscent of the historic struggle with which this book began: 'Their cry is the same as that of the old Sardari malcontents' viz., that the Raj is theirs and not ours, and that they intend to fight for it and get it.'[83] It symbolizes the continued form of conjugated violence, 'historically inherited inequalities of power, which enable dominant groups and the state to control the adverse incorporation of Adivasis and Dalits in the capitalist economy'.[84] The conjugated violence that is evident in the form of discriminatory legislations such as the land bank and land acquisition were frequently invoked in Adivasi areas (Figure 5.8).[85]

Figure 5.7 Protest against the Supreme Court judgment on the Forest Rights Act (FRA), July 2019

Source: Photograph by Mithilesh.

Figure 5.8 Protest against the Forest Rights Act (FRA) judgment
Source: Photograph by Mithilesh.

I also think that these attempts to procure the land (in the case of the Pathalgadi movement) not only disrupt the existing system of governance but also attack the *landscape of memory*. I draw upon Tim Ingold's work to define the landscape as a mode of representation. He considers the landscape as a form of *dwelling perspective* where 'landscape is constituted as an enduring record of—and testimony to—the lives and works of past generations who have dwelt within it, and in doing so, have left there something of themselves'.[86] This is indeed helpful to explain the *resistance memory* of *pathalgadi*s, who considered an attack on land as an attack on the *landscape* that is built on the memory of their ancestors and constitutes their lifeworld. It gives the impression that is palpable in the visual of Ramji Munda in the banner of protest and perhaps in the multiple banners held by indigenous peoples (Māori and First Nations, amongst others) across the world against outsiders.

In the case of the Pathalgadi movement, visuals served as a powerful medium to build a register of protest. It also generated wide-scale mobilization by inscribing provocative statements on the slabs. This underscored the method of using visuals as a medium of politics that captured the landscape of memory. In the narrative, I try to demonstrate the use of the landscape of memory through pictures that I took during my fieldwork and towards the end of the movement.

Visuals as Memory Archives
Environment of Memory I

> In indigenous language, the one word may mean country, hearth, everlasting home, totem, place, lifesource, spirit centre and much more. When I speak of the earth, I may also be speaking of my shoulder or side, of my grandmother, or brother. Removed from our lands, we are literally removed from ourselves.
>
> —Leo van der Vlist quoting indigenous peoples[87]

On 24 September 2018, a collaborator and I drove to Sail Rakab village, situated about 40 miles from the regional capital, Ranchi. On leaving the city, the landscape changes drastically. When I invoke landscape here, I do not refer to nature. The landscape is the environment; nature is one of the components that constitute the landscape. Unlike statues and memorials, a landscape is not an ideal built environment. It is a phenomenon that is 'ever-unfolding' and always 'in-making'.[88] A landscape therefore is a radically different concept. In that sense, Sail Rakab is an environment, not the site of memory.[89]

As we turned left from a well-pitched and broad four-lane asphalt road on National Highway 20 to enter Sail Rakab village, the roads seemed to change. Giant good-carriage buses loaded with sand and coal disappeared. The bustling noise of the extraction business fell into silence along an empty road, and the bulging couch grass (*Elymus repens*) began to rub against the sides of our faces as we drove on our motorbike along a narrow passage. Soon after, we were confronted by a giant stone slab (Figure 5.9). It was green with words painted on it in white. This slab was no ordinary milestone. It was a massive 8–11-foot-tall stone slab surrounded by bamboo canes.

Reading the first line of the words written on the slab filled me both fear and surprise. It read 'non-judicial area'. I re-read it. It said 'non-judicial area'. I could now sense the seething anger as well as the scale of the movement. Unlike the classic portrayal of Adivasis as the 'backwards other' in the nationalist and modern imagination, where they emerge as subjects of modernity projects for the nation, here the Adivasis have shown and challenged these grotesque stereotypes. They have used excerpts from the state's primary document, the Constitution of India, demonstrating use of what Alf Nilsen calls 'legalism from the below'.[90] It occurred to me how resistance is not only displayed as forms of physical movements as in forms of opposition claimed by blockades and marches but also folded in gesturing

Figure 5.9 A *pathalgadi* slab in Sail Rakab, Khunti district

Source: Photograph by the author.

through words. Two ideas seemed apparent to me as I stood reading the slab. One was resistance as the practice of pedagogy, where the Adivasis have refused to suffer what Bob Scholte describes as 'epistemocide'—a state of denial someone's knowledge.[91] The Adivasis were articulating their claims by appropriating the established legal norms meant to safeguard their interests in the areas. Second, and more interestingly, the Adivasis have drawn on their historical memory, an old burial ceremony—a social custom as a template to protest the incursion of the state into their area.

These slabs established the primacy of the *gram sabha*, 'open assemblies that constitute an integral part of a system of decentralized participatory local government in India'.[92] It also suggests what I would call, borrowing from Signe Howell's idea, the 'battle of cosmologies'.[93] Howell's ethnographic work in Indonesia explored the effects of Catholicism on the community in the region, where 'hierarchy is treated both as a model of value, conveyed through asymmetrical relations, and as a system of social organization'.[94] Her research suggests that Catholicism fails to establish equality because it seeks legitimacy through the ideology of egalitarianism, while Lio *adat* (indigenous religion) suggests that the 'whole is considered superior to the individual'.[95]

Furthermore, when people felt an evident hierarchy in *adat*, they accepted it merely because the whole was respected over the individuals. Signe argues: 'Catholicism and Catholic priests' attempts to merge the two, through the ideology and practices of inculturation, fail to capture the people's imagination and emotions.'[96] This is an interesting point to elaborate and draw an analogy with the invocation of 'my village, my rule' by the *pathalgadi*s. As Howell's idea of the social whole led to the battle of cosmologies, it can also be argued that the cosmic structure of Adivasis that focuses on the notion of landscape as a social whole has led to this resistance. To explain what suggests that the resistance is related can be thought as a site of cosmic structure, I will slightly digress to examine why *pathalgadi*s took up *pathalgadi*.

As an old burial practice, the stone slab was evident in the account of Hoffman, where he recounts that 'Sasandiriko horonkokoa pata' (Their burial stones are title-deeds of the Munda race).[97] I would argue here that these burial stones, as also present in *pathalgadi*, represent not only a marker of territory but also an artefact of memory that defines the social cohesion of the community. It produces an affective and cosmological relationship of the human and the land and makes an environment—the landscape of memory. It establishes the hierarchy as a social whole, where the land is customary law, but it also holds the community vis-à-vis the *bonga*s. The presence of this relationship between the land, the human and the *bonga* is woven into the fabric of life—for instance, the idea of *paromrenko* (another world) that explains *bonga*s who dwell in the same world. However, *paromrenko* is distinguished by the sense of being. It is not another world (hell or heaven). This establishes the presence of the spirit (*bonga*) in different things in the environment. Hoffman, who was seminal in framing the CNTA legislation and writing volumes on Mundas, recollects the same:

> They [spirits] dwell in the huts of their nearest relatives, in *streams, rivulets, tanks, ponds, rocks, forests, fields and mountains of their villages*, and Singbonga, the lord of them all, is explicitly declared to be everywhere and see everything.... According to Mundas, sense perception is the only bar between us from them. Bongas are those living beings, which, though firmly believed in as existing and influencing us for good, or evil, can neither be seen nor heard nor perceived: though *fluttering about everywhere*, they are, so far as sense perception goes, just as if they were not.[98]

This suggests that the conceptual world of the Adivasi community cannot possibly separate between human, nature and spirit. The spirit co-constitutes the lifeworld of Adivasis. This also raises an important point about the restricted imagination that emerges from the anthropocentric definition of culture. It not only explains the culture from the worldview of human beings but also separates the environment (nature, spirit) from it. Within the cosmos of Adivasis, where *jal, jungle aur jameen* constitute the lifeworld of the community, it is erroneous to draw such binaries. Doing so, I suggest, also effaces the importance of *place as a memory* that forms the landscape. It isolates the lived experience—the intimacy, touch and sensorial attachment with the place.

In other words, as Ingold writes, 'a place owes its character to the experiences it affords to those who spend time there—to the sights, sounds and indeed smells that constitute its specific ambience. Moreover, these, in turn, depend on the kinds of activities in which its inhabitants engage.'[99] However, the notion of a distinction between nature, culture and human goes back to Eurocentric ideas of property. It is intrinsically tied to the origins of property law. Nicole Graham explores the same phenomena and suggests: 'People–place relations were translated into systems of property and measured against the standard of English property law as though those people–place relations or property systems were culturally and geographically non-specific.'[100]

These laws in their local form translate into the property rights that disenfranchise the community from co-constituting the worldview. Furthermore, 'people–place relations were not compared in terms of differentials but in terms of the degree of attainment of a universal [English] standard.'[101] It is with this articulation of the binary between people and place that laws within colonial India introduced a new way of thinking about property. This has had a direct impact on forest-dwelling communities. The Pathalgadi movement, in some sense, suggests that the tension has roots in the definitions of the land and property. It does so by using a traditional template against the modern state. The following discussion focuses on the use of law and the response from the state.

Environment of Memory II

As soon as I finished reading the notice on the stone slab, we moved further barefoot into the stretch of the village surrounded by an elephant corridor and spotted another slab (Figure 5.10). The placement of slabs was strategic. Each faced the main road of entry into the village in the incoming direction. Both the slabs that I surveyed displayed used articles from the Constitution except one that read 'non-judicial areas' on it. On both slabs, the use of Article 19(6) and Article 244(1) of Schedule 5 was the most interesting. These two Articles provide safeguards against interference in the Scheduled Tribe areas. For instance, Article 19(6) states:

> Nothing in sub-clauses (d) and (e) of the said clause shall affect the operation of any existing law in so far as it imposes, or prevents the State from making any law imposing reasonable restrictions on the exercise of any of the rights conferred by the said sub-clauses either in the interests of the general public or for the protection of the interests of any Scheduled Tribe.[102]

Clause (d) states 'to move freely throughout the territory of India' and clause (e) states 'to reside and settle in any part of the territory of India'.[103] This suggests that *pathalgadi*s were using the existing law—that is, Schedule 5—in Sail Rakab (Khunti district) and other areas to establish norms meant to safeguard the rights of Scheduled Tribes. However, it emerged as a provocation for the state. This is primarily because the movement drew upon an old belief and a cult popular amongst Adivasis in western India.

The Sati Pati cult in Gujarat 'denounces Government of India' and 'believes that natural resources like forest land and rivers were gifted by Queen Victoria to Keshri Singh, their founder, pre-independence. They disassociate themselves with

Figure 5.10 *A pathalgadi* slab in Khunti district
Source: Photograph by the author.

any activity propagated by the local, state or central government.'[104] The disregard for the government within the Pathalgadi movement emerged from seeking refuge in Constitutional remedies—an approach unique to the resistance in this part of the region. It became what Nandini Sundar calls 'Constitutional Messianism', where Adivasis have drawn 'outlandish' features from 'heaven's light' (*sati pati*). However, it has 'a strong kernel of truth to it, which resonates with people whose daily lives have been made difficult by an ignorant and indifferent bureaucracy'.[105] In my conversations, I found *sati pati* at best a partial account of the movement, if not a deviation to the *pathalgadi*s. Gopal Munda, a resident in Khunti district, expressed his disagreement with the orientation towards *sati pati*, casting their ideals as a deviation from traditional Munda groups, more specifically Sarna Dharam and their demands. Much of this tension is still brewing in the region and was captured recently in a report by Deepanwita Gita Niyogi, where an activist spoke of Hindutva influence on *sati pati* and asserted: 'Not observing Adivasi festivals and developing a different tradition signifies that these people are going in a different direction. Incidentally, *sati pati* is spreading at a time when tribals are demanding the Sarna religious code.'[106]

However, the circulation of rumours produced a number of narratives about the movement. In fact, upon finishing my field visits, narratives—not facts— dominated the flow of information. Rumour became an effective tool of political mobilization.[107] Various reports selectively highlighted the more outlandish features of the movement. Words such as 'non-judicial' on the slabs, which were used as a form of provocation, drew attention but also severely damaged the movement. By the middle of 2018 the movement had begun to come under massive pressure. A variety of allegations, charges and crackdowns were used by the state.

Responses from the State: Opium and the Sedition

On 5 March 2019, Gladson Dungdung, a well-known social activist, interviewed the lead figure in the Pathalgadi movement. I did not have access to the area due to safety issues and compliance with ethical guidelines. The region was badly affected by militancy, and staying there would have been dangerous. I therefore had to rely on Dungdung's interview as a source to build a narrative.[108] In the interview, Sukhram Munda, also the headman of Kochang village (Khunti district), denied the claim that Pathalgadi was unconstitutional. He asserted: 'In fact, we have carved the Constitutional provision on the stone slab to educate and make aware our Adivasis. Pathalgadi is our tradition. We install stone slabs on many social and cultural occasions.'[109] Denying the claims made by other leaders of Pathalgadi, who had asked Adivasis to boycott the government's schemes, Sukhram, in fact, said: 'I have given my land for a school free of cost, a health sub-centre is being run in my house for the last couple of decades, and an Aanganvadi centre was also in my house.'[110] However, he seemed enraged about the land grab in the area.

Responding to the land acquisition, he said: 'After Kochang gang-rape incident, a police camp was set up in the school of my village. I have given land for the school free of cost, but another 14 decimals of my land were grabbed for construction of toilet for *jawan*s [constables] without my consent or any compensation.'[111] On 6 July 2019, two unidentified persons shot Sukhram Munda down.[112] His death brought many people out onto the streets. However, the various allegations and charges against many people remain to be heard in court.

The responses of the BJP government led by chief minister Raghuvar Das came in the form of two significant allegations. First, it was alleged that the movement was an attempt to safeguard the business of opium cultivation in the region: 'Opium is cultivated in 2,700 acres of land in Jharkhand, of which 1,500 acres, that is, almost 58% of the total area, falls in the Khunti district alone.'[113] Second, the government charged various people under the secession laws in the immediate aftermath of the movement, and several people were booked under sedition laws.[114] The scale of the sedition charges is enormous—as many as 30,000 people, which is roughly 10 per cent of people in Khunti district, have been brought within the scope of the law.[115]

The movement raises severe concerns about unresolved questions concerning land politics in the state (Figure 5.11). The region has witnessed several resistance movements throughout its history to highlight the same. However, this has not received a sufficient democratic and institutional response. Pathalgadi is not a movement that can be quelled using laws such as sedition, which is primarily meant to be used against 'anti-national' activities. Pathalgadi is a register of protest that draws on historical memory and tension and enables a mode to articulate the rights of Adivasis. It is a form of conjugated violence because the state does not use effective and democratic means of redress in cases where land contains mineral resources. In fact, most of the laws that have roots in the colonial order have received further extension and support in post-colonial India in order to develop industrial corridors. Notably, as Sundar observes, 'laws dealing with expropriation of land and resources away from groups, which formerly controlled them, were violent in themselves and the maintenance of "law and order" part of a coercive order rather than any law'.[116] These arrangements therefore allow the state to use unsuitable laws, often casting the whole group of people as 'anti-national' and continuing to harness the legacy of colonialism. Various groups protested the disproportionate use of harsh laws (such as sedition) to sabotage the movement. These groups of people who work in the various organizations came together under the Jharkhand Janadhikar Mahasabha (JJM), a civil society, which submitted a memorandum to the Governor with the following demands:

Echoes from the Graveyard

Figure 5.11 A newspaper clipping capturing the congregation of Adivasis on the eve of a *pathalgadi* installation. Men, armed with traditional weapons, are performing customary rituals.

Source: *Hindustan Times*, Ranchi, 26 February 2018.

1. The government must immediately withdraw all frivolous FIRs [first information reports] filed against the thousands of unnamed residents of Khunti and activists on charges of sedition. It must also undertake a judicial inquiry into the charges framed against the named people in the FIRs. It must make public all the evidence that formed the basis for these FIRs and the evidence collected in all related inquiries since then.

2. The government should undertake a judicial inquiry into the violence unleashed by security forces in Ghaghra and other villages and ensure punitive action against the personnel responsible for the human rights abuses. It must ensure compensation to victims of human rights violations in these villages.

3. The government should initiate dialogue with representatives of the Pathalgadi villages, Adivasi organisations and experts on the Constitution.

4. The government must ensure immediate implementation of all provisions of the Fifth Schedule and PESA in letter and spirit.[117]

These demands targeted the charges, a judicial inquiry for a fair trial and the implementation of Constitutional rights enshrined under Schedule 5. Along with the memorandum there was a general atmosphere of intimidation of activists, including the recent attack on Stan Swamy, who works for the rights of Adivasis, and on the PESA and the Land Acquisition Act. The JJM also demanded 'an immediate end to the raids, dropping of all false charges against human rights activists across the country and release of those who are arrested. This harassment is politically motivated and wholly unjustified.'[118]

The responses from the state have not sufficiently addressed any of the issues. There was a state election due by the end of 2019, and such issues posed a significant challenge to the regional parties. However, the movement draws our attention to unresolved tensions regarding the land and the law. It demonstrates various possibilities to understand the structural conflict. Singh suggests that it is developing in two ways: 'the government which is trying to assert its authority', while 'the Adivasis in the villages appear oblivious to the nuances of the present politics, but they continue to repose a deep faith in their customary practices and traditional systems'.[119] This is useful to understand the sub-national sentiment that remains prevalent in this region. However, a sense of deep distress underlies the movement, emerging from the attack on the environment of memory: the land, the spirit (*bonga*) and the legacy of self-governance.

Following the relentless repression, I visited some of the villages in Khunti district during the last leg of my field research to trace the vestiges of the movement. The visit was driven by the desire to understand the linkages between memory, the movement and Birsa Munda. The movement had obviously begun from Birsa's hometown and mobilized the struggle of *jal, jungle aur jameen*. Besides, Birsa, both within the movement and outside, is used as a metaphor to assert *khuntkhatti* rights.[120] To examine the relationship between Birsa and the memory of rebellion, the following section explores the Adivasi territorial notions of belonging in the region. In doing so, I argue that the politics of memory in predominantly Adivasi constituencies emerges at the intersection of cultural milieu (such as burial practices), resistance and the image of the past. This allows the Adivasis to articulate their political desire for territorial power and resentment against the onslaught of neo-liberal policies. It encompasses a range of issues folded into the image of the past that is mobilized in the resistance.

Flickering Hope at the Margin: Birsaites, Forgotten Tales of Rebellion and the State

> We survive with the memory of Birsa Munda. We do not have anything to lose. We do not sing and dance. We are not ordinary Adivasis. We are Birsaite Adivasis: those who do not eat non-vegetarian or drink *hadia*. We have strict rules of living…. Memory of Birsa makes us survive (Figure 5.12).
>
> —Sombari, in an interview[121]

12 June 2019, Charid (Khunti)

After having met a few Birsaites at a day-long function held at Ulihatu (Khunti) marked by a procession, chanting and singing on Birsa's martyr day (9 June), I gathered some information to meet more Birsaites—those who follow Birsa. Having by now spent months in Jharkhand for field research fraught with unexpected turns of events ranging from political visits in Ulihatu to Pathalgadi, I was beginning to feel the significance of Birsa, who at once remained an empty signifier (for the state to manipulate) while also working as a unifying force in resistance movements. Memory, as for this research, I am aware can never be one thing. Later, on 12 June, a collaborator and I arrived in Charid (Khunti), a village divided into two *tola*s (units). In one of our first visits to a house in the *chotka tola* (smaller unit), we were received by Sombari. Fresh grains had been spread out and left to dry under the sun on a veranda, while the corner of the veranda was circled by a *tulsi* (holy basil) plant. Sombari, perhaps in her 50s, had piercing eyes with a cotton white saree draped around her body as she slowly chanted hymns about Birsa. As she spoke there was a constant attempt to self-identify as a Birsaite Adivasi. Tempted by my question about the environment (land, spirit and memory) as I sat down opposite the door to her small one-room clay house, she said:

> We think God exists in everything: *forest, wind, water*. God resides in this *environment*. We get together every Thursday at my place to worship our Birsa. We chant to remember Birsa Munda. We do not have his ideal. We do not follow *daan dakshina* [religious charity]. We have his memory.[122]

Sombari described her worldview as an omnipresent force that exists in the environment: *forest, wind, water*. Assuring me of her beliefs, she invited us for a chanting session the following month. We sat down for a few hours, mostly rambling through descriptions of her everyday live as a Birsaite. As soon as we

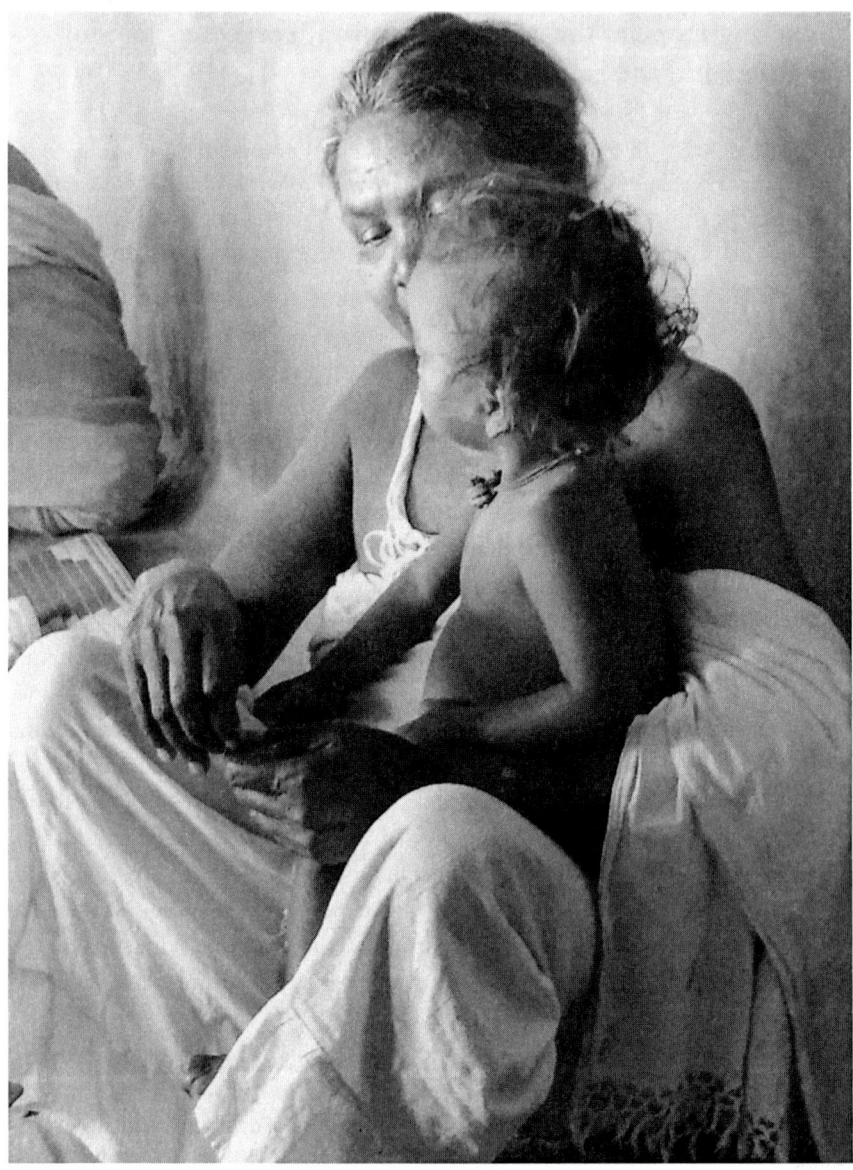

Figure 5.12 A Birsaite recounting her story of everyday life of remembering Birsa

Source: Photograph by the author.

left her to find other people, she screamed at us: 'I don't consider you *diku*. Come back for the chanting.'[123] In that moment, having spent months in the region, I felt the strong, deep-rooted, almost jolting rush of close acceptance. But I was also disheartened to find no other Birsaite families nearby (Figure 5.13). However, we heard an older man at a distance, calling to us.

Bosu Pahan, an old man in his late 60s, identifies himself as one of the 'true Birsaites'.[124] He offered us a seat on his open veranda strewn with dry forage and jackfruit leaves. As we settled down, he began to give an illustrative description of his heritage. Not only did his face beam with a sense of pride but his voice also became joyful. He said that the true identity of a Birsaite is symbolized by a flag hoisted at their house. He said: 'Look around. I have a flag hoisted.' I turned around and saw a tricolour Indian flag. Seen from afar, it looked somewhat unusual. I asked him why it looked different. He calmly told me that he has not cleaned it in a while. Meanwhile, his son, Nile, joined the conversation. Nile was asked by his father to show us a document that establishes everything about Birsaism as claimed by Pahan.

Figure 5.13 Birsaites congregated at Birsa Munda's house to observe the anniversary of his death, 9 June 2019

Source: Photograph by the author.

Reflecting on his identity and ideas of a native, Nile explained that he had a range of documents (supplemented by memory) to trace and establish his heritage in Charad in Khunti district. The impression of Pathalgadi that generated suspicion—defined by the need to have proof—was looming large in our conversation. The legal battles are deeply rooted in causes of the historical tension in this region (as is shown in Chapter 2) and goes back to the British Empire, which 'was defined by a pervasive legalism and an abiding concern that colonial rule be formally embedded in a rule of law.'[125] Claiming that the *khatian* (records) bear his name, he insisted that we look at some materials that establish his community as more than *just* Adivasis. *Khatian*s play a vital role in ascertaining the historical records of the native. Macpherson, in his survey of land rights in Porahat, underlines the primacy of *khatian* in establishing the *khuntkhatti* rights of Mundas (Figure 5.14). He notes:

Figure 5.14 A Birsaite household in Khunti district

Source: Photograph by the author.

> As to the method employed in recording Mundar Khuntkattidars—all whose names appear in the *Khatians* are named in the records-of-rights. The Mundari *khuntkhattidar* must be in possession of land in the village. No attempt could be made to indicate the actual ancestral lands. In many cases claims to be recorded were made by landless *bhuinhars* now residing in other villages, because they feared that unless recorded, they henceforth are not be allowed to bury in their own village, but they do not satisfy the legal definition.[126]

These historical bearings remain significant. Meanwhile, Nile rushed out of the room with a document in his hand (Figure 5.16). He said: 'You see this document—it lays out the foundations for Birsaism. It is an old document. We remember Birsa through this document. It makes us who we are and how we live.'[127] The 23-page document outlined various interesting descriptions of Birsa Munda and his life. Two key features were prominent in the document. First, it did not situate the role of Adivasiness. It foreclosed any possibility to recognize Birsa as an Adivasi at all—outlining characteristics in so far it highlights his messianic charisma. Second—although inconsistent with historical facts such as the description of his movement—the document emphasized the role of Birsa in shaping the nation.

Jhanda (flag) formed an interesting part—for instance, on page 21 of the document, the flag has 'three colours with no chakra in it', as pointed out by Bosu. The slogan that follows is 'Gae Mata ki jai. Governor Sarkar ki jai. Pandit Jawaharlal Nehru ki jai' (Long live the Cow Goddess. Long live the Governor. Long live Nehru) (Figure 5.15). Interestingly, it claimed that Gandhi was a reincarnation of Birsa Munda—a popular impression found in Tana Bhagat, a group which preaches that 'the Oraon religion should be freed of evils like ghost-finding and exorcism, belief in *bhut*s [spirits], animal sacrifice and drinking'.[128]

Nationalist sentiment in the representation of Birsa Munda, both among Birsaites and in the memorialization process by the state, is invariably dominant. Two factors drive the identification with the nation. First is an absence of substantial historical records to establish the political ideology of the movement. Second, it reflects a conscious effort to frame Birsa as an anti-colonial icon, politically frozen, upon whom to direct historical emotions and struggle including rebellions against the *zamindars*. The valorization of Birsa saved them from being charged as anti-national. This was also evident when Bosu mentioned his friend in a nearby village who was not troubled during the police raids regarding the Pathalgadi case. In fact, the Birsaite family had had a hand pump installed in their courtyard as a

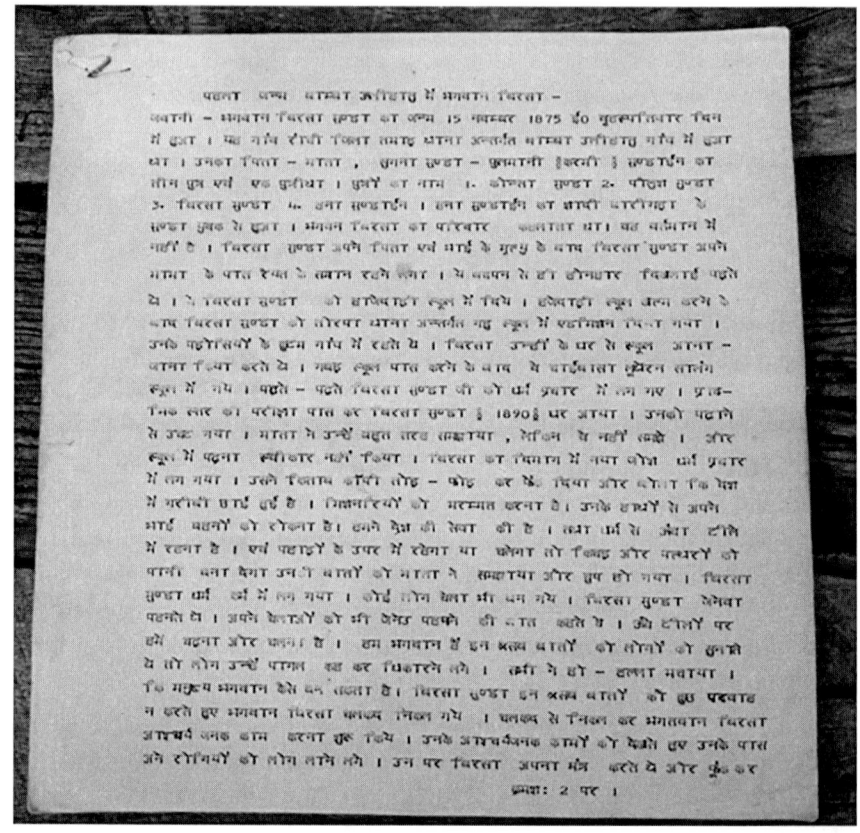

Figure 5.15 A document explaining Birsa Munda's history and the traits of Birsaism

Source: Photograph by the author.

part of the government scheme. This was because they had hoisted a flag at their house (Figure 5.16).

Besides, the document also performs a mnemonic and political function. It is mnemonic because it embodies 'concrete traces of the past. Instrumental to consensual notions about the past, they help define memory itself.'[129] Inconsistent with the historical facts, the documents nonetheless organizes the Birsaite lifeworld. It effectively grants Birsaites a place in the nationalist past which offers refuge in troubled times today. They negotiate with the state through symbolic acts (flags), documents and narratives, which, in turn, allows them to be represented in the 'imagined community' of the nationalist past.[130] Memory through commemorative practices plays a significant role here by dovetailing the broader aspirations of nationalism to regional histories that are far more plural and diffused. For instance,

Figure 5.16 A Birsaite house in Khunti district

Source: Photograph by the author.

Birsaites' constant attempts to hover between the plains of national unity through the symbolic flag and documents enable them to draw out a distinct ideal of political space. In their work on memory and nationalism, Katharine Hodgkin and Susannah Radstone assert:

> In nationalist movements and in achieved nations alike, the appeal to memory articulates the narrative of the nationalist past, and enjoins its subject to recognise and own it.... Memory is thus at the heart of nationalist struggles, transmitted from one generation to the next as a sacred injunction.... [It] is also one of the major mobilizing forces in the modern nation state.[131]

However, such identification with the nation is a political act. Birsa's own political method in the past is noticeable in the attitude of Birsaites today. For instance, a report noted that Birsa invoked a puritan practice to an extent that jeopardized ordinary non-Birsaite Mundas. Hoffman notes:

> A belief in Birsa as the saviour of the Munda race, associated possibly with glimmerings of the New Testaments picked by their family … leaving the Christians on one side, the great majority of heathen *Mundas are now against Birsa* (thanks to the two experiences they have had of a police occupation of their tract of the country).[132]

Historically, Birsaites have mobilized their political ambition under this religious canopy. In other words, religion is not neatly distinct from the political. It is indeed the 'sacral polity', as Alpa Shah puts it, that defines the social structure of Mundas in Chota Nagpur.[133] The reflection of such an attitude is evident in the way Hoffman recalls: 'I did not fully realize the danger of an armed rebellion … although I saw the necessity of laying hand on the man who, under the garb of religion, had assumed a purely political role of high ambition.'[134] Religious practice driven by puritan and political ambition served a varied purpose. It 'allowed the Birsaites to accumulate in their house any amount of arms' during the movement.[135] In that sense, the 'sacral polity' within the Birsaite worldview offers a different version of political consciousness. To locate the political consciousness of Birsa within the contemporary political dispensation, I sought to meet more members of the community.

Birsaites, **Pathalgadi** *and the State*

As the day was drawing to dusk, Bosu very insistently took us to Birsaite families who lived across the farmland in another *tola*. We walked through a vast field across patches of cracked soil. An elevated mud bridge divided each field. Looking across the fields while we walked under the sweltering sun, the absence of water was glaringly evident. There had been an uproar in Jharkhand in 2018 due to the depletion of groundwater levels. Predominantly an agrarian belt, Adivasis in the remote villages of the state are now suffering the most. As we reached another *tola*, we found a cluster of houses with a flag hoisted. Bosu gathered his friends, and we were invited to sit inside the house had that suffered heavy water seepage through the roof during the rains. There was a single room for six members of the family to share.

By this time I had begun to feel more comfortable about asking political questions. Eight members from three different families joined us. Birju took the lead to speak in Hindi with us while occasionally translating the conversation but was frequently interrupted by an elderly woman sitting across the room. She found it unusual that we had come to talk about Birsa. Birju made some remarkable observations about Birsaites. He said: 'We are not political people. We pray and live in the most minimal condition for humans to survive.' I insisted on knowing about his job and income. He quickly replied: 'I am self-employed. I work on the piece of land that belongs to us.'

Upon being asked about the absence of electricity in the house and the access to the free gas (cylinder) scheme, Birju seemed hesitant. While we waited for his reply, he turned around to discuss something in Mundari with his fellow men. Over the years I have come to understand the lack of trust Adivasis hold against outsiders when they are questioned about government schemes. A series of false charges and regular intimidation lie at the heart of this suspicion. Bagicha, a research institute later run by Stan Swamy, prepared a comprehensive list of falsely framed Adivasi youths and raised questions about serious human-rights violations. The report showed that of the youths under trial in Jharkhand, 97 per cent of those who are arrested in connection with Maoists' militancy and Naxalite violence have nothing to do with them.[136]

Aware of the political climate, Birju chose to respond in evasive ways. He insisted that his reply might disappoint me: 'I do not have access to electricity, and I do not want it. It entails a complex process of document verification that I cannot undergo.' Furthermore, he explained: 'I spoke with the dealer [contractor], and he needs me to have a certain document such as Aadhaar to access these services. I cannot do this. If it is an *anudaan* [free service] policy for the poor, then give it free. They are doing it to make us all have our Aadhaar.' Unlike Bosu, who holds a range of documents, Birju expressed his disagreement with policies demanding identity documents. The Aadhaar card is a unique twelve-digit identification card that takes a person's biometric details such as fingerprints, eye scans and demographic information to create a national database. The card has stirred serious debate, and even though it is not mandatory, an increasing number of services require it. People in Jharkhand have faced serious issues, especially in accessing rationed food, due to the absence of the Aadhaar card. In his findings on the card, Kunal Purohit reports: 'The state has seen 19 starvation deaths, the highest in any Indian state since 2015. One district in Jharkhand, Garhwa, has seen three deaths in that period.'[137] The report offers the list of nine deceased persons who were all invariably denied access to rations due to the absence of the Aadhaar card.[138] This has created panic amongst those who remained suspicious of proof and identity.

Birju's disagreement with policies such as Aadhaar is rooted in deep suspicion towards any 'proof of residency': 'Adivasis mulwaasi hai' (Adivasis are original settlers). Ideological basis for the Pathalgadi movement also reflects similar sentiment. The ideological differences with the machinery of the state, said Birju, are important to understand:

> We have information about how much money was allotted to this block. It was 16,000 crores. We have seen it on a friend's phone. The contractor is making a fool out of us. We cannot be forced to make Aadhaar or produce any document to access anything. I would rather die of starvation than make such a card.

I insisted he explain why he feels so resentful about having a national identity card that grants easier access to schemes. He said:

> It will require us to declare our land and address. It is not only about Aadhaar. Other policies such as Indira Aawas Jogna that makes it compulsory agreement and seek our *khaata* [account] details. There are so many *rashid*s [tickets] that are issued by the government. I cannot get this. It needs revenue tickets. If our land is sold, what will we do? I am not sure what it would do to our heritage and us. The only asset that we own is our ancestral land.

This underlines the wariness shown towards *diku*s (outsiders). For Birsaites, who otherwise display symbols of nationalism such as the flag, documents establishing their identity are unfathomable and affiliation to leaders is incomprehensible. The identity that is secured through the revenue ticket and cards allows the state to recognize them as native. It seems to give primacy to the *outsider*—the state. I think this is most primal to the conflict—the village is their kingdom, and it is under their rule. People in the region do not recognize or at least are invariably suspicious of the institutional structure and tenets of procedural democracy that governs the nation outside the boundaries of the *disum*. This is evident in the *pathalgadis*' story as well as that of Birju.

Therefore, a story about the politics of memory that mobilizes Birsa Munda as an anti-colonial figure has various facets. On one level it is appropriated into mainstream party politics, where Birsa becomes a significant symbol of nationalism through a closed form, a politically laden memorialization process. However, Birsa's memory also reinvigorates the spirit of *abua disum, abua raj*. Both Pathalgadi and Birju display the latter sentiment and are unified in their political ideology folded in historic angst about the *saheblok* and the government. It is also reminiscent of the Sardari *ladai*—the resistance in a new frame. While the former (Pathalgadi) took up a violent form of mobilization and emphasized the militant outlook of Birsa, the latter reflects a passive form of resistance. Common to both is an ideological force to protect the landscape of memory from the *diku*s.

Summary

This chapter presented the working of memory through a case study of the Pathalgadi movement. It has shown different strands of a movement that in the end took a radical turn. In doing so, it displayed an essential use of memory drawn from the customary practice of the community. As artefacts and mnemonic sites of memory, graveyards within the movement became a marker of territorial claims. This echoed the voices from the past—where colonial officials had also underscored this phenomenon. Even though the movement had had outlandish features and exhibited an aggressive approach, it certainly succeeded in establishing the links between the struggles of the past and those of the present.

In tracing the links to the past, the movement also highlighted the lack of institutional measures and safeguards to ensure the protection of land within contemporary legislative arrangements. It showed the active interest of the state in expanding the industrial corridor and promoting companies that have wrought havoc on the region. An impressive range of new categories of development and amendments—the land bank and the new Jharkhand Right to Fair Compensation and Transparency in Land Acquisition, Rehabilitation and Resettlement (LAA Amendment) Act, 2017—now define the landscape of burgeoning conflict.[139] Fundamentally, these new changes confront the existing protectionary laws such as the CNTA and the SPTA. To remove the possibility of a hindrance to the extension of development projects, the state government has *attempted* to dilute these laws. An attempt to dilute such protective legislation proved to be deleterious for the state. Adivasi groups have demonstrated complete defiance towards the change.

Similarly, the Pathalgadi movement repudiated the land bank and amendments to the Land Acquisition Act.

Fundamentally, this chapter highlighted the gap in our understandings of land. I suggested that there are two main problems. First, for the community, the land is not merely a tradable asset—it is one of the components of the broader landscape of memory. The landscape of memory consists of a variety of elements, such as heritage and the 'belonging' of the dead. The attack on land is therefore an attack on the cosmological order of the community. Second, there is a prevalent sentiment amongst the community that continues to treat any form of intervention in self-rule as an attack by outsiders. The community derives its sovereignty from their self-rule within the village. The power of control and governance lies with traditional authority such as the *pahan*.

The resistance highlighted a unique characteristic of post-colonial India. In particular, the Pathalgadi movement displayed the limits of memorialization politics by reversing it. It upset the usual order of political mobilization, where a subaltern icon such as Birsa Munda is invoked to validate the power of the state. *Pathalgadi*s mobilized the memory of the past to assert their resistance against the colonial order—where resistance is rooted not in 'opposition to the effects of power' but rather in the form of 'struggle against the privilege of knowledge'.[140] In establishing the resistance, they used a modern strategy—referring to the Constitution of India that guarantees the rights of Adivasis. This is evident in strategies used by Adivasis elsewhere.[141]

Notes

1. Tim Ingold, 'Temporality of the Landscape', *World Archaeology* 25, no. 2 (1993): 152–74, pp. 152–53.
2. A. Kumar Giri, 'Lifeworlds and Living Words', *Social Change* 49 (2019): 241–56.
3. Anjana Singh, 'Many Faces of the Pathalgadi Movement in Jharkhand'. *Economic and Political Weekly* 54, no. 11 (2019): 28–33.
4. *Report on the Settlement of the Estate of the Maharajah of Chota Nagpur*, shelf mark no. IOR P/W 397, Page 46, British Library, London (emphasis mine).
5. John-Baptist Hoffman, *Mundarica Encyclopedia*, vol. 13. New Delhi: Gian Publishing House, 1912, p. 3868.
6. Subhashis Das, 'The Hargarhis of Jharkhand: A Brief Study of the Megaliths of Jharkhand', *Chitrolekha International Magazine on Art and Design* 5, no. 1 (2015): 2–21.
7. The burial grounds were treated as common property during the settlement of the land in Chota Nagpur. They are also free of rent. See *Report on the Settlement of the Estate of the Maharajah of Chota Nagpur*.

8   Das, 'The Hargarhis of Jharkhand'.
9   Howard Williams, 'Cremation and Present Pasts: A Contemporary Archaeology of Swedish Memory Grove', *Mortality* 16, no. 2 (May 2011): 113–30, p. 114.
10 Ibid.
11 Howard Williams, 'The Emotive Force of Early Medieval Mortuary Practices', *Archaeological Review from Cambridge* 22, no. 1 (2007): 107–23, p. 109.
12 'The Chota Nagpur Tenancy Act being Act 6 of 1908 with notes, judicial rulings framed under the act by J. Reid', shelf mark T 7377, British Library, London.
13 See M. Topno, 'Funeral Rites of the Mundas', *Anthropos* (1955): 715–34.
14 John-Baptist Hoffman, *Mundarica Encyclopedia*, vol. 2 (New Delhi: Gian Publishing House, 1912), p. 3869.
15 Alpa Shah has an interesting description of this conflict drawing on the forest policies that are enforcing the conflict. See Alpa Shah, *In the Shadows of the State: Indigenous Politics, Environmentalism and Insurgency in Jharkhand, India* (New Delhi: Oxford University Press, 2011).
16 Topno, 'Funeral Rites of the Mundas', p. 729.
17 Ibid.
18 Ken Taylor, 'Landscape and Memory: Cultural Landscapes, Intangible Values and Some thoughts on Asia', Research School of Humanities, Australian National University, Canberra, 2008.
19 'The Chota Nagpur Tenancy Act being Act 6 of 1908' (emphasis mine).
20 Ibid.
21 Barbara Verado, 'Rebels and Devotees of Jharkhand: Social, Religious and Political Transformation among the Adivasi of Northern India', PhD dissertation, London School of Economics and Political Science, University of London, 2003, p. 96 (emphasis mine).
22 Ibid.
23 Elsewhere the concept of 'memory law' is deeply associated with the legislation that addresses the denial of the Holocaust in the context of Europe. I do not use it in the same sense.
24 Nicholas Dirks, *Castes of Mind: Colonialism and the Making of Modern India* (Princeton, NJ: Princeton University Press, 2001).
25 Kaushik Ghosh, 'Indigenous Incitements', In *Indigenous Knowledge and Learning in Asia/Pacific and Africa*, ed. D. Kapoor and E. Shizha, pp. 35–46 (New York: Palgrave Macmillan, 2010).
26 Dirks, 'Castes of Mind', p. 60.
27 Ibid., p. 75.
28 Ghosh, 'Indigenous Incitements', p. 40 (emphasis mine).
29 Ibid.

30 Kaushik Ghosh, 'Between Global Flows and Local Dams: Indigenousness, Locality, and the Transnational Sphere in Jharkhand, India', *Cultural Anthropology* 21, no. 4 (2006): 501–34, p. 508.
31 Ibid.
32 See Ghosh, 'Between Global Flows and Local Dams', p. 508.
33 Ingold, 'Temporality of the Landscape'.
34 For the visual content, see Koustav De, 'Gaon Chodab Nahi (We Will Not Leave Our Village)', YouTube video, 28 March 2009, www.youtube.com/watch?v=8M5aeMpzOLU&t=108s (accessed on 20 December 2019). See the appendix for the translation and transliteration.
35 Alpa Shah, Jens Lerche, Richard Axelby, Dalel Benbabaali, Brendan Donegan, Jayaseelan Raj and Vikramaditya Thakur (eds.), *Ground Down by Growth: Tribe, Caste, Class and Inequality in 21st Century India* (London: Pluto Press, 2017).
36 See Shah, Lerche, Axelby, Benbabaali, Donegan, Raj and Thakur (eds.), *Ground Down by Growth*.
37 Amarnath Tewary, 'The Pathalgadi Rebellion', *The Hindu*, 13 April 2018, www.thehindu.com/news/national/other-states/the-pathalgadi-rebellion/article23530998.ece (accessed on 20 December 2019).
38 Mona Lilja, 'The Politics of Time and Temporality in Foucault's Theorisation of Resistance: Ruptures, Time-Lags and Decelerations', *Journal of Political Power* 11, no. 3 (2 September 2018): 419–32, p. 422.
39 James Clifford, 'Indigenous Articulations', *Contemporary Pacific* 13, no. 2 (2001): 469–90.
40 Malini Nambiar, 'Making the Gram Sabha'. *Economic and Political Weekly* 36, no. 33 (2001): 3114–17, p. 3114.
41 Ibid., p. 3115.
42 See 'The Provisions of the Panchayats (Extension to the Scheduled Areas) Act, 1996' (New Delhi: Ministry of Tribal Affairs, Government of India, 1996).
43 Subhra Tuhin, 'The Pathalgadi Movement: An Overview', Sanhati, 30 October 2018, http://sanhati-india.org/2018/10/30/the-pathalgadi-movement-an-overview (accessed on 2 January 2020).
44 Singh, 'Many Faces of the Pathalgadi Movement in Jharkhand'.
45 Ibid., p. 29.
46 Virginius Xaxa, 'Is the Pathalgadi Movement in Tribal Areas Anti-Constitutional?'. *Economic and Political Weekly* 54, no. 1 (2019): 10–12.
47 Ibid., p. 10.
48 Ibid., p. 11.
49 P. K. Dutta, 'Pathalgadi Movement, a Rebellion against the Government with Opium Taint', *India Today*, 27 June 2018, https://www.indiatoday.in/india/story/

pathalgadi-movement-jharkhand-khunti-1270963-2018-06-27 (accessed on 20 December 2019).

50. D. Sarkar, 'Pathalgadi Masterminds Arrested in Kochang Gangrape of 5 Tribal Girls', *Hindustan Times*, 22 July 2018, https://www.hindustantimes.com/india-news/pathalgadi-masterminds-arrested-in-kochang-gangrape-of-5-tribal-girls/story-iTwScm2DOeytFNkZgrXQdJ.html (accessed on 15 January 2020).

51. For a detailed alternative narrative of the rape, refer to this report that contains the testimony of one of the survivors: Javed Iqbal, 'Jharkhand Gang-Rape Survivor's Account Upends Narrative of Pathalgadi Role', *The Wire*, 26 July 2018, https://thewire.in/rights/jharkhand-pathalgadi-movement-gang-rape-police-firing (accessed on 15 January 2020).

52. 'Declaration of 5th Schedule' (New Delhi: Government of India, n.d.), https://tribal.nic.in (accessed on 5 January 2020). These criteria are not spelled out in the Constitution of India but have become well established. They embody principles followed in declaring Excluded and Partially Excluded Areas under the Government of India Act, 1935, Schedule B of recommendations of the Excluded and Partially Excluded Areas Sub Committee of Constituent Assembly and the Scheduled Areas and Scheduled Tribes Commission, 1961.

53. See 'Fifth Schedule Areas: Provisions as to the Administration and Control of Scheduled Areas and Scheduled Tribes' (New Delhi: Government of India, 1996).

54. Sudha Vasan, 'Shifting the Terrain of Struggle: Critically Evaluating the Forest Rights Act', in *First Citizens: Studies on Adivasis, Tribals, and Indigenous Peoples in India*, ed. Meena Radhakrishna, pp. 255–79 (New Delhi: Oxford University Press, 2016), p. 255.

55. For an elaborate discussion on the subject, see Sharachchandra Lele, 'Understanding Current Forest Policy Debates through Multiple Lenses: The Case of India', *Ecology, Economy and Society-the INSEE Journal* 2, no. 2 (2019): 21–30.

56. Prakash Kashwan and Rahul Ranjan (eds.), 'Introduction' (Special Issue: Echoes from the Woods: At the Crossroads of Forest Struggles and Human Rights in Postcolonial India), *International Journal of Human Rights* 25, no. 7 (2021): 1089–93.

57. Arpitha Kodiveri, 'Land Banks in India: Who Benefits?', Thomas Reuters Foundations, 5 February 2019. http://news.trust.org/item/20190205105527-r5onz (accessed on 15 November 2019).

58. 'Jharkhand Industrial and Investment Promotion Policy 2016' (Ranchi: Government of Jharkhand, 2016), pp. 14–66 (emphasis mine).

59. Ibid.

60. 'Indian Forest Report, 2011: Jharkhand' (New Delhi: Government of India, 2011).

61. David Stuligross, 'Resources, Representation, and Authority in Jharkhand, India', *Asia Pacific Viewpoint* 49, no. 1 (2008): 83–97, p. 87.

62. Ibid.

63 'General, Social and Economic Sectors, Government of Jharkhand' (New Delhi: Social Welfare, General Sector Ministries and Constitutional Bodies, 2018), p. 4.

64 Ibid.

65 This was a global investment meet for mica mining organized by the Jharkhand government in 2017. The campaign was named 'Momentum Jharkhand'.

66 Singh, 'Many Faces of the Pathalgadi Movement in Jharkhand', p. 29.

67 *Economic Times*, '2017 Brought Multi-Crore Investment Proposals to Jharkhand', 30 December 2017, https://economictimes.indiatimes.com/news/politics-and-nation/2017-brought-multi-crore-investment-proposals-to-jharkhand/articleshow/62305228.cms (accessed on 20 January 2020).

68 *The Pioneer*, 'Over 100 Investment Proposals for Momentum Jharkhand-3: CS', 5 October 2017, https://www.dailypioneer.com/2017/state-editions/over-100-investment-proposals-for-momentum-jharkhand-3-cs.html (accessed on 20 January 2020). For a fuller account, see Aruna Chandrashekhar, 'Jharkhand Villagers Ask Why They Should Lose Land for Adani Project Supplying Power to Bangladesh', *Scroll.in*, 13 June 2018, https://scroll.in/article/882342/jharkhand-villagers-ask-why-should-they-lose-land-for-adani-project-supplying-power-to-bangladesh (accessed on 20 January 2020).

69 To access the report, see 'Land Bank', Government of Jharkhand, jamshedpur.nic.in/landbank/ (accessed on 20 January 2020).

70 The category of 'deemed forest' is maintained in the document in Figure 5.5.

71 Ibid., p. 66.

72 For literature on the importance of the forest as 'sacred groves', see M. D. Subash Chandran and Madhav Gadgil, 'Indigenous Vision: People of India Attitudes to the Environment', *India International Centre Quarterly* 19, nos. 1–2 (1992): 183–87.

73 Prakash Kashwan, *Democracy in the Woods: Environmental Conservation and Social Justice in India, Tanzania, and Mexico* (New Delhi: Oxford University Press, 2017), pp. 132–44. For a rich ethnographic work on 'sacred groves' in Jharkhand, see Lea Schulte-Droesch, *Making Place through Ritual: Land, Environment and Region among the Santhal of Central India* (Berlin: De Gruyter, 2018).

74 Ishan Kukreti, 'Tribal Affairs Ministry's Report on FRA Riddled with Discrepancies', Down to Earth, 14 May 2019. https://www.downtoearth.org.in/news/forests/tribal-affairs-ministry-s-report-on-fra-riddled-with-discrepancies-64589 (accessed on 19 January 2020).

75 Tariq Anwar, 'Jharkhand's Land Bank: Injustice to Adivasis Continues', *Newsclick*, 18 June 2018, https://www.newsclick.in/Jharkhand-Land-Bank-Adivasis-Tribes-Revenue-Land-Reforms (accessed on 19 January 2020).

76 Ibid.

77 Gladson Dungdung, 'Land Bank and Forest Rights', Adivasi Hunkar: Amplifying the Voice of the Indigenous Peoples of India, 2019, https://adivasihunkar.

com/2019/03/05/i-was-forced-to-sign-on-the-land-acquisition-papers-sukhram-munda (accessed on 19 January 2020).

78 K. Sivaramakrishnan, *Modern Forests: Statemaking and Environmental Changes in Colonial Eastern India* (California: Standford University Press, 1999), p. 31.

79 Ibid.

80 Judith Butler, 'Merely Cultural'. *Social Text* 52–53 (Autumn–Winter 1997): 265–77.

81 The name of the person is pseudonymous.

82 Ishan Kukreti, 'Does the Supreme Court Order Mean the Eviction of Forest Dwellers Right Away?', *Down to Earth*, 22 February 2019, https://www.downtoearth.org.in/news/forests/does-the-supreme-court-order-mean-eviction-of-forest-dwellers-right-away--63315 (accessed on 19 January 2020).

83 From A. Forbes, Esq, CSI., Commissioner of the Chota Nagpur Division to the Chief Secretary to the Government of India, Bengal, IOR/L/PJ/6/532, J&P 268, British Library, London.

84 Jens Lerche and Alpa Shah, 'Conjugated Oppression within Contemporary Capitalism: Class, Caste, Tribe and Agrarian Change in India', *Journal of Peasant Studies* 45, nos. 5–6 (19 September 2018): 927–49, p. 935.

85 For rampant use of the Land Acquisition Act as a medium to dilute the rights of Adivasis, refer to Rahul Ranjan, 'Unravelling the Narratives of Adivasi Dispossession: A Case Study of Land Acquisition in Nagri Village, Jharkhand', *Development* 60, nos. 3–4 (2017): 227–34. Also see Nikita Sud, 'State, Scale and Networks in the Liberalisation of India's Land', Working Paper Number 207, QEH Working Paper Series QEHWPS207, Queen Elizabeth House, University of Oxford, 2016.

86 Ingold, 'Temporality of the Landscape', p. 152.

87 Leo van der Vlist quoting indigenous peoples. See Leo van der Vlist, *Voices of the Earth: Indigenous Peoples, New Partners and the Right to Self-Determination in Practice* (Amsterdam: International Books, 1994), p. 22.

88 Ingold, 'Temporality of the Landscape'.

89 In this conceptualization, I disagree with Pierre Nora's idea of memory. He conceptualizes memory as a fixed entity. See Pierre Nora, 'Between Memory and History: Lieux de Memoire', *Representations* 26 (Spring 1989): 7–24.

90 Alf Gunvald Nilsen, *Adivasis and the State: Subalternity and Citizenship in India's Bhil Heartland* (Cambridge: Cambridge University Press, 2018), p. 171.

91 Bob Scholte, 'Reason and Culture: The Universal and the Particular Revisited', *American Anthropologist* 86, no. 4 (1984): 960–65.

92 Paromita Sanyal and Vijayendra Rao, *Oral Democracy* (Cambridge: Cambridge University Press, 2018), p. 1.

93 Signe Howell, 'Battle of Cosmologies: The Catholic Church, Adat, and "Inculturation" among Northern Lio, Indonesia'. *Social Analysis* 60, no. 4 (1 January 2016): 21–39.

94 Ibid., p. 21.

95 Ibid.

96 Ibid., p. 22.
97 John-Baptist Hoffman and E. Lister, 'Special Memorandum on the Land System of the Munda Country', in *Encyclopaedia Mundarica*, vol. 8 (reprint), ed. John-Baptist Hoffman and A. V. Emelen (New Delhi: Gyan Publishing House, 2015); *Report on the Settlement of the Estate of the Maharajah of Chota Nagpur* (India Land Settlement Reports: Bihar, Chota Nagpur District) (Calcutta: Bengal Secretariat Press, 1888), shelf mark: P/W 397, p. 225.
98 John-Baptist Hoffman, *Encyclopedia Mundarica*, vol. 1, 1908, p. 614, shelf mark no. IOR 14178.e.47, British Library, London (emphasis mine).
99 Ingold, 'Temporality of the Landscape', p. 155.
100 Nicole Graham, *Lawscape: Property, Environment, Law* (New York: Routledge, 2011), p. 38.
101 Ibid.
102 For Article 19, see Constitution Society, 'PART III: Fundamental Rights', www.constitution.org/cons/india/p03019.html (accessed on 15 February 2020).
103 Ibid.
104 Maitri Porecha, 'Not Just Netaji Cult, Sati Pati in Gujarat Denounces the Government of India', *DNA*, 9 June 2016, https://www.dnaindia.com/india/report-forget-netaji-sect-sati-pati-cult-stakes-ownership-to-entire-india-2221404 (accessed on 5 February 2020).
105 Nandini Sundar, 'Pathalgadi Is Nothing but Constitutional Messianism so Why Is the BJP Afraid of It?', *The Wire*, 16 May 2018, https://thewire.in/rights/pathalgadi-is-nothing-but-constitutional-messianism-so-why-is-the-bjp-afraid-of-it (accessed on 5 February 2020).
106 Deepanwita Gita Niyogi, 'Rise of Sati Pati Cult in Jharkhand', Pulitzer Center, https://pulitzercenter.org/stories/rise-sati-pati-cult-jharkhand (accessed on 9 February 2020).
107 Shahid Amin, 'Gandhi as Mahatma: Gorakhpur District, Eastern UP 1921–2', in *Selected Subaltern Studies*, ed. Ranajit Guha and Spivak Gayatri Chakravorty, pp. 335–39 (New Delhi: Oxford University Press, 1988). Also see Georges Lefebvre, *The Great Fear of 1789: Rural Panic in Revolutionary France*, trans. Joan White (New York: Vintage Books, 1973).
108 Gladson Dungdung, 'I Was Forced to Sign on the Land Acquisition Papers: Sukhram Munda', Adivasi Hunkar, 5 March 2019, https://adivasihunkar.com/2019/03/05/i-was-forced-to-sign-on-the-land-acquisition-papers-sukhram-munda (accessed on 15 February 2020).
109 Ibid.
110 Ibid.
111 Ibid.
112 Sudeep Chakravarti, 'The Anatomy of a Tribal Uprising in Jharkhand', *Livemint*, 11 July 2019, https://www.livemint.com/opinion/columns/opinion-the-anatomy-of-a-tribal-uprising-in-jharkhand-1562777976997.html (accessed on 1 Jan 2020).

Also see Swati Parashar and Anju Topno, 'Patthalgarhi Challenges the Republic in Its Own Backyard', *Indian Express*, 8 April 2018, https://indianexpress.com/article/opinion/patthalgarhi-jharkhand-challenges-the-republic-in-its-own-backyard-5128458 (accessed on 25 February 2020).

113 Singh, 'Many Faces of the Pathalgadi Movement in Jharkhand', p. 31.

114 *Scroll.in*, 'Jharkhand: Police File Sedition Cases against 20 People for Their Role in Pathalgadi Protests', 30 July 2018, https://scroll.in/latest/888494/jharkhand-police-file-sedition-cases-against-20-people-for-their-role-in-pathalgadi-protests (accessed on 25 February 2020).

115 *Scroll.in*, 'Activists Protest Repression of Tribals Engaged in Pathalgadi Movement', 22 July 2019, https://thewire.in/rights/pathalgadi-movement-jharkhand-tribals (accessed on 25 February 2020).

116 Nandini Sundar, 'Laws, Policies and Practices in Jharkhand', *Economic and Political Weekly* 40, no. 41 (2005): 4459–62, p. 4459. Also see Vinita Damodaran, 'Indigenous Agency: Customary Rights and Tribal Protection in Eastern India, 1830–1930', *History Workshop Journal* 76, no. 1 (October 2013): 85–110.

117 *Sabrang*, 'Every 10th Adivasi of Jharkhand's Pathalgadi Area Have Been Charged with Sedition', 22 July 2019, https://sabrangindia.in/article/every-10th-adivasi-jharkhands-pathalgadi-area-have-been-charged-sedition (accessed on 1 March 2020).

118 Jharkhand Janadhikar Mahasabha, 'Harassment of Activists—I', *Economic and Political Weekly* 54, no. 24 (2019): 4–5.

119 Singh, 'Many Faces of the Pathalgadi Movement in Jharkhand', p. 32.

120 Anumeha Yadav, 'In Jharkhand, a Tribal Assertion Met with Fierce Police Crackdown', *Aljazeera*, 30 September 2018, https://www.aljazeera.com/indepth/features/jharkhand-tribal-assertion-met-fierce-police-crackdown-180929223820429.html (accessed on 15 March 2020).

121 Sombari, in a personal interview with the author, Ranchi, 12 June 2019.

122 Ibid (emphasis mine).

123 Ibid.

124 Bosu Pahan, in a personal interview with the author, Ranchi, 12 June 2019.

125 Elizabeth Kolsky, 'The Colonial Rule of Law and the Legal Regime of Exception: Frontier "Fanaticism" and State Violence in British India', *American Historical Review* 120, no. 4 (October 2015): 1218–46.

126 T. S. Macpherson, 'Records of Rights in Pargana Porahat 1905–1907', shelf mark IOR/V/27/314/119, British Library, London.

127 Nile, in a personal interview with the author, Ranchi, 12 June 2019.

128 Sangeeta Dasgupta, 'Mapping Histories: Many Narratives of Tana Pasts', *Indian Economic and Social History Review* 53, no. 1 (2016): 99–129, p. 99.

129 Barbie Zelizer, 'Reading the Past Against the Grain: The Shape of Memory Studies', *Critical Studies in Mass Communication* 12 (2013): 214–39.

130 Benedict Anderson, *Imagined Communities: Reflections on the Origin and Spread of Nationalism* (London: Verso Publication, 2006 [1983]).

131 Katharine Hodgkin and Susannah Radstone, 'Patterning the National Past', in *Memory, History, Nation: Contested Pasts*, ed. Katharine Hodgkin and Susannah Radstone, pp. 169–74 (New Brunswick: Transaction, 2006), p. 169.

132 Extract from a letter from H. C. Streatfield, Esq., Deputy Commissioner of Ranchi, dated Camp Bangaon, the 4th 1900 (J&P 224) (emphasis mine).

133 Shah, *In the Shadows of the State*.

134 Rev. Fr. J. Hoffman, Catholic Missionary of Sarwada to the Commissioner of the Chota Nagpur Division, 14th January 1900, file: 534, enclosure 4, British Library, London.

135 Ibid.

136 See Bagaicha Research Team, 'Deprived of Rights over Natural Resources, Impoverished Adivasis Get Prison', Sanhati, 2 February 2016, http://sanhati.com/excerpted/16044/. In the recent past, Swamy was accused of being an 'urban Naxal' under the new lexicon of the Indian state. He faced two raids at his home and is now being tried under the sedition laws. See Rajendran Narayanan and Debmalya, 'Father Stan Swamy, Children and the Unholy State', *The Wire*, 3 September 2018, https://thewire.in/rights/stan-swamy-jharkhand-adivasis-undertrials-pesa-uapa (accessed on 15 March 2019).

137 Kunal Purohit, 'In India, Welfare Politics Trumps Poll Rhetoric', *Devex*, 22 May 2019. https://www.devex.com/news/in-india-welfare-politics-trumps-poll-rhetoric-94927 (accessed on 20 March 2020).

138 See V. G. Bhatnagar, 'Starvation Deaths of Three Children in UP, Bihar Highlight State Govt Apathy', *The Wire*, 11 September 2018, https://thewire.in/rights/starvation-deaths-three-children-up-bihar (accessed on 20 March 2020).

139 The Indian Social Institute, New Delhi, published an extensive report on four Indian states including Jharkhand that have a concentrated population of Adivasis/Scheduled Tribes. The report made some staggering observations about the Land Acquisition Act. It highlighted serious gaps in the implementation of the Rehabilitation clause and the use of the old Act. It states:

> The Forest Act, 1927 was extensively used to acquire land in Jharkhand. Of the total 1035 projects, 914 development projects (constituting 88.31% of the whole) were notified for acquisition in the period 1947–50. The highest number of projects in this period was notified in the district of Ranchi—125 projects (13.68%). In the period 1991–2007, 117 projects (constituting 11.30% of the total) were notified for acquisition. Again, the highest number of projects were notified in the district of Ranchi—48 projects (41.03%). Of the total 549776.5 acres of land acquired in Jharkhand in the period of study, the largest acquisition of land was from private lands (415983.2 acres), followed by forest lands (63818.77 acres) and then from uncategorized land (55602.34 acres).

See ActionAid, Indian Social Institute (New Delhi) and Laya, 'Resource Rich Tribal Poor: Displacing People, Destroying Identity in India's Indigenous Heartland' (New Delhi, 2008), p. 40. Also see Sud, 'State, Scale and Networks in the Liberalisation of India's Land'.

140 Lilja, 'The Politics of Time and Temporality in Foucault's Theorisation of Resistance'.

141 Uday Chandra, 'Flaming Fields and Forest Fires: Agrarian Transformations and the Making of Birsa Munda's Rebellion', *Indian Economic and Social History Review* 53, no. 1 (2016): 1–30.

CHAPTER 6

Conclusion

Tracing the Lineage of Memory in the Book

The story of Birsa Munda in this book is that of a *transitioning*—the transition from systemic exploitation to the advent of new forms of law—and that of extractive industries. It is a narrative that marks the transition to post-colonial Jharkhand. It speaks of discontinuity; yet it also admits to great continuities.[1] Politics then was organized by the 'lost Munda *raj*', a reclamation trope of Adivasis to secure *abua disum*. It displayed the complex process of transitioning: the making of sociopolitical fabric through *encounters* with the new institutional enterprise (colonial administration), violent caste orders (*zamindars*) and the theological carriers (missions).

The book briefly outlined the historical account of the land conflict that emerged from a series of new kinds of interventions, surveys and laws, missionization, and *zamindari* exploitation in the late 19th century. The historical contingencies frame the narrative of the historical memory of the region. This historical memory of the *ulgulan* presents a response to not only systemic violence but also the transition of power. In such a transition narrative, the book has identified a few nodal points to understand the contemporary articulation of Birsa's memory. Memory emerged as both a methodological and epistemic tool to illustrate the continuing effects of colonialism, the everyday politics of Adivasi memory and the enmeshing of the state in the shadows of the *ulgulan*. I have engaged with three specific 'sites of memory': statues, memorials and the Pathalgadi movement. The specific characteristic of each site explains its political use.

Birsa Munda, Adivasi icons at large and their legacy of anti-colonial struggle contain in themselves *resistance* as the primal force. In the wake of new political conditions—unabated wide-scale land dispossession, attempts at diluting protectionary legislations (such as the CNTA) and the normalization of *development* as the critical vocabulary in Adivasi regions, which has adverse effects on their lifeworld—any efforts to suspend or remove the force of resistance in portrayals of the anti-colonial icon is simply a betrayal of their heritage. In turn, I proposed in this book that memorialization should incorporate newer forms of the aesthetic of rebellion that mainstream the political urgencies.

Statues, memorials and a whole range of objects are far from being an isolated passive object for the aesthetic display of memory. In fact, they are also a manifestation of political ideologies and widespread entangled corporate interests. Beyond the political use of the built environment that brings the sacred, the historical and the political onto the canvas of memory, these sites of memory should endeavour to initiate a dialogue that places the changing lives of Adivasis at the heart of affective provocation in politics. The Adivasi community has shown this possibility by using facets of the Pathalgadi movement. It dovetailed mobilization of village history and traces of the past together into the contemporaneous character of political urgency.

The historical accounts about the customary traditions (for instance, T. S. Macpherson's land record) are evidently present in the fabric of this new protest movement. This is not new. My research has simply outlined it. Adivasis have lived it and continue to do so. They have used the past as it is. That is to say, the past never ceased to exist in an act; it always remained as an excess—an unfolding process, an unfinished process—of remembering. Jacques Derrida's idea of the text with an edge illustrates this passage, where text sometimes overruns and 'spoils boundaries and forces us to extend the accredited notions of a text'.[2] Text becomes an unfinished corpus of writings and has 'a fabric of traces [read: memory] referring endlessly to something other than itself, to other differential traces'.[3] Similarly, the historical register (texts or archives) always remains a limited corpus of writings that is mobilized by the traces of memory. The use of stone slabs (*pathal*) by Adivasis as territorial markers is a trace of memory that emerges as an *excess*—insisting on us moving beyond administrative demands to the framing of grievances, anger and emotion.

Memory Manifesto: Anti-colonialism as a Transnational Struggle

Memory and subalternity mark the political landscape of Jharkhand in this book. In thinking about subaltern memory, elements of incommensurability—that is, angst towards outsiders, the complex articulation of sub-national grievances (*pathalgadi*) and cosmovision about the landscape—are translated in turn into the commensurable language of the state. This fundamentally expands the limited provocation of 'can the subaltern speak?'. Instead of dwelling on the ideas and thoughts that emerge from resistance movements and the Adivasi lifeworld, the state perceives the past as a distant object—making it an eventful 'thing' in time. In this framework of time and event, the Adivasi past is imagined predominantly through either the community's contribution to the nation-making project or its so-called selective version of anti-colonial past.

Inadequate attention is paid to the structure of hearing; in this case, what kind of memorialization does the community imagine for its past and its biographer of memory (Birsa)? Who are the participants? How do they design the architecture of memory? Much of this reflects serious unresolved and long-standing problems with structures of speech and listening to the subaltern voice—both figuratively and literally. I would like to reflect upon them as not alternative models but cotangent positions that constitute the epistemic foundation of speech.

I hesitate to propose an alternative model primarily because it assumes my position—and, for that matter, the position of any scholar, especially non-indigenous—at the centre and reproduces the historical epistemic injustices that relegate Adivasi knowledge to secondary sources used as footnotes. I also do not advocate the new approach towards any epistemic inquiry such as a memory project in graded and vertically arranged formations of knowledge. The epistemic inquiry, in turn, should allow for flattening of the surface of our own understanding about people and their social habitus. Moving forward, I propose two key manifestos for thinking about a radical form of memory politics. These models are reflections of my accumulated learning from the Adivasi knowledge system as a *saathi* (friend) and a *sadan* (non-Adivasi) or at least attempting to learn from it as I grow as an individual.

Manifesto: Script for the Counter-memorial

First, we should think about symbolic representation of the past through a dialogical approach. In this approach, it is unnegotiable that the core participants should consist of members of the community (Adivasis, for instance, in India) who not only design the format of remembering but also use their cosmovision and experiences to define the content. Amongst others, the dialogical approach would help us to pay close attention to the ways in which the built environment can become acts of speech in non-verbal form, inviting various responses from the viewer as a provocative space. Unlike statues and memorials, which somehow remain passive objects for public display, the dialogical approach can be used to construct counter-memorials. The counter-memorial model flattens the surface of historical time and reorganizes the structure of remembering. It unveils new ways of speaking about, listening to and thinking with various *modes of remembrance* that primarily belong to those being represented—and not us, the researchers, the outsiders. The first place to think about engagement is resolutely submitting to the empire of knowledge that Adivasi heritage has to offer'. Borrowing from the work of Quentin Stevens and others on Aboriginal Australian memory work, the counter-memorial can be understood as a model that invites 'close, multi-sensory visitor engagement; and, rather than being didactic, [invites] visitors to work out the meanings for themselves'.[4] Essentially, it would not only situate the use of material memory as a source of *telling history* but also disrupt the coloniality of power held and controlled by the outsiders.

This coloniality of power operates in microcosm—for instance, we 'claim' our expertise on ideas and histories that do not write themselves on us. We need to suspend this strain of ownership and allow the community to help us learn from their experience. We can only write from a position of solidarity, as I mentioned in the preface: solidarity that is not patronage but a meaningful engagement and admission to our privilege and how it enables us to do this work; solidarity that is sought by people who are written about; solidarity that is contingent on an equal relationship highlighting the visceral caste orders, gendered violence and oppression of Adivasis that continue to define large parts of the country. It is through a combination of these admissions that 'abstract objects' of material memory move away from the 'conventional representation and figuration and its rethinking of the visitor's encounter with the art object' to manifest the material inequalities and changing landscape of memory.[5]

The Pathalgadi movement, in many respects, has already shown the possibility of a counter-memorial template in real polity, showcasing many lives of the land—that is, as Nikita Sud has recently argued, 'the land far from fixed, unchangeable'.[6] *Pathalgadi*s and the Adivasi community in a wider schema of protest in post-colonial India not only mobilized 'legalism from below' but also situated the primacy of collective memory. *Pathalgadi*s emerged as the subaltern counter-hegemony.[7] They laid out their memory manifesto by situating their agency in defining the landscape and posing it as an 'experiential counterweight and a disruption of received wisdom of everyday tyranny'.[8] Innovative methods and the creative use of language disrupted the continuum of modern and traditional dialectic in which the state has continued to perceive the Adivasi community. In fact, the movement disrupted the popular representation of resistance—that is, violence—and highlighted the structural problem in the process of hearing, underlining the importance of incommensurability that defines the landscape. The use of an abstract material object as a critical tool clearly reflected 'indigenous people's sense of living under ongoing colonial projects and not just colonial legacies'.[9] They succeeded in demonstrating a counter-memorial as a way of *doing politics*. The accommodation of the counter-memorial presupposes the contemporary character and relevance of the subject (in this case, Birsa Munda). This leads me to explain how we can situate Birsa and his anti-colonial ideals beyond the confines of colonial records and memorialization.

Manifesto: Pathways to Anti-colonialism and Thinking about Subaltern Present Past

The vitality of history—as both a discipline and an idea that we continuously mobilize to set a background—must allow us to think of a 'plurality of times existing together', rendering the agency of those being written about visible.[10] The book has shown the perils of thinking about history as a linear idea by demonstrating, for instance, the atypical nature and limitation of archival sources that exclusively provide the official narrative to describe Birsa and the political life of his ideas. Notably, as Priyamvada Gopal, in her recent work, has argued, anti-colonialism is radically democratic and redistributive in nature and does not merely seek to oust the colonizer but also reflects on indigenous tyrannies.[11] In effect, anti-colonialism seeks to capture the wider dimensions of resistance, reflection and critical stances from within.

The official framing of Birsa, for instance, in the contemporary landscape, fails to address how the subaltern resists and negotiates with the modern state that embodies colonial values. It also shows that anti-colonialism must transcend the temporal fixation with colonial confines and build into the contemporary articulation of *jal, jungle aur jameen*. The use of memory in the Pathalgadi movement demonstrated the possibility of framing the spirit of anti-colonialism as transcendental in the approach to contesting the coloniality of power. Here, subaltern memory is both disruptive and redistributive, reflecting the political history of the canon (Birsa) as well as offering a contemporaneous articulation.

The Political Life of Memory offers various possibilities. While on the one hand the state produces and circulates a selective narrative, on the other hand the Adivasi community have shown the limits of the state and articulated the historical memory of Birsa within the contemporary landscape. It is possible to imagine a new array of memory work in times to come as movements sprawl across the country and intensify against the emerging repression and the narratives of the Munda *raj* begin to take new forms.

Notes

1   Ranabir Samaddar, *Memory, Identity, Power: Politics in the Junglemahals, 1800–1950* (New Delhi: Orient Blackswan, 2013 [1998]).
2   Harold Bloom, De Paul Man, Jacques Deridda, Geoffrey H. Hartman and J. Hillis Miller, *Deconstruction and Criticism* (London: Routledge and Kegan Paul, 1979), pp. 83–84.
3   Ibid., p. 84.
4   Quentin Stevens, Karen A. Franck and Ruth Fazakerley, 'Counter-monuments: The Anti-monumental and the Dialogic', *Journal of Architecture* 17, no. 6 (2012): 951–972, p. 954.
5   Quentin Stevens, 'Nothing More Than Feelings', *Architectural Theory Review* 14, no.2 (2009): 156–72, p. 159.
6   Implication of this phrase, as Sud highlights in the book, is not to fetishize the land but to recognize the various forms, meaning and ideas it occupies in the lives of people. See Nikita Sud, *The Making of Land and the Making of India* (Oxford: Oxford University Press, 2021).
7   Alf Gunvald Nilsen, *Adivasis and the State: Subalternity and Citizenship in India's Bhil Heartland* (Cambridge: Cambridge University Press, 2018), p. 171.
8   Ibid., p. 143.
9   Jodi A. Byrd and Michael Rothberg, 'Between Subalternity and Indigeneity', *Interventions* 13, no. 1 (2011): 1–12.
10 Dipesh Chakrabarty, *Provincializing Europe: Postcolonial Thought and Historical Difference* (New Jersey: Princeton University Press, 2000).
11 Ibid.; Priyamvada Gopal, *Insurgent Empire Anticolonial Resistance and British Dissent* (London: Verso, 2019).

Appendix

Part 1

डोमबारी बुरु चेतान रे
Dombari buru chetan re
डोमबारी बुरु चेतार रे
Dombari buru chetar re
ओकोए दुमाङ रूतानाको सुसुनताना ।
Aokoe dumand rutanako susuntana
डोमबारी बुरु लातार रे
Dombari buru lata re
चिमाए बिगुल साङितानाको सांगिलाकादा ॥
Chimaye bigul saaritanaku sangilakada
डोमबारी बुरु चेतार रे
Dombari buru chetar re
बिरसा दुमाङ रूतानाको सुसुनताना ।
Birsa dumaad rutanako susuntana
डोमबारी बुरु लातार रे
Dombari buru lataar re,
सायोब बिगुल साङितानाको सांगिलाकादा ॥
Saayob bigul saaritanaku sangilakada
जोनोम दिसुम नागेनेगे
Janoom disum naagenege
बिरसा दुमाङ रूतानाको सुसुनताना ।
Birsa dumaand dumaad rutanako susuntana

गोली चालाओ नागेनेग
Goli chalao naagenege
डोमबारी पहाड़ पर
On the hills of Dombari
डोमबारी पहाड़ के ऊपर
On the top of Dombari
कौन मांदर बजा रहा है, लोग नाच रहे हैं ।
Who is playing the mandar, who is dancing there
डोमबारी पहाड़ के नीचे
On the foothills of Dombari
कौन बिगुल बजा रहा है, लोग ऊपर ताक रहे हैं
Who is playing bigul? People drifted up to the hills
डोमबारी पहाड़ के ऊपर
Atop Dombari Hill
बिरसा मांदर बजा रहा है, लोग नाच रहे हैं ।
Birsa is playing the mandar, people are dancing to it!
डोमबारी पहाड़ के नीचे
On the foothills of Dombari
साहब बिगुल बजा रहा है, लोग ऊपर ताक रहे हैं॥
Sahib is playing bigul, people are looking up to him

जन्म देश के लिए ही
Born for the nation
बिरसा मांदर बजा रहा है, लोग नाच रहे हैं ।
Birsa is playing the mandar, people are dancing to it!
गोली चलाने के लिए ही
Shoot the bullets
सायोब बिगुल साड़िताानाको सांगिलाकादा ॥
Saayob bigul saaritaanako saangilakada hai
गोली बारूद चाबाजाना
Goli barud chabajaana
बिरसा दुमाङ रूतानाको सुसुनताना ।
Birsa dumaad rutanako susuntana
डोमबारी बुरु चेतान रे
Dombari buru chetan re
जोनोम दिसुम आबुआ:को काकालाताना ॥
Jonom disum abua:ko kakalatana
साहब बिगुल बजा रहा है, लोग ऊपर ताक रहे हैं ॥
Sahib is playing bigul, people are looking up to him
गोली बारूद खत्म हुए
Guns have no bullets left
बिरसा मांदर बजा रहा है, लोग नाच रहे हैं ।
Birsa is playing the mandar, people are dancing to it!
डोमबारी पहाड़ के ऊपर लोग
People are at the top of Dombari Hill
'जन्म देश हमारा है' को गूंजित कर रहे हैं ॥
A country is born, is chanted

Part 2

गाँव छोड़ब नहीं, जंगल छोड़ब नहीं,
Gaon chodab nahin, jungle chorab nahin
We will not leave our village, we will not leave our jungle

माए माटी छोड़ब नहीं, लड़ाई छोड़ब नहीं, [...]
Mae maati chodab nahin, ladai chodab nahin, [...]
We will neither leave our motherland; we will fight for it as long as we can

जल जंगल जमीन छोड़ी हमीन कहाँ जाए,
Jal, jungle, jameen chodi humeen kahaan jaaye,
Where shall we go leaving behind our land, water and forest?

विकास के भगवान बता, हम कैसे जान बचाए ...
Vikas ke bhagwan bata, hum kaise jaan bachaae
O god of development, tell us how to save our lives

Glossary

Aadhaar card	a 16-digit identification card issued by the government of India
aaakrosh	angst
adi	belonging to the past
Adi Dharma	Adivasi religion
Adivasi	indigenous autochthonous people
Adivasi Mahasabha	Great Council of the Indigenous Peoples
Adivasiyat	indigeneity
akhra	a meeting place in Munda and Oraon villages
bazaar	marketplace
bhagwan	god
bhagawani	follower of god—in this case, Birsa
bhuinhar	original Munda settler
bhuinhari	land tenure of a *bhuinhar*
Birsa Mrig Vihar	deer park named after Birsa Munda
Bonga	spirit
dewani	a powerful ruler
dhangar	skilled Kols (Adivasis)
dharam	religion
Dharti Aba	Father of the Land
diku	outsider
disom	Munda village
dewani	powerful government
diwas	day
gram sabha	village assembly
gram panchayat	rural grassroots-level institution

Glossary

hadia	rice beer
horo	man
hul	revolution
jagirdar	servant of *raja*s
jal, jungle and jameen	water, forest and land
jangir	handcuff
jati	caste; social stratification based on religion in Hindus
johar	greetings
jungli	savage, wild
kasba	locality
khatian	record of rights
khuntkhattidar	original clearer of land in a village
Kol	a word used by the British to describe Ho Adivasis of Kolhan region
mafia *raj*	mafia regime
mahila panchayat	women's council
mandar	drum
Munda	name of a tribal community
munda	headman of a village
nawab	an imperial governor
pahan	village priest
panch	five
panchayat	village council
parha	self-governance system amongst Adivasis
pathalgadi	erection of stone slabs
patta	record of rights
patti	wider organization of *parha*s
pergunah	fiscal unit of administration
raiyat	tenant
raj	rule
raja	king
sadan	resident; a Hindu largely belonging to other backward castes living with Adivasis for a very long time
Sardari *ladai*	a movement against the British started by Munda *sardar*s between 1858 and 1895 CE
saheb	a word used to denote the British
Sangh Parivar	Family of Organizations, an umbrella term referring to the collective group of Hindu nationalist organizations produced by the Rashtriya Swayamsevak Sangh (RSS)
samadhi sthal	sepulchre site

sarna	sacred grove
sasandiri	a gravestone placed flat over the burial bones in a *sasan*—that is, burial place
sati pati	heaven's light
Shiv *charcha*	meetings organized to discuss the greatness of Lord Shiva
singbonga	sun god
talab	pond
tola	locality
ulgulan	uprising
Unnati Sabha	Improvement Society
upanayana	a ritual ring of sacred thread worn by Hindus
vananchal	forest-dwelling state
vanvasi	forest dwellers
varna	each of the four Hindu castes comprising Brahmins, Kshatriyas, Vaisyas and Sudras
vasi	resident
zamindar	landlord

Bibliography

Primary Sources

Archives

British Library, London

India Office Records and Private Papers

J&P, Judicial Files (1880–1900)

Records of the Church Missionary Society, Cadbury Research Library, University of Birmingham

Overseas (Missions) Series (OMS) 1803–1934.

North India Mission

The Harold Turner Collection

National Archives, New Delhi

Home Office Records, Foreign Proceedings 1893.

Government Reports and Documents

ActionAid, Indian Social Institute (New Delhi) and Laya. 'Resource Rich Tribal Poor: Displacing People, Destroying Identity in India's Indigenous Heartland'. New Delhi, 2008. www.actionaidindia.org. Accessed on 15 November 2019.

'Fifth Schedule Areas: Provisions as to the Administration and Control of Scheduled Areas and Scheduled Tribes'. New Delhi, 1996.

'Centrally Sponsored Scheme of Establishment of Ashram Schools in Tribal Sub-Plan Areas'. New Delhi, 2008. https://www.india.gov.in/scheme-establishment-ashram-schools-tribal-sub-plan-areas. Accessed on 11 January 2020.

'Declaration of 5th Schedule'. New Delhi, n.d., https://tribal.nic.in/. Accessed on 15 December 2019.

'General, Social and Economic Sectors, Government of Jharkhand'. New Delhi: Social Welfare, General Sector Ministries and Constitutional Bodies, 2018.

Ghose, Joyita. 'Standing Committee Report Summary Working of Ashram Schools in Tribal Areas'. New Delhi, 2014. https://www.prsindia.org/sites/default/files/parliament_or_policy_pdfs/1393414764_SCRSummary-WorkingofAshramSchoolsinTribal Areas.pdf. Accessed on 15 January 2017.

'Census of India 2011: Jharkhand'. Jharkhand, 2011.

'Indian Forest Report, 2011: Jharkhand'. New Delhi, 2011.

'Jharkhand Industrial and Investment Promotion Policy 2016'. Ranchi, 2016.

Judicial Academy, Jharkhand. *Handbook on Land Law*. Ranchi, n.d. https://www.jajharkhand.in. Accessed on 15 March 2019.

'Land Bank'. Government of Jharkhand. https://www.jamshedpur.nic.in/landbank. Accessed on 30 November 2019.

Ministry of Home Affairs. 'The Bihar Reorganisation Act, 2000'. https://www.indiacode.nic.in/bitstream/123456789/2001/1/200030.pdf. Accessed on 20 June 2020.

Ministry of Panchayati Raj (Government of India). 'Mandate of the Ministry of Panchayati Raj'. https://pesadarpan.gov.in/en. Accessed on 1 May 2019.

Planning Commission. 'Scheduled Tribe'. http://planningcommission.nic.nic.in/data/datable/data_2312/databook.pdf. Accessed on 15 June 2018.

Rangarajan, C. *Report of the Expert Group to Review the Methodology for Measurement of Poverty*. New Delhi: Planning Commission, Government of India, 2014.

Report of the Indian Statutory Commission: Selections from Memoranda and Oral Evidence by Non-officials, part 1. Calcutta: Government Printing, 1930.

Report on the Settlement of the Estate of the Maharajah of Chota Nagpur (India Land Settlement Reports: Bihar, Chota Nagpur District). Calcutta: Bengal Secretariat Press, 1888.

Revenue Department, Government of Bengal. *Final Report on the Settlement of the Kolhan Government Estate in District Sighbhum*. Calcutta: Bengal Secretariat Press, 1898.

'TD Tenders from Jharkhand Tender Notice – 8798021'. Tender Detail. https://www.tenderdetail.com/Indian-Tenders/TenderNotice/8798021/481855ad-27e8-4569-b778-96cf45c9499d$development-of-ulihatu-and-dombari-buru-hill-as-heritage-tourism-destination-khunti-district. Accessed on 1 February 2019.

'The Provisions of the Panchayats (Extension to the Scheduled Areas) Act, 1996'. New Delhi: Ministry of Tribal Affairs, Government of India, 1996.

Unpublished Sources

Verado, Barbara. 'Rebels and Devotees of Jharkhand: Social, Religious and Political Transformation among the Adivasi of Northern India'. PhD dissertation. London School of Economics and Political Science, University of London, 2003.

Chandra, Uday. 'Millenarian Dreams, Modern Aspirations: Tribal Community-Making and Contentious Politics in Colonial Chotanagpur'. Working Paper WP 14-01, ISSN 2192-2357, Max Planck Institute for the Study of Religious and Ethnic Diversity, Göttingen, Germany, April 2014, https://www.mmg.mpg.de/60983/wp-14-01. Accessed on 24 January 2017.

Ghosh, Kaushik. 'The Modernity of Primitive India Adivasi Ethnicity in Jharkhand and the Formation of a National Modern'. PhD dissertation. Department of Anthropology, Princeton University, Princeton, NJ, 2006.

Sud, Nikita. 'State, Scale and Networks in the Liberalisation of India's Land'. Working Paper Number 207, QEH Working Paper Series QEHWPS207, Queen Elizabeth House, University of Oxford, 2016.

Peñarrocha Giménez, Carmina. 'Rescuing the Identity of the Adivasis from Their Invisibility: The Encounter between Jesuits and the Indigenous Peoples of India'. PhD dissertation, Doctoral Programme 14003, Development Cooperation, Universitat Jaume, Castellón de la Plana, Spain, 2017.

Standing, Hilary. 'Munda Religion and Social Structure'. PhD dissertation. School of Oriental and African Studies (SOAS), University of London, n.d.

Published Sources

Adas, Michael. *Prophets of Rebellion: Millenarian Protest Movements against the European Colonial Order*. Cambridge: Cambridge University Press, 1979.

Alexievich, Svetlana. *Second-Hand Time*. New Delhi: Juggernaut Books, 2016.

Alfred, Taiaiake, and Jeff Corntassel. 'Being Indigenous: Resurgences against Contemporary Colonialism'. *Government and Opposition* 40, no. 4 (2005): 597–614.

Amin, Shahid. 'Gandhi as Mahatma: Gorakhpur District, Eastern UP 1921–2'. In *Selected Subaltern Studies*, edited by Ranajit Guha and Spivak Gayatri Chakravorty, pp. 335–39. New Delhi: Oxford University Press, 1988.

Anderson, Benedict. *Imagined Communities: Reflections on the Origin and Spread of Nationalism*. London: Verso Publication, 2006 (1983).

Anderson, Edward, and Christophe Jaffrelot. 'Hindu Nationalism and the "Saffronisation of the Public Sphere": An Interview with Christophe Jaffrelot'. *Contemporary South Asia* 26, no. 4 (2 October 2018): 468–82.

A. S. 'Containing the Jharkhand Movement'. *Economic and Political Weekly* 14, no. 14 (1979): 648–50.

Assmann, Jan. 'Collective Memory and Cultural Identity'. *New German Critique* 65 (Spring–Summer 1995): 125–33.

Banerjee, Prathama. *Politics of Time: 'Primitives' and History-Writing in a Colonial Society*. New Delhi: Oxford University Press, 2006.

———. 'Writing the Adivasi: Some Historiographical Notes'. *Indian Economic and Social History Review* 53, no. 1 (2016): 131–53.

Bara, Joseph. 'Alien Construct and Tribal Contestation in Colonial Chhotanagpur: The Medium of Christianity'. *Economic and Political Weekly* 44, no. 52 (2009): 90–96.

———. 'Colonialism, Christianity and the Tribes of Chhotanagpur in East India, 1845–1890'. *South Asia: Journal of South Asia Studies* 30, no. 2 (2007): 195–222.

———. 'Western Education and Rise of New Identity Mundas and Oraons of Chotanagpur, 1839–1939'. *Economic and Political Weekly* 32, no. 15 (1997): 785–90.

Barrett, Michele. 'Subalterns at War'. In *Can the Subaltern Speak? Reflections on the History of an Idea*, edited by Rosalind C. Morris, pp. 156–78. New York: Columbia University Press, 2010.

Bates, Crispin (ed.). *Mutiny at the Margins: New Perspectives on the Indian Uprising of 1857*. New Delhi: SAGE Publications, 2013.

———. 'Race, Caste and Tribe in Central India: The Early Origins of Indian Anthropometry'. *Edinburgh Papers in South Asian Studies* 3, no. 3 (1995): 2–35.

Bates, Crispin, and Alpa Shah. *Savage Attack: Tribal Insurgency in India*. New Delhi: Social Science Press, 2014.

Baviskar, Amita. *In the Belly of the River: Tribal Conflicts over Development in the Narmada Valley*. New Delhi: Oxford University Press, 1997.

Bayly, C. A. *Indian Society and the Making of the British Empire*. Cambridge: Cambridge University Press, 1990.

Bell, Duncan. 'Mythscapes: Memory, Mythology, and National Identity'. *British Journal of Sociology* 54, no. 1 (2003): 63–81.

Belli, Malia. 'Monumental Pride Mayawati's Memorials in Lucknow'. *Ars Orientalis* 44 (2014): 85–109.

Bera, Gautam Kumar. *The Unrest Axle: Ethno-Social Movements in Eastern India*. Kolkata: Mittal Publications, 2008.

Berger, Peter L., and Thomas Luckmann. *The Social Construction of Reality*. New Delhi: Penguin Books, 1991.

Béteille, André. 'The Concept of Tribe with Special Reference to India'. *European Journal of Sociology* 27, no. 2 (1986): 297–318.

Bevernage, Berber. 'Tales of Pastness and Contemporaneity: On the Politics of Time in History and Anthropology'. *Rethinking History* 20, no. 3 (2 July 2016): 352–74.

Blake, Emma Sardinia. 'Nuraghi: Four Millennia of Becoming'. *World Archaeology* 30, no. 1 (1998): 59–71.

Bloom, Harold, De Paul Man, Jacques Deridda, Geoffrey H. Hartman and J. Hillis Miller. *Deconstruction and Criticism*. London: Routledge and Kegan Paul, 1979.

Bond, Lucy, Stef Craps and Pieter Vermeulen. *Memory Unbound: Tracing the Dynamics of Memory Stduies*. New York: Berghahn Books, 2017.

Boym, Svetlana. 'Nostalgia and Its Discontents'. *Hedgehog Review* 9, no. 2 (Summer 2007): 7–18.

Bradley-Birt, and Francis Bradley. *Chota Nagpore: A Little Known Province of the Empire*. New Delhi: Asian Educational Services, 1998 (1903).

Bergmann, Sigurd. 'Religion in the Built Environment: Aesth/Ethics, Rituals, and Memory in Lived Urban Space'. In *The Sacred in The City*, edited by Liliana Gómez and Walter Van Herck, pp. 73–95. London: Bloomsbury, 2012.

Briggs, Charles L. 'Anthropology, Interviewing, and Communicability in Contemporary Society'. *Current Anthropology* 48, no. 4 (2007): 551–80.

Buettner, Elizabeth. 'Cemeteries, Public Memory and Raj Nostalgia in Postcolonial Britain and India'. *History and Memory* 18, no. 1 (2006): 5–42.

Butalia, Urvashi. *The Other Side of Violence*. Chapel Hill, NC: Duke University Press, 2000.

Butler, Judith. 'Merely Cultural'. *Social Text* 52–53 (Autumn–Winter 1997): 265–77.

Byrd, Jodi A., and Michael Rothberg. 'Between Subalternity and Indigeneity'. *Interventions* 13, no. 1 (2011): 1–12.

Carey, Matthew. *Mistrust: An Ethnographic Theory*. Chicago: HAU Books, 2017.

Carrin, Marine, and Harald Tambs-Lyche. *An Encounter of Peripheries: Santals, Missionaries, and Their Changing Worlds, 1867–1900*. New Delhi: Manohar Publication, 2008.

Césaire, Aimé. *Discourse on Colonialism*, translated by Joan Pinkham. New York: Monthly Review Press, 2000.

Chakrabarty, Dipesh. 'A Small History of Subaltern Studies'. In *A Companion to Postcolonial Studies*, edited by Henry Schwarz and Sangeeta Ray, pp. 467–85. Oxford: Blackwell Publishing, 2007.

———. 'Minority Histories, Subaltern Pasts'. *Postcolonial Studies* 1, no. 1 (1998): 15–29.

———. *Provincializing Europe: Postcolonial Thought and Historical Difference* (New Jersey: Princeton University Press, 2000).

———. 'Subaltern Studies and Postcolonial Historiography'. *Nepantla: Views from South* 1, no. 1 (2000): 9–32.

Chandra, Uday. 'Flaming Fields and Forest Fires: Agrarian Transformations and the Making of Birsa Munda's Rebellion'. *Indian Economic and Social History Review* 53, no. 1 (2016): 1–30.

———. 'Towards Adivasi Studies: New Perspectives on "Tribal" Margins of Modern India'. *Studies in History* 31, no.1 (2015): 121–27.

———. 'Marxism, Postcolonialism and the Spectre of Universalism'. *Critical Sociology* 43, nos. 4-5 (2015): 599–610.

Chandra, Uday, Geir Heierstad and Kenneth Bo Nielsen. *The Politics of Caste in West Bengal*. Oxon: Routledge, 2016.

Chandran, M. D. Subash, and Madhav Gadgil. 'Indigenous Vision: Peoples of India Attitudes to the Environment'. *India International Centre Quarterly* 19, nos. 1–2 (1992): 183–87.

Chatterjee, Partha. 'After Subaltern Studies'. *Economic and Political Weekly* 47, no. 39 (2012): 44–49.

———. *The Nation and Its Fragments: Colonial and Postcolonial Histories*. Princeton, NJ: Princeton University Press, 1993.

———. *The Politics of the Governed: Reflections on Popular Politics in Most of the World*. New York: Columbia University Press, 2004.

Cheah, Pheng. *Spectral Nationality: Passages of Freedom from Kant to Postcolonial Literatures of Liberation*. New York: Columbia University Press, 2003.

Chibber, Vivek. *Postcolonial Theory and the Spectre of Capital*. New York: Verso Books, 2013.

Chiriyankandath, James. 'Colonialism and Post-Colonial Development'. In *Politics in the Developing World*, edited by Peter Burnell, Vicky Randall and Lise Rakner, pp. 29–43. Oxford: Oxford University Press, 2017.

Chowdhury, Indira. 'Oral Traditions and Contemporary History Event, Memory, Experience and Representation'. *Economic and Political Weekly* 49, no. 30 (2014): 54–59.

Clifford, James. 'Indigenous Articulations'. *Contemporary Pacific* 13, no. 2 (2001): 469–90.

Clifford, James, and George E. Marcus. *Writing Culture: The Poetics and Politics of Ethnography*. Berkeley and Los Angeles: University of California Press, 1986.

Coulthard, Glen Sean. *Red Skin, White Masks: Rejecting the Colonial Politics of Recognition*. Minneapolis, MN: University of Minnesota Press, 2014.

Cohn, Bernard S. 'Representing Authority in Victorian India'. In *The Invention of Tradition*, edited by Eric Hobsbawm and Terry Ranger, pp. 165–211. Cambridge: Cambridge University Press, 1983.

Comaroff, Jean, and John Comaroff. 'Christianity and Colonialism in South Africa'. *American Ethnologist* 13, no. 1 (February 1986): 1–22.

———. *Of Revelation and Revolution: Christianity, Colonialism and Consciousness in South Africa*. Chicago: University of Chicago Press, 1991.

———. *Law and Disorder in the Postcolony*. Chicago: University of Chicago Press, 2006.

Connerton, Paul. 'Seven Types of Forgetting'. *Memory Studies* 1, no. 1 (January 2008): 59–71.

Cubit, Jeoffrey. *History and Memory*. Manchester: Manchester University Press, 2007.

Damodaran, Vinita. 'Colonial Constructions of the 'Tribe' in India: The Case of Chotangapur'. *Indian Historical Review* 33, no. 1 (2006): 44–75.

———. 'Environment, Ethnicity and History in Chotanagpur, India, 1850–1970'. *Environment and History* 3, no. 3 (1997): 273–98.

———. 'History, Landscape, and Indigeneity in Chotanagpur, 1850–1980'. *South Asia: Journal of South Asia Studies* 25, no. 2 (2002): 77–110.

———. 'Indigenous Agency: Customary Rights and Tribal Protection in Eastern India, 1830–1930'. *History Workshop Journal* 76, no. 1 (October 2013): 85–110.

Danius, Sara, Stefan Jonsson and Gayatri Chakravorty Spivak. 'An Interview with Gayatri Chakravorty Spivak, Sara Danius and Stefan Jonsson'. *Boundary* 20, no. 2 (2012): 24–50.

Das, Subhashis. 'The Hargarhis of Jharkhand: A Brief Study of the Megaliths of Jharkhand.' *Chitrolekha International Magazine on Art and Design* 5, no. 1 (2015): 2–21.

Dasgupta, Sangeeta. 'Mapping Histories: Many Narratives of Tana Pasts'. *Indian Economic and Social History Review* 53, no. 1 (2016): 99–129.

———. 'Heathen Aboriginals, Christian Tribes and Animistic Races: Missionary Narratives on Oraons of Chotanagpur in Colonial India'. *Modern South Asian Studies* 50, no. 2 (2016): 437–78.

———. 'The Journey of an Anthropologist in Chhotanagpur'. *Indian Economic and Social History Review* 42, no. 2 (2004): 165–98.

Dasgupta, Sangeeta, and Daniel J. Rycroft. *The Politics of Belonging in India: Becoming Adivasi*. New Delhi: Routledge, 2011.

Derne, Steve. 'Religious Movement as Rite of Passage: An Anlaysis of Birsa Movement'. *Contributions to Indian Sociology* 19, no. 2 (1985): 251–68.

Devi, Mahasweta. *Aranyer Adhikar (Forest Rights)*. Calcutta: Karuna Prokashini, 2001.

———. *Chotti Munda and His Arrow*. New Delhi: Blackwell Publication, 2003.

Dirks, Nicholas. *Castes of Mind: Colonialism and the Making of Modern India*. Princeton, NJ: Princeton University Press, 2001.

Dudai, Yadin, and Micah G. Edelson. 'Personal Memory: Is It Personal, Is It Memory?' *Memory Studies* 9, no. 3 (2016): 275–83.

Dumont, Louis. *Essays on Individualism: Modern Ideology in Anthropological Perspective*. Chicago: University of Chicago Press, 1986.

Ekka, Vincent. "Lessons from the Institution of 'Indigenous Self-Governance'". In *Being Adivasi: Existence, Entitlements, Exclusion*, edited by Abhay Xaxa and G. N. Devy, pp. 80–93. New Delhi: Rupa Publications, 2021.

Erll, Astrid. *Memory in Culture*, translated by Sara B. Young. London: Palgrave Macmillan, 2011.

———. 'Re-Writing as Re-Visioning Modes of Representing the "Indian Mutiny" in British Novels, 1857 to 2000'. *European Journal of English Studies* 10, no. 2 (2006): 163–85.

———. 'Travelling Memory'. *Parallax* 17, no. 4 (2011): 4–18.

Erll, Astrid, Nünning Ansgar and Sara B. Young. *Cultural Memory Studies: An International and Interdisciplinary Handbook*. Berlin: Walter de Gruyter, 2008.

Frykenberg, Robert Eric. 'Introduction: Dealing with Contested Definitions and Controversial Perspectives'. In *Christians and Missionaries in India: Cross-Cultural Communication since 1500*, edited by Robert Eric Frykenberg, pp. 1–33. Michigan: William B. Eerdmans Publishing Company, 2003.

Geertz, Clifford. *The Interpretation of Cultures Selected Essays*. New York: Basic Books Inc., 1973.

Ghosh, Kaushik. 'Between Global Flows and Local Dams: Indigenousness, Locality, and the Transnational Sphere in Jharkhand, India'. *Cultural Anthropology* 21, no. 4 (2006): 501–34.

———. 'Indigenous Incitements'. In *Indigenous Knowledge and Learning in Asia/Pacific and Africa*, edited by D. Kapoor and E. Shizha, pp. 35–46. New York: Palgrave Macmillan, 2010.

Ghuyre, Govind Sadashiv. *The Scheduled Tribes: The Aborigines So-Called and Their Future*. Bombay: Ramdas Bhatkal for Popular Prakashan, 1963.

Giri, A. Kumar. 'Lifeworlds and Living Words'. *Social Change* 49 (2019): 241–56.

Gopal, Priyamvada. *Insurgent Empire: Anticolonial Resistance and British Dissent*. London: Verso, 2019.

Graham, Nicole. *Lawscape: Property, Environment, Law*. New York: Routledge, 2011.

Gramsci, Antonio. *Selections from Prison Notebooks: Antonio Gramsci*, translated by Quintin Hoare and Geoffrey Nowell Smith. London: Lawrence and Wishart, 1971.

Guha, Ranajit. *Dominance without Hegemony: History and Power in Colonial India*. Cambridge, MA: Harvard University Press, 1997.

———. *Elementary Aspects of Peasant Insurgency in Colonial India*. Durham, NC: Duke University Press, 1999.

———. 'On Some Aspects of the Historiography of Colonial India'. In *Subaltern Studies*, vol. 1: *Writings on South Asian History and Society*, ed. Ranajit Guha, pp. 37–44. Delhi: Oxford University Press, 1982.

———. 'Prose of Counter Insurgency'. In *Selected Subaltern Studies*, edited by Ranajit Guha and Gayatri Chakravarty Spivak, pp. 45–85. Oxford University Press, 1988.

Gupta, Akhil. 'Imagining Nations'. In *Companion to the Anthropology of Politics*, edited by David Nugent and Joan Vincent, 267–81. Oxford: Blackwell Publishing, 2007.

———. *Red Tape: Bureaucracy, Structural Violence, and Poverty in India*. Durham, NC: Duke University Press, 2012.

——— (ed.). *Subaltern Studies*, vol. 1: *Writings on South Asian History and Society*. Delhi: Oxford University Press, 1982.

Gupta, Sanjukta Das. 'Rethinking Adivasi Identity: The Chota Nagpur Tenancy Act (1908) and Its Aftermath among the Hos of Singhbhum'. In *Adivasi in Colonial India: Survival, Resistance and Negotiation*, edited by Biswamoy Pati, pp. 88–111. New Delhi: Orient Blackswan, 2011.

Halbwachs, Maurice. *The Collective Memory*, 1941. Chicago: University of Chicago Press.

Hardiman, David. *The Coming of the Devi: Adivasi Assertion in Western India*. Oxford: Oxford University Press, 1987.

Hardt, Michael, and Antonio Negri. *Empire*. Cambridge, MA: Harvard University Press, 2000.

Hartog, François. 'Time and Heritage'. *Museum International* 57, no. 3 (2005): 7–18.

Hobsbawm, Eric. *Primitive Rebels*. Manchester: University of Manchester Press, 1959.

Hobsbawm, Eric, and Terence Ranger. *The Invention of Tradition*. Cambridge: Cambridge University Press, 1983.

Hodges, Matt. 'Reinventing "History"?' *History and Anthropology* 26, no. 4 (11 September 2015): 515–27.

Hodgkin, Katharine, and Susannah Radstone. 'Patterning the National Past'. In *Memory, History, Nation: Contested Pasts*, edited by Katharine Hodgkin and Susannah Radstone, pp. 169–74. New Brunswick: Transaction, 2006.

Hoffman, John-Baptist. *Encyclopedia Mundarica*, vol. 2. New Delhi: Gian Publishing House, 1912.

———. *Encyclopedia Mundarica*, vol. 13. New Delhi: Gian Publishing House, n.d.

Hoffman, John-Baptist, and E. Lister, 'Special Memorandum on the Land System of the Munda Country'. In *Encyclopaedia Mundarica*, vol. 8 (reprint), edited by John-Baptist Hoffman and A. V. Emelen. New Delhi: Gyan Publishing House, 2015.

Howell, Signe. 'Battle of Cosmologies: The Catholic Church, Adat, and "Inculturation" among Northern Lio, Indonesia'. *Social Analysis* 60, no. 4 (1 January 2016): 21–39.

Hunter, William Wilson. *The Imperial Gazette of India*. Oxford: Oxford University Press, 1881.

Hunter, William Wilson, James Sutherland Cotton, Sir Richard Burn, William Meyer and Great Britain India Office. *The Imperial Gazetteer of India*, vol. 21. Oxford: Oxford Publication, 1908.

Ingold, Tim. 'Temporality of the Landscape'. *World Archaeology* 25, no. 2 (1993): 152–74.

———. 'That's Enough about Ethnography!' *HAU: Journal of Ethnographic Theory* 4, no. 1 (2014): 383–95.

Jaffrelot, Christophe. *The Hindu Nationalist Movement and Indian Politics (1925–1990)*. London. C. Hurst & Co. Publishers, 1996.

Jaoul, Nicolas. 'Learning the Use of Symbolic Means: Dalits, Ambedkar Statues and the State in Uttar Pradesh'. *Contributions to Indian Sociology* 40, no. 2 (2006): 175–207.

Jazeel, Tariq. 'Subaltern Geographies: Geographical Knowledge and Postcolonial Strategy'. *Singapore Journal of Tropical Geography* 35, no. 1 (2014): 88–103.

Jha, Jagdish Chandra. *The Tribal Revolt of Chota Nagpur (1831–1832)*. Patna: Kashi Prasad Jayaswal Research Institute, 1987.

———. 'The Kol Rising of Chotanagpur (1831–33): Its Causes'. *Proceedings of the Indian History Congress* 21 (1958): 440–46.

Jharkhand Janadhikar Mahasabha. 'Harassment of Activists—I'. *Economic and Political Weekly* 54, no. 24 (2019): 4–5.

Johnson, Nuala. 'Cast in Stone: Monuments, Geography, and Nationalism'. *Environment and Planning D: Society and Space* 13, no. 1 (12 October 2006): 51–65.

Jones, Andrew. *Memory and Material Culture*. Cambridge: Cambridge University Press, 2007.

Kaiwar, Vasant. *The Postcolonial Orient: The Politics of Difference and the Project of Provincialising Europe*. Leiden: Brill, 2014.

Kannan, K. P. 'How Inclusive Is Inclusive Growth in India?' *Indian Journal of Labour Economics* 55, no. 1 (2012): 33–60.

Karlsson, Bengt G., and T. B. Subha. *Indigeneity in India*. New York: Columbia University Press, 2006.

Kasabova, Anita. 'Memory, Memorials and Commemoration'. *History and Theory* 47, no. 3 (2008): 331–50.

Kashwan, Prakash. *Democracy in the Woods: Environmental Conservation and Social Justice in India, Tanzania, and Mexico*. New Delhi: Oxford University Press, 2017.

Kashwan, Prakash, and Rahul Ranjan. 'Introduction' (Special Issue: Echoes from the Woods: At the Crossroads of Forest Struggles and Human Rights in Postcolonial India)'. *International Journal of Human Rights* 25, no. 7 (2021): 1089–93.

Kerketta, Jacinta. *Angor*. Kolkata: Adivaani, 2016.

Khilnani, Sunil. *Incarnations: India in 50 Lives*. London: Allen Lane, 2016.

Khosla, G. D. *The Murder of the Mahatma*. Mumbai: Jaico Publishing House, 1965.

Kikon, Dolly. 'Jackfruit Seeds from Jharkhand: Being Adivasi in Assam'. *Contributions to Indian Sociology* 51, no. 3 (2017): 313–37.

Kiro, Santosh. *The Life and Times of Jaipal Singh Munda*. Ranchi: Prabhat Publications, 2018.

Koselleck, Reinhart. *Future Past: On the Semantics of Historical Time*, translated by Keith Tribe. New York: Columbia University Press, 2004.

———. *The Practice of Conceptual History: Timing History, Spacing Concepts*, translated by Hayden White. Stanford: Stanford University Press, 2002.

Kolsky, Elizabeth. 'The Colonial Rule of Law and the Legal Regime of Exception: Frontier "Fanaticism" and State Violence in British India'. *American Historical Review* 120, no. 4 (October 2015): 1218–46.

Kujur, Ignes. *Jharkhand Do Mujane Par*. n.d. n.p.

Kumar, Sanjay, and Praveen Rai. 'Shrinking Political Space for the Jharkhand Mukti Morcha'. *Economic and Political Weekly* 44, no. 33 (2009): 24–29.

Lahiri-Dutt, Kuntala, Radhika Krishnan and Nesar Ahmad. 'Land Acquisition and Dispossession: Private Coal Companies in Jharkhand'. *Economic and Political Weekly* 47, no. 6 (2012): 39–45.

Lee Klein, Kerwin. 'On the Emergence of Memory in Historical Discourse'. *Source: Representations* 69 (Winter 2000): 127–50.

Lee, Richard E. 'Lessons of the Longue Durée: The Legacy of Fernand Braudel'. *Historia Crítica* 69 (July–September 2018): 69–77.

Lefebvre, Georges. *The Great Fear of 1789: Rural Panic in Revolutionary France*, translated from the French by Joan White. New York: Vintage Books, 1973.

Lele, Sharachchandra. 'Understanding Current Forest Policy Debates through Multiple Lenses: The Case of India'. *Ecology, Economy and Society-the INSEE Journal* 2, no. 2 (2019): 21–30.

Lerche, Jens, and Alpa Shah. 'Conjugated Oppression within Contemporary Capitalism: Class, Caste, Tribe and Agrarian Change in India'. *Journal of Peasant Studies* 45, nos. 5–6 (19 September 2018): 927–49.

Lewis, Adam Gary. 'Ethics, Activism and the Anti-Colonial: Social Movement Research as Resistance'. *Social Movement Studies* 11, no. 2 (April 2012): 227–40.

Lilja, Mona. 'The Politics of Time and Temporality in Foucault's Theorisation of Resistance: Ruptures, Time-Lags and Decelerations'. *Journal of Political Power* 11, no. 3 (2 September 2018): 419–32.

Ludden, David. *Reading Subaltern Studies: Critical History, Contested Meaning and the Globalization of South Asia*. London: Anthem Press, 2001.

Macaulay, Thomas Babington. 'Minute of 2 February 1835 on Indian Education'. In *Macaulay, Prose and Poetry*, selected by G. M. Young, pp. 721–24. Cambridge, MA: Harvard University Press, 1957.

Mahato, S. *A Hundred Years of Christian Missions in Chotanagpur since 1845*. Ranchi: Chotanagpur Christian Publishing House, 1971.

Mahuika, Rangimarie. 'Kaupapa Māori Theory Is Critical and Anti-colonial'. *MAI Review* 3 (2008): 1–16.

Majeed, Javed. *Ungoverned Imaginings James Mill's 'The History of British India and Orientalism'*. London: Clarendon Press, 1992.

Marschall, Sabine. 'Collective Memory and Cultural Difference: Official vs. Vernacular Forms of Commemorating the Past'. *Safundi: The Journal of South African and American Studies* 14, no. 1 (2013): 77–92.

Marvasti, Amir B. *Qualitative Research in Sociology*. New Delhi: SAGE Publications, 2011.

Marx, Karl. *Capital*, vol. 1. New York: Penguin, 1990.

McLean, Stuart. 'Materiality and Culture'. In *International Encyclopedia of the Social and Behavioral Sciences: Second Edition*, edited by James D. Wright, pp. 765–71 (Amsterdam: Elsevier, 2015). https://doi.org/10.1016/B978-0-08-097086-8.12207-X. Accessed on 9 August 2022.

Medina, Jose. *The Epistemology of Resistance: Gender and Racial Oppression, Epistemic Injustice, and Resistant Imaginations*. Oxford: Oxford University Press, 2013.

Morton, Timothy. *Ecology without Nature: Rethinking Environmental Aesthetics*. Cambridge, MA: Harvard University Press, 2007.

Morris, Rosalind C. (ed.). *Can the Subaltern Speak? Reflections on the History of an Idea*. New York: Columbia University Press, 2010.

Mosse, David. *The Saint in the Banyan Tree*. California: University of California Press, 2012.

Mullick, S. Bosu. 'Preface'. In *Adi-Dharam: Religious Beliefs of the Adivasis of India*, edited by Ram Dayal Munda, pp. 7–12. Calcutta: Advaani, 2014.

Munda, R. D. *Adivasi Astitva aur Jahrkhandi Asmita ke Sawaal*. 2nd edition. Ranchi: Rumbul, 2018.

Munda, R. D., and B. P. Keshari. 'Recent Developments in the Jharkhand Movement'. *India International Centre Quarterly* 19, no. 3 (1992): 71–89.

Munda, R. D., and Norman Zide. 'Revolutionary Birsa and Songs Related to Him'. *Journal of Social Research* 12, no. 2 (1969): 37–60.

Munda, R. D., and S. Bosu Mullick. *Jharkhand Movement: Indigenous Peoples' Struggle for Autonomy in India*. Copenhagen: International Work Group for Indigenous Affairs, 2003.

Nathan, Dev, and Virginius Xaxa. *Social Exclusion and Adverse Inclusion: Development and Deprivation of Adivasis in India*. New Delhi: Oxford University Press, 2012.

Nambiar, Malini. 'Making the Gram Sabha'. *Economic and Political Weekly* 36, no. 33 (2001): 3114–17.

Nandy, Ashis. *The Intimate Enemy: Loss and Recovery of Self under Colonialism*. New Delhi: Oxford University Press, 1983.

Nilsen, Alf Gunvald. *Adivasis and the State: Subalternity and Citizenship in India's Bhil Heartland* (Cambridge: Cambridge University Press, 2018).

———. *Politics from Below: Essays on Subalternity and Resistance in India*. New Delhi: Aakar Books, 2017.

Nora, Pierre. 'Between Memory and History: Les Lieux de Mémoire'. *Representations* 26 (Spring 1989): 7–24.

Lazarus, Neil. 'Introducing Postcolonial Studies'. In *The Cambridge Companion to Postcolonial Literary Studies*, edited by Neil Lazarus, pp. 19–40. Cambridge: Cambridge University Press, 2004.

Lennox, Corinne, and Damien Short (eds.). *Handbook of Indigenous Peoples' Rights*. London: Routledge, 2016.

O'Brien, Daniel B. Cruise. *Symbolic Confrontations: Muslims Imagining the State in Africa*. London: Palgrave Macmillan, 2003.

O'Hanlon, Rosalind. 'Recovering the Subject Subaltern Studies and Histories of Resistance in Colonial South Asia'. *Modern Asian Studies* 22, no. 22 (1988): 189–224.

O'Keeffe, Tadhg. 'Landscape and Memory: Historiography, Theory, Methodology'. In *Heritage, Memory and the Politics of Identity: New Perspectives on the Cultural Landscape*, edited by Yvonne Whelan and Niamh Moore, pp. 3–18. Hampshire: Ashgate Publishing Limited, 2007.

Ohlström, Marcus, Marco Solinas and Olivier Voirol. 'On Nancy Fraser and Axel Honneth's Redistribution or Recognition? A Political-Philosophical Exchange'. *Iris* 3, no. 5 (2011): 205–21.

Ortner, Sherry B. 'Resistance and the Problem of Ethnographic Refusal'. *Comparative Studies in Society and History* 37, no. 1. (1995): 173–93.

Pandey, Gyanendra. *Remembering Partition: Violence, Nationalism and History in India*. New Delhi: Cambridge University Press, 2001.

———. 'Subaltern Citizens and Their Histories'. *Interventions* 10, no. 3 (2008): 271–84.

Parmar, Pooja. *Indigeneity and Legal Pluralism in India: Claims, Histories, Meanings*. New Delhi: Cambridge University Press, 2016.

———. 'Undoing Historical Wrongs: Law and Indigeneity in India'. *Osgoode Hall Law Journal* 49, no. 3 (2012): 491–525.

Pink, Sarah. *The Future of Visual Anthropology: Engaging the Senses*. London: Routledge, 2006.

Portelli, Alessandro. 'The Peculiarities of Oral History'. *History Workshop Journal* 12, no. 1 (1981): 96–107.

Porter, Andrew. *European Imperialism, 1860–1814 (Studies in European History)*. London: Macmillan Press, 1994.

Prakash, Amit. *Jharkhand: Politics of Development and Identity*. New Delhi: Orient Blackswan, 2001.

Prakash, Gyan. 'The Impossibility of Subaltern History'. *Nepantla: Views from South* 1, no. 2 (2000): 287–94.

Quijano, Aníbal. 'Coloniality and Modernity/Rationality'. *Cultural Studies* 21, nos. 2–3 (March 2007): 168–78.

Radhakrishna, Meena. *First Citizens: Studies on Adivasis, Tribals, and Indigenous People in India*. New Delhi: Oxford University Press, 2016.

Radstone, Susannah. 'Memory Studies: For and Against'. *Memory Studies* 1, no. 1 (2008): 31–39.

Rajan, Rajeswari Sunder. 'Death and the Subaltern'. In *Can the Subaltern Speak? Reflections on the History of an Idea*, edited by Rosalind C. Morris, pp. 117–38. New York: Columbia University Press, 2010.

Raman, Bhavani. *Document Raj: Writing and Scribes in Early Colonial India* (South Asia across the Disciplines). Chicago: University of Chicago Press, 2012.

Rana, L. N. 'The Adivasi Mahasabha (1938–1949): Launching Pad of the Jharkhand Movement'. *Proceedings of the Indian History Congress* 53, no. 3 (1992): 397–405.

Ranciere, Jacques. *The Politics of Aesthetics: The Distribution of the Sensible*. London: Continuum International Publishing House, 2004.

Ranjan, Rahul. 'Mini-India: The Politics of Migration and Subalternity in the Andaman Islands'. *Postcolonial Studies* 24, no. 3 (19 August 2018): 1–3.

———. 'Unravelling the Narratives of Adivasi Dispossession: A Case Study of Land Acquisition in Nagri Village, Jharkhand'. *Development* 60, nos. 3–4 (2017): 227–34.

Rao, Rahul. 'What Do We Mean When We Talk About Statues?' 10th Africa Day Memorial Lecture, 2018. https://www.ufs.ac.za/docs/default-source/ufs-news-list/read-lectures-here.pdf. Accessed in September 2022.

Raza, Ahmed. *Chotnagpur Tenancy Act: A Handbook on Tenancy Law in Jharkhand*. New Delhi: Human Rights Law Network, 2015.

Rege, Sharmila. *Against the Madness of Manu*. New Delhi: Navayana, 2013.

Risley, H. H. 'The Study of Ethnology in India'. *Journal of Anthropological Institute of Great Britain and Ireland* 20 (1891): 235–63.

———. *The Tribes and Castes of Bengal: Ethnographic Glossary*, vol. 1. Calcutta: Bengal Secretariat Press, 1891.

Roy, R. N. Pandey. *Manual of Chhotanagpur Tenancy Laws*, vol. 2. Calcutta: Rajpal and Company, 2001.

Roy, S. C. *The Mundas and Their Country*. Calcutta: Kuntaline Press, 1912.

———. *The Oraons of Chota Nagpur: Their History, Economic Life and Social Organisation*. Ranchi: Thacker, Spink and Company, 1915.

Roy, Srila, and Alf Gunvald Nilsen. *New Subaltern Politics: Reconceptualizing Hegemony and Resistance in Contemporary India*. New Delhi: Oxford University Press, 2015.

Runia, Eelco. 'Burying the Dead, Creating the Past'. *History and Theory* 46, no. 3 (2007): 313–25.

Russell, Robert Vane. *The Tribes and Castes of the Central Provinces of India*. London: Macmillan, 1916.

Rycroft, Daniel J. *Representing Rebellion: Visual Aspects of Counter-Insurgency in Colonial India*. New Delhi: Oxford University Press, 2006.

———. 'Capturing Birsa Munda: The Virtuality of a Colonial-Era Photograph'. *Indian Folklore Research Journal* 1, no. 4 (2004): 53–67.

———. 'Anthropological Archives and "Chiasmic" Time in Modern India'. *Irish Journal of Anthropology* 19, no. 2 (Autumn–Winter 2016): 46–68.

———. 'Locating Adivasi Politics: Aspects of "Indian" Anthropology after Birsa Munda'. *Anglistica AION* 19, no. 1 (2015): 133–46.

———. 'Looking Beyond the Present: The Historical Dynamics of Adivasi (Indigenous and Tribal) Assertions in India–Part II: Indian Confederation of Indigenous and Tribal Peoples'. *Journal of Adivasi and Indigenous Studies (JAIS)* 2, no. 1 (2015): 1–10.

Sa, Fidelis de. *Crisis in Chota Nagpur, with Special Reference to Judicial Conflict between Jesuit Missionaries and British Government Officials, November 1889-March 1990*. Bangalore: Redemptorist Publication, 1975.

Sabin, Margery. 'In Search of Subaltern Consciousness'. *Prose Studies* 30, no. 2 (2008): 177–200.

Sachichidanda. 'Social Change in Chotanagpur'. *Bulletin of the Bihar Tribal Research Institute* 6, no. 2 (1964): 220–39.

Said, Edward. *Orientalism*. London: Routledge & Kegan Paul Ltd, 1978.

———. 'Invention, Memory, and Place'. *Critical Inquiry* 26, no. 2 (2000): 175–92.

Saito, Hiro. 'From Collective Memory to Commemoration'. In *Handbook of Cultural Sociology*, edited by John R. Hall, Laura Grindstaff and Ming-cheng Lo, pp. 629–38. London: Routledge, 2010.

Samaddar, Ranabir. *Memory, Identity, Power: Politics in the Junglemahals, 1800–1950*. New Delhi: Orient Blackswan, 2013 (1988).

Samson, Colin, and Carlos Gigoux. *Indigenous Peoples and Colonialism: Global Perspectives*. Cambridge: Polity Press, 2017.

Sanyal, Kalyan. *Rethinking Capitalist Development: Primitive Accumulation, Governmentality and Postcolonial Capitalism*. New Delhi: Routledge, 2007.

Sanyal, Paromita, and Vijayendra Rao. *Oral Democracy*. Cambridge: Cambridge University Press, 2018.

Sarkar, Sumit. *Modern India 1885–1947*. London: Palgrave Macmillan, 1989.

Sarkar, Tanika. 'Nationalist Iconography: Image of Women in 19th Century Bengali Literature'. *Economic and Political Weekly* 22, no. 47 (1987): 2011–15.

Savyasaachi. 'Primitive Accumulation, Labour, and the Making of "Scheduled Tribe", "Indigenous", and Adivasi Sensibility'. In *First Citizens: Studies on Adivasis, Tribals, and Indigenous Peoples in India*, edited by Meena Radhakrishna, pp. 53–76. New Delhi: Oxford University Press, 2016.

Schaffer, Kay, and Sidonie Smith. 'Conjunctions: Life Narratives in the Field of Human Rights'. *Biography* 27, no. 1 (2004): 1–24.

Scholte, Bob. 'Reason and Culture: The Universal and the Particular Revisited'. *American Anthropolgist* 86, no. 4 (1984): 960–65.

Schulte-Droesch, Lea. *Making Place through Ritual: Land, Environment and Region among the Santhal of Central India*. Berlin: De Gruyter, 2018.

Scott, James C. 'Everyday Forms of Resistance'. *Copenhagen Journal of Asian Studies* 4, no. 1 (24 November 2017): 33–62.

Seal, Anil. *Locality, Province and Nation: Essays on Indian Politics 1870 to 1940*. Cambridge: Cambridge University Press, 1973.

Sengupta, Nirmal. *Fourth World Dynamics: Jharkhand*. Kolkata: Authors Guild Publications, 1984.

Sen, Asoka Kumar. *Indigeneity, Landscape and History: Adivasi Self-fashioning in India*. New Delhi: Routeldge, 2018.

Shah, Alpa. 'Alcoholics Anonymous: The Maoist Movement in Jharkhand, India'. *Modern Asian Studies* 45, no. 05 (2011): 1095–1117.

———. 'Ethnography? Participant Observation, a Potentially Revolutionary Praxis'. *HAU: Journal of Ethnographic Theory* 7, no. 1 (2017): 45–59.

———. *In the Shadows of the State: Indigenous Politics, Environmentalism and Insurgency in Jharkhand, India*. New Delhi: Oxford University Press, 2011.

———. '"Keeping the State Away": Democracy, Politics, and the State in India'. *Journal of the Royal Anthropological Institute* 13, no. 1 (2007): 129–45.

———. *Nightmarch: Among India's Revolutionary Guerillas*. London: Hurst Publications, 2018.

———. 'Religion and the Secular Left: Subaltern Studies, Birsa Munda and Maoists'. *Anthropology of This Century* 9 (2014): 1–12.

———. 'The Agrarian Question in a Maoist Guerrilla Zone: Land, Labour and Capital in the Forests and Hills of Jharkhand, India'. *Journal of Agrarian Change* 13, no. 3 (2013): 424–50.

———. 'The Labour of Love: Seasonal Migration from Jharkhand to the Brick Kilns of Other States in India', *Contributions to Indian Sociology* (n.s.) 40, no. 1 (2006): 91–118.

Shah, Alpa, Jens Lerche, Richard Axelby, Dalel Benbabaali, Brendan Donegan, Jayaseelan Raj and Vikramaditya Thakur (eds.). *Ground Down by Growth: Tribe, Caste, Class and Inequality in 21st Century India*. London: Pluto Press, 2017.

Shourie, Arun. *Missionaries in India: Continuities, Changes, Dilemmas*. New Delhi: ASA Publications, 1994.

Singh, Anjana. 'Many Faces of the Pathalgadi Movement in Jharkhand'. *Economic Political Weekly* 54, no. 11 (2019): 28–33.

Singh, Jai Pal. 'Jai Jharkhand! Jai Adivasi! Jai Hind!' In *Jharkhand Movement: Indigenous Peoples' Struggle for Autonomy in India*, edited by S. Bosu Mullick and R. D. Munda, pp. 2–14. Copenhagen: International Work Group for Indigenous Affairs, 2003.

Singh, K. S. *Birsa Munda and His Movement (1872–1901)*. Centennial Edition. Kolkata: Seagull Books, 2002.

Singh, K. M., M. S. Meena, R. K. P. Singh, Abhay Kumar and Anjani Kumar. 'Rural Poverty in Jharkhand, India: An Empirical Study Based on Panel Data'. MPRA

Paper. Munich Personal RePEc Archive, Munich, 2012. https://mpra.ub.uni-muenchen.de/45258. Accessed on 24 January 2018.

Sinha, Amita. 'Colonial and Post-Colonial Memorial Parks in Lucknow, India: Shifting Ideologies and Changing Aesthetics'. *Journal on Landscape Architecture* 50, no. 2 (Autumn 2010): 60–71.

Sinha, S. P. *Conflict and Tension in Tribal Society*. New Delhi: Concept Publication Company, 1994.

———. *Life and Times of Birsa Bhagwan*. 2nd edition. Ranchi: Bihar Tribal Research Institute, 1997.

Sinha, Subir, and Rashmi Verma. 'Marxism and Postcolonial Theory: What's Left of the Debate?' *Critical Sociology* 43, no. 4–5 (2015): 545–58.

Sinha, Nitin, 'Fluvial Landscape and the State: Property and the Gangetic Diaras in Colonial India, 1790s-1890s', *Environment and History* 20, no. 2 (May 2014): 209–37.

Sivaramakrishnan, K. *Modern Forests: Statemaking and Environmental Changes in Colonial Eastern India*. California: Standford University Press, 1999.

Sowvendra Shekhar, Hansda. 'Sarna-Hindu Theology: A Study of Some Cults, Gods and Worship in Jharkhand'. *The Apollonian* 4, nos. 1–2 (2017): 94–106.

Spiegel, Gabrielle M. 'Memory and History: Liturgical Time and Historical Time'. *History and Theory* 41, no. 2 (2018): 149–62.

Spivak, Gayatri Chakravorty. 'Can the Subaltern Speak?'. In *Colonial Discourses and Post-Colonial Theory: A Reader*, edited by Patrick Williams and Laura Chrisman, pp. 66–111. New York: Columbia University Press, 1994.

———. 'Can the Subaltern Speak?'. In *In Marxism and the Interpretation of Culture*, edited by Cary Nelson and Lawrence Grossberg, pp. 271–313. Chicago: University of Illinois Press, 1988.

———. *The Spivak Reader: Selected Works of Gayatri Chakravorty Spivak*, edited by Donna Landry and Gerald MacLean. New York: Routledge, 1996.

Standing, Hilary. 'Postcolonial Theory and the Specter of Capital'. *Cambridge Review of International Affairs* 27, no. 1 (2014): 184–98.

———. 'The New Subaltern: A Silent Interview'. In *Mapping Subaltern Studies and the Postcolonial*, edited by Vinayak Chaturvedi, pp. 324–45. London: Verso, 2000.

Stevens, Quentin. 'Nothing More Than Feelings'. *Architectural Theory Review* 14, no. 2 (2009): 156–72.

Stevens, Quentin, Karen A. Franck and Ruth Fazakerley. 'Counter-Monuments: The Anti-Monumental and the Dialogic'. *Journal of Architecture* 17, no. 6 (2012): 951–72.

Stewart-Harawira, Makere. *The New Imperial Order: Indigenous Responses to Globalization*. London: Zed Books, 2005.

Stoler, Ann Laura. *Along the Archival Grain: Epistemic Anxieties and Colonial Common Sense*. Princeton, NJ: Princeton University Press, 2009.

Stuligross, David. 'Resources, Representation, and Authority in Jharkhand, India'. *Asia Pacific Viewpoint* 49, no. 1 (2008): 83–97.

Sud, Nikita. *The Making of Land and the Making of India*. Oxford: Oxford University Press, 2021.

———. 'State, Scale and Networks in the Liberalisation of India's Land'. *Environment and Planning: Politics and Space* 35, no. 1 (2016): 76–93.

Sundar, Nandini. 'Laws, Policies and Practices in Jharkhand'. *Economic and Political Weekly* 40, no. 41 (2005): 4459–62.

Taylor, Ken. 'Landscape and Memory: Cultural Landscapes, Intangible Values and Some thoughts on Asia'. Research School of Humanities, Australian National University, Canberra, 2008.

Tarlow, Sarah. *Bereavement and Commemoration: An Archaeology of Mortality*. Oxford: Blackwell Publishers, 1999.

Tartako, Gary Michael. *Dalit Art and Visual Imagery*. New Delhi: Oxford University Press, 2012.

Tete, S. J. Peter. *A Missionary Social Worker in India: J.B. Hoffamn, The Chota Nagpur Tenancy Act and the Catholic Co-Operatives 1893–1928*. Roma: Universita Gregoriana Editrice, 1984.

———. *Constant Lievens and the Catholic Church in Chotanagpur*. Ranchi: Archbishop's House, 1993.

Thapar, Romila. 'Early Indian History and the Legacy of DD Kosambi'. *Economic and Political Weekly* 43, no. 30 (25 July 2008): 43–51.

Thiong'o, Ngũgĩ wa. *Decolonising the Mind: The Politics of Language in African Literature*. Nairobi: East African Publishing House, 1981.

Thrift, Nigel. 'Intensities of Feeling: Towards a Spatial Politics of Affect'. *Geografiska Annaler* 86, no. 1 (2004): 57–78.

Tillin, Louise. *Remapping India: New State and Their Political Origins*. New Delhi: Oxford University Press, 2013.

———. *Remapping India: New States and Their Political Origins*. New Delhi: Oxford University Press, 2013.

Topno, M. 'Funeral Rites of the Mundas'. *Anthropos* (1955): 715–34.

Tota, Anna Lisa, and Trever Hagen (eds.). *Routledge International Handbook of Memory Studies*. London: Routledge Publications, 2015.

Upadhyay, Videh. 'Water Law and the Poor'. In *Legal Grounds: Natural Resources, Identity, and the Law in Jharkhand*, edited by Nandini Sundar, pp. 132–56. New Delhi: Oxford University Press, 2009.

Vansina, Jan. 'For Oral Tradition (But Not against Braudel)'. *History in Africa* 5 (1978): 351–56.

Varma, Rashmi. 'Primitive Accumulation'. *Third Text* 27, no. 6 (2013): 748–61.

Vasan, Sudha. 'Shifting the Terrain of Struggle: Critically Evaluating the Forest Rights Act'. In *First Citizens: Studies on Adivasis, Tribals, and Indigenous Peoples in India*, edited by Meena Radhakrishna, pp. 255–79. New Delhi: Oxford University Press, 2016.

Vionnet, Claire. 'From Experience to Language towards an Affected and Affective Writing: A Conversation with Tim Ingold'. *TSANTSA* 23 (2018): 82–90.

Vishwanath, Rupa. *The Pariah Problem: Caste, Religion and the Social in Modern India*. New York: Columbia University Press, 2014.

Viswanathan, Gauri. *Outside the Fold: Conversion, Modernity, and Belief*. Princeton, NJ: Princeton University Press, 1998.

Vitebsky, Piers. *Living Without the Dead*. Noida: HarperCollins Publishers, 2018.

———. 'Loving and Forgetting: Moments of Inarticulacy in Tribal India'. In *The Scheduled Tribes and Their India: Politics, Identities, Policies, and Work*, ed. Nandini Sundar, pp. 168–95. New Delhi: Oxford University Press, 2016.

Vlist, Leo van der. *Voices of the Earth: Indigenous Peoples, New Partners and the Right to Self-Determination in Practice*. Amsterdam: International Books, 1994.

Weiner, Myron. *Sons of the Soil: Migration and Ethnic Conflict in India*. Princeton, NJ: Princeton University Press, 1978.

Williams, Howard. 'Cremation and Present Pasts: A Contemporary Archaeology of Swedish Memory Grove'. *Mortality* 16, no. 2 (May 2011): 113–30.

———. 'Death, Memory, and Material Culture: Catalytic Commemoration and the Cremated Dead'. In *The Oxford Handbook of the Archaeology of Death and Burial*, edited by S. Tarlow and L. Nilsson Stutz, pp. 195–208. Oxford: Oxford University Press, 2013.

———. 'The Emotive Force of Early Medieval Mortuary Practices'. *Archaeological Review from Cambridge* 22, no. 1 (2007): 107–23.

Winter, Jay. 'The Generation of Memory: Reflections on the "Memory Boom" in Historical Studies'. *Archives and Social Studies: A Journal of Interdisciplinary Research* 1 (March 2007): 363–97.

Xaxa, Virginius. 'Formation of Adivasi/Indigenous Peoples' Identity in India'. In *First Citizens: Studies on Adivasis, Tribals, and Indigenous People in India*, edited by Meena Radhakrishna, pp. 33–52. New Delhi: Oxford University Press, 2016.

———. 'Is the Pathalgadi Movement in Tribal Areas Anti-Constitutional?'. *Economic and Political Weekly* 54, no. 1 (2019): 10–12.

Yazzie, Robert. 'Indigenous Peoples and Postcolonial Colonialism'. In *Reclaiming Indigenous Voice and Vision*, edited by Marie Ann Battiste, pp. 39–49. Vancouver: University of British Columbia, 2000.

Young, Robert J. C. 'Postcolonial Remains'. *New Literary History* 43, no. 1 (2012): 19–42.

Zehmisch, Philip. *Mini-India: The Politics of Migration and Subalternity in the Andamans Islands*. New Delhi: Oxford University Press, 2017.

Zelizer, Barbie. 'Reading the Past Against the Grain: The Shape of Memory Studies'. *Critical Studies in Mass Communication* 12 (2013): 214–39.

Online Sources

AKHRA Ranchi. 'Naachi Se Baanchi: Film on Ram Dayal Munda (2017)'. YouTube video, 2:04, 12 March 2018. https://www.youtube.com/watch?v=dGPuFcbGVns. Accessed on 10 March 2019.

Bagaicha Research Team. 'A Study of Undertrials in Jharkhand'. Sanhati, 2 February 2016. http://sanhati.com/excerpted/16044. Accessed on 24 February 2019.

———. 'Deprived of Rights over Natural Resources, Impoverished Adivasis Get Prison'. Sanhati, 2 February 2016, http://sanhati.com/excerpted/16044/. Accessed on 15 November 2019.

Cambridge Dictionary. 'mausoleum', https://dictionary.cambridge.org/dictionary/english/mausoleum. Accessed on 10 September 2019.

Constitution Society. 'PART III: Fundamental Rights'. https://www.constitution.org/cons/india/p03019.html. Accessed on 3 January 2019.

Damodaran, Vinita. 'Sacred Landscapes: Mining, Globalisation and the Environmental History of Eastern India'. Centre for World Environmental History, University of Sussex, http://www.sussex.ac.uk/cweh/research/sacredlandscapes. Accessed on 1 May 2019.

De, Koustav. 'Gaon Chodab Nahi (We Will Not Leave Our Village)'. YouTube video, 28 March 2009. www.youtube.com/watch?v=8M5aeMpzOLU&t=108s. Accessed on 10 October 2019.

Deepanwita Gita Niyogi, 'Rise of Sati Pati Cult in Jharkhand'. Pulitzer Center. https://pulitzercenter.org/stories/rise-sati-pati-cult-jharkhand. Accessed on 21 December 2021.

Dungdung, Gladson. 'Adivasis on the March: Crisis and Cultural Genocide in Tribal India'. Adivasi Hunkar, 14 March 2019. https://www.adivasihunkar.com/2019/03/14/adivasis-on-the-march-crisis-and-cultural-genocide-in-tribal-india. Accessed on 11 February 2021.

———. 'I Was Forced to Sign on the Land Acquisition Papers: Sukhram Munda'. Adivasi Hunkar, 5 March 2019. https://adivasihunkar.com/2019/03/05/i-was-forced-to-sign-on-the-land-acquisition-papers-sukhram-munda. Accessed on 11 February 2020.

———. 'Land Bank and Forest Rights'. Adivasi Hunkar, 5 March 2019, https://adivasihunkar.com/2019/03/05/i-was-forced-to-sign-on-the-land-acquisition-papers-sukhram-munda. Accessed on 11 February 2020.

Katyayan, Rashmi. 'Dombari Buru Cetanare: Ram Dayal Munda'. YouTube video, 5:08, 21 August 2012. https://www.youtube.com/watch?v=rDDhh2COUHU. Accessed on 15 September 2019.

Lexico (Oxford English Dictionary). s.v. 'commemoration'. https://en.oxforddictionaries.com/definition/commemorate. Accessed on 22 April 2019.

Singh, Rajiv. 'India at 70: Why Freedom Fighter Birsa Munda's Village in Jharkhand Is Still in Fetters', Kractivist, 14 August 2017, https://kractivist.org/india-at-

70-why-freedom-fighter-birsa-mundas-village-in-jharkhand-is-still-in-fetters. Accessed on 7 July 2019.

Tuhin, Subhra. 'The Pathalgadi Movement: An Overview, 2018'. Sanhati, 30 October 2018. http://sanhati-india.org/2018/10/30/the-pathalgadi-movement-an-overview. Accessed on 19 July 2019.

UNESCO World Heritage Convention. 'Mausoleum of First Qin Emperor' (UNESCO: World Heritage List, Lington Country, Shaanxi Province, 1987). https://whc.unesco.org/en/list/441. Accessed on 1 May 2019.

Index

abua disum (father of the land), 3–4
abua disum, abua raj (my village, my rule), 110, 111, 142, 247
activism, 9, 106, 114
activists, 23, 29, 106, 115, 141, 170, 171, 174, 235, 236, 255n115
Adas, Michael, 13
Adi Dharma, 12, 120, 121, 170
Adivasi
    movement, 25, 105
    studies, 9, 10, 38n22
    violence against, 33
Adivasi Mahasabha, 21, 26, 27, 41n87, 42n88, 43n123, 43n126
adivasi, political vocabulary, 21–22
'Adivasi studies,' 9
administrators and ethnographers, 60
aesthetic, 24, 38n19, 93–97, 101, 102, 104, 106–08, 111, 113, 114, 122, 124, 125, 128, 130, 131, 137, 138, 140, 146n32, 149n77, 153, 172, 186, 220, 259
affect, 16, 38n19, 73, 155, 164, 194, 224
affective, 8, 24–25, 29, 34, 38n19, 51, 95–102, 111, 124, 139, 140, 145n18, 153, 155, 159, 164, 165, 188, 194, 196, 197, 224, 229, 259
agrarian crisis and anti-colonialism, 66
akhra, 44n138, 118, 149n76, 171, 174
allegations, 233, 234
All Jharkhand Students Union (AJSU), 28
AJSU Party, 28, 102, 112, 146n40
Anglo-European legal system, 73
anti-colonialism, 5–7, 25, 66, 224, 259, 262
    'actualization of freedom itself', 7
    counter-memorial, 260–62
    epistemic and ideological formation, 6
    of ethnic nationalism, 6
    Hindu-caste imagination, 6
    history of Adivasis, 7–8
    liberation and independence, 7
    thingification, 7
    transnational struggle, 259
    violence and coercion, 7
arrest, 67, 75, 76, 77, 78, 177, 202, 236, 245, 251n50
attack
    attack on, 68, 126, 127, 177, 224, 226, 236, 248

Index   **291**

Ayushman Bharat (National Health Promotion Scheme) (2018), 129, 130, 151n102

backwardness, 18, 192, 218
Bara, Joseph, 42n89, 59, 84n67, 84n69
Barla, Dayamani, 2n3, 114, 149n68, 150n88, 174
battle of cosmologies, 225, 229, 253n93
Bharatiya Janata Party (BJP), 28, 30, 31, 102, 106, 118, 122, 130, 146n41, 147n42, 151n105, 157, 169, 170, 180, 234, 254n105
bhuinhari (tenants), 68–73, 177, 202n83
Bhutkheta, 68
Bihar, 27, 30, 37n5, 39n37, 44n148, 52, 53, 105, 150n84, 204n100, 254n97
Bihar Land Reforms Act (1950), 105
billboards, 129–31, 163, 172, 185
Birsa
  Bhagwan, 12, 14, 37n5, 39n39, 75, 76, 86n101, 86n112, 95, 96, 107, 169
  land legislations, 66, 125
  mammoth statue, regional political elite and fieldnotes, 102
  memory and heritage, 113, 125
  movement, 5, 6, 9, 14, 15, 22, 25, 28, 35, 39n28, 50, 54, 79, 93, 105, 144n3
  statues, 100, 101
  ulgulan, 5, 16, 17, 23, 52, 76
  voice of resistance, Dayamani Barla, 114
Birsa Chowk, 122, 123, 142
Birsaism, 12, 239, 241, 242
Birsaites, 10–12, 15, 22–23, 76, 88n148, 113, 163–65, 176, 179, 180, 183, 184, 187, 196, 207, 237, 239, 241–46
Birsa Memorial in Ranchi, Jharkhand, 4
Birsa Munda
  and anti-colonialism, 6–8
  brief biography, 10–13
  iconography, 24–25
  and memory, 3–6, 8–9
Birsa Seva Dal, 27
Birsa *ulgulan*, 4, 5, 17, 23–24, 49, 52, 76, 114, 116, 126, 131, 148n59, 158, 167, 174, 183, 193, 196, 258
Bongaism, 12, 121
British
  Library, 2n1, 35, 39n31, 80n20, 82n21, 82n30, 82n31, 83n42, 83n51, 84n57, 84n60, 85n81, 85n86, 86n104, 86n110, 86n111, 87n114, 87n120, 87n122, 88n138, 88n140, 88n143, 89n153, 89n159, 89n160, 89n150, 150n85, 200n28, 202n80, 203n83, 203m84, 205n133, 248n4, 249n12, 253n83, 254n98, 255n126, 256n134
  Raj, 4, 25, 62–64, 78, 116
built environment, 5, 94, 95, 96, 98, 108, 111, 118, 140, 142, 144n11, 144n13, 155, 157, 166, 172, 196, 197, 227, 259, 260
burial, 36, 118, 145n21, 153, 154, 158, 160, 173, 177, 208, 209, 211–14, 229, 236, 248n7
  territorial claims, 211
Buru, 36, 119, 174–76, 179, 180, 183, 187, 188, 191, 195, 204n111, 205n131
Buru Bonga, 119, 159

canon, 10, 79, 137, 157, 189, 192, 193, 196, 262
Carrin, Marine, 51
caste, 6, 18–20, 32, 33, 36, 39n27, 40n69, 57, 58, 66, 68, 69, 86n107, 94, 96, 124, 137, 138, 139, 140, 141, 143, 149n63, 152n114, 152n116, 193, 200n33, 202n83, 203n86, 212, 224, 249n24, 250n35, 253n84, 258, 261
Cave-Browne, Reverend John, 62
Césaire, Aimé, 7, 38n14
Chandra, Uday, 5, 6, 23, 37n7, 38n22, 42n103, 43n107, 46n172, 85n94, 204n109, 257n141
Charter Bill, 54
Chatterjee, Partha, 32, 37n11, 43n114, 46n162, 157, 199n22
Chiriyankandath, James, 25, 43n115
Chota Nagpur
  Chota Nagpur Tenancy Act (CNTA) (1908), 13, 20, 31, 68, 72, 83n39, 105, 106, 118, 124, 147n53, 211, 213, 216, 218, 220, 221, 230, 247, 259
  Chota Nagpur Tenure Act II (1869), 68
  improvement society, 21, 26, 89n42
  sasandiri, 208–11
Christianity, 10, 13–15, 42n89, 55, 59, 60, 61, 63, 64, 66, 75, 81n13, 81n17, 84n69, 85n75, 158, 176, 209
Christian missionaries, 23, 26, 56
Christian Missionary Society, 35–36, 86n99, 206n134
Church Missionary Society (CMS), 58
Collin, E. W., 53
colonial India, 17–21
commemoration, 36, 98, 114, 125, 128, 131, 140, 144n10, 145n21, 154–59, 161, 163, 164, 166, 171, 174, 179, 183, 193, 196, 197, 198, 198n5, 198n6, 198n44, 206n136
Communist Party of India (Marxist–Leninist), 27
Compensatory Afforestation Fund Management and Planning Authority (CAMPA), 218
Constituent Assembly (1946), 26
Constitution of India, 26, 45n150, 124, 185, 208, 217, 227, 248, 251n52
counter-memorial, 260–62
cultural imperialism, 51, 57, 58, 84n66
cultural revivalism, 27–31

Dalikatari, 68
Dalit icons and statue politics
  canonization, 137
  material memory, 137
  time and memory, 138
Damodaran, Vinita, 19, 28, 41n77, 44n135, 74, 80n6, 84n73, 87n123, 88n131, 88n132, 150n97, 204n101, 255n116
Dasgupta, Sangeeta, 14, 38n22, 39n38, 60, 81n20, 83n55, 84n71, 255n128
decolonization process, 9
dhangar, 57, 58
dharam (religion), 10
Dharti Aba, 12, 14, 39n31, 66
dikus (outsiders), 7, 51
Dirk, Nicholas, 61, 84n74, 212, 24n24, 249n26
Dombari Buru, 36, 174–76, 179, 180, 183, 187, 188, 191, 195, 204n111, 205n131, 264, 265
Dombari Hill, 49, 131, 153, 175, 180–82, 184–86, 188, 191, 193, 195, 264, 265

Index   293

Elementary Aspects of Peasant Insurgency, 23

Elementary Aspects of Peasant Insurgency in Colonial India, 16

empire of ethnography, 59

encounter, 3, 4, 7, 15, 27, 51, 56, 64, 78, 81n14, 94, 95, 97, 126, 145n18, 163, 176, 203n98, 211, 258, 261

Encyclopaedia Mundarica, 39n31, 151n98, 200n28, 254n97

English law (the Chota Nagpur Tenancy Act [CNTA]), 72

environment of memory, 227, 231, 236

episodic, 35, 166, 189

ethnographic method, 102

ethnographic refusal, 24, 43n108

ethnography

of memory, 36

'exploitative and anti-Adivasi', 27

'Final Report on the Survey and Settlement Operations', 82n21, 82n32, 83n48, 85n89, 85n93, 87n115, 87n116, 88n137

folk memory, 173, 189, 192

Forbes, A., 1, 2n2, 76, 77, 88n138, 88n143, 89n153, 176, 202n80, 205n133, 253n83

Forest Act (1878), 67

forest democracy, 215

Gossner School in Chaibasa, 11

Gossner Evangelical Lutheran Church, 57, 83n97

Government of India Act (1935), 24

*gram panchayat*s (rural grassroots-level institutions), 15, 40n49, 103, 147n44, 215

grassroots-level mobilization, 103

graveyard, 35, 177, 194, 207–09, 211, 212, 247

Guha, Ranajit, 16, 17, 22, 23, 32, 40n55, 45n153, 80n2, 80n5, 87n129, 89n129, 254n107

Gupta, Sanjukta Das, 20, 41n80, 82n29, 147n53

hadia (rice beer), 3

'Heathen Soul'

cultural imperialism, 57, 58

history of Chota Nagpur, 52

mission, school and English education, 59

mutiny and missionaries, 55

skirts of civilization, 55

Hindu

caste, 6, 18, 19, 39n27, 54, 57, 141, 143, 175

society, 18, 152n114

historical memory, 35, 50, 56, 78, 79, 95, 108, 110, 116, 174, 176, 188, 197, 208, 229, 234, 258, 262

historical records, 5, 50, 60, 79, 189, 240, 241

Hobsbawm, Eric, 16

Hoffman, John-Baptist, 12, 13, 22, 39n31, 67, 73, 75, 76, 83n39, 84n104, 87n128, 121, 127, 150n85, 159, 200n28, 209, 212, 229, 230, 244, 248n5, 249n5, 254n97

Horo, N. E., 27

Indian Forest Act VII (1882), 74

Indian independence movement, 9

Indian National Congress (1940), 24

indigeneity, 26, 31, 35, 42n90, 43n117, 45n154, 46n180, 83n46, 130, 150n89, 150n97, 213, 215, 263n9

individual and collective memory, 164, 172
insurgency, 16

jal, jungle aur jameen (water, forest and land), 1, 5, 52, 79, 116, 121, 122, 137, 141, 173, 215, 230, 236, 262
Jha, J. C., 54
Jharkhand
    Jharkhand Coordination Committee (JCC), 28–29
    Jharkhand Mukti Morcha (JMM), 27–29, 44n131, 169
    Jharkhand Panchayati Raj Act (2001), 134
    Jharkhand Party, 27–28, 41n86
    Jharkhand's political struggle, 25–27

Khunti, 10, 11, 15, 36, 126, 128–30, 136, 153, 164, 167, 178–80, 184, 185, 191, 210, 211, 214, 216, 228, 231–37, 240, 243
khuntkatti, 14, 39n36, 68, 74, 211, 241
    khuntkhattidar, 20, 72, 208, 209, 241
knowledge, 19, 20, 32–35, 61, 62, 73, 74, 115, 144n7, 155, 174, 177, 185, 193, 207, 214, 229, 248, 260, 261
Kolhan Settlement Act (1867), 53
Kols, 21, 53–65, 67, 69, 70–73, 83n37, 85n91, 87n122
Kol uprising (1829), 52

Land Acquisition Act, 31
landlords (*zamindars/manjhihas*), 4, 7, 12–13, 21, 50, 53, 54, 57, 64–74
landscape of memory, 122, 150n86, 177, 193, 197, 207, 212, 225, 226, 229, 247, 248, 261

Life and Times of Birsa Bhagwan, 14
lifeworld, 34, 46n176, 94, 98, 118, 121, 122, 126, 127, 139, 151n99, 171, 180, 185, 192, 193, 198, 207, 209, 210, 214, 221, 224, 226, 230, 242, 259, 260
litigation process, 64

Macaulay, Thomas Babington, 51, 81n16
Macpherson, T. S., 208, 240, 255n126, 259
Mahatoai, 68
Mahto, Sudesh, 28, 102, 109, 147n43, 147n50, 148n60, 150n92, 160, 161
Maoists, 3, 22–23, 31, 36n2, 42n92, 113, 128, 130, 134–36, 151n99, 152n112
material inequalities, 34, 36, 103, 261
material memory culture, 96–100
memorialization, 4–5, 8–9, 28, 34, 36, 79, 80, 94, 95, 99, 100, 106, 143, 154, 157, 158, 164, 168, 171, 172, 188–90, 192, 193, 197, 224, 241, 247, 248, 259, 260, 262
memorial pillar, 36, 153, 154, 183–89
memory
    material, 5, 92–102, 113, 131, 137–38, 140, 144n14, 153
    politics, 5, 8–9, 24, 34, 36, 79
memory and Birsa Munda, 3–6, 8–9
memory archives
    environment of memory, 227–33
    opium and sedition, 233–36
memory manifesto, 259–61
'messianic'/'millenarian' beliefs, 12
Ministry of Tribal Affairs (MoTA), 222, 250n42
missionaries, 7, 10, 12–13, 23, 26–27
moral alibis, 51

Index   **295**

Mullick, Samar Bosu, 29, 39n25, 42n88, 42n122, 148n61
Munda, Jai Pal Singh, 21, 25–26, 87n41, 107, 126, 143
Munda *raj*, 22–23, 49–51, 66, 75, 177–79, 258, 263
Munda, Ram Dayal, 12, 39n25, 44n138, 205n131
Municipal Corporation of Ranchi, 3

Narmada Bachao Andolan (NBA), 106
narration and design of the statue, 108–11
narrative of remembrance, 168–71
nationalism, 5–7, 25, 32, 35, 45n150, 80n4, 85n87, 114, 130, 141, 146, 147n41, 152n119, 153, 157, 158, 168, 169, 172, 193, 205n123
nationalizing memory, 107
Nilsen, Alf Gunvald, 34, 38n22, 46n177, 227
non-Adivasi, 30, 36, 102, 104, 113, 142, 182, 260

Onasch, Reverend H., 63
Ortner, Sherry, 24

*pahan*s (village priests), 119–21, 208, 248
Pahnai, 67
Panchayats (Extension to the Scheduled Areas) (PESA) Act (1996), 158, 250n42
parha (self-governance amongst Adivasis), 15
participants, 9, 34, 116, 142, 192, 197, 260
Patel statue, 106
Pathalgadi movement. *See also* battle of cosmologies
 defined, 215, 216

description, 214
forest democracy, 215
land bank, 219–24
legislative measures and violation, 217–19
mapping, 216
Permanent Settlement Act, 54
petitions, 63–67, 73, 80n6, 218
political life
 Birsa, 24–25, 68–70
politics of visibility, 24
post-colonial, 3, 6, 9, 17–18, 25, 32–35, 38n22, 43n115, 46n166, 62, 79, 99, 111, 116, 124, 144n10, 145n27, 146n32, 152n116, 154, 157, 180, 188–93, 224, 234, 248, 258, 261
post-colonial capital, 189–93

*raiyat*s, 31, 68, 106
Rana, L. N., 27
reassemblements, 17
red files, 211–14
Reid, J., 65
*reja*s (casual labourers), 3
revitalization moment, 14
Roche, H. J., 77
Roy, S. C., 10, 13–14, 37n6, 38n22, 39n25, 42n88, 46n174
'rude barbarians', 58
Rycroft, Daniel J., 24, 38n22, 43n109, 44n141, 80n7, 88n136, 148n59, 172n23

Sahee, Lall Lokenath, 70
Sail Rakab, 36, 79, 80, 126, 167, 174, 177, 178–80, 183–86, 197, 227, 228, 231
sal (*Shorea robusta*), 119–21
*samadhi sthal*s, 5, 153, 154, 160–63

Santhal Parganas Act (1949), 105
Santhal Pargana Tenancy Act (SPTA) (1949), 124, 216, 221, 247
Santhal rebellion, 52
Sardari
   Sardari agitation, 14, 76
   Sardari *ladai*, 11, 49, 67–78
      end of the rebellion, 78, 79
      and spectre of surveys, 68–78
   Sardari movement, 69
Sarhul, 118–122
sarna, 118–19, 150n84, 233
sasandiri, 36, 177, 178, 208, 214, 229
Scott, James, 8, 16, 38n20
Seal, Anil, 49, 80n3
'semi-savage foolishness', 12, 13, 75
Sen, Asoka Kumar, 55, 124, 207
Shah, Alpa, 18, 36n2, 40n73, 42n91–96, 44n146, 85n47, 128, 151n99, 162, 200n99, 201n62, 244, 249n15, 250n35, 253n84
Shiv *charcha*, 22
Sidhu Kanhu (Santhal rebellion) (1855), 52
Simon Commission, 25–27
Singh, Anjana, 215, 216, 248n3
Singh, K. S., 22, 39n24, 39n26, 39n29, 40n46, 151n99
Singh, Kumar Suresh, 65, 66
Sinha, Subir, 33, 46n166
Sinha, Surendra Prasad, 14
Sivaramakrishnan, K., 74, 88n133, 223, 253n78
Society for the Propagation of the Gospel (SPG), 61
solidarity, 7, 36, 103, 104, 112–15, 135, 178, 182, 262

Spivak, Gayatri Chakravarty, 31, 45n153, 46n173, 87n129, 99, 145n27, 254n107
stakeholders and architecture, 155, 156
statues, 5–6, 8, 29, 34, 94–97
stone slabs, 5, 6, 35, 153, 175–81, 208, 209, 210, 214, 224, 233, 259
subaltern
   subaltern memory, 6, 8, 50, 96, 142, 157, 158
   subalternity, 34, 38n22, 45n153, 46n177, 95, 114, 259, 260, 263n9
   subaltern studies, 9, 31–32
symbolism shift, 111–13

Tambs-Lyche, Harald, 51
theatrics and emotions, 163–68
*thikeddar*s (contractors and farmers), 65
thingification, 7
tribal, 15–16, 19, 38n22, 114, 119, 125, 130

Ulihatu village, 10, 39n23, 95, 115
   13 October 2018, 128–37
United Nations Working Group on Indigenous Populations (UNWGIP), 29
United Progressive Alliance (UPA), 130
upper-caste Hindus, 18, 39n25, 39n27, 57, 175

vananchal (forest-dwelling state), 30
Varma, Rashmi, 192, 205n124

weaving theory, 34–35

Xaxa, Virginius, 18, 41n75, 149n72, 216, 250n46